Ancient India

Ancient India
New Research

edited by

Upinder Singh and Nayanjot Lahiri

OXFORD
UNIVERSITY PRESS

OXFORD
UNIVERSITY PRESS
YMCA Library Building, Jai Singh Road, New Delhi 110 001

Oxford University Press is a department of the University of Oxford. It furthers the University's objective of excellence in research, scholarship, and education by publishing worldwide in

Oxford New York

Auckland Cape Town Dar es Salaam Hong Kong Karachi Kuala Lumpur Madrid Melbourne Mexico City Nairobi New Delhi Shanghai Taipei Toronto

With offices in

Argentina Austria Brazil Chile Czech Republic France Greece Guatemala Hungary Italy Japan Poland Portugal Singapore South Korea Switzerland Thailand Turkey Ukraine Vietnam

Published in India
by Oxford University Press, New Delhi

First published 2009
Second impression 2010

ISBN-13: 978-0-19-806028-4
ISBN-10: 0-19-806028-9

Typeset in Adobe Garamond Pro 11/12.7
by Sai Graphic Design, New Delhi110 055
Printed in India at Pauls Press, New Delhi 110 020
Published by Oxford University Press
YMCA Library Building, Jai Singh Road, New Delhi 110 001

This book is dedicated to the
memory of Devahuti and Damodar Singhal
for their commitment to history
and to Manana

Contents

Figures

Tables

Appendices

Preface and Acknowledgements

This book emerged out of the initiative of the Devahuti Damador Svaraj Trust, which was established in 1990, to further the legacy of Professors Devahuti and Damodar Singhal.

Devahuti (1929–1988) was a renowned scholar of ancient Indian and early Southeast Asian history and taught at the Universities of Malaya and Adelaide, Australia, and at the University of Delhi. Her works as a writer/editor include *Harsha: A Political Study* (three editions), *India and Ancient Malaya*, *Problems of Indian Historiography*, *Bias in Indian Historiography*, *Historical and Political Perspectives*, and *The Unknown Hsüan-Tsang*. Damodar Prasad Singhal (1925–1986) was a lecturer in history at the University of Malaya and later, professor of history at the University of Queensland, Australia, from where he retired as Professor Emeritus. His books include *India and World Civilization* (2 vols); *Nationalism in India and Other Historical Essays*; *The Annexation of Upper Burma, India and Afghanistan: A Study in Diplomatic Relations, 1876–1907*; and *A History of the Indian People; Pakistan; Buddhism in East Asia*; *Modern Indian Society and Culture*; and *Gypsies: Indians in Exile*.

Since its inception, the Devahuti Damodar Svaraj Trust, under its organization named Manana, has supported several projects in the areas of Indian history, philosophy, and culture. The Devahuti-Damodar Library at Greater Kailash has an old and valuable collection of more than 6,364 titles on modern and ancient Indian history and related areas of Southeast, East, and Central Asia. Apart from its excellent collection of books, what sets it apart is that it is a library which welcomes readers from all walks of life with open arms. The Trust has also been involved in the publication of journals, books, and other printed materials; helping scholars in research and preparation of books for publication; holding workshops, seminars, public lectures, and nominating scholars to attend the same; providing scholarships and fellowships; running a support school for underprivileged children; assisting libraries, and organizing ancillary and administrative work connected with the above. The activities of the Trust show how the initiatives of two dedicated people—the founder, Veena Sachdev, and her colleague, Anshu Dogra, who is now the executive director of Manana—can make a difference.

In September 2004 Veena approached us for ideas for a seminar or workshop on ancient Indian history. We discussed various possibilities with our former teacher, P.S. Dwivedi. In view of the spirit of the Trust she had founded, we felt that we had to think of an event that would be meaningful and off the beaten track. The result of our various discussions was the workshop held in the India International Centre on 27–28 August 2005. It did turn out to be an academic event with a difference. The usual hierarchies were reversed as older scholars listened carefully and reacted to the ideas and work of younger scholars who ranged from undergraduate to postgraduate students and scholars. We are grateful to Veena Sachdev, Anshu Dogra, and the staff of Manana for attending to all the organizational details with such efficiency and care.

The essays in this book are essentially reworked versions of some of the papers presented at that workshop. Perhaps this can be one of a series of publications which showcase the ideas and research of a younger generation of scholars working on different aspects of the history of ancient and early medieval India.

UPINDER SINGH AND NAYANJOT LAHIRI

Introduction

UPINDER SINGH AND NAYANJOT LAHIRI

THE ESSAYS in this volume cannot be simply introduced in terms of either a unity of theme or a similarity of source material. There is historiography, there are archaeological writings ranging from prehistory to the archaeology of medieval temples, and there are contributions that are anchored in texts and inscriptions. This volume brings together new research that reflects certain approaches that are recognized as central to the study of ancient India. There are essays on individual and institutional initiatives in the production of archaeological knowledge; surface surveys as a means of reconstructing the archaeological history of micro-regions; subsistence practices and palaeoenvironments of macro-regions; and the use of material remains to recreate variegated religious landscapes. The interrogation of ancient texts in creative and nuanced ways, to reveal the complex relationship between ideas, norms, and social and political practice is another significant thread, as is an emphasis on the need to generate histories that are more socially inclusive. There is also a strong awareness of the fact that although the correlation of archaeology and texts is desirable, the enterprise is fraught with many difficulties that must be addressed rather than ignored.

ARCHAEOLOGY, PREHISTORY, AND PROTOHISTORY

The first essay of this book by Sanjukta Datta investigates the history of archaeology in Bengal, and the interface of official and non-official institutional and individual endeavours in that area during the late nineteenth and early twentieth century. Although this is not the place to review previous research on the history of Indian archaeology, there is a notable trend towards examining the development of archaeology in British India through a close analysis of the perspectives and work of Indian antiquarians and archaeologists in different regions, at different points of time, anchoring the analysis firmly in the colonial context. Exemplifying this trend, Datta describes the activities and writings of a range of Indian scholars who were devoted to the recovery of the pre-modern past of Bengal.

These were Bengali scholars whose primary focus was Bengal, but Datta demonstrates that they also wrote about other parts of India and attempted to weave the history of this region into the larger narrative of Indian history. Rajendralala Mitra, whom she describes as the 'first professional Bengali archaeologist', is one polymath whose formidable repertoire admirably exemplifies this. Mitra was the author of many works, including two major studies on the art and antiquities of Orissa and Bodh Gaya, and many antiquities he collected from these areas were donated by him to the Indian Museum, Calcutta. He was an editor of Sanskrit texts and of inscriptions. He was also the first Indian president of the Asiatic Society of Bengal (in 1885), and the first cataloguer of the entire range of objects in the possession of the Society.

In the twentieth century, the relationship of the Archaeological Survey of India—a government department of archaeology—and scholars associated with antiquarian and archaeological societies was especially close. Names like Ramaprasad Chanda and Nanigopal Majumdar are usually remembered in the history of Indian archaeology as officers of the Survey and as authors of volumes published as *Memoirs of the Archaeological Survey*, which continue to be usefully mined by scholars of the Indian past even today. However, before they were co-opted by the Archaeological Survey, both these scholars were active members of the Varendra Research Society, established at Rajshahi in 1910 by Kumar Sarat Kumar Ray of the Dighapatiya royal family. Pioneers like Akshay Kumar Maitra who wrote on the archaeology of Bengal in the vernacular, and other scholars like Rakhaldas Banerji who wrote in English and Bengali, and were associated with private societies and also employed by the Archaeological Survey, organizations like the Bangiya Sahitya Parishad, which were seriously interested in recovering all kinds of archaeological remains and became repositories of manuscripts and artefacts collected by its members—all these are explored and woven by Datta into a rich tapestry which showcases and analyses the approaches and interests of Indians in a British Indian province.

It is striking, though, that advances in the field of prehistory appear to have had little impact on the research interests of the scholars and organizations discussed in Datta's essay. This also remains true for the Delhi region, the geographical focus of the second essay in this volume by Mudit Trivedi. In the writings of pioneer explorers like Alexander Cunningham and documenters of monuments and sites like Maulvi Zafar Hasan, the prehistory of Delhi remains a blank. The presence of Stone Age sites on the hillsides of Delhi first came to be recognized in the 1970s, and since then their pervasive presence has been underlined through surface collection and excavation.

Trivedi's own work is focused on a small segment of the Delhi ridge. His study is, in fact, an exposition of what has emerged from essentially a one-man survey of the roughly 1,500 acres of the Aravalli hills enclosed within the campus of Jawaharlal Nehru University. What makes this survey distinctive is the way in which one individual (Trivedi) has successfully extracted unknown dimensions of the prehistory of this landscape through a careful and meticulous surface exploration. The essay combines a close examination of the landscape and the prehistoric remains that it yielded, with the available geological information. Instead of the general division of this micro-region into mountainous and alluvial segments, the landscape is shown as being made up of three different geomorphological elements—Aravalli hills, Yamuna alluvium, and aeolian deposits. Most importantly, the interleaving of the Delhi quartzite rocks with sediments that represent deposits of aeolian sands from the Thar is discussed at length, as are the implications of this for the artefacts that are scattered across this surface. Perhaps this is the first publication where a threefold geological division of the Delhi region and its ramifications for understanding the site formation and the weathering of prehistoric artefacts has been undertaken.

Trivedi also carefully studies the archaeology of the Aravalli landscape. With reference to the palaeolithic phase of prehistory, quartzite was the preferred raw material for the production of Acheulian artefacts, although rare specimens of sandstone and quartz are also found. The reasons why some of these stone tools bear a red stain while others are marked by a yellow-brown patination are discussed, as is the cause for differential abrasion on their surface. The time frame for these assemblages is roughly placed between 350,000 to 128,000 years ago. The younger microlithic complex was fashioned in a different context in terms of location as well as raw material. Ridges which provided clear views of the landscape and edges of large and small ravines formed the favoured locales of microlith users. The presence of prehistoric humans is mainly reflected in the form of scatters of microliths of crystal and clear quartz, with rare examples of artefacts made from ferruginous nodules and sandstone. Trivedi has also made the first discovery of petroglyphs in the Aravalli belt of Delhi, and while they are difficult to date, their spatial contiguity to microlithic scatters suggests that they may have been contemporaneous with microlith-using communities.

If Trivedi's work is based on a micro-region, Shibani Bose offers a macro-perspective of a large region, namely, the Middle Gangetic Plains. She offers a synthesis of the available archaeobotanical evidence in order to explain the patterns of human exploitation of plants from the mesolithic till the first phase of the early historic period (around the third century BC). Wild and cultivated varieties of rice have been identified at rock shelter sites and at sites situated in the Ganga alluvium, along with a broad spectrum of wild vegetal food. As Bose's overview of the dates suggests, these hunter-gatherers coexisted with early agriculturists. The peninsular edge of the central plains has revealed early neolithic strata representing rice-producing communities. The essay draws attention to the recent excavations at Lahuradeva in Uttar Pradesh, which have revealed that early rice cultivation was not confined to the Vindhyan hills, but extended into the Gangetic alluvium.

If the documentation of the early presence of rice is one important element in the human–plant interaction in the Middle Gangetic Plains, the other is the sheer variety of crops that were cultivated at sites ranging from neolithic Chirand and Senuwar in Bihar to Tokwa and Jhusi in Uttar Pradesh. The diversification of the agricultural tradition seems to have continued into the neolithic–chalcolithic phase. The diversity of cereal varieties—rice, wheat, barley, millet, pulses—is interesting in itself, as is the presence of several other plant species. An instance in point is that *bhang* (*Cannabis sativa*) was enjoyed in the late second millennium BC by the inhabitants of Imlidih Khurd (in Uttar Pradesh) and Senuwar (in Bihar). There is also unequivocal evidence that some of the exotic plants and trees present in the repertoires of advanced agricultural societies of the Ganga plains may have come through contacts with contemporaneous cultures in other regions. The range is fascinating—from grapes and dates at Narhan to Himalayan *deodar* at Senuwar.

This diversity has important implications for understanding the evolution of the agricultural geography of the Ganga valley. Bose's essay clearly underlines that no one culture or one society can claim to be the harbinger or pioneer in the creation of a strong agricultural base in this area. For instance, the trajectory of cultural development in eastern Uttar Pradesh clearly differs from the manner in which village cultures in Bihar evolved. What is common to them is that, in more ways than one, they represent a kind of watershed for the advent of stable agricultural societies in their respective tracts. In fact, the palaeobotanical remains from Iron Age and early historic cultures clearly indicate the creation of a diverse and stable agrarian base by neolithic–chalcolithic farmers. The crops that later came to support an early historic urban base in the Ganga plains were first farmed by these third and second millennia BC cultivators.

LITERARY AND ARCHAEOLOGICAL LANDSCAPES OF DEATH

While the first three essays in the volume focus exclusively on India north of the Vindhyas, Uthara Suvrathan takes us to the Vidarbha region of eastern Maharashtra. The importance of landscape not merely as a background to human actions but as a central element that also shapes them is well recognized in archaeology today. The imaginative ways in which the landscape can be perceived is highlighted in Suvrathan's analysis of mortuary practices as representations of commemorative strategies. These strategies are identifiable in terms of the location and composite character of the Vidarbha megaliths, from *c.* 1000 BC till *c.* AD 300. While megaliths are concentrated in those parts of Vidarbha that have rich mineral deposits, and the habitation-cum-burial sites are frequently located in areas with fertile soil and on the banks of perennial rivers, burials also took place in wastelands and forested areas. Within each site, again, megaliths are generally grouped in two or more locations, which is suggestive of multiple clans or families. The range of artefacts buried with the dead clearly represented an attempt to include the range of items used by individuals during their lifetime, although the social person being commemorated certainly influenced the diversity of funerary furniture, as the case of Mahurjhari suggests.

With regard to the temporal dimension, Suvrathan explores the short- and long-term scales in order to recover the meanings that surround the megaliths. In the immediate context, the same burials can be viewed in various ways, depending on the time when the interment took place. For instance, the high point of ritualized activities in the case of primary burials occurred immediately after the death of the individual, while in the case of secondary interment, there is the likelihood of a staggered scale of ritualization. The long-term perspective, on the other hand, underlines the fact that although megalithic burials reflect the material culture of that time, the pottery—Black and Red Ware—which is commonly found in megalithic burials, is not peculiar to it. In fact, as Suvrathan argues, there is no distinguishing feature that helps differentiate the Black and Red Ware of the chalcolithic from that of the megalithic.

Inspired by ideas about the manner in which landscapes are imaged in literary traditions, the final section of Suvrathan's essay examines the ways in which Vidarbha has been conceptualized in texts and inscriptions. The Puranas and the Mahabharata are trawled, and this in turn demonstrates that such texts contain useful historical information about this region, as also its integration into textual mythologies and events. In legends, Vidarbha refers to a territory (a *janapada* of the Deccan) and to a people with specific customs and language (with Vaidarbhi described as a kind of diction). Essentially, then, as Suvrathan argues, it is necessary to see historic landscapes as being configured in different ways, ranging from material features related to the experiences and lives of people, to the images available in texts.

The idea of landscape as a physical and conceptual category is also central to Meera Visvanathan's analysis in the next chapter. She too explores literary and archaeological landscapes of death, but those belonging to a different chronological, geographical, and cultural milieu. The literature she delves into is early classical Tamil literature, popularly referred to as Sangam literature. Her essay basically tries to locate martial heroism and the relationship between death and fertility within the larger historical context of early historic south India. Along the way, several hypotheses come up for questioning: the nature of the polity and the relationship between war, plunder, and agriculture.

The *akam* and *puṟam* poems reveal a striking diversity of geographical, experiential, and emotional landscapes. This is confirmed to some extent by the archaeological data from megalithic habitation and burial sites of the period, one of the most important of which is Kodumanal. Visvanathan moves to and fro between textual and archaeological sources. Although she recognizes the importance of material evidence, as she points out, 'what slips from the archaeological record is the voice of the poet'. In fact, the voice of the poet commands our attention in her essay, and this gives it a distinctive flavour.

Reconstructing the experience of people living in ancient times requires attentiveness to the textures and nuances of sources. The *tiṇai*—poetic landscapes—of the Tamil poems cannot be read simplistically as factual descriptions of communities and ecological zones. As Visvanathan rightly points out, they have to be understood as highly complex literary devices, aesthetic constructs within which the poets structured experience in relation to landscape. This point can form the basis of a larger question: to what extent do the Sangam poems, with their preoccupation with themes of love and heroic death, in fact represent the everyday reality of ordinary people? Issues of the poet–patron relationship, and the place and role of this poetry in the larger socio-political context become crucial in order to address these questions.

RECONSTRUCTING RELIGIOUS LANDSCAPES THROUGH ARCHAEOLOGY AND ARTEFACTS

We move to a different region and a different theme with Susan Verma Mishra's essay. Mishra emphasizes the importance of archaeology in reconstructing the history of religions, and, instead of focusing on one particular religion, she chooses to explore the interrelation and interaction of different traditions—brahmanical, Buddhist, and Jaina. The main sites discussed include Amreli, Devnimori and Shamalaji, Nagara, Valabhi, Akota, and Vadodara. The evidence includes structural remains, sculptures, and inscriptions. Excavations at Devnimori revealed a Buddhist complex, but the site has also yielded a large number of Śaiva shrines and sculptures, revealing the variety of focii of popular worship from the third/fourth to the seventh/eighth century. Vadodara and Akota have yielded evidence of Jainism and the worship of brahmanical deities, showing elements of continuity over many centuries. The coexistence of different religious traditions in a region is one thing, but the nature of the relationship between them can take many different forms and requires further exploration.

Mishra emphasizes the need to look at religious establishments within their larger political, social, and economic contexts. Regarding the issue of political patronage, she points out that in Gujarat, the majority of shrines do not appear to have been connected with royalty. The essay also examines archaeological data pertaining to the resources that sustained the places where major religious establishments were located, especially the evidence of agriculture, crafts, and trade. It questions the long-held connection between the rise and decline of Buddhism, and the ebb and flow of urbanism and trade.

Shivani Agarwal shifts the focus to the interpretation of a particular type of artefact—the ubiquitous and often ignored terracotta figurine. A special focus of interest are the female terracottas, which have for far too long been routinely interpreted and labelled as 'mother goddesses'. Agarwal gives an overview of female terracottas from the two important sites of Mathura and Ahichchhatra against the larger background of interpretations of early Indian religions. She emphasizes the need to study such artefacts in their own right instead of being carried away with making cross-cultural parallels or looking into literary texts for their identification. As for the larger socio-economic context of the production of terracotta figurines, it is now well established that mass-produced terracottas were related to demand generated in urban centres.

Terracottas had different functions in ancient times, and a religious one cannot be presumed. Many of the animal figurines, for instance, were probably toys. Even in the case of some of the female figurines, which, from their sheer form, appear to have a cultic significance, a strong case can be made to consider them as representations of various goddesses rather than a primeval, unchanging Great Goddess. Archaeological evidence proves that the worship of such goddesses—along with the worship of *nāgas*/*nāgī*s and *yakṣas*/*yakṣī*s—was an important part of popular religion, probably cutting across sectarian divides, over many centuries. Terracotta tanks and shrines too had an important place, and seem to have been used in domestic rituals. Issues that merit further inquiry are the relationship of terracottas with other artefacts, and their regional specificities and profiles.

While it is possible to trace the patterns of continuity and change in terracotta art, the problems in understanding the nature and function of these figurines remain. Context is crucial, but the problem is that the context of finds is often unknown. In most cases, the artefacts have not been found in the course of archaeological excavation and they are often completely dislocated from their original locale.

HISTORICIZING AND ENGENDERING TEXTS

The last two essays in this book focus squarely on texts. Shonaleeka Kaul represents a fresh approach towards the historical analysis of

Sanskrit *kāvya* and the city. The vast corpus of kāvya literature of the first millennium has been treated in two broad ways by historians. One approach is to consider it a stereotyped product of the poetic imagination and to either completely ignore it or give it scant importance as historical source material. Another approach is to use it in a positivistic manner, extracting empirical data from it. As for urban history, historians and archaeologists who have worked on urbanism in ancient and early medieval India have tended to focus on issues such as the definition of urbanism, settlement patterns, urban features such as specialized crafts and trade, and long-term patterns of urban emergence, growth, and decline. It is against this background that Kaul simultaneously makes a strong case for a different approach towards textual analysis, urban history, and social history, placing the roles and relationship of men and women centre-stage.

Kaul is sensitive to the conventions of the genre of texts she deals with, but insists that the archetypes these texts construct are rich in meaning and can be subjected to fruitful historical analysis. Her focus is on urban behaviour, especially the behaviour of men and women as social and sexual beings. Ranging across various texts of the first millennium, such as the *Mṛcchakaṭikaṁ*, *Caturbhāṇī*, and *Kāmasūtra*, she explores two key kāvya archetypes—the *nāgaraka* (man-about-town) and the *gaṇikā* (courtesan). An exploration of these two models of urban behaviour leads into an inquiry into the relationship between pleasure and culture, especially the ambivalences and paradoxes inherent between them in the case of the gaṇikā. Kaul extends her argument to offer the hypothesis that the nāgaraka and gaṇikā symbolize the tensions between *kāma* and *dharma*.

Devika Rangachari's essay too focuses on issues related to gender, but within the context of a region and a more specific time frame. It makes a scathing indictment of the manner in which secondary literature has minimized the important political role played by women in early medieval Kashmir. The main body of the chapter analyses three texts—Kalhana's *Rājataraṅgiṇī*, Kṣemendra's *Samayamātṛkā*, and the *Nīlamatapurāṇa*—in order to reconstruct the different forms this role assumed. It is important to note that although these texts belong to Kashmir and to early medieval times, they belong to three very different genres.

Rangachari points out that the *Rājataraṅgiṇī* is a rich source of information on gender relations. Kalhaṇa, in fact, treats women as historically relevant figures and speaks of them exercising political power directly as well as indirectly. Of the women rulers of early medieval Kashmir—Yaśovatī, Sugandhā, and Diddā—the last is the most famous. Rangachari examines their exercise of political power, and their role as donors and builders. Apart from royal women, many non-royal women too make an appearance in the *Rājataraṅgiṇī*. Rangachari argues that certain aspects of the picture of gender relations reflected in this text are confirmed by the other two sources. The *Samayamātṛkā*, which dilates on the activities and adventures of Kaṅkālī, testifies to the social and political roles played by prostitutes. The *Nīlamatapurāṇa*, for its part, corroborates Kalhaṇa's indication that non-royal women wielded power in the political sphere. Rangachari attributes the evidence of female power in Kashmir to the gap between theory and practice. Like Kaul, she points to the difficulty of extracting historical descriptions from normative texts such as the Dharmaśāstras. But theory and practice are not two opposite and unrelated points on a scale; they have to be seen as being in constant dialogue with each other.

On the basis of her analysis of the three texts, Rangachari argues that women had wrested a 'largely autonomous space' for themselves within the contemporary society and polity. Whether this space was, indeed, largely autonomous is debatable, but she does successfully demonstrate that the apparent irrelevance or invisibility of women in writings on early medieval Kashmir is more the result of the indifference of secondary scholarship rather than the silence of primary sources. Women are not invisible in the sources—you just have to look for them. The question that still remains is: within an overarching patriarchal framework, why do we see women exercising political power in some socio-political contexts rather than in others?

Collectively, the nine essays that comprise this book do, in our opinion, raise fresh, interesting questions and represent new, emerging directions of research. They highlight the need to interrogate the construction of archaeological and historical knowledge, to meticulously uncover and analyse the empirical data generated by archaeology, to connect literary and archaeological data in a new manner, and to devise new ways of historicizing texts. Above all, the volume presents tangible evidence for the deep commitment and scholarship of a group of young researchers to the study of ancient India.

1. Artefacts and Antiquities in Bengal
Some Perspectives within an Emerging Non-official Archaeological Sphere

Sanjukta Datta

This essay discusses the emergence of a non-official archaeological sphere in Bengal during the late nineteenth century and early decades of the twentieth century. In the history of archaeology in Bengal, the institutional backgrounds of those who pioneered research ranged from the Archaeological Survey of India, whose character and work are reasonably understood, to the initiatives taken by the local educated elite and private bodies of antiquarian scholars, whose contributions have generally been less appreciated in standard accounts of Indian archaeology. For this reason, we will specially focus on the two leading non-official institutions of the time—the Bangiya Sahitya Parishad in Calcutta and the Varendra Research Society, Rajshahi, and scholars such as Akshay Kumar Maitra, Haraprasad Sastri, Nagendranath Basu, Ramaprasad Chanda, Rakhaldas Banerji, and Nanigopal Majumdar—all of whom were associated with one or both of these bodies. Within this framework, we will touch upon issues such as the history of discoveries from a few sites in West Bengal and Bangladesh; the different approaches to material remains; and the manner in which archaeology was used as a tool in the construction of a regional identity of Bengal, based on language, religion, and culture. It should be mentioned that the word 'private' used in the context of archaeology in Bengal in the period under review refers to non-official endeavours; it does not imply being outside the public sphere. In fact, one notes that scholars from Bengal were constantly straddling the official and non-official domains.

By the early decades of the twentieth century, the colonial channels open to English-educated Bengalis for pursuing antiquarian/ archaeological research included the Asiatic Society of Bengal, the Indian Museum, and the Archaeological Survey of India. From the second half of the nineteenth century, Rajendralala Mitra (1822–1891) started playing an active role in the Asiatic Society of Bengal—the pioneering institution of Indological research formed in 1784. Mitra himself was a polymath and a path-breaker in ways more than one. He was the first professional Bengali archaeologist and laid the foundation for the study of Indian antiquities not only by Bengalis, but Indians at large through the publication of his two-volume *The Antiquities of Orissa* (1875–80) and *Buddha-Gaya: The Hermitage of Śākya Muni* (1878). He was also the first Indian to be elected president of the Asiatic Society in 1885. During his years in the Society, Mitra edited and commented on inscriptions in the *Journal of the Asiatic Society of Bengal*, edited Sanskrit texts in its *Bibliotheca Indica* series, and published catalogues of the Society's collection of manuscripts, books, and antiquities (Fig. 1.1).[1] Haraprasad Sastri (1853–1931), about whom we shall have much to say later, succeeded Mitra as editor of the *Bibliotheca Indica* in 1885. He was also very successful as the Society's director (from 1891 onwards) for conducting operations

FIGURE 1.1: Raja Rajendralala Mitra

in search of Sanskrit and vernacular manuscripts. He procured more than 8,000 manuscripts from various places, including several towns and villages of Bengal, and the Darbar Library in Nepal. Like Mitra, Sastri became president of the Asiatic Society in 1919.[2] Several other Bengali scholars engaged in archaeology kept up the institutional link that Mitra had first strongly established with the Society.

Right from its inception as the Museum of the Asiatic Society of Bengal in 1814, the Indian Museum in Calcutta acquired remains of ancient monuments, sculptures, inscriptions, and coins for its archaeological/ethnological section. Since 1832, Indians—some of them Bengalis—began donating objects to the Museum. Rajendralala Mitra, for example, deposited in the Museum's archaeological gallery the antiquities obtained from his surveys in Bodh Gaya and Orissa in the 1870s. Much earlier, in 1849, Mitra had also prepared the first catalogue of what was then known as 'curiosities' in the Museum. This catalogue listed the entire range of objects in the possession of the Asiatic Society, including coins and inscriptions. In 1907, two young Bengali scholars, Rakhaldas Banerji (1885–1930) and Nilmani Chakravarti, joined the Indian Museum as archaeological assistants under Theodor Bloch, the archaeological superintendent of the Eastern Circle of the Archaeological Survey of India and also in charge of the archaeological section of the Museum (Fig. 1.2). Banerji assisted Bloch in preparing the *Supplementary Catalogue of the Archaeological Collections of the Indian Museum*, which was published in 1911 after the latter's death.[3]

One observes that by the early twentieth century, those who joined the Indian Museum developed connections with the Archaeological Survey and vice versa. Banerji joined the Archaeological Survey as excavation assistant to the Director General John Marshall in 1910 and remained attached to it until his sudden dismissal as superintendent of the Eastern Circle in 1926. Undoubtedly, the apogee of Banerji's career in the Survey was marked by the excavations he conducted at Mohenjodaro in Sind in 1922–3. During the last two years of his service in the Survey he explored the sites of Mahasthangarh and Ghoraghat, and surveyed the monuments of Murshidabad and Dhaka in Bengal.[4] Prior to Banerji's stint, one of the earliest Indian field archaeologists, Purna Chandra Mukharji, had been personal assistant to Bloch in the Bengal Circle till 1903.[5] In 1917, Ramaprasad Chanda (1873–1942), secretary of an archaeological society—Varendra Research Society—in north

FIGURE 1.2: Nilmani Chakravarti

Bengal, joined the Survey as a scholarship holder to equip himself to direct his society's independent excavations.[6] Because of Chanda's exceptional abilities, Marshall wanted to co-opt him in the Survey, but that did not happen. Later in 1921, on Marshall's request, Chanda joined the archaeological section of the Indian Museum. He retired as superintendent of this section in 1932. His colleague at the Varendra Research Society, Nanigopal Majumdar (1897–1938) also remained a trainee archaeologist, working at Mohenjodaro, but unlike Chanda, was immediately absorbed into the Survey. In the 1920s and 1930s Majumdar worked extensively in Sindh, where, in fact, he was killed in 1938. In the mid-1930s, as superintendent of the Eastern Circle of the Survey, he unearthed remnants of ancient temples from sites in Bengal such as Mahanad in Hughli district, Baigram in Dinajpur district, and Medh near Mahasthangarh in Bogra district. In 1931, he was appointed assistant superintendent of the archaeological section of the Indian Museum, and like Chanda, became superintendent soon after. In 1937 he published *A Guide to the Sculptures in the Indian Museum, Parts I and II.*[7]

While the aforementioned instances show that Bengali intellectuals became increasingly involved with official institutions of archaeological research, many of them, however, could not completely identify themselves with the colonial/European character of these bodies. Perhaps a major reason for this dissonance lay in the fact that these establishments did not adequately assist in constructing what had by then become significant in the historical context of Bengal—a regional identity. This is further borne out in the manner in which the spurt in private archaeological research in Bengal from the late nineteenth century can be located within the rubric of the educated Bengali elite's search for a regional identity. In the 1860s and 1870s, patriotism and growing anti-British feelings among the Bengalis found expression through the medium of Bengali literature, newspapers, and theatre.[8] *Amrita Bazar Patrika*, a patriotic Bengali weekly, was started against this background in 1868. A number of patriotic plays (many of them dealing with the oppression and injustice of indigo planters and magistrates) were staged, beginning with Dinabandhu Mitra's *Nil-Darpan*, which ultimately led to the passage of the repressive Dramatic Performances Act in 1876, prohibiting the staging of certain plays. With the Swadeshi Boycott movement of 1905–6 marking a watershed in the Bengali intelligentsia's quest for identity, there was again a great upsurge in nationalist newspapers, songs, plays, historical research, and art movement.[9]

Like language, literature, theatre, and art, a search for Bengal's material past too was identified as a means of retrieving its lost glory. The greatest champion of this idea was Bankimchandra Chattopadhyay (1838–1894), one of the earliest Bengali novelists and a pillar of modern Bengali prose, who emerged as an indomitable source of strength for the first generation of scholars in the forefront of historical-archaeological research in Bengal. Subsequently, Bankim's mantle was assumed by Rabindranath Tagore (1861–1941).[10] In 1880, Bankimchandra wrote in Bengali that Bengal desperately needed a history, and this history had to be written by every Bengali.[11] He also criticized Rajendralala Mitra for not engaging himself in retrieving the archaeology of Bengal although he was, in the latter's opinion, the most capable among both Bengali and European archaeologists.[12] Bankim set the trend of writing in both English and Bengali. This was soon adopted by his young contemporaries such as Romesh Chunder Dutt (1848–1909), and Akshay Kumar Maitra (1861–1930), and by the early twentieth century came to define the academic output of Bengali scholars writing on archaeology. Bengali scholars made conscious efforts to disseminate historical and archaeological knowledge in the vernacular as they believed that this would generate patriotism among fellow Bengalis.[13] Thus, Bengali articles on archaeology began to be juxtaposed with diverse subjects in journals started for the serious reading public, such as Rajendralala Mitra's *Bibidartha Sangraha*, Bankimchandra's *Bangadarshan*, Rabindranath Tagore's *Bharati*, and Ramananda Chattopadhyay's *Prabasi* to name a few. In addition, many scholars of archaeology wrote historical novels, plays, and lexicons in their mother tongue, traced the history of the Bengali script, popularized science, and evolved a technical vocabulary in Bengali. Another important point to note is that Bengal in the third quarter of the nineteenth century had many proponents of Hindu nationalism, including Bankimchandra.[14] Historians and archaeologists influenced by this strain strove to recover a Hindu past for Bengal.

On 29 April 1894, an organization called the Bengal Academy of Literature (which had been founded a year earlier with the aim of promoting Bengali language and literature) was reorganized as the Bangiya Sahitya Parishad. Its founder-members included wealthy patrons like Maharaja Benoy Krishna Deb Bahadur of Sovabazar and scholars like Haraprasad Sastri. Soon after its establishment, the Bangiya Sahitya Parishad introduced a quarterly Bengali research journal called the *Sahitya Parishad Patrika*,[15] much like the *Journal of the Asiatic Society of Bengal* but more restricted in scope in terms of content and contributors. Within a short span, the Sahitya Parishad emerged as a very popular literary platform, but what is more significant from our perspective is that this body also gave an immense impetus to archaeological research. In 1894 itself, antiquarian research was established as one of its goals. This entailed searching and editing old manuscripts, looking for stone and copper inscriptions, stone seals, coins, and sculptures, recovering their contents and histories, and, finally, locating the objects' individual histories within a larger historical framework.

Haraprasad Sastri, whom we discussed earlier in the context of the Asiatic Society, greatly contributed to archaeological research in the Bangiya Sahitya Parishad, not least of all by regularly providing antiquarian remains (Fig. 1.3). He was one of the founder-members of the Parishad and remained its president for several terms. Interestingly, Sastri was not a professional archaeologist but a Sanskrit scholar who had developed a keen interest in ancient palaeography and sculpture.[16] In the 1915 volume of *Epigraphia Indica*—the Archaeological Survey

FIGURE 1.3: Haraprasad Sastri

of India's journal on inscriptions—Sastri edited the AD fourth-century Susunia rock inscription of Candravarman (Bankura district, West Bengal) and engaged in the debate concerning the issuer's royal family. While this article was undoubtedly a product of his serious interest in the subject, one cannot overlook the role played by the Parishad in sustaining this interest. The Susunia inscription had been first edited, in Bengali, by one of Sastri's colleagues at the Parishad, Nagendranath Basu (1866–1938) in the *Sahitya Parishad Patrika*, and Sastri's edition of it, in English, was based on the impressions supplied by yet another colleague, Rakhaldas Banerji.[17] Sastri, who had a mentor in Bankimchandra, wrote extensively on the histories of Bengali language, literature, script, and the scope of Bengali in education and intellectual pursuits. For a few years he worked as an assistant translator with the Bengal government and as librarian of the Bengal library. In the early 1920s, Haraprasad headed the Bengali and Sanskrit departments of Dhaka University. Sastri's experience at the Asiatic Society, of searching and editing manuscripts, which we mentioned earlier, stood him in good stead on at least two counts. First, it supplied him with the material for his own researches on the Bengali language and script, on Mahāyāna Buddhism in Bengal, and so on. Largely on the basis of eleven manuscripts in the Bengali script discovered by him, and particularly a genre of songs called *Charja Geeti* composed by Buddhist monks in one such manuscript found at the Darbar Library in Nepal, Sastri traced back the antiquity of the Bengali script to at least the tenth century. In 1916, he published *Bauddha Gana O Doha* by editing these songs along with three other Buddhist works. His concern with the history of Buddhism was also reflected in his historical novel *Bener Meye* ('The Merchant's Daughter'), which described the complex process of interaction between Buddhists and Hindus in eleventh-century Bengal. Second, the Asiatic Society experience equipped Sastri to lead the Bangiya Sahitya Parishad's search for ancient manuscripts, their edition, publication, and study. The discussion on a large number of such manuscripts collected from different parts of Bengal formed one of the *Sahitya Parishad Patrika*'s thrust areas.

The *Patrika* also contained articles on local history, many of them written on the basis of newly discovered coins and inscriptions. Among those who wrote in this journal on the history and archaeology of Bengal in the early decades of the twentieth century, mention may be made of Nagendranath Basu, Nalini Kanta Bhattasali, Rakhaldas Banerji, Radhagovinda Basak, Ramesh Chandra Majumdar, and Suniti Kumar Chatterji.

For a long time Nagendranath Basu, honorary archaeological surveyor of the Mayurbhanj estate of Orissa and the first honorary curator of the Parishad's museum, edited the *Patrika* (Fig. 1.4). He also edited a number of ancient texts published by the Parishad. Greatly influenced by Haraprasad Sastri, he donated to the organization's museum many artefacts collected during his tours in different parts of eastern India. One of these was the Susunia grant of Candravarman, mentioned earlier. He also loaned edicts to the Parishad when it held its exhibitions (the twelfth-century AD Bangarh grant of Mahipāla during the 1911–12 exhibition, for instance) and sometimes involved colleagues in deciphering inscriptions. Sastri's influence on Basu was not limited to the latter's activities within the Sahitya Parishad. For example, in 1894 at the Asiatic Society where Sastri had introduced him, Basu delivered a number of lectures on the antiquities of Bengal. Basu was also a member of the philological committee of the Asiatic Society. Like his mentor, he went on to collect a large number of ancient Bengali manuscripts, including more than 200 family records, which later formed the corpus of

FIGURE 1.4:
Nagendranath Basu

the Bengali department of Calcutta University. The issue of Bengali identity had affected Basu strongly enough for him to write the multi-volume *Banger Jatiya Itihas* ('The National History of Bengal'). While these volumes were essentially about the ancient histories of different families in Bengal, they also discussed several archaeological relics found in the province.[18] In some ways, Basu's compilation of the first Bengali encyclopaedia—the twenty-two-volume *Bangla Bishwakosh* (the last volume of which was published in 1911) and an English–Bengali dictionary *Shabdendu Mahakosh* (1884)—was in tandem with the *Sahitya Parishad Patrika*'s pioneering role in introducing the study of the sciences in the vernacular and preparing *paribhasha*s or Bengali definitions of technical terms.

The Bangiya Sahitya Parishad witnessed its most intense phase of activity roughly around the years of the Swadeshi Boycott movement, when Ramendrasundar Tribedi (1864–1919) was secretary between 1904 and 1911.[19] Tribedi was a staunch patriot who worked towards involving women in the Swadeshi Boycott movement. He described the Parishad's search for literary and material remains of Bengal's past as a *sadhana* (dedicated endeavour) to recognize the true identity of the motherland. From 1905–6 onwards, the Parishad began establishing its branches in different parts of Bengal (such as Rangpur, Rajshahi, Mymensingh, and Barisal) and beyond in areas with Bengali-speaking populations (Bhagalpur, Varanasi, Meerut, and Agra). One such branch that was very successful was the Rangpur Sahitya Parishad in north Bengal. It established itself as a centre for local historical-archaeological research, built up a museum to house its veritable collection of sculptures and manuscripts, and published a quarterly literary journal, *Rangpur Sahitya Parishad Patrika*, which carried articles on local historical relics, unpublished manuscripts, and folklore of north Bengal. People with deep love for their local heritage coupled with genuine pride in a Bengali identity played a crucial role in such branches of the Parishad. Nalini Kanta Bhattasali (1888–1947), who later became curator of the Dacca Museum[20] and prepared a classic catalogue of the museum's sculptures, was closely associated with the Parishad's branch at Dhaka. In 1916, while still a student, Prafulla Kumar Sarkar (1892–1977) established the Nadia Sahitya Parishad and engaged himself in recovering the archaeological remains of Nadia district. He surveyed the mound of Ballaldhibi there along with K.N. Dikshit, superintendent of the Archaeological Survey, and worked towards bringing it under the Survey's purview.

While institutions like the Sahitya Parishad nurtured the making of a regional identity, they were not divorced from the larger nationalist aspirations. In the winter of 1906–7, when the Indian National Congress session was held in Calcutta, an exhibition on crafts and agriculture was organized on the occasion. The Parishad lent to this exhibition rubbings of copper and stone inscriptions, terracotta and metal sculptures, photographs of historical sites and temples, old illustrations, ancient manuscripts, and objects used by littérateurs—all of which had trickled into the Parishad since its inception. In the aftermath of the popular interest generated by the exhibition, some members emphasized the need for a permanent museum.[21] Ramendrasundar Tribedi proposed that this historical-literary museum should be named Romesh Bhavan in memory of Romesh Chunder Dutt, the first president of the Bangiya Sahitya Parishad. The Parishad justified the need for another local museum in Calcutta on the basis that the Indian Museum was cramped for space and could not find sufficient accommodation for archaeological exhibits. In addition, it felt there was enough scope for private archaeological explorations without infringing on the provisions of the Treasure Trove Act or the Ancient Monuments Act. Tribedi hoped that the

Museum would grow into what he called 'a National museum of our own which we may look upon with pride'.[22] In April 1912 the museum was formally established as an independent wing of the Parishad.[23]

Perhaps one who had the greatest association with the museum was the Parishad's assistant secretary Rakhaldas Banerji, who as mentioned earlier was employed in the Archaeological Survey of India and the Indian Museum. Banerji graduated in history from Presidency College, Calcutta, and thereafter obtained his masters in history from Calcutta University in 1910 (Fig. 1.5). Having worked on catalogues in the Indian Museum and the Asiatic Society,[24] and mastered several languages and scripts (including Sanskrit under Haraprasad Sastri), Banerji had sound foundations for a career in archaeology, unlike many of his contemporaries in Bengal who drifted into archaeology from other disciplines. Perhaps this accounted for his equal expertise in archaeological exploration and excavation, epigraphy, numismatics, and the study of sculptures. He was a prolific bilingual writer who wrote fourteen monographs and more than 300 articles. Over the years, he also edited and re-edited more than eighty inscriptions. In 1914, he wrote the first Indian vernacular work on numismatics—*Prachin*

FIGURE 1.5: Rakhaldas Banerji

Mudra, Part I, in Bengali. Banerji's other notable work on Bengal was his two-volume *Bangalar Itihas*—a history of Bengal from prehistoric times to the end of Muslim rule, published in 1915.[25] While Banerji, like the others, was conscious about reinforcing a Bengali identity, he was also convinced that the history of Bengal had to be seen as a small part of the history of India, as what he called 'a chapter in the history of *uttarapatha*'. Thus, at the end of each chapter in *Bangalar Itihas* there was an appendix that summarized the larger history of the nation during the period covered. In his posthumously published *Eastern Indian School of Medieval Sculpture* (1933), he identified a distinct artistic school in early medieval Bengal, marked by the Pāla and Sena period sculptures (*c.* eighth to twelfth centuries AD). These periods as a whole remained Banerji's particular focus of research within the larger project of recovering the pre-Islamic history of Bengal. Banerji's academic output was matched by his publication of more than half a dozen historical novels in Bengali, among which *Sasanka* (1914), *Dharmapala* (1915), and *Moyukh* (1916) dealt with Bengal. In Banerji's scheme of things, Śaṣāṅka, king of Gauḍa, was the first harbinger of the independence of Bengal and Bengalis, while the Pāla ruler Dharmapāla marked the apogee of that independence. Banerji also wrote a number of articles on Bengali theatre and advised directors staging historical plays.

In the early years of the Parishad's museum, Banerji procured a large number of artefacts and helped in organizing its exhibitions. More importantly, he published *A Descriptive List of Sculptures and Coins in the Museum of the Bangiya Sahitya Parishad* in 1911 (the year in which Bloch's *Supplementary Catalogue* was also published). The collection of the museum had grown steadily, and by such time included 248 archaeological artefacts. The bulk of the donations came from the rulers of Dighapatiya, Kassimbazar, Lalgola, and Natore, but more humble sources such as Maulavi Khair-ul-Anam, a teacher at the Hare School, Calcutta, and Janaki Nath Gupta, a professor at Ripon College, Calcutta, were not altogether missing. Banerji's catalogue mentioned stone and bronze images of the Buddha, Bodhisattva, Tārā, Viṣṇu, Śiva, and Durgā, Jaina icons, carved brick panels, enamelled bricks, copper plates, door jambs, votive stūpas, terracotta medallions, palm leaf manuscripts, and coins—largely obtained from Bengal, Bihar, Assam, and Nepal.[26] For Banerji, his association with the museum proved very fruitful as much of the material of his subsequent writings emerged from it. The best example of this is *The*

Origins of the Bengali Script which was published as a monograph in 1919. At the suggestion of Ramendrasundar Tribedi and with the help of Basanta Ranjan Ray, the custodian of the manuscript collection of the Parishad, Banerji had written this as an essay in Bengali. Tribedi had wanted to publish the article in the Parishad's journal, but at the initiative of Asutosh Mukherjee, Vice Chancellor of Calcutta University, the essay was translated into English and awarded the University's Jubilee Research Prize in 1913.[27]

Like the Bangiya Sahitya Parishad, and yet qualitatively different from it, was another non-official body promoting archaeological research in Bengal in general and the Varendra region of north Bengal in particular. This was the Varendra Research Society established at Rajshahi, north Bengal, in 1910 by Kumar Sarat Kumar Ray (1876–1945), a scion of the Dighapatiya royal family, Akshay Kumar Maitra, a leading lawyer and historian of Rajshahi, and Ramaprasad Chanda, then a teacher at the Rajshahi Collegiate School (Figs 1.6 and 1.7). Sharing a passion for history and archaeology, the three in April 1910 went on their first exploratory tour of Bengal to collect archaeological materials from areas adjacent to Rajshahi town, accompanied by Rakhaldas Banerji and Ramkamal Sinha

FIGURE 1.6: Akshay Kumar Maitra

FIGURE 1.7: Ramaprasad Chanda

from Calcutta. The tour was an immense success as they were able to collect thirty-two relics, including a distinct Sena period life-size image of Pārvatī from Mandoil. While things had moved smoothly so far, a tussle now emerged over the custodianship of these relics. Banerji wanted to carry these to the Indian Museum. While Sinha mooted for the Sahitya Parishad, Sarat Ray and other notables of Rajshahi, such as the honorary secretary of the local branch of the Bangiya Sahitya Parishad, Shashadhar Ray, wanted these to remain in the town. The problem was resolved when Sarat Kumar Ray decided to establish a centre for archaeological research in Rajshahi—the Varendra Research Society. It was formally inaugurated in September 1910 and registered as an association four years later. In 1916, Sarat Ray financed a building for the society on a piece of land gifted by his elder brother. In addition, through a monthly contribution of Rs 200, Sarat Ray sustained the society's ambitious programme of exploring ancient sites, collecting and preserving antiquities discovered in the course of such explorations, acquiring and publishing rare manuscripts, researching on the cultural and political history of early Bengal, and regularly publishing results of these researches. From

1917, the Bengal government began to give the society an annual grant of Rs 1,200.

Sarat Ray and his colleagues followed up the first tour with several successful antiquarian explorations in different areas of Varendra. To house the antiquities collected in the course of these tours and those acquired from elsewhere, the Society built a museum which was formally opened to the public in November 1919. This had one of the most impressive collections of Bengal sculpture in terms of the sheer number and the historical value of individual pieces. The first catalogue of its sculptures, published in 1919, listed as many as 465 specimens. Its epigraphic collection included some of the earliest inscriptions of undivided Bengal, like the Dhanaidaha copper plate inscription of the Gupta ruler Kumaragupta I and the five Gupta period copper plate sale deeds from Damodarpur.

Successful explorations encouraged the Varendra Research Society to undertake limited excavations around Rajshahi. The most important of these was the joint excavation in 1923 with Calcutta University (largely financed by the University) under the direction of D.R. Bhandarkar at Paharpur, at the site of the ninth-century Somapura Buddhist monastery, now in Bangladesh. Unfortunately, within two months (during which a few rooms at the south-west corner of the monastery enclosure together with the adjoining part of the courtyard had been excavated), this project fell apart. The Archaeological Survey, under the stewardship of Rakhaldas Banerji, revived it in 1925–6, albeit acrimoniously. There were charges and counter-charges on the question of ownership of recovered sculptures. The crux of the conflict was the professional competence of private bodies. Earlier, the Society had excavated a mound at Cossipur, 8 km from Balurghat in erstwhile Dinajpur district (1911), the Pradyumneshvar/Padumshahar tank at Deopara, almost 26 km from Rajshahi town (1917–18), and the site of Mahisantosh, popularly known as Mahiganj, under Patnitala police station, 5 km south of Balurghat in erstwhile Dinajpur district (1916).

In order to understand how the Varendra Research Society went about its excavations, one may turn to an article by A.K. Maitra in a popular Bengali journal *Sahitya* in 1916, describing the events leading to the society's excavation at Mahisantosh, the excavation itself, and the relics unearthed.[28] According to Maitra, in 1911, while surveying the ruins around Balurghat, on the invitation of the local elite, members of the Society had also visited the ruins of Mahisantosh. It contained a fortified area with a mud moat, an old dargah encircled by brick walls, a mound covered in vegetation and brick-stone debris, and many old tanks. At the topmost point of this mound (which had not been mentioned in any of the earlier accounts of Mahisantosh written by English scholars), the upper portions of two or three stone pillars were found. On the walls of the dargah were attached two 'Islamic' stone inscriptions, which had already been deciphered. When Maitra revisited Mahisantosh five years later, he found the smaller inscription missing and the larger one lying on the ground. So he contributed some money and urged the public to subscribe towards the conservation of the site. To further stem the destruction, pillars from the mound were removed to the Society's museum. A few days later when Sanskrit inscriptions were identified on two stone pillars and destroyed iconic remains were discovered on a few stone plaques, the Varendra Research Society decided to conduct excavations on this mound at Mahisantosh. Sarat Ray, Ramaprasad Chanda, Akshay Kumar Maitra, and others reached Mahisantosh once the permission to excavate had been obtained from the zamindar owning the land. The excavation involved a number of related activities: surveying Mahisantosh and ruins nearby, collecting local traditions associated with the site, preparing maps of the ruins, photographing the southern portion of the mound before and after the dig, deciding on the exact location and method of the dig, and finally selecting and cataloguing the unearthed finds. Among the artefacts yielded by the excavation, inscribed pillars were the most notable, of which two contained two identical lines inscribed in Sanskrit. The sculptures of Viṣṇu, Mahiśāsuramardinī, and Sūrya that were unearthed had been damaged with their limbs broken off, their rear smoothed out and embellished with Islamic ornamentation. The stones seemed to have come from Hindu and Buddhist temples nearby.

Islamic reuse of stone relics from Hindu places of worship appeared as a recurrent theme in Akshay Maitra's writings. He noticed, for example, that the gate and steps of the *mimbar* (pulpit) of the Adina mosque at Pandua in Maldah district were probably built with stones gathered from temples.[29] Maitra had been drawn to history from an early age, but at the same time found colonial historical accounts to be extremely biased. He, therefore, thought of ways to redress it by presenting a balanced account in Bengali. Although proficient in English, he chose to write in Bengali, and two-thirds of his published works are in that language. He was a lawyer by profession, but did not take up practice seriously. Instead, he devoted himself to literary and historical works—all of which consciously projected a heroic, Hindu identity of Bengal. For example, in a poem titled 'Bangavijaya Kavya', young Maitra challenged the view that the Sena ruler Lakṣmaṇasena had fled when Bakhtiyar Khilji, an ambitious Turk officer under Muhammad Ghori, had attacked Bengal in the thirteenth century. In 1899 Maitra began publishing, on Tagore's advice, the first Bengali historical quarterly, titled *Aitihasik Chitra*, but it was extremely short-lived. Through the writings of fellow-Bengalis, the journal tried to make the Bengalis aware of their own history and Tagore saw it as 'preparing for the holy war to free the history of our country from bondage'.[30] For Maitra, the pre-Muslim history of Gauḍa (north Bengal), which he reconstructed through his book *Gauda Under the Hindus* (1902) and through articles in Bengali journals *Bangadarshan*, *Prabasi*, and *Sahitya*, constituted the true heritage of modern Bengalis. In this process of reconstruction, Maitra generously used archaeological relics from north Bengal such as pillars, old tanks, inscribed stone pieces, architectural members, and sculptures as his instrument. In the years of the Swadeshi Boycott movement, he completely identified his archaeological research with the creation of a regional identity. He also published his historical novel *Mir Kasim* in the midst of this movement. It is interesting to note that Maitra, although a champion of Hindu identity of Bengal, based two of his extremely popular novels—*Siraj-ud-daulah* (1897)[31] and *Mir Kasim* (1905)—on Muslim protagonists.

It was under the guidance of Maitra that for thirty years, researches of the Varendra Research Society were regularly published in its annual reports and memoirs. Maitra had conceived the publication of an eight-volume compendium on north Bengal titled *Gaudavivaranmala*, of which only two were published: *Gaudarajamala* by Ramaprasad Chanda in 1911, and *Gaudalekhamala* by himself in 1912. The *Gaudarajamala*, written by Ramaprasad Chanda, was the first publication of the Varendra Research Society. It was also the first history of the region to be written solely on the basis of epigraphic evidence. Ramaprasad Chanda was a versatile scholar in the mould of Rakhaldas Banerji. His notable contributions were in anthropology, art, and architecture, but he was also adept at archaeological exploration, excavation, palaeography, and the history of ancient Indian religions. Around 1905, Chanda had got acquainted with Sarat Kumar Ray and A.K. Maitra while teaching at the Rajshahi Collegiate School, and this led to the formation of the Varendra Research Society. At the Society, Chanda performed secretarial jobs, but more significantly, he also handled the total collection of its museum, of which archaeological material formed the first group. He had been stirred by the publication of Herbert Risley's *Census Report of 1901*, which rather arbitrarily divided the people of India into seven racial groups. So he began his own research, and in a few years started publishing articles refuting the former's claims. One such article, on the origin of races in Bengal, was published in the journal *East and West* in 1907. Encouraged by Sarat Kumar Ray and Ramendrasundar Tribedi, Chanda continued his research, whose results, based on compilation of anthropometric data and examination of early traditions preserved in ancient Indian literature, were published by the Varendra Research Society as *Indo-Aryan Races* in 1916. This, among other things, opposed Risley's theory of the Mongolo-Dravidian origin of Bengalis. In 1919, Chanda joined the department of ancient Indian history and culture of Calcutta University and later headed its nascent anthropology department. In 1920, he was elected fellow of the Asiatic Society, and remained its anthropological secretary for many years. Unlike most scholars under review, he did not write much in Bengali. Till 1930 most of his studies were published in the annual reports and memoirs of the Survey. One of the best examples of this is the *Beginnings of Art in Eastern India with Special Reference to the Sculptures in the Indian Museum, Calcutta*, which was published in 1927 as Memoir number 30. Chanda's expertise in iconography was well acknowledged and led the British Museum to commission him to catalogue Indian sculptures in its collection. This was published from London as the *Medieval Indian Sculptures in the British Museum* (1936).

In 1929, the Varendra Research Society published the third volume of *Inscriptions of Bengal,* written by its museum's erstwhile curator Nanigopal Majumdar (Fig. 1.8). While the *Gaudalekhamala* had discussed copper plates issued by the Pāla rulers, this contained seventeen edited inscriptions of the subsequent Candra, Varman, and Sena rulers of Bengal. Three years earlier, the Society had published Majumdar's book on the Nalanda copper plate of Devapaladeva. Majumdar was an exceptional epigraphist who began deciphering and editing inscriptions, in both Bengali and English, in journals like the *Indian Antiquary* and the *Bangiya Sahitya Parishad* while still

FIGURE 1.8: Nanigopal Majumdar

a Sanskrit Honours' student at Sanskrit College, Calcutta. In 1920 Majumdar obtained his master's degree in ancient Indian history and culture from Calcutta University and then taught in this department for a few years. He edited several important inscriptions of ancient and early medieval Bengal including the sixth-century AD grant of Mahārājādhirāja Vijayasena discovered from the Mallasarul village in Bardhaman district. This was edited for the first time in the 1935–6 volume of the *Epigraphia Indica*. Two years later, Majumdar wrote about it in the *Bangiya Sahitya Parishad*. His soundness as an epigraphist prompted John Marshall and Alfred Foucher to employ him to edit, classify, and discuss the 800-odd inscriptions published in their three-volume *Monuments of Sanchi* (1940). While he was curator of the Varendra Research Museum between 1924 and 1927, Majumdar described in the museum's annual reports the recent sculptural acquisitions of the museum such as stone figures of Viṣṇu, Sūrya, and Umā-Maheśvara. One unique sculpture that came to the museum in 1925 during Majumdar's curatorship was the gold-plated bronze sculpture of Manjuśrī in the Gupta style discovered at Balai Dhap near Mahasthan in Bangladesh. Nanigopal Majumdar published a detailed description of this along with its first illustrations in the October 1926 issue of *The Modern Review*.

Having profiled the two leading non-official bodies engaged in archaeological research, it is worth noting that both enjoyed an active interface. Sarat Kumar Ray of the Varendra Research Society had been introduced to the Sahitya Parishad by his science tutor Ramendrasundar Tribedi, and he played a proactive role in this institution, including obtaining from Maharaja Manindra Chandra Nandy of Kassimbazar the land on which a permanent building of the Parishad was built in 1908. A.K. Maitra too had a long relationship with the Parishad, which involved lending copper plate inscriptions from north Bengal for the Parishad's exhibitions and donating artefacts to its museum, culminating in his appointment as vice-president of the Parishad in 1918. At one point, an understanding was reached between the two bodies on the demarcation of their respective areas of archaeological exploration: while the latter concentrated on the Rarh region of south-west Bengal, the former explored the Varendra area of north-east. A special Rarh Anusandhan Samiti was set up within the Bangiya Sahitya Parishad, which in 1913–14 decided to work on the Basuli temple in the Chhatna village and the Susunia rock inscription in Bankura district.[32] The archaeological traditions that the Bangiya Sahitya Parishad and the Varendra Research Society nurtured were integrally linked to their search for local/regional history, although this did not preclude their attempt to relate the local histories to the larger history of the province, the nation, and at times, even areas beyond the subcontinent.[33] Maitra was convinced that 'the main source of the history of the entire Bengali people may be traced through the *Varendra-maṇḍala* in the period before the advent of Muslim rule',[34] and Haraprasad Sastri clearly believed that a full-fledged history of Bengal is possible if one compiles the histories of villages in every district.[35]

Although one notices a broad convergence between the Sahitya Parishad and the Varendra Research Society on issues such as the ambit of archaeological explorations, the range of archaeological activities sponsored by them, and the way archaeology was used by them to shape the creation of a modern Bengali identity, there were differences in the way material remains were viewed by these two institutions as also individual practitioners of archaeology in Bengal. One cannot, however, visualize these two non-official bodies with their associated scholars as exclusive camps with their distinctive approaches to archaeology. For Maitra, Banerji, and Chanda, history had to be grounded in verifiable facts and, in the process of historical analysis (that involved an objective, scientific examination of these facts), there had to be a primacy of archaeological, epigraphic, and numismatic sources over textual or oral evidence. Therefore, they challenged the historicity of Bengal's genealogical literature, the *kulagranthas*/*kulajis*, through which one could trace a history of the evolution of Bengal's brahmanical social structure. What this group of scholars particularly questioned was the existence of a king named Ādiśūr in the remote past who was believed to have invited five brahmans from Kanauj—the ancestors of modern Bengali Varendra and Radhiya brahmans—to migrate to Bengal. This was largely because there was no epigraphic, numismatic, or archaeological data to corroborate these references to Ādiśūr.[36] Haraprasad Sastri and Nagendranath Basu on the other hand staunchly supported the historicity of the *kulagranthas*, which they identified as a rich source of Bengal's social history. In an article published in 1917 in the Bengali journal *Utbodhan*, Sastri was dismissive of the 'scientific historians' (translation mine) who doubted the historicity of Ādiśūr. For the Sahitya Parishad, which was essentially a literary organization, archaeological artefacts, language, literature, and customs of the people were all related subjects of study. Its museum not only housed the archaeological relics that we discussed in the context of Banerji's catalogue, but manuscripts and memorabilia of Bengali literati such as their letters, documents, writing accessories, and even their apparel. Yet the most valuable category of objects in the collection of the Parishad were ancient and medieval manuscripts, which, like archaeological relics, were viewed as testaments of the past that needed to be collected and preserved. For the Varendra Research Society, on the other hand, archaeological explorations/excavations in north Bengal remained its primary focus.

While Bengal forms an important case study for the development of a non-official archaeological sphere, in no way was this unique to Bengal. Like Bengal, its eastern neighbour Assam witnessed a similar growth of popular consciousness from the last decades of the nineteenth century, which was reflected in the proliferation of journals, newspapers, and societies for the promotion of Assamese language, literature, and history. The Kamrupa Anusandhan Samiti was one such society formed in 1912 to investigate the antiquities of Assam. It built up a sizeable collection of sculpted stone images, ancient architectural relics, terracotta plaques, and stone and copper plate inscriptions. From 1933, it started the *Journal of the Assam Research Society* which published, in line with the Society's strong tradition of epigraphic studies, newly-discovered inscriptions. Through the efforts of two of its members, Mahamahopadhyaya Padmanath Bhattacharya Vidyavinoda and Pandit Hemachandra Goswami, the society acquired quite a few copper plate and rock inscriptions of the ancient kings of Kāmarūpa. On the basis of these discoveries, in 1931, Padmanath Bhattacharya published the earliest compilation of historical inscriptions of the pre-Ahom kings of Assam titled *Kamarupashasanavali*. A towering figure in the non-official sphere, Bhattacharya had formed the Bangasahitya—Anushilani Sabha in Gauhati in 1908 to enlighten Bengal about the 'real' history of Assam. It was later transformed into the Gauhati branch of the Bengali Literary Association. Like the Kamrupa Anusandhan Samiti, the Sabha was patronized by both European scholars and local intellectuals like Hemchandra Goswami and Mahamahopadhyay Dhireshwar Bhattacharya Kaviratna.[37]

In conclusion, what has emerged in the process of this discussion is that while it is convenient to categorize the archaeological enterprise of the late nineteenth and early twentieth century as 'colonial' and 'native', and establish a stark contrast between the two, this exercise has its limitations because, in reality, archaeological practice was a medley of things. What has not been adequately highlighted in most histories of Indian archaeology is that although Indian scholars were stereotyped as 'ignorant natives', lacking the potential to internalize official training and incapable of pursuing historical-archaeological research on their own, there were cases where official bodies developed working relationships with indigenous scholars and non-official bodies. The relationship that developed between the Varendra Research Society and the Archaeological Survey/Indian Museum, for example, did not remain uniformly cordial, but ultimately the latter could not overlook the Varendra Research Society as a potential recruitment bank. For the majority of scholars, the official establishments offered the opportunity to work on a larger canvas. Such scholars continuously straddled both the spheres and, hence, their contributions and legacy cannot be pigeonholed as either 'native' or as part of the colonial apparatus.

ACKNOWLEDGEMENTS

This essay would not have been possible without the support of Nayanjot Lahiri, Upinder Singh, Gautam Sengupta, Saktidas Roy, Sunil Das, and my parents. I am grateful to the Bangiya Sahitya Parishad, Kolkata, for the photographs.

NOTES

1. Upinder Singh, *The Discovery of Ancient India: Early Archaeologists and the Beginnings of Archaeology*, New Delhi: Permanent Black, 2004, pp. 325, 327–8.
2. Haraprasad Sastri's biographical details are based on Narendra Nath Law (ed.), *Haraprasad Memorial Volume*, The Indian Historical Society, 9(1), 1933.
3. This was an updated version of the *Catalogue and Handbook of the Archaeological Collections of the Indian Museum* prepared by zoologist John Anderson in 1882–3, who was then the superintendent of the Museum. For the history of the Indian Museum see Tapati Guha-Thakurta, *Monuments, Objects, Histories: Institutions of Art in Colonial and Postcolonial India*, New Delhi: Permanent Black, 2004, pp. 52–3, 73, 76–7, 99, 113–14.
4. The biographical details about Rakhaldas Banerji are based on the introduction in Asit Bandopadhyaya and Bishwanath Mukhopadhyaya (eds), *Rakhaldas Bandopadhyaya Rachanabali*, vol. 1, Calcutta: Paschimbanga Rajya Pustak Parishad, 1988.
5. Singh, *Discovery of Ancient India*, p. 316.
6. During his training, Chanda accompanied the Archaeological Survey of India excavation team to sites like Sarnath, Mathura, and Taxila, and aided in the preparation of a catalogue of archaeological material preserved in the Sanchi Museum. Two of his works—*Dates of the Votive Inscriptions of the Stupa of Sanchi* (1919) and *Archaeology and Vaishnava Tradition* (1920)—were published as memoir numbers 19 and 20 of the Survey, respectively. For biographical details about Chanda, see, Narendranath Bhattacharya's introduction in *The Indo-Aryan Races: A Study of the Origin of Indo-Aryan People and Institutions*, Calcutta: *Indian Studies: Past & Present*, 1969. Also see Nayanjot Lahiri, *Finding Forgotten Cities: How the Indus Civilization was Discovered*, New Delhi: Permanent Black, 2005, p. 187.
7. For biographical details on Majumdar, see Mallar Mitra, 'Nanigopal Majumdar', in Gautam Sengupta (ed.), *Purabritta: An Anthology of Articles on Archaeology and Local History*, vol. 1, Calcutta: West Bengal Government, Directorate of Archaeology, [1807] 2000, pp. 421–39.
8. Sumit Sarkar, *Modern India*, 1885–1947, New Delhi: Macmillan India Limited, 1983, p. 83.
9. Sumit Sarkar, *The Swadeshi-Boycott Movement in Bengal: 1903–1908*, New Delhi: People's Publishing House, 1973, pp. 496–7.
10. Mukhlesur Rahman (ed.), *Journal of the Varendra Research Museum: A.K. Maitra Number*, vol. 7, 1981–2, p. 34.

11. Quoted in Gautam Sengupta, 'Bangalir Pratnatattva, Banglar Pratnatattva', in Sengupta (ed.) *Purabritta*, vol. 1, p. 3.
12. Although two of Mitra's works, which are mentioned earlier, did not focus on Bengal, he did occasionally write on aspects of Bengal's archaeology such as the ancient relics of Pandua in Maldah district of West Bengal and coins found in Muhammadpur in erstwhile Jessore district of Bangladesh. See Sengupta, 'Bangalir Pratnatattva, Banglar Pratnatattva', Sengupta (ed.) *Purabritta*, vol. 1, p. 2.
13. A Bengali literary journal *Bandhab*, started in 1874, wrote in its first editorial that the enrichment of the mother tongue is closely associated with overall development and enrichment of the whole nation. Quoted in Tapti Roy, 'Disciplining the Printed Text: Colonial and Nationalist Surveillance of Bengali Literature', in Partha Chatterjee (ed.), *Texts of Power: Emerging Disciplines in Colonial Bengal*, Calcutta: Samya with Centre for Studies in Social Sciences, 1996, p. 56.
14. Sarkar, *Modern India*, p. 84. One of the most prominent advocates of this school of thought was Nabagopal Mitra who, with the backing of the Tagore family, organized an annual Hindu *mela* from 1867 onwards for the promotion of unity and national feeling among Hindus. See R.C. Majumdar, 'Rajendralal Mitra as a National Leader', in *Rajendralal Mitra: 150th Anniversary Lectures*, Calcutta: Asiatic Society, 1978.
15. Brojendranath Bandopadhyay, *Parishad Parichay 1300–1356*, Calcutta: Bangiya Sahitya Parishad, 1949 (1356).
16. He taught Sanskrit at Sanskrit College in Calcutta and later became its principal in 1900. He also briefly headed the Sanskrit department at Presidency College, Calcutta.
17. H.P. Sastri, 'Susunia Rock Inscription of Chandravarman', *Epigraphia Indica*, vol. XIII, 1915–16, p. 133.
18. Tarapada Santra, 'Bangalar Anchalik Itihas Charcha: Ekti Samiksha', in Sengupta (ed.), *Purabritta*, vol. 1, p. 84.
19. Ramendrasundar Tribedi taught physics and chemistry at Ripon College, Calcutta, and went on to become principal (1903–19). He inspired a whole generation of scholars both within the Parishad (such as Rakhaldas Banerji) and beyond. He was extremely passionate about the Bengali language—always lecturing and publishing in Bengali, and twice even declining to give guest lectures in English at the Calcutta University. See A.K. Mukhopadhyay, 'Ramendrasundar Tribedi: A Scientist's Philosophical Quest', in A.K. Mukhopadhyay (ed.), *The Bengali Intellectual Tradition from Rammohun Roy to Dhirendranath Sen*, Calcutta: K.P. Bagchi & Company, 1979, pp. 174–97.
20. The Dacca Museum was set up in 1914 with government funding, but in its early years at least quite a few sculptures that formed its collection were chance finds obtained in the course of non-official excavations conducted by local enthusiasts. See Nalinikanta Bhattasali, *Iconography of Buddhist and Brahmanical Sculptures in the Dacca Museum*, New Delhi: Aryan Books International, 2001, pp. vi–vii.

21. Samir Kumar Mukhopadhyay, 'Art Museums in Calcutta', in Pratapaditya Pal (ed.), *Changing Visions, Lasting Images: Calcutta through 300 Years*, Bombay: Marg Publications, 1990, p. 96.
22. See Ramendrasundar Tribedi's introduction in Rakhaldas Banerji, *Descriptive List of Sculptures and Coins in the Museum of the Bangiya Sahitya Parishad*, Calcutta: Bangiya Sahitya Parishad, 1911.
23. Sunil Das, 'Sahitya Parishader Atma', *Desh*, 67 (19), 2000, p. 32.
24. In 1910 Banerji had published the *Catalogue of Inscriptions on Copper Plates in the Collection of the Asiatic Society of Bengal.*
25. A distinctive feature of this book is that Banerji included in his reckoning the prehistory of the subcontinent and beyond. This was unlike his contemporaries who completely overlooked the prehistoric phase.
26. See Banerji, *Descriptive List*, pp. 1–18.
27. Lahiri, *Finding Forgotten Cities*, p. 194.
28. Translated from A.K. Maitra, 'Varendra Khanan Bibaran', *Sahitya*, January–April, 1916 (Magh–Chaitra, 1323). Reprinted in his Ghosh and Bhattacharya (eds), *Uttarbanger Puratattva Sangraha*, Calcutta: Pratiti Prakashani, 1984.
29. A.K. Maitra, 'The Stones of Varendra', *The Modern Review*, VII (6), 1910, p. 91.
30. Lahiri, *Finding Forgotten Cities*, p. 187.
31. For Maitra, Siraj-ud-daulah was a tragic hero who had been misrepresented by the British. Maitra was a member of the Calcutta Historical Society Committee set up to probe into Holwell's 'black hole' episode on the alleged atrocities of Nawab Sira-ud-daulah during his invasion of Calcutta in June 1756. In his report submitted in 1916, Maitra dismissed the episode as a 'gigantic hoax'. See Rahman, *Journal of the Varendra Research Museum*, vol. 7, p. 35.
32. Guha-Thakurta, *Monuments, Objects, Histories*, pp. 126–7.
33. The Varendra Research Society explored the role of Bengal in the expansion of ancient Indian culture in South-East Asia. A.K. Maitra observed how Garuda was the carrier of Vishnu in both Bengal and Java, and how the art of Gauda influenced the art of Java. See, O.C. Gangoly, 'Museum of the Varendra Research Society, Rajshahi (Bengal)', *The Modern Review*, XXVII (2), 1920, pp. 184–5, and A.K. Maitra, 'Garuda, the Carrier of Vishnu in Bengal and Java', *Rupam*, vol. 1, pp. 2–7.
34. See Akshay Kumar Maitra's editorial preface to Ramaprasad Chanda's *Gaudarajamala*, Calcutta: Nababharat Publishers, 1975.
35. Quoted by Santra, 'Bangalar Anchalik Itihas Charcha', in Sengupta (ed.), *Purabritta*, vol. 1, p. 70.
36. See Chanda, *The Indo-Aryan Races*, pp. 88–94. These scholars had several problems with the kulaji texts such as their date of composition, authorship, and inconsistencies in several accounts. See Kumkum Chatterjee, 'The King of Controversy: History and Nation-making in Late Colonial India', *American Historical Review*, 110 (5), 2005, pp. 1454–75.
37. Nayanjot Lahiri, *Pre-Ahom Assam: Studies in the Inscriptions of Assam between the Fifth and the Thirteenth Centuries AD*, New Delhi: Munshiram Manoharlal, 1991, pp. 6–8.

REFERENCES

Books and Articles in English

Banerji, Rakhaldas, *The Origins of the Bengali Script*, Calcutta: University of Calcutta, 1919.

———, *Descriptive List of Sculptures and Coins in the Museum of the Bangiya Sahitya Parishad*, Calcutta: Bangiya Sahitya Parishad, 1911.

Bhandarkar, D.R., B.Ch. Chhabra, and G.S. Ghai (eds), *Corpus Inscriptionum Indicarum volume III: Inscriptions of the Early Gupta Kings*, New Delhi: Archaeological Survey of India, 1981.

Bhattasali, Nalini Kanta, *Iconography of Buddhist and Brahmanical Sculptures in the Dacca Museum*, New Delhi: Aryan Books International, 2001.

Chakrabarti, Dilip K., *Colonial Indology: Sociopolitics of the Ancient Indian Past*, New Delhi: Munshiram Manoharlal, 1988.

———, *A History of Indian Archaeology, from the Beginning to 1947*, New Delhi: Munshiram Manoharlal, 1988.

———, *India, An Archaeological History: Palaeolithic Beginnings to Early Historic Foundations*, New Delhi: Oxford University Press, 1999.

———, *Archaeology in the Third World: A History of Indian Archaeology Since 1947*, New Delhi: D.K. Printworld, 2003.

Chanda, Ramaprasad, *The Indo-Aryan Races: A Study of Indo-Aryan People and Institutions*, Calcutta: Indian Studies: Past & Present, 1969.

Chatterjee, Kumkum, 'The King of Controversy: History and Nation-making in Late Colonial India', *American Historical Review*, 110 (5), 2005, pp. 1454–75.

Chatterjee, Partha (ed.), *Texts of Power: Emerging Disciplines in Colonial Bengal*, Calcutta: Samya with Centre for Studies in Social Sciences, 1996.

Datta, Asok (ed.), *History and Archaeology of Eastern India*, New Delhi: Books and Books, 1998.

Gangoly, Ordhenda Coomar, 'The Museum of the Varendra Research Society, Rajshahi (Bengal)', *The Modern Review*, XXVII (2), 1920, pp. 177–91.

Ganguly, Manamohan, *Handbook To The Sculptures in the Museum of the Bangiya Sahitya Parishad*, Calcutta: Bangiya Sahitya Parishad, 1922.

Guha-Thakurta, Tapati, *Monuments, Objects, Histories: Institutions of Art in Colonial and Postcolonial India*, New Delhi: Permanent Black, 2004.

Guide book to the Archaeological and Literary Exhibits at the Bangiya Sahitya Parishad on the occasion of the visit of H.E. Lord Carmichael, Governor of Bengal on 2nd February, 1915, Calcutta: Bangiya Sahitya Parishad, nd.

Lahiri, Nayanjot, *Pre-Ahom Assam: Studies in the Inscriptions of Assam between the Fifth and the Thirteenth Centuries AD*, New Delhi: Munshiram Mahoharlal, 1991.

———, *Finding Forgotten Cities: How the Indus Civilization was Discovered*, New Delhi: Permanent Black, 2005.

Law, Narendra Nath (ed.), *Haraprasad Memorial Volume*, The Indian Historical Society, 9 (1), 1933.

Maitra, Akshay Kumar, 'Garuda, the Carrier of Vishnu in Bengal and Java', *Rupam*, vol. 1, pp. 2–7.

Maitra, Akshay Kumar, 'The Stones of Varendra', *The Modern Review*, VII (6), 1910, pp. 588–90.

———, 'The Stones of Varendra', *The Modern Review*, VIII (1), 1910, pp. 89–91.

Majumdar, N.G., 'A Gold-plated Bronze From Mahasthan', *The Modern Review*, XL (4), 1926, pp. 425–7.

Majumdar, R.C., 'Rajendralal Mitra as a National Leader', in *Rajendralal Mitra: 150th Anniversary Lectures*, Calcutta: The Asiatic Society, 1978.

Mukhopadhyay, A.K., 'Ramendrasundar Tribedi: A Scientist's Philosophical Quest', in A.K. Mukhopadhyay (ed.), *The Bengali Intellectual Tradition from Rammohun Roy to Dhirendranath Sen,* Calcutta: K.P. Bagchi, 1979, pp. 174–97.

Mukhlesur, Rahman, *Sculpture in the Varendra Research Museum: A Descriptive Catalogue*, Rajshahi, Varendra Research Museum, 1998.

——— (ed.), *Journal of the Varendra Research Museum: A.K. Maitra Number*, vol. 7, 1981–2.

Mukhopadhyay, Samir Kumar, 'Art Museums in Calcutta', in Pratapaditya Pal (ed.), *Changing Visions, Lasting Images: Calcutta through 300 Years,* Bombay: Marg Publications, 1990, pp. 91–108.

Poddar, Arabinda, *Renaissance in Bengal: Search for Identity*, Simla: Indian Institute of Advanced Study, 1977.

Sarkar, Sumit, *The Swadeshi-Boycott Movement in Bengal: 1903–1908*, New Delhi: People's Publishing House, 1973.

———, *Modern India, 1885–1947*, New Delhi: Macmillan India, 1983.

Sastri, Haraprasad, 'Susunia Rock-inscription of Chandravarman', *Epigraphia Indica,* vol. XIII, 1915–16, p. 133.

Singh, Upinder, *The Discovery of Ancient India: Early Archaeologists and the Beginnings of Archaeology*, New Delhi: Permanent Black, 2004.

Varendra Research Society, Annual Report for the year 1926–27, Rajshahi: Varendra Research Society.

Books and Articles in Bengali

Bandopadhyay, Asitkumar and Bishwanath Mukhopadhyay (eds), *Rakhaldas Bandopadhyay Rachanabali*, vol. 1, Calcutta: Paschimbanga Rajya Pustak Parishad, 1988.

Bandopadhyay, Brojendranath (ed.), *Parishad Parichay 1300–1356*, Calcutta: Bangiya Sahitya Parishad, 1356 BS (1949).

Banerji, Rakhaldas, *Prachin Mudra*, Calcutta: Bengal Medical Library, 1915.

———, *Bangalar Itihas,* vol. 1, Calcutta: Dey's Publishing, [1915] 1987.

Basu, Nagendranath, *Banger Jatiya Itihas, Brahmana Kanda*, Part 2, Varendra Brahmana Bibarana, Calcutta: Viswakosh, 1927 (1334 BS).

Chanda, Ramaprasad, *Gaudarajamala,* Calcutta: Nababharat Publishers, 1975.

Chatterji, Suniti Kumar (ed.), *Haraprashad Rachanabali, 1853–1931*, Calcutta: Eastern Trading Company, 1956.

Das, Sunil, 'Bangiya Sahitya Parishader Atma', *Desh*, 67th year, vol. 19, 22 July 2000, p. 3236.

Kumar, Madanmohan, *Bangiya Sahitya Parishader Itihas, prothom porbo*, Calcutta: Bangiya Sahitya Parishad, 1381 BS (1974).

Maitra, Akshay Kumar, *Gaudalekhamala: Rajshahi: Varendra Anusandhan Samiti,* 1319 BS (1912).
———, *Gauder Katha*, Calcutta: Sahityalok, 1390 BS (1983).
———, *Uttarbanger Puratattva Sangraha,* edited by Anandagopal Ghosh and Malaysankar Bhattacharya, Calcutta: Pratiti Prakashani, 1984.
Majumdar, Nanigopal, 'Mallasarule prapta Vijaysener tamrasasan', *Sahitya Parishad Patrika,* 44th year, no. 1, 1344 BS (1937), pp. 17–21.
Sengupta, Gautam (ed.), *Purabritta: An Anthology of Articles on Archaeology and Local History*, vol. I, Calcutta: West Bengal Government, Directorate of Archaeology, Baisakh 1807 (May 2000).

2. On the Surface Things Appear to be...
Perspectives on the Archaeology of the Delhi Ridge

Mudit Trivedi

This essay presents the preliminary report of a small-scale archaeological survey that explored a controlled segment of the Delhi Aravallis, a landscape from which a great deal of archaeological evidence had previously been reported. The survey sought to inquire into questions related to distribution and context, and the results presented here hope to provide a geo-archaeological picture to frame extant archaeological cultures. The archaeological presence in the region is primarily threefold, beginning with extensive Acheulian artefacts to a microlithic complex and ending expectedly with the intermingled hinterlands of Delhi's many medieval cities.[1]

The 'Delhi ridge', immortalized in public memory by the dramatic scenes of the siege of 1857, have been comprehended geologically in the manner of one summary and romanticized description. In one of the defining narratives of the social geography of twentieth-century India, the Delhi ridges are described as 'lean but wiry fingers', a well-known phrase coined by Spate and Learmonth, sinking into the young alluvium of the Ganga–Yamuna doab. This picture aptly allegorized the very nation, as the old but resilient stood proud in a sea of change all around.[2] While this picture has framed all archaeological understandings of the region, this essay shall try and demonstrate that the geological pasts of the Delhi region are far more complex. Reconstructing palaeo-landscapes in the Delhi region being an all too challenging task, this chapter merely tries to reconstruct the broad processes and correlate them to phases of hominin occupation.

The region surveyed is the campus of the Jawarharlal Nehru University, which has protected about 1,500 acres of land from the rapidly expanding urban sprawl of Delhi. The area is typical of the

Aravallis in the region, with a number of low parallel rocky ridges, populated by acacias and within which a diverse range of fauna persists even today as a fragile reminder of past ecosystems. The ridges are capped by series of distinctive tor or boulder-like formations. In the areas where no university constructions have hitherto encroached, varied archaeological landscapes are nestled within these ridges. The foremost of these is an extensive distribution of Acheulian artefacts commonly observed on the surface. In addition to these, a subsequent microlithic culture is profusely evident with upwards of twenty discrete scatters. Medieval ceramics are by and large rare, but point to the marginal worlds of the many medieval cities around, most specifically that of Lal Kot.

This essay is an argument in surface archaeology and follows upon the work of Zarine Cooper, agreeing that the interpretation of surface artefacts is 'a challenge and not a deterrent'.[3] It hopes to place itself within that tradition of reaching beyond the world of well-defined sites into those dimensions of human material behaviour which constitute a landscape. This study and the survey have many limitations that must be made clear at the outset. The survey was conducted by one person and, thus, selection effects may be very high. Survey intensity was variable and subject to dense vegetation and rugged topography, under best conditions though return-transect lines 5 m distant from the previous were attempted. This also has the additional drawback of being unable to present any quantitative artefact analysis at this stage.

ANCIENT ROCKS AND YOUNG SEDIMENTS

All archaeological situations confront us with a dual challenge. At the microlithic scatters of this survey, for example, we encounter at one level the result of cultural processes. Some people, at some point(s) of time, chose a particular location in the landscape after having chosen particular type(s) of stone, and set about flaking them to produce whatever they desired. Yet the temporal distance between these actions and our documentation bring in the inexorable claims of geological time and demonstrate the relentless action of natural processes. All manner of geomorphological processes—including sedimentation, fluvial transport, and redeposition, colluvial motion distributing artefacts down a slope, or aeolian sedimentation laying a blanket over them—are but a few examples in the manner in which sites may be altered after they have been constituted. Trampling underfoot by animals or complication by human action in the interim by addition and mixing of recent materials or by removal or destruction are all distinct and oft-encountered processes. These varied processes of site formation, embodying the cultural and natural history of artefacts are an essential exercise in archaeological source criticism.[4] In excavations, the process itself yields much sedimentological information, which answers many of these questions. When inquiring into a scattering of archaeological presences over the surface of a large area, the task becomes one of landscape geomorphology, concentrating upon earth surface processes. An exercise in surface archaeology such as the current must, therefore, necessarily engage with the processes of landscape evolution over the long term.

The archaeology of hominin communities over at least the last million years in the subcontinent makes it apparent that our evidence for colonization bears distinct regional trends. The attempt to explain these patterns of differential distributions over differing lengths of time and varying extents of space has led to an interest in even greater temporal and spatial frames. It has been argued that the geological evolution of units in the subcontinent is useful and key in assessing the resources, climatic regimes, and, thus, 'potential' for hominin occupation of certain regions. The implications of such explorations are significant not only for the purposes of modelling and understanding why prehistoric communities may have dispersed in certain manners, but also for helping us visualize better their tasks of resource selection and utilization. It has been demonstrated that the Purana and Gondwana basins display structural qualities as being resource rich and climatically stable, and, thus, 'core' areas.[5] In a supplemental manner, on a smaller and more directly empirical scale, similar consideration of local geology can present us with information on climate, raw materials such as stone, as well as the nature and form in which these may have been present at the time of occupation.

This section will try and respond to these two broad agenda of site formation processes and long-term geological constraints by providing a geo-archaeological description for the Delhi region. In doing so, it will provide a summary of the relevant aspects of the geological past of the region, beginning from the earliest periods of rock formation to the deposition of the youngest Holocene sediments, attempting to highlight the archaeological implications of each. Considering the geological history of the Delhi region takes us back to the earliest period of rock formation in the history of the Earth. Deep within the crust in the study region, the complex known as the Banded Gneissic Complex (approximately 3 billion years old) dates to the Archaean period and underlies the entire peninsular shield. It is in the subsequent period, the Proterozoic (from 2,500 to 600 million years ago), when much of the secondary deposition and formation of rocks occur.[6] The Delhi ridges, composed of tough quartzites, are known to date to this period. From traces remaining in the structure of these metamorphosed quartzites we can deduce some information about the parent sandstones of the Archaean period. Geochemical studies of the weathering status of the parent sandstone and the observation of preserved features such as ripple marks, current beddings, and mud cracks in the quartzites suggest that the sandstones themselves were deposited under very special conditions and were subsequently not subject to much reworking. Given this, it has been suggested that these sandstones were deposited in an extremely stable environment that was marine and marginal, such as one would expect on the coastline of a large continent. Thus, the sandstones are amongst those that are termed 'supermature', being heavily weathered, and, thus, very rich in quartz (silicas) and poor in other minerals, as well as being uniformly deposited without reworking.[7] This depositional environment seems to have exerted important control over the manner in which these sandstones were subsequently metamorphosed and transformed.

The margins of continental plates are volatile regions and likely sites for some of the most spectacular of geological processes which occur at the interaction of two plates. The interaction of two plates is often the pivotal cause for orogeny or mountain building. The range of hills which we call the Aravallis is remnants of a mighty range, upthrust in three major phases of orogeny during the Proterozoic. Of these three, the Delhi phase defines a supergroup of many local formations, of which the quartzites of the Delhi region are a typical example. These rocks are veritably those which are also definitive of the Aravallis, and run from Delhi through to Gujarat constituting the main Aravalli Hills mountain belt. As the exposure of these ancient mountains is scarce near the Delhi region, most studies of rocks from this age have been done for areas where more of the formations are still exposed, such as in southern Rajasthan and Gujarat. The North Delhi Fold Belt remains comparatively less understood in the sense of the basins it constituted and the broad events of its post-uplift history. Within the Delhi region and its surroundings, complex histories of episodes of uplift, deformation, and transformation of the landscape are nonetheless visible in traces. In addition to such processes as well as those of denudation and erosion, the Aravallis of the period are recognized as being veritable laboratories of metavolcanic activity. These are broadly understood as stimulated by a variety of tectonic causes from various sites in the basic continental rift.[8] As an example of how different this period was, traces of palaeo-volcanisms are petrified and preserved in the rocks around the town of Sohna, approximately 30 km to the south-east of Delhi.[9]

After the stabilization of this mighty landscape of mountains, which itself could date back a billion years, a last episode of major rock formation occurred, bearing tremendous implications for the hominin communities of much later times. The intensely metamorphosed landscape was abruptly stirred from its depths, and igneous rocks rose and came to be present as intrusives punctuating the landscape. While the set of rocks known as the Erinpura granites are the most distinctive for the Aravallis, they have remained sub-surface in the survey area. Two classes of intrusives are characteristic of the Delhi region, quartz and pegmatite, which are both exhibited as veins. The quartz veins are particularly significant and occur as distinct and recognizable forms, optically discernible into the common names of crystal or glassy quartz, as well as the more turbid varieties.[10] Characteristically, as a crystalline silica, quartz flakes extremely well and this is the reason why microlith-producing communities favoured the region. Additionally, it appears that the cooling history of the metamorphosed quartzites may also have produced small and indifferent quartz nodules within the quartzites, which are often exposed as the quartzite weathers, and may have also served as an alternative source of crystalline rock.

The foregoing discussion has attempted to provide a skeletal outline of only the most major units in the bedrock geology of the Delhi region. Making this description relevant to the observed landscape involves transgressing a vast period for which we simply do not have any visible geological records. The situation presents us with a tremendous challenge, particularly because at least one part of the senile topography of the Aravallis is ancient and has borne witness to much change of geological setting.[11] It is the very last of these, the extension of the Himalayan foreland basin by the young and vigorous depositional regimes of the Ganga and Yamuna, which has masked the old and laid a soft cover of alluvium over any older landforms and deposits. There is considerable evidence which suggests the tremendous implication of this transformative sequence of depositions: it is suggested that the Delhi ridge extends under the surface up to Hardwar. It is estimated that the depth of sediments within the capital varies from nil, as on the ridges, to well in excess of 200 m as we approach the river. As incised sections of any depth greater than a couple of metres are almost non-existent, our knowledge of this archive of sedimentation remains at the stage where seismic estimates of depth are the only gauge.[12] It is the recognition of this lack of exposure of dated core samples in addition to the massive unconformity, or gap, in our geological archive that is essential to all tasks of reconstructing the palaeo-landscape. More specifically, it leaves us handicapped and without traces into most part of the quaternary.

The basic root of all the landforms of the ridge areas in Delhi and the rugged topography has been diagnosed as being in an iron impurity that is carried by the quartzite bedrock. The presence of geochemically significant proportions of pyrite (FeS_2) in the quartzites has led to an uncharacteristic process of extensive and intensive chemical weathering. The quartzites demonstrate a dramatic manifestation of this basic process, whereby on the progress of the weathering front deeper into it, a series of extremely weathered and friable to moderately weathered zones are left behind. These are observed commonly on extremely large scales and are visible in a series of weathering rinds or skin-like layers. Typically, these proceed from a grey unweathered core to a white moderately weathered section, and to a red section where weathering has proceed to the extent that inter-grain bonds are so weak that the stone has disintegrated and become sand-like. These sands are recognized as excellent construction material, especially for the infilling of foundations and roads, and have been quarried extensively in the Delhi region, thus earning their name from one such location on the south-eastern border of Delhi called Badarpur.[13]

This erosional peculiarity of the Delhi quartzites has exerted a strong control over the dominant aspects of the geomorphology of the Delhi ridge. It is hypothesized that the action of meteoric water initiated this process of weathering from cracks and faults that existed. The disintegrative end of the process contributed to the widening of such initial sites, thus extending the weathering process over most of the bedrock. It is only where particularly resistant quartzites are encountered that the process seems to result in small and large spheroidal quartzite blocks which dominate the landscape. These distinctive tor formations cap most ridges and impart a rugged and austere quality to the landscape. The spheroidal form is imparted to the quartzite by the removal of the rinds by subsequent erosion, leaving a sphere-like resistant core. Sheet rock and bedrock in general can be seen to have been weathered extensively to a depth of many metres in cases, especially on tablelands where subsequent erosion of the outermost rinds has not occurred. This is easily visible in sections exposed at quarries. The gentle slopes of the parallel ridges in the study region have created situations such that, in most cases, the outermost sandy rinds have been washed away and transported towards the lower areas of the slope. Such processes are visible and active in every monsoon.

The valleys in between the lineaments of the study region too were thought to correlate directly to this general paradigm of ancient rock and alluvium. Recent work has demonstrated that this picture has entirely failed to recognize an entire sedimentary unit of tremendous implications. The valleys enclosed by the lineaments of the local Aravallis are simply too far above the flood plains and the megafans of the Gangetic system to have had any correlation with them. The highest reach of alluvial deposition in the region reaches a height approximately 30 to 40 m below the level at which the ridge lineaments enclose sediments (roughly 245 to 255 m).[14] A systematic study based on the geochemical components of these sediments has now conclusively established that they are neither derived from the local quartzites or any of its weathering products; nor do they bear the signature of the Yamuna alluvium. Instead, they bear the physical and chemical signatures of being a typically aeolian sediment, that is, entrained into the air at a remote location and deposited by prevalent wind conditions upon the Delhi ridge at some point of time. The geochemical signature, as determined by analysis despite alteration over transport selection and other processes, has suggested an origin of these sands with the Thar.[15]

The activation and past periods of tremendous intensification of the Thar have been issues of great interest and debate in the quaternary science of the subcontinent. The paradigm of the 1960s, anxious that the desert was advancing and extended eastwards, presumed it to be of recent origin, possibly within Holocene times. Since then it has been repeatedly established that the Thar is an ancient landform, and has undergone a complex history of intensification and stabilization, expansion as well as retreat. It is currently presumed that major aeolian processes are at least 200,000 years old in the core areas of the desert, and they may be older still. One major indicator of these variations in time, space, and intensity was argued to be the presence of stabilized fossil dunes, a system of which was reported as close as the suburb of Gurgaon (approximately 12 km from the study region). It appears that the greatest maximal extent of this complex, which refashioned almost the entire north-western half of the subcontinent, was not synchronous with that of other major desert systems such as the Sahara and the Kalahari, or the Australian deserts. While this has been suggested to have occurred after the last glacial maximum in the case of the Thar, it has been difficult to construct a single chronology for the march of the Thar, or its retreat, as significant regional variation appears to have occurred.[16]

The aeolian component within the study region appears in a twofold manner. The wind-blown deposition has occurred in the form of both a thin blanket over the entire landscape as well as their consolidation by slope wash into thick sections in the valleys between the lineaments. Thus, the aeolian sediment has formed thin sections of soil, from a couple of inches to many feet, smoothening out depressions on the ridges themselves. But more impressively, these have filled in and raised the valley floors, providing veritable pediments at the foot of the otherwise rugged and tor-littered ridges. These sediments generally bear a rich yellow-brown colour and are, typically for wind-blown sediments, often massive and unconsolidated. Local topographic drainages have dissected and gullied these sediments, exposing large sections. The only constraint that field observations suggest about this aeolian sedimentation is that these appear to have been deposited in a concerted phase when climatic regimes transported large quantities to the region. Exposed sections in the region can be relatively large, up to 15 m, and appear to be uninterrupted by any paleosols, that is, periods when deposition was slow enough or had ceased for long enough to allow for an episode of the generation of soil which would have left traces behind. In this sense, then, the sediments that have been fluvially reworked by slope wash are not true 'loess' in a geological sense, but still constitute a useful paleo-climatic proxy record (Fig. 2.1).

While the lack of a precise chronology for this sedimentary unit greatly limits our interpretation, the aeolian sediments bear very important implications for the landscape and the artefacts it

FIGURE 2.1: Massive sections of gullied unconsolidated fluvio-aeolian sediments exposed by modern quarrying. The boar family provides scale

harbours. The processes of slope wash, especially as rills, are highly active for pieces of small mass. For example, the detritus of the red and weathered quartzite rinds are extensively redistributed along rills and slope washes. The fate of many microlithic scatters situated on slopes appears to have been the same, and the smallest pieces of debitage, unless cemented into locally flat or stable sediments, have been washed away into the valley at times to a distance of up to 10 to 15 m. While most angular shatter seems to have suffered such a fate, a majority of flake-sized debitage and core pieces are generally less likely to have travelled very far and are usually constrained. Many other scatters are on flat tablelands and have undergone less movement. This combination of colluvial action by slope wash, heightened by the effects of aeolian sedimentation, appears to have had an even gentler affect on larger sized clasts. Pieces about the size of the typical palaeolith are distributed across the slopes in a manner suggesting little motion down the slopes, nor is there typically much abrasion or rolling into a rounded form as is the common pattern in a fluvial situation. By and large, the distribution of heat spalls exfoliating off from quartzitic tors provide a good measure of such actions, constituting a spall landscape around a tor. Smaller pieces are likely to have travelled further and been more dispersed. An important feature exhibiting control over these site formation processes is the nature of bedding in the metastructure of the quartzites and its subsequent deformation. Often, sets of tors at different elevations along the slope have been affected by the aeolian mantle so as to produce an almost stepped terrain, thus effectively providing barriers in the paths of colluvial displacement. Within limits then, what appears to be the case is that in the upper reaches of these modest lineaments, the landscapes are ancient. While the bedrock has weathered into tors, the outermost rinds washed away and even as aeolian sediments have found a niche in centimetre-scale depressions, much else has remained the same. Heat spalls reside close to the areas from where they peeled off. Provided that the context is relatively undisturbed and the artefact size relatively large, it appears that artefacts, especially palaeoliths, too have not themselves moved very much. Much in the manner of a tiger's skin, there are areas within the study region which in a weak sense make the case for palaeo-landscape preservation (Fig. 2.2).[17]

In between these other areas that are potentially significant, there lies a sea of recent alluvium. In the past, a rough chronology of old and new alluvial, the *khadar* and *bangar*, was in use, indeed even in the toponyms of villages, to describe the older alluvial plain, and the new and active zone. Recent years have seen the publication of a comprehensive model which describes the evolution of the Indo-Gangetic basin and its different morphotectonic units, and most significantly, has used multi-site luminescence dates to generate a chronological framework for these broad periods and processes of sedimentation. The mass of alluvium that seems to have buried

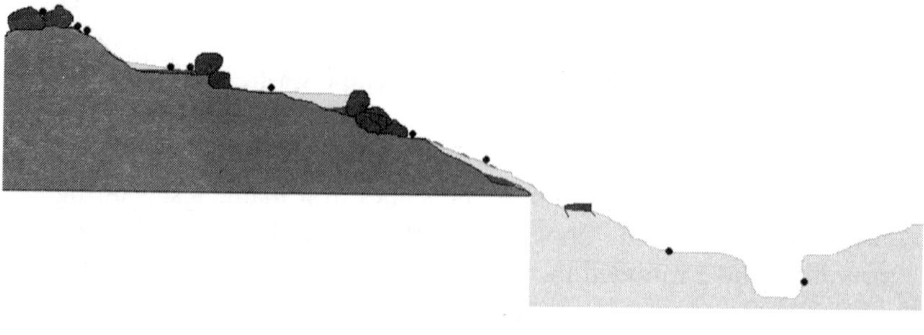

FIGURE 2.2: Schematic profile of typical ridge and valley in the survey region depicting observable extents of bedrock and aeolian sedimentation

the Aravallis of the larger Delhi area seems to have been from the Yamuna Megafan, which is overlain or associated with that of the upland interfluve surface. These broad units themselves are tentatively suggested to have been associated with the global climatic changes referred to as marine oxygen isotope stage 5 (OIS) and past OIS 3 correlating to the periods between 120 and *c.* 40 ka.[18]

This larger picture has resulted in a complex succession of sediments towards the plains as one moves away from the extant ridges. Yet it must be stressed that the two sedimentary units share an extremely complex relationship. The study region is a tableland-like exception as the lineaments circumscribe the valleys in between them. Other areas where the local relief of the Aravallis was lower may have recorded a more complex interaction between aeolian pediment-colluvial deposits and the higher reaches of the interfluve sedimentation. Instances where the alluvium overlies the aeolian sediments have been reported and bear testimony to such processes. It is such sections that may be useful in providing geo-chronological constraints on these processes by means of OSL chronologies. This section has tried to demonstrate that the geomorphology of the Delhi region is significantly threefold and not merely restricted to the received wisdom of the bipolar mountain alluvium understanding. Further, the nature of the erosional quartzite landscapes and the aeolian deposition upon them have constrained site formation processes considerably especially in cases of favourable slope topography. Given these features, the surface archaeology of the region attains a special degree of importance as it bears possible traces for patterns of landscape use by hominin communities. Since only colluvial action and minimal sorting by such sedimentation have been active as post-depositional processes, those artefacts found distributed on the gentler of the ancient slopes may still retain significant information. It has also sought to highlight that the alluvial plains are amongst the youngest landscapes of the subcontinent. The Aravalli highlands of the region must be contextualized within the vast percentage of the landscape of the Delhi region, which has undergone massive transformations and we do not know enough about them to attempt a fuller reconstruction of landscape and climate change. Yet, as the next sections will try and demonstrate, these thin tiger stripes where the palaeo-landscape has undergone fathomable and little change, can be usefully interrogated to work towards a more complete description of the prehistoric archaeology of the region. It is in this effort that much of the foregoing geological engagement shall be brought to bear upon the evaluation of these cultures.

THE ACHEULIAN OCCUPATION OF THE HIGHLANDS

The palaeolithic of the Delhi region has a relatively long history of repeatedly being a surprise and a revelation. Numerous archaeologists have been all but a bit taken aback to have been able to pick up Acheulian artefacts, often in numbers, by just going for a stroll on any of the outcrops of the Delhi ridge. Artefacts have shown a strong correlation with the highlands and were picked up on the surface of various Aravalli outcrops, including the study region and elsewhere. Two studies are definitive and provide very different levels of information. The survey work by Chakrabarti and Lahiri[19] is foundational. A brief survey of the Aravallis of the region resulted in the reporting of many localities, particularly invaluable as many of these have been subsequently swallowed by the urban sprawl. The extensive surface collections, further explorations, as well as excavations at one of these, the site of Arangpur by Ota and Sharma[20] in the early 1990s provide the much needed establishment of the magnitude and significance of one of these localities. These excavations yielded an impressive tool collection of more than 300 artefacts besides much reported 'debitage and waste materials'. If these two studies together establish the significance of the Delhi palaeolithic complex, an even greater regional context of sorts is laid by the famous Thar complex of the palaeolithic, which has seen extensive investigation in the last two decades.[21] It is against this existing quantum of data that this section will try and address the issues of geomorphic contexts for the palaeoliths, the raw material selection, and speculate on possible patterns of acquisition. Before attempting a general appraisal of the artefact collection, several qualifications about the nature of this sample must be made clear. The total sample is small and is of two kinds. The first category of tools has been collected from the surface of the study region, often in isolation or even seemingly in association with one another in a range of geomorphic context. The second set of artefacts was recovered from the excavated remains of a construction site for a new academic complex being built in the heart of the survey region. While the destruction of this second valuable 'site' as opposed to the thin distributions across the landscape is much lamented, it has provided an extremely useful and complementary set of evidence and once again makes the case for urgent legislation about salvage archaeology in India. These two halves of the collection make for an intriguing, if admittedly small, sample set and allow for the consideration of a wide range of post-depositional complexities.[22]

The Delhi palaeolithic provides us with another opportunity to address the issue of quartzite as a favoured and much utilized raw material in the Indian palaeolithic record. A recent synthesis has highlighted the patterning of this information by pointing out the influence of the form (rounded or angular) in which quartzites are usually available as well as the average clast sizes.[23] It is in this context that even the most preliminary consideration of the Delhi palaeolithic proves to be extremely challenging. Owing to the processes of pyrite dissolution-led weathering, we know that much of the country quartzite would have presented itself even to the palaeolithic communities as weathered and with much unusable rinds. It is in this context that the exfoliating tor formations which present local resistant and tougher rock attain greater significance. The exfoliation processes would have presented the hominin knappers with an extensive spall landscape (that is, a littering of rocks cleaved under the action of heat) as well as the tor itself. Even the most preliminary of replication experiments have suggested that the local heat spalls are not good candidates for the production of bifaces. They appear to have been weakened by the processes of chemical weathering, often the tracks of iron rich solutions travelling through the rock as well as the coating of grains being optically visible. The spalls are thus prone to unexpected snap fractures.[24] In this context, it is suggested that quartzite acquisition may have had to begin by quarrying directly from a tor or large spheroid, subsequent to which large pieces may have been used to directly produce bifaces or, indeed, to fire large flat blanks upon which tools were made. While all this is admittedly still at the realm of speculation rather than quantified observations, the nature of the recovered tools and pre-forms suggests that localities within the Delhi region may actually be locations where large parts, if not most or even 'all' of the reduction sequences of biface production, may be documented at once. It appears unlikely that anything except a hard stone hammer, most likely of the same quartzite, was used in the reduction processes (Fig. 2.3).

Further dimensions of complexity in the use of raw materials in the Delhi paleolithic are suggested by the utilization of fine-grained yellow sedimentary rock, which has been identified as a tuffaceous sandstone which affords good conchoidal fractures. It is unclear as

FIGURE 2.3: A typical section at the construction site. The black line on the section to the right illustrates the contact between the aeolian sediment and the weathering quartzites. The arrow indicates one of the few locations of a resistant section of unweathered quartzite which the labourer is manually removing

to what tools were made out of this raw material, but a few informal core-like artefacts suggest that they were being used for the production of small flakes.[25] The rock type is uncommon in the Delhi region and has only one known exposure reported from the extensive tablelands near the town of Sohna, where other evidences of palaeo-volcanism intruding into the country rock have also been noted.[26] While closer outcrops probably do exist, none were encountered within the survey region.[27] Additionally, a single biface produced on quartz suggests that raw material procurement and utilization patterns had other significant aspects, of which this study has only scratched the surface.

One of the most impressive shared characteristics is the completely unabraded condition of practically all artefacts (three bifaces make for an important exception and are discussed later). As a result, most artefacts from varying conditions of recovery demonstrate considerable detail of surface features such as flake scars. One major trend of the sample links their post-depositional histories to the simple phenomenon of patination (the deposition of minerals onto the outer surface of a rock, thus altering its appearance). A small selection of artefacts appears to have been in contact only with a tor-like resistant bedrock and have largely remained unpatinated. The tools from the construction site appear to have undergone a period wherein they were in prolonged contact with a stable and progressively weathering quartzite formation. It appears that the very bedrock upon which they were produced may have subsequently weathered through to the red friable stage of loose sands or such weathering in the immediate surroundings was redistributed so as to bury them. In either case, the net result is the deposition of an iron (ferric-rich) solution upon the surfaces of the artefacts, imparting them a red stain.

In complete contrast to these two forms of patination, there also appears to have been more complex alternative life histories for artefacts 'discarded' in locations where later aeolian sedimentation proceed to envelope them, or colluvial motion brought them into contact with such deposits. It is here that a number of processes seem to be differentially active at once. The surface which is buried, that is, in contact with the sediment itself, appears to be attaining a yellow-brown staining without much alteration to its physical relief, which continues to exhibit flake scars and any other features. The exterior surface, in complete contrast, records a high degree of abrasion and severe to moderate loss of features. The tentative interpretation of this is a picture of aeolian erosion by abrasion and/or by colluvial wash affecting only the exposed upper surface of the artefact (Fig. 2.4).

FIGURE 2.4: Selection of hand-axes demonstrating the variation in patinations regimes. From left to right, the first specimen illustrated barely any patination and was recovered from a location where it had been in contact with bedrock alone. The second specimen is from the construction site and had been buried within the weathering rinds of the quartzite. The third and fourth are images of the dorsal and ventral of the same artefact demonstrating the complex history it underwent. The dorsal appears extremely abraded while the ventral still retains a substantial degree of surface features and their details

The reason why simple and universal aspects of palaeolithic artefacts such as surface patination have been addressed at length here lies in the observation that across the landscape, they seem to retain spatial information as well. The limited nature of colluvial action for typical biface-sized clasts, together with this dramatic pattern of variation in the patination regimes, is combined with a clear and observed correlation with the sedimentary units they were seen to be in contact with at the time of recovery. In combination these are here suggested to be the primary manifestation and index of the conditions of landscape preservation. In other words, there seems to be a case to argue that despite the long periods of intervening time, there has been little movement in the position of artefacts after they were last transported by hominin agency, past or recent. The appearance of a group of artefacts within a 20 m^2 region appears to suggest that a certain area of a slope capped with multiple sets of tors was used to produce large flakes and proceed some distance in their reduction as both large blank flakes as well as biface production discards have been recovered from the surface alone. While these are only the most general examples of surface distributions of artefacts in one small region, it is possible that they may be suggestive of a truly significant spatial record, albeit necessarily subject to the tentativeness of all surface archaeology, when examined over larger more extensive tableland-like situations.[28] It is hoped to develop a strategy of lithic analyses that will respond fruitfully to the nature and small size of the sample. In the following discussion, therefore, all observations about the assemblage are necessarily qualitative. Hand-axes seem to have probably been the most important tool type that the hominins authoring the assemblage were interested in producing. Two distinct forms appear to congeal from within the sample. It appears that a common method of producing these hand-axes was to remove a flake of approximately biface-sized proportions from a core type or from a quarried part of a tor that cannot be currently commented upon. It appears that the knappers fired such blanks that often bore a flat platform, about 1.5 cm across, which in some cases is not removed in the whole process of lithic reduction from these generally thin flakes (thicknesses up to 2.5 cm). The basic aim here seems to have been to produce a thin slab-like clast merely a few centimetres greater in length and breadth than the desired biface, and of approximately the desired thickness. A second set of more diminutive hand-axes seem to have been produced from thicker flakes and are known mainly from abandoned pre-forms. This is suggested by the indifferent marginal flaking or the evident loss of usable platform, and especially from the snap fracture at the distal that seems to have resulted from knapping errors. At the construction site, for example, a combination of many of these examples was found, abandoned at both early and later stages of the reduction process. Additionally, the flakes removed during this process were also recovered, again from different stages of the process, from a context that suggests that had the site been excavated, refitting pieces may have been obtained and would have allowed for a more complete and valuable understanding of the reduction process, and possibly even its spatial dynamics over the living floor (Figs 2.5 and 2.6).[29]

It is from the construction site alone that classical and less typical cleavers were recovered. In addition, core technologies are also solely known from the salvaged artefacts. The site appeared to demonstrate two main types of broadly informal core technologies resulting in polyhedral and discoidal core types. There is an example of a core rejuvenation flake from the latter form. The sense of lament at the loss of information from the site is only heightened by the additional recovery of what appears to be utilized and unutilized end-flakes, as well as what can only be termed broken ends of hand-axe-like bifaces seemingly again resulting from knapping errors. The presence of these types from across the known spectrum of the Acheulian is only augmented by the addition of types recovered elsewhere within the survey, which include large flake blanks, small discoidal tools, as well as scrapers on flakes.

Investigations into the palaeolithic over the last two decades have foregrounded the importance of the patterning of data, especially from the level of the locality upwards towards regional connections. It is here that the significance and potential of the Delhi region for the Indian palaeolithic may be assessed and appreciated. The large area survey by Chakrabarti and Lahiri has clearly demonstrated that the landscape is littered with (surface) localities.[30] The basic geo-archaeological contexts of these localities and associations to topographic and natural features such as palaeo-drainages needs to be further understood. The reconstruction of this will necessarily include the need to generate much more high-precision information, beginning from a more intensive survey towards locating and

FIGURE 2.5: A selection of hand-axes, pre-forms, and fragments (dorsal and ventral views) from the survey (top row) and the construction site (bottom row)

understanding their geomorphological setting. Comparisons and connections will perhaps remain none too meaningful unless a multivariate and systematic statistical comparison can be made across a number of these assemblages. Additionally, without geological

FIGURE 2.6: Selection of flakes (dorsal and ventral views) documenting various stages of the reduction process at the construction site

information about depositional and erosional regimes that go deeper into the quaternary than merely the last 130,000 years at the most, it remains difficult to describe landscape evolution in the larger region.

It is towards the larger region and the larger picture of the palaeolithic of north and central India that the Delhi complex holds out a set of questions which are extremely important and yet cannot be resolved at this stage. An extreme difficulty in even trying to make suggestions about the larger connections of this complex lies in the current inability in providing any chronological limits to this complex. Despite this, the report of extensive exposures of Acheulian tools at the similarly island-like exposure of the Govardhan Hill, near Mathura, some 150 km to the south-east, appear suggestive.[31] While next to nothing is known of the artefacts collected from Govardhan, it is towards the well-documented and much studied Thar complex that the most important connections of the Delhi palaeolithic may lie. The relationship of this complex to that already described for the Thar complex of sites (Didwana, Singi Talav) seems to offer much potential in terms of artefacts analysis and even perhaps in terms of assemblage variation with respect to bifaces as well as core technologies.[32] However, all such connections and comparisons cannot even be begun to be discussed in detail until we arrive at some form of geo-chronological constraints for the Delhi palaeolithic complex and which of the various stratified Thar Palaeolithic cultures it could possibly be coeval with. The typical stratigraphical position of these assemblages seems to be defined upon, or very near, a previous quartzite bedrock layer, which has subsequently weathered significantly. While an estimation of time depths is not possible at this stage, it may tentatively be suggested that these assemblages correlate to a time frame broadly between OIS 9 to 6, that is, approximately 350,000 ya to 128,000, and it appears unlikely to be any younger than that. Despite these limitations, it is hoped that the foregoing discussion has contributed meaningfully to the description of the Delhi palaeolithic complex. It is also hoped that future research can lend some much-needed chronological and analytical precision and description to the information presented here. As a final point, it is important to note that the location of the complex on the subcontinental scale too has significant implications. It appears to have the potential to contribute meaningfully to the currently active and stimulating debates over the models and most likely paths of the colonization of the Indian subcontinent. This is particularly the case as most synthetic accounts and reviews of the Indian palaeolithic have not considered the complex at all. Equally, it suggests a basic reorientation in the manner in which that of the north-west has been typified. While no doubt the palaeolithic is characterized by the Thar complex, it appears for reasons of habitat, resources, and in the broadest sense 'setting', the Aravallis too can make an equal claim. Until we have more information about the plains and the seemingly extensive archaeological pasts they conceal, the defining aspect of the Delhi palaeolithic complex retains its place in its own landscape, of the Aravalli highlands.

SENSE IN A SCATTER: THE MICROLITHIC COMPLEX

In introducing the second major category of artefacts recovered in the survey, the microliths, it is important to direct attention towards the tremendous temporal and spatial distribution of blade-oriented, or in a broader sense chipped stone, artefacts. It is recognized that the archaeological record of the subcontinent from after the end of the Middle palaeolithic involves a general shift to such industries of small blade-based tools which differ widely in the way local situations, that is, needs as well as lithic practices, informed the constitution of these much varied assemblages. While this understanding has structured the understanding of later/Upper palaeolithic, a second and equally forceful recognition has come to frame our understanding of such artefacts from the other end of their temporal distribution, from far within the historical context. A number of case studies from Dihar in West Bengal or from the Vijayanagara area survey have helped establish that chipped stone strategies had continued relevance and were utilized for local needs in very different times and locations.[33] Such recognition of the broad and varied contexts are necessary for historiographic and practical reasons. They help us step out of stagist formulae of prehistory such as the mesolithic, which have questionable inherent explanatory capacities from the South Asian record embodying such versatility and 'persistence' of chipped lithic traditions. Bringing these to bear upon the situation on the ground, the microlithic assemblage of the Delhi region is unknown from all excavated cultural sequences in the region, and by this fact and by its wide distribution seems to define itself as a separate unit. For these reasons, by which various categories of material evidence come to define them, this essay shall refer to this cultural complex as simply that of the microlithic scatters, as the reference to the loosely defined wastes of lithic reduction embodies their presence in the landscape best.

The microlithic scatters of the survey are presented here only in qualitative terms.[34] Even at this level, however, it is possible to attempt a description of these distinctive mass of debitage and flakes fired on quartz quarried from local veins or nodules that punctuate the local quartzite. In many of the scatters that sit on stabilized terrains and have not been subjected to distribution down or across a slope by wash processes it is often possible to discern different stages of lithic reduction by examination of the debitage. Thick cortical and badly fracturing flakes are sometimes present in scatters, especially those that sit at the lip of a nodule or vein. In others, core-like pieces and many blank flakes seem to be distributed within an extremely small area, perhaps suggestive of a single knapping episode in contrast to the former, where more complex associations may be presumed. In still other scatters it appears that only final stage tool production was being practised as only angular shatter and very fine flakes can be observed.

Even without a statistical description, it appears that the object of the industry was primarily oriented towards the production of blade-like flakes, a striking category of which were parallel-sided, thin, and appear to have been minimally retouched or altered. Another broad template appears to have been recorded in the production of thicker and less strictly controlled set of flakes upon which a whole variety of side-scrapers were produced often with extensive and deft retouching of various types.[35] A variety of cores seems to have been used, varying from some informal discoidal cores to the more common single-platform cores for the production of blades. Significantly, a number of flakes that are struck laterally appear to be for the purpose of rejuvenating such cores and producing fresh platforms have also been identified. Additionally, many pieces suggest a dual-platform type of strategy for similar purposes of core maintenance, where a fresh margin seems to have been provided by removing a thick flake from the surface opposite the erstwhile platform. Such flakes bearing a series of flake removal scars towards their distal end have also been commonly observed. The two broad grades of quartz available in the region (crystal or clear quartz and the more turbid or milky quartz) were both utilized. The former seems to exhibit marginally better fracture, especially in the production of thin blades. Two geo-archaeological constraints seem to operate upon the utilization of these raw materials. Despite their extremely high resistance to processes of weathering, the intense pyrite dissolution-led weathering of the surrounding country quartzites has led to the development of cortical surfaces up to many centimetres from the surface of quartz, which unpredictably affects fracture. Often the largest flakes at scatters are merely those removing such cortical sections to reach a usable surface. Another factor influencing the fracture dynamics seems to lie in the specifics of these small veins and their cooling history as intrusives. Even though large blocks can easily be quarried from veins, as appears to have been the case, fractures can initiate

FIGURE 2.7: A selection of scrapers from the microlithic assemblage. All working edges oriented towards left

normally (in a predictable conchoidal manner) and then terminate in unexpected manner along planes extant within the matrix of the quartz. Such complications may have dictated the preferential selection of large blocks from certain sources and not others while they all appear visually to be much the same (Fig. 2.7).

While these features but merely provide the most skeletal account of the processes of microlithic production, it is the diversity of artefacts beyond the quartz shatter that lends the scatters a definitive cultural identity in the field. The quartzite weathering mechanisms described in the first section also produce, under stable conditions, an extremely iron-rich precipitate upon the outermost rind. In themselves indices of massive erosional pasts and possibly of palaeo-humidity as well, these precipitate formations have attained, at times, considerable proportions to the order of many centimetres. Such deposits are understandably rare and have been located in only two or three places in the survey. Yet, despite its relative rarity, such iron-rich pieces are in evidence and are invariably present at most scatters. The natural cleavage of these pieces shows a rough and granular section, in contrast to the 'polish' or worn sections of many pieces that appear to have acquired that sort of condition by way of deliberate abrasion.[36] In addition to such pieces, nodular iron-rich pieces too appeared to have been brought to these microlithic scatters. A singular example of a flake produced on such material is suggestive of the exploitation of these exceptional deposits as well.

Further, two more categories of cultural artefacts add different levels of complexity. The first relates to a single find of a completely exhausted, diminutive, and multifaceted core on the tuffaceous sandstone. The raw material seems to be transported especially as this core was utilized till no longer possible and to much greater degree than any observed quartz core (Fig. 2.8). The second category of artefacts is in contrast to the rarity of the tuffaceous sandstone present at almost every scatter. The presence of heavily eroded, rolled, and

FIGURE 2.8: Various faces of the multi-directional core fashioned from the tuffaceous sandstone

fragmentary pieces of pottery at many scatters has provided another register of cultural complexity to these lithics. The ceramics seem to have been made from particularly well-levigated clay, with few inclusions except from being extremely micaceous as well as being well fired. In addition, they have been reduced to a condition where form has been extremely rare to discern, and as such any correlation with known broad ceramic types of the excavations in the Delhi region has not been possible.[37]

If the ceramics leave the investigation into the microliths with more questions than answers, there are also a number of other aspects: broadly, more intangibles than features concretely established. The locational aspects of the scatters themselves are suggestive of many such aspects of social organization that can at this stage be merely described. In more than one case within a small area of 200 m^2 there exist a number of small discrete scatters. In other areas, scatters adjoining nodules seem to have been the sites for a greater volume of knapping than a number of smaller discrete scatters, possibly single-use, which circumscribe such large ones. Further, the microlithic scatters demonstrate a sense of the landscape in their locations and many of them regularly are distributed along the tors that cap the ridges and afford clear and commanding views of the landscape. A similar rationale seems to have informed the location of others along the lip of the large and small ravines that carve up the topography of the study region. An additional level to these symbolisms is suggested by the widespread and frequent distribution of petroglyphs, bruised into the red weathering rind of friable quartzite-derived sands. These petroglyphs, by their manner of occasional conjunction with quartz veins and/or microlithic scatters, seem to suggest a contemporaneity and authorship with the microliths using communities, but nothing concrete can be said regarding this relationship. It is only the shared sense of landscape between the scatters and the petroglyphs that can be seen as any evidence for a connection.

The stratigraphic relationship of this cultural complex to the preceding palaeolithic, and to the period of the maximal aeolian deposition is frustratingly difficult to establish. The scatters are all either cemented into thin sections of aeolian sediment or are alternatively found stabilized on locations practically 'amidst tors' or on the bedrock itself. Where they are found in section, as has been observed and reported earlier, those sections are found to be presumably those that had been constituted by wash into the valleys. Thus, the observation of microliths somewhere in the middle of aeolian sediments does not appear to be one which presents us with primary context, but rather an opportunity with which to establish a *terminus ante quem* by methods of luminescence.[38] Without that level of information, only a most preliminary hypothesis can be suggested here. Since no palaeosols have been reported nor observed as interrupting the aeolian sedimentation anywhere in the Delhi region, the microlith-using communities appear to have inhabited the region before the major phase of this intensified deposition. From what is known of the extension of the Thar towards the larger region, the two last phases of heightened and maximal aridity has been postulated in general terms at the 11 to 13 Kya and 4 to 2 Kya BP boundaries.[39] The two main projects that are seriously required for a better characterization of the microlithic complex are a statistical investigation of the assemblage as well as the development of a comprehensive chronology for the aeolian deposition.

CONCLUSIONS

The Delhi ridge encloses within its folds a vast time scale. Within the space of a couple of metres, one can walk across from small strips of ancient landscapes on to young sediments. It is because of these processes of landscape transformation that a complex range of archaeological cultures from palaeoliths to medieval ceramics can be recovered from the surface. This essay has been unable to make a contribution to the vast amount of evidence that exists for medieval interventions in the landscape. The archaeology of stone quarrying and of the varied ceramics as well as the landscape discourses embodied in many monuments—most notably associated with the closest citadel of Lal Kot—remain an unfulfilled agenda.

This study has attempted to argue that the Delhi palaeolithic complex is an important record for how we understand the Indian palaeolithic. The preliminary study here hopes to indicate that the complexity of the record of a small segment of a once far more extensive mountain range has considerable implication and much further scope for study. Renewed excavations as well as geo-chronological work are direly needed to advance our knowledge of the palaeolithic complex as well as to enable us to approach the authors of the microliths with more clarity. This essay has wrestled with appearances on the surface of a landscape. The questions it has hoped to raise now require an investigation that can complement this by going beyond it.

ACKNOWLEDGEMENTS

While this is only an initial and exploratory study, it would not have been possible without the guidance and support of many people. Without the guidance, advice, and patient support of Himanshu Prabha Ray this essay would never have taken form. Nayanjot Lahiri took time out repeatedly to show me artefacts recovered during her survey as well as to clarify various matters. Upinder Singh advised on what direction the essay should take, and graciously allowed a very generous period of time for its revision. J.K. Tripathi's patience and enthusiasm in discussing his work and clarifying all misgivings, from the most basic to the more subtle geochemical points, is gratefully acknowledged. I am also thankful to Milap C. Sharma who solved all problems as soon as they arose, and without whom it would not have been possible to implement the survey. He provided me with the GPS unit, the basic map, and the Munsell soil colour chart, and made it possible for this survey to attempt to be professional. Ravi Korisettar visited the sites, clarified the most initial problems, and subsequently provided much sound advice and corrected many glaring errors. I am tremendously indebted to him for not only pointing out the errors, but also for often demonstrating how one should consider the evidence. Parth Chauhan took time out of a busy schedule to visit the sites and see the artefacts. I thank him for all his encouragement and for readily answering all questions as well as sending copies of his essays. Jinu Koshy has helped in many more ways than he knows by making hitherto incomprehensible aspects of lithics seem lucid and clear. M.V. Pradeep Kumar was equally present and witness to the thrill of the initial discoveries and in his subsequent absence he was deeply missed. I wish to thank my parents and brother for always being tremendously supportive and tolerating long periods of absence and longer periods of frustration. Radhika Govindrajan has known this work at the level of every stone from every day, and it would not have been possible without her support.

NOTES AND REFERENCES

1. The alluvial plains away from the ridges record a complex and rich pattern of shifting settlements from the late Harappan horizons through the phase of the Painted-Grey Ware. A large early historic settlement was excavated at the Purana Qila, and early medieval and medieval period ones have been excavated within the citadels of Lal Kot and Tughlaqabad respectively. It seems fair to presume continuous occupation in the region for at least the last 4,000 years. For a synthetic account of these various cultures, see Upinder Singh, *Ancient Delhi,* New Delhi: Oxford University Press, 1999.
2. O.H.K. Spate and A.T.A. Learmonth, *India and Pakistan: A General and Regional Geography,* London: Methuen, 1967.
3. Zarine Cooper, *Prehistory of the Chitrakot Falls*, Pune: Ravish Publishers, 1997, p. 1.
4. M.D. Petraglia, 'Pursuing Site-formation Research in India', in S. Wadia, R. Korisettar, and V.S. Kale (eds), *Quaternary Environments and Geoarchaeology of India* (Geological Society of India Memoir 32), Bangalore: Geological Society of India, 1995, pp. 440–65.
5. R. Korisettar, 'Toward Developing a Basin Model for Paleolithic Settlement of the Indian Subcontinent: Geodynamics, Monsoon Dynamics, Habitat Diversity and Dispersal Routes', in M.D. Petraglia and B. Allchin (eds), *The Evolution and History of Human Populations in South Asia and Inter-disciplinary Studies in Archaeology, Biological Anthropology, Linguistics and Genetics,* Dordrecht: Springer, 2007, pp. 69–96. Also, R. Korisettar, 'Geoarchaeology of Purana and Gondwana Basin of Peninsular India: Peripheral or Paramount', *Proceedings of Indian History Congress,* Presidential Address, Section of Archaeology, Sixty-fifth session, Bareilly, 2004, pp. 1–40.
6. Two volumes that describe most of the data and debates over the Aravallis are A.B. Roy (ed.), *Precambrian of the Aravalli Mountains, Rajasthan, India,* (Geological Society of India Memoir 7), Bangalore: Geological Society of India, 1988; and A.B. Roy and S.R. Jakhar, *Geology of Rajasthan, Northwest India: Precambrian to Recent,* Jodhpur: Scientific Publishers, 2002.
7. All geochemical data and arguments about the weathering of the quartzites and the nature of the ridge sediments presented in this essay draws upon the prolonged and sustained investigation of J.K. Tripathi from his 1997, 'Geochemical Aspects of Weathering of Rocks and Sediments of South Delhi Area', unpublished PhD Thesis, Delhi: Jawaharlal Nehru University.

   While the large corpus of publications produced by Tripathi's research project are interrelated, they are cited where most appropriate. In this case, refer to J.K. Tripathi, and V. Rajamani, 'In Situ Maturation of Sediments within the Weathering Profiles: An Evidence from REE Behaviour During Weathering of the Delhi Quartzites', *Current Science*, 76 (12), 1998, pp. 1255–8.

8. Z.S.H. Abu-Hamatteh, 'Geochemistry and Tectonic Framework of Proterozoic Mafic Metavolcanics of Aravalli-Delhi Orogen, NW India', *Chemie der Erde Geochemistry*, 62 (2), 2002, pp. 123–44.
9. S.C. Awasthi and M. Prasad, 'Palaeovolcanism in Sohna Area, Gurgaon Dist. Haryana', *Records of the Geological Survey of India*, 15 (7 and 8), 1992, pp. 1–3.
10. A. Tyagi, 'Mineralogical and Geochemical Changes Leading to the Formation of Clay Deposits in the Mehrauli Area, South Delhi', unpublished PhD Thesis, Delhi: University of Delhi makes the suggestion that the quartz and pegmatite intrusives of the Delhi region broadly coincide with the known chronology of the intrusion of the Erinpura granites into the Delhi series.
11. It appears that the Delhi region would have lain on the margins of some sort of a basin that evolved from the Proterozoic that was to the west of it and was bracketed by the Aravallis. Yet, the manner in which the landscape has been transformed since the collision of the Indian and Asian shields, especially in the last 2 million years, renders it virtually impossible to comprehend the previous dispensation of the terrain in any great detail.
12. A range of studies now addresses the complexity of fluvial sedimentary succession, driven by the consideration that the depth of these sediments is thought to contribute and heighten seismic sensitivity in the capital. K.S. Rao and D. Neelima Satyam, 'Liquefaction Studies for Seismic Microzonation of Delhi Region', *Current Science*, 92 (5), pp. 646–54. Also, for a review of many other studies, Y. Pandey and R. Dharmaraju, 'Subsurface Map of Delhi', http://www.gisdevelopment.net/application/urban/agglomeration/urbana0002pf.htm, accessed 11 June 2008.
13. J.K. Tripathi and V. Rajamani, 'Weathering Control over Geomorphology of Supermature Proterozoic Delhi Quartzites of India', *Earth Surface Processes and Landforms*, 28 (13), 2003, pp. 1379–87.
14. Further, the surrounding quartzite ridges show little signs of fluvial action, and those that exist are the work of local topographic drainages from the slopes rather than those carved out by a major sediment load-bearing river like the Yamuna. Additionally, the slopes of the ridges even above the valley floor in small depressions and hollows demonstrate small cemented sections of sediments.
15. J.K. Tripathi, and V. Rajamani, 'Geochemistry of Loessic Sediments on the Eastern Fringe of the Thar Desert, Rajasthan, India: Its Implication to Exogenic Processes', *Chemical Geology*, 155 (3–4), 1999, pp. 265–78.
16. A vast geological literature exists on the evolution of the Thar, and in addition, a considerable body of articles now reports or speculates on correlation between the Thar and shifting archaeological distributions. The most significant of these efforts establishing that the Thar was an ancient landform of changing and fluctuating dynamics is Bridget Allchin, A. Goudie, and K. Hegde, *The Prehistory and Palaeogeography of the Great Indian Desert*, London: Academic Press, 1978. Subsequently, V.N. Misra *et al.*, 'Radiometric Dating of a Quaternary Dune Section, Didwana, Rajasthan', *Man and Environment*, vol.

XIII, 1989, pp. 19–23. A recent review is found in R.P. Dhir, S.N. Rajaguru, and A.K. Singhvi, 'Desert Quaternary Formations and Their Morphostratigraphy: Implications for the Evolutionary History of the Thar', *Journal Geological Society of India*, 43 (4), April 1994, pp. 435–47.

17. While the ridge in the study region may bear out the argument made above, the table land ridges of the Asola sanctuary and the extensive Harchandpur ridge suggest other dimensions of such processes that still need to be worked out in greater detail and surveyed intensively. At the same time, it is important to recognize that many ridges afford steep slope angles and generate colluvial action of a much higher order as well. These are most often regions which appear to be completely non-artefactual.
18. For the best statement on the model of sedimentation, see I.B. Singh, 'Late Quaternary History of the Ganga Plain', *Journal of the Geological Society of India,* 64(4), 2004, pp. 431–54, and references to the same author cited therein. For the geo-chronological data in support of the model, P. Srivastava, I.B. Singh, M. Sharma, and A.K. Singhvi, 'Luminescence Chronometry and Late Quaternary Geomorphic History of the Ganga Plain, India', *Palaeogeography, Palaeoclimatology, Palaeoecology*, 197 (1), 2003, pp. 15–41. The numerous and disconnected palaeo-channels in the entire region south and north of Delhi document a complex record of fluvial change in terms of depositional features to erosional and incising into existing active zones and in addition also document the control exerted by neo-tectonics over this activity. The palaeo-channels of the Yamuna are all now understood as being relatively recent and may correspond more closely to the terminal Pleistocene or even the Holocene rather than to the era of the Acheulian settlers.
19. D.K. Chakrabarti and N. Lahiri, 'A Preliminary Report on the Stone Age of Delhi and Haryana', *Man and Environment*, vol. XI, 1987, pp. 109–16. Altogether, they report 43 different localities providing an invaluable and unmatched investigation of the region.
20. The extensive two-season long explorations and excavations at Arangpur have been published in a number of sources. Annual reports are available in the *Indian Archaeology: A Review* for the years 1990–1 and 1991–2. *Indian Archaeology: A Review*, New Delhi: Archaeological Survey of India, 1994 and 1995. A monograph was published containing a description of the project and its execution by A.K. Sharma, *Prehistoric Delhi and its Neighbourhood*, New Delhi: Aryan Books International, 1993. An important metrical study of the artefacts was published by A.K. Sharma and S.B. Ota, 'Anangpur: The Paleolithic Site Near Delhi', in B.U. Nayak and N.C. Ghosh (eds), *New Trends in Indian Art and Archaeology: S.R. Rao's 70th Birthday Felicitation Volume*, New Delhi: Aditya Prakashan, 1992, vol. I, pp. 1–13.
21. The representative work on the Thar complex are Allchin *et al.*, *The Prehistory and Palaeogeography of the Great Indian Desert*; V.N. Misra, S.N. Rajaguru, D.R. Raju, H. Raghavan, and C. Gaillard, 'Acheulian Occupation and Evolving Landscape Around Didwana in the Thar Desert, India', *Man and Environment*, vol. VI, 1982, pp. 72–86; and V.N. Misra, 'Geoarchaeology of

the Thar Desert', in S. Wadia, R. Korisettar, and V.S. Kale (eds), *Quaternary Environments and Geoarchaeology of India* (Geological Society of India Memoir 32), Bangalore: Geological Society of India, 1995, pp. 210–30.

22. The collection strategy employed in the survey for the palaeoliths is necessarily a far cry from crawl surveys that would have been ideal but are impractical over the rugged terrain. Whatever artefacts were encountered in the course of the survey were collected, but only after the recording of their individual locations by GPS. Even if this level of data may be superfluous in itself, it is combined with other recorded information, such as the surface of the artefact in contact with the sedimentary surface, what sort of sedimentary surface this was, and whether the artefacts had been buried to any depth. Estimations of colluvial motion or erosion in the immediate vicinity as well as any modern disturbances such as the laying of pipes or quarrying were also recorded. Every time an artefact was located, a consistent attempt was made to search a 10 to 15 m^2 region around it intensively for any other artefacts.
23. P. Chauhan, 'Paleolithic Exploitation of Rounded and Sub-angular Auartzites in the Indian Subcontinent', in B. Blades and B. Adams (eds), *Lithic Materials and Paleolithic Societies*, Blackwell, forthcoming.
24. Importantly, it has been suggested that at Attirampakkam spalls did constitute a viable objective piece, which was utilized for the production of Acheulian bifaces. The record from even within the survey area seems complex and does not unequivocally suggest that all reduction systematically ignored spalls, but it seems unlikely that they were considered a significant objective piece/core to begin reduction with.
25. The yellow tuffaceous sandstone was found in association with the palaeoliths only at the construction site. While quantities of the flaked material were found at the site, it is perhaps best to advance a sense of caution about its exploitation by the palaeolithic communities as no other indication of this is available except from the disturbed building constructions. As is reported further in the essay, there is evidence that the microlithic communities did utilize the rock as well.
26. Awasthi and Prasad, 'Palaeovolcanism', pp. 1–3.
27. The abundance of good quality vein quartz and nodules seems suggestive, and while no tools associated with the palaeolithic were encountered in the course of the survey, such tools are reported but not described from the site of Arangpur. Sharma (*Prehistoric Delhi*) distinguishes between quartzite and fine-grained as well as coarse-grained 'sandstones' as the raw materials for bifaces.
28. The study of site formation processes here has admittedly remained largely anecdotal rather than quantified. The main study, which the general attempt at description draws upon, is R. Jhaldiyal, 'Surface Wash Processes and Their Impact on Stone Age Sites', *Man and Environment*, XXIII (1), 1998, pp. 81–92, as well as K. Padayya, R. Jhaldiyal, and M.D. Petraglia, 'Geoarchaeology of the Acheulian Workshop at Isampur, Hunsgi Valley, Karnataka', *Man and Environment*, XXIV (1), 1999, pp. 167–84. It is suggested here that the western fringe of the Aravallis may eventually, upon more sustained survey, reveal a distribution similar to that described for Raisen in terms of surface Acheulian

clusters. Jerome Jacobsen, 'Early Stone Age Habitation Sites in Eastern Malwa', *Proceedings of the American Philosophical Society*, 119 (4), 1975, pp. 280–97.

29. I am tremendously indebted to a number of conversations with Jinu Koshy about palaeolithic technology and knapping for having made me sensitive to many of these issues and aspects. Without his insights it would not have been possible to raise these issues at all. All responsibility for inaccuracies and errors is, of course, solely my own.
30. Chakrabarti and Lahiri, 'A Preliminary Report on the Stone Age of Delhi', pp. 109–16.
31. This information reported indifferently in the *Indian Archaeology: A Review* is detailed in Sharma, *Prehistoric Delhi*, p. 6.
32. Even the most preliminary consideration of the known core technologies from sites in the Thar and Aravallis suggests important dimensions of variability. As our knowledge about these assemblages, their relative chronologies and the role core technologies played in them statistical comparisons across regions as demonstrated for the Levant may prove fruitful. I.J. Wallace and J.J. Shea, 'Mobility Patterns and Core Technologies in the Middle Paleolithic of the Levant', *Journal of Archaeological Science*, XXXIII (9), 2006, pp. 1293–309.
33. Hannah V.A. James and M.D. Petraglia, 'Modern Human Origins and the Evolution of Behavior in the Later Pleistocene Record of South Asia', *Current Anthropology*, vol. 46 (Supplement, December), 2005. See D.K. Chakrabarti, *India: An Archaeological History*, New Delhi: Oxford University Press, 1999, p. 94 for a discussion on early historic and medieval microliths from Bankura district, West Bengal. Also, K.D. Morrison, 'Historicizing Foraging in Asia: Power, History, and Ecology of Holocene Hunting and Gathering', in Miriam Stark (ed.), *The Archaeology of Asia*, Malden, MA: Blackwell, 2005.
34. A more ambitious programme of statistical description is planned and a comprehensive research design for the depopulation of some scatters to generate this data is under preparation. The general method adopted in the survey was to record a GPS location for each scatter and provide a rough estimate of the extant surface size of the scatter making note of the extent to which surface processes had redistributed or washed away the materials. Observations over two monsoons suggest that much sorting occurs during the rains, but relative motion is often only a function of topography and the angle of the quartzite slopes or of the gullied aeolian deposits. Sampling of artefacts from scatters was restricted to a minimum collection of standard types and cores or core fragments. Some estimation of the average density and size of the typical shatter was attempted at a general level, but may not approximate the statistical reality in any sense. It is hoped that a systematic and controlled depopulation of a scatter or set of scatters shall allow a better description of the industry and by hopefully yielding refitting pieces shall allow for an understanding of the many stages of the reduction process.
35. Some pieces that resemble broken points have been located, but it is unlikely that the artefact type, if actually present at all, would have been a significant part of the assemblage. If any artefact represents the assemblage, it is the wide variety of scrapers.

36. Informal grinding against a quartzite piece of such iron-rich hematite-like pieces readily offers 'rust'-like powder. Beyond the suggestion that they possibly served as a source for pigment, it is difficult to state why such materials were used. The texture of the material being a precipitate varies greatly from affording reasonable step fractures to being primarily grainy and crumbling on percussion.
37. Given the extremely small size of most body sherds, it has been extremely difficult to describe the ceramics, but some broad and decorated rims are available. The defining characteristic of the pottery appears to be its extremely weathered condition, to the extent that it gives off its 'ochre' or surface colouring even on the slightest of contact. Traditionally, accounts of Indian prehistory are not attuned to the presence of such complexes, but startlingly similar evidence is reported quite frequently. F. R. Allchin notes the repeated finds of ceramics with microlithic scatters at a number of sites and remarks upon the difficulty of correlating them easily. Allchin suggests a broad correlation with the sites of Ahar, Gilund, and the Berach Basin. F.R. Allchin, 'Appendix: Pottery and Miscellaneous Finds', in Allchin *et al.*, *Prehistory and Paleogeography of the Great Indian Desert*. Also S. Mishra, M. Jain, S.K. Tandon, A.K. Singhvi, P. P. Joglekar, S.C. Bhat, A. A. Kshirsagar, S. Naik, and A. Deshpande-Mukherjee 'Prehistoric Cultures and Late Quaternary environments of the Luni Basin around Balotra', *Man and Environment*, XXIV (1), 1999, pp. 39–50, similarly report that the site of Manawara I where a culture known from microliths, ceramics, bones, and shell was subsequently covered over by an advancing aeolian deposit sometime between 3,400 and 2,800 years ago.
38. Such as in the fluvio-aeolian section as reported at Lakkarpur by Chakrabarti and Lahiri, 'A Preliminary Report', pp. 109–16.
39. Dhir *et al.*, 'Desert Quartenary Formations', p. 446.

3. Human–Plant Interactions in the Middle Gangetic Plains

An Archaeobotanical Perspective (From the Mesolithic up to c. *Third Century* BC*)*

Shibani Bose

Structurally, the central segment of the vast Gangetic plains, the Middle Ganga Plains (24°30'N–27°50'N and 81°47'E–87°50'E), is a massive alluvial expanse bounded by the Himalayan foothills in the north and the Vindhyan ranges in the south, the Ganga–Yamuna confluence in the west, and the Bengal and Bihar border in the east. Covering the northern part of Allahabad district and Pratapgarh, Sultanpur, Jaunpur, and Varanasi districts of Uttar Pradesh[1], and the divisions of Tirhut, Bhagalpur (excluding Kishanganj subdivision and including only the Godda subdivision), and Patna in Bihar, (leaving out the area above 150 m in the south),[2] it may be defined 'as simply what is left between the Upper Gangetic Plains and Bengal : roughly the eastern third of Uttar Pradesh and the northern half of Bihar'[3] (Fig. 3.1). The Ganga, originating in the Himalayas, is the river that dominates the topography of the area, and is the recipient of all drainage lines like the Sai, Gomati, Ghaghara, Gandak, Kosi, and their numerous seasonal tributary systems.[4]

Devoid of rock, ordinary alluvium predominates the geology of the region. The average depth of alluvium is 1,300 m to 1,400 m and is clearly divisible into the older (Pleistocene) alluvium known as *bhangar* (Fig. 3.2) and the younger alluvium, *khadar*. The terminal of the bhangar constituted the bank of the Ganga when it was actually forming this area and gradually receding southwards to form the deposit of the khadar.[5]

FIGURE 3.1: Study area with administrative divisions

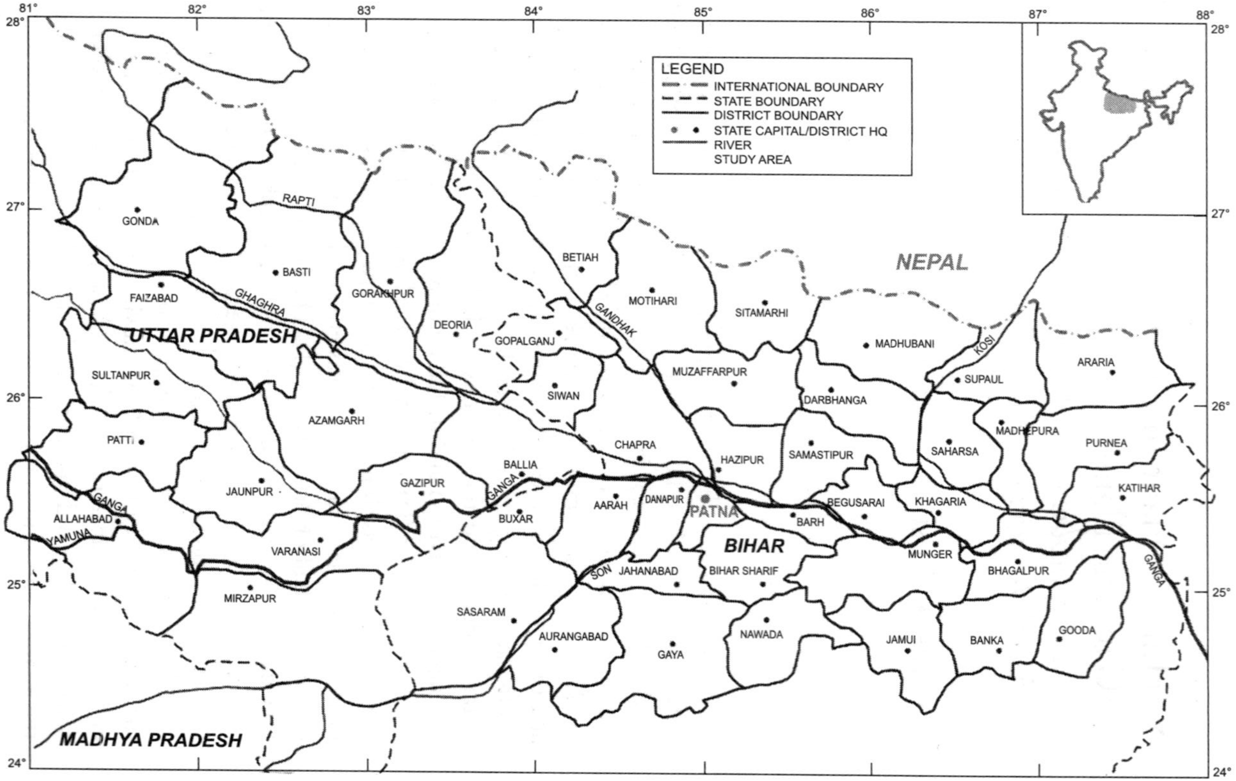

FIGURE 3.2: Exposed sections of the bhangar showing a succession of four deposits

As regards the genesis of this fluvial landscape, investigations conducted by the University of Allahabad, led by G.R. Sharma, and subsequently amplified by the Lucknow University, have revealed that the structure of the Gangetic plains and the various formations constituting it suggest a volatile history during the Stone Age. A deep depression is believed to have existed between the Himalayas in the north and the plateau in the south up to the Pleistocene era. The detritus brought down by the Himalayan and the Vindhyan rivers slowly filled this up.[6] Geologically speaking, therefore, the Middle Gangetic Plains are very young, the surface having been built up by the silting action of its streams during the late Pleistocene and early Holocene times.[7]

A type-section of the Ganga showing geological formations of the late Pleistocene and early Holocene reveals four distinct layers made by the Ganga before it started cutting its bed to form the present channel. Preliminary observations of these formations and their tentative correlation with the Belan section have furnished some idea of the palaeo-climate of the region. Sharma[8] suggests that in the case of the Belan, in the course of the formation of the top two aeolian layers, correlated with the sandy soil capping the Pleistocene deposits of the Ganga, there was a change in climate, ushering in an extremely dry phase. The rivers of the Vindhyas, which had been building up their flood plains during the late Pleistocene started flowing in much narrower channels, resulting also in the deepening of the old channel. A contemporary and parallel change is said to have affected the Ganga as well, which then formed the most recent sandy deposit of its plain. The river, which had been building its valley since its arrival in the plains down the Himalayas, suddenly started cutting its bed and receding further south to its present course. In the course of its withdrawal to its present course, many of the meanders of the old courses were converted into ox-bow lakes, enclosing recently formed sandy silty alluvium (Fig. 3.3). With the onset of the mild climate of the Holocene, the marshy land or water-locked Ganga alluvium gradually turned into good grasslands and sprouted new types of grasses and plants.[9] Rich food resources in the Gangetic plains and population pressure in the Vindhyas are suggested to have provided

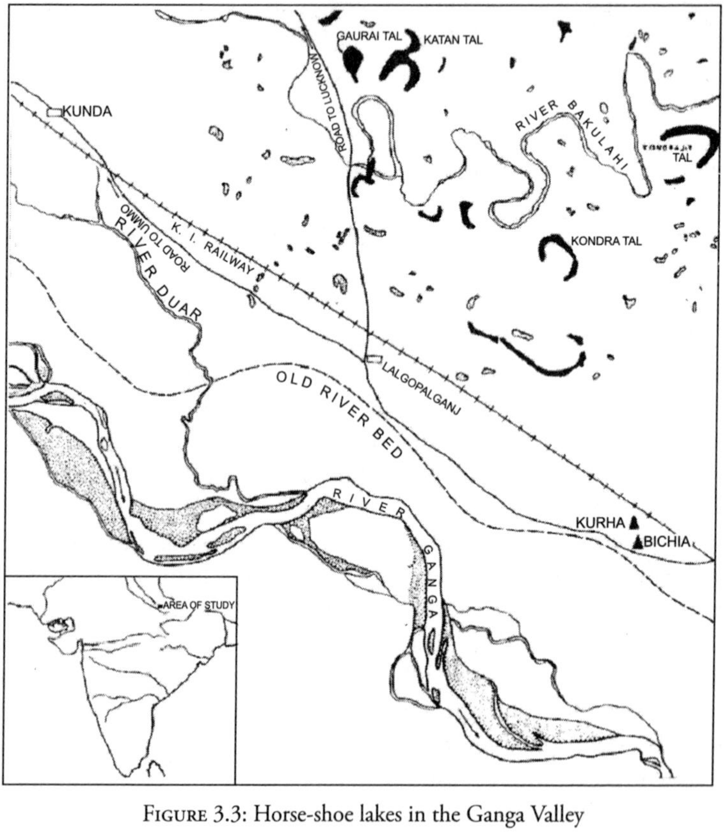

FIGURE 3.3: Horse-shoe lakes in the Ganga Valley

the decisive impulse for the migration of Stone Age humans from the Vindhyas to the more hospitable regions of the Ganga alluvium.[10.]

More recently, climate and tectonic changes have been studied by I.B. Singh of Lucknow University, with reference to their role in shaping the geomorphic features of the Ganga plains, whereby it has been argued that its present geomorphic features are the result of changing climate and base-level adjustments (sea-level changes) during the last 128 Ka (late Pleistocene–Holocene period).[11] Palynological studies[12] have also aided the reconstruction of palaeo-climatic trends, recent ones being the study of the Sanai Tal, which forms a part of the meander cut-off and abandoned channel belt system in Rai Bareli district, Uttar Pradesh,[13] Basaha lake, Unnao, Misa Tal, Lucknow, and the Lahuradewa lake deposit in the Sarayupur region of the Central Ganga Plains in Sant Kabir Nagar district, Uttar Pradesh.[14]

It is also worthwhile to note how recent research, apart from documenting the impact of anthropogenic activity on the evolution of this fluvial landscape, has also underlined the antiquity of human activity in the Ganga plains. In the Middle Ganga Plains, marked by ox-bow lakes and rivulets originating from them, there are indications that during the first arrival of Stone Age humans in the area, the present geomorphological features had come into existence and the bigger rivers like the Ganga, Yamuna, Gomati, and Sai were flowing in their present courses. The first colonizers of the Gangetic plains were the late upper palaeolithic and early mesolithic groups.[15.] A review of the habitation pattern during the latest Pleistocene–Holocene by Singh[16] revealed a number of fossil-rich horizons and artefacts in early contexts. Particularly interesting is the crucial evidence of human activity documented[17] from the Kalpi section of the Yamuna river, where the sediments yielded rich vertebrate fossils, namely, an elephant tusk, shoulder blade of an elephant, molars of *Equus*, bovids, *Bos, Elephas, Hippopotamus*, and skeletal parts of crocodiles and turtles. A large number of bone fragments showed signs of human workmanship that was rather crude and seemed to be of late palaeolithic affinity (Figs 3.4a, 3.4b, and 3.4c). The evidence clearly indicated human occupation of the site. Along with the vertebrate fossils, several specimens of human femur were also retrieved. These displayed cut marks at the distal end resembling pencil sharpening, which had been neatly made and polished. Though precise dating of the event is not available, its sediments and the rich fauna indicated its deposition during the humid climate of 28–33 Ka.

Archaeological research conducted in the Middle Gangetic Plains has brought to light various dimensions of the Holocene cultures of the region. As a result of these investigations, considerable data for the reconstruction of the environment and human adaptations is now available. This essay endeavours to synthesize available archaeobotanical evidence relevant to the understanding of human–plant interactions within the chronological framework of Holocene cultures spanning the mesolithic till the first phase of the early historic period up to *c.* third century BC in the Middle Ganga Plains and the eastern Vindhyas. A glance at the botanical remains retrieved from archaeological sites in the region (Fig. 3.5), however, suggests that though a large number of them have yielded evidence of plant resource utilization, a thorough documentation of all plant remains, together with a critical evaluation of the data, is still perhaps unavailable to us in the case of many sites. In most cases, one has to contend with only preliminary results that are limited to a record of the presence or absence of particular plant species as the final reports are yet to be published. Within the confines of the evidence available through archaeological journals and individual publications, the present essay will attempt to reconstruct the vegetational environment of humans in the ancient past together with patterns of exploitation of this environment and their implications for subsistence practices through the centuries surveyed. Apart from presenting a synoptic

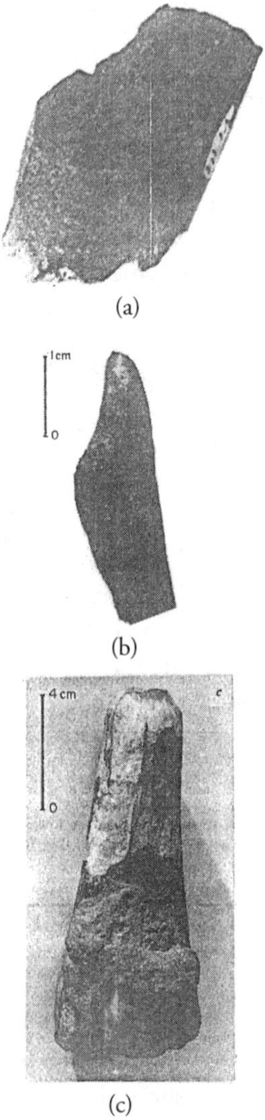

FIGURE 3.4: a) A bone splinter showing peeling effect
b) A piece of bone with sickle-shaped edge
c) Distal end of metacarpal showing peeling effect

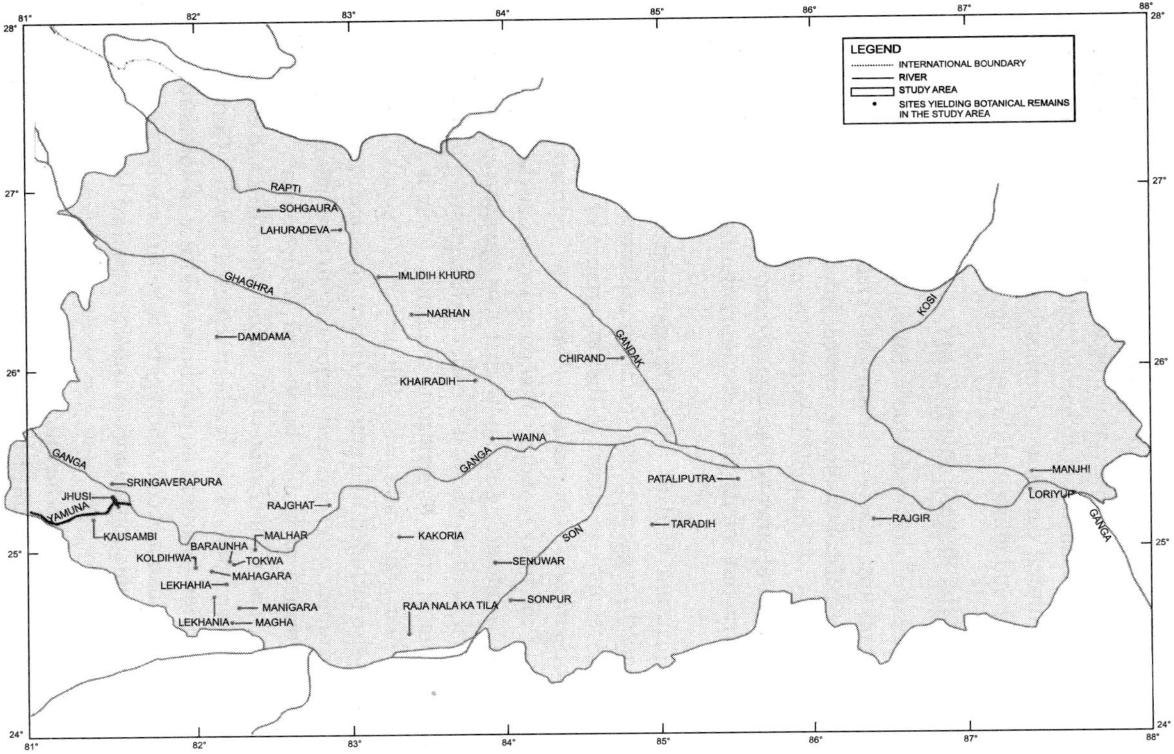

FIGURE 3.5: Sites yielding botanical remains in the study area

view of the patterns of utilization of economically important plants during different cultural phases of the Holocene, the essay will also delve into intra-site botanical variability over time in relation to ecological opportunities and archaeobotanical evidence hinting at cultural contacts and interactions between diverse cultural regions. The botanical remains from archaeological sites in the region together with their cultural details and implications have been tabulated in Appendix 3.1 and illustrated through Figs 3.6, 3.7, and 3.8.

MESOLITHIC PLANT ECONOMY

In the context of the mesolithic cultures of the region, though the picture seems unsatisfactory for want of a greater number of stratified sites yielding palaeobotanical evidence, inferences drawn from the available corpus of botanical information, together with analysis of lithic artefacts and other archaeological data, have considerably aided the reconstruction of its plant economy during the period under discussion.

The quantum of data from Damdama in district Pratapgarh, Uttar Pradesh, suggests broad-spectrum exploitation of wild vegetal food. The assemblage attests to the importance of wild species like goosefoot/*bathua (Chenopodium album*) and purslane (*Portulaca oleracea*) in the food economy of ancient settlers at the site. In this context, it is interesting to know that *Chenopodium album* occurs as an annual weed in wheat and barley fields, growing preferably in the mud drains made for irrigating the fields. There is also evidence of millet-like grains and wild jujube/*ber (Ziziphus*).[18] Botanical retrievals also included wild grasses (*Heteropogon contortus* and several of indeterminate type) and seeds belonging to three additional plant groups identified to family: buckwheat (*Polygonaceae*), nightshade (*Solanaceae),* and mint (*Labiatae).* A single carbonized and extremely poorly preserved grain of rice has been reported as well.[19] Contrary to Kajale's assertion regarding no conclusive evidence of domestic plant species at Damdama, recent findings by K.S. Saraswat have indicated that the mesolithic inhabitants at the site exploited both cultivated and wild rice.[20]

Investigations at the mesolithic rock shelter site of Lekhahia of the Kaimur hills confirmed both the wild and cultivated strains of rice (*Oryza rufipogon* and *Oryza sativa).* The identified assemblage also included wood charcoal remains of *Anogeissus pendula* and *Lagerstroemia speciosa* together with *Callicarpa arborea. Anogeissus*

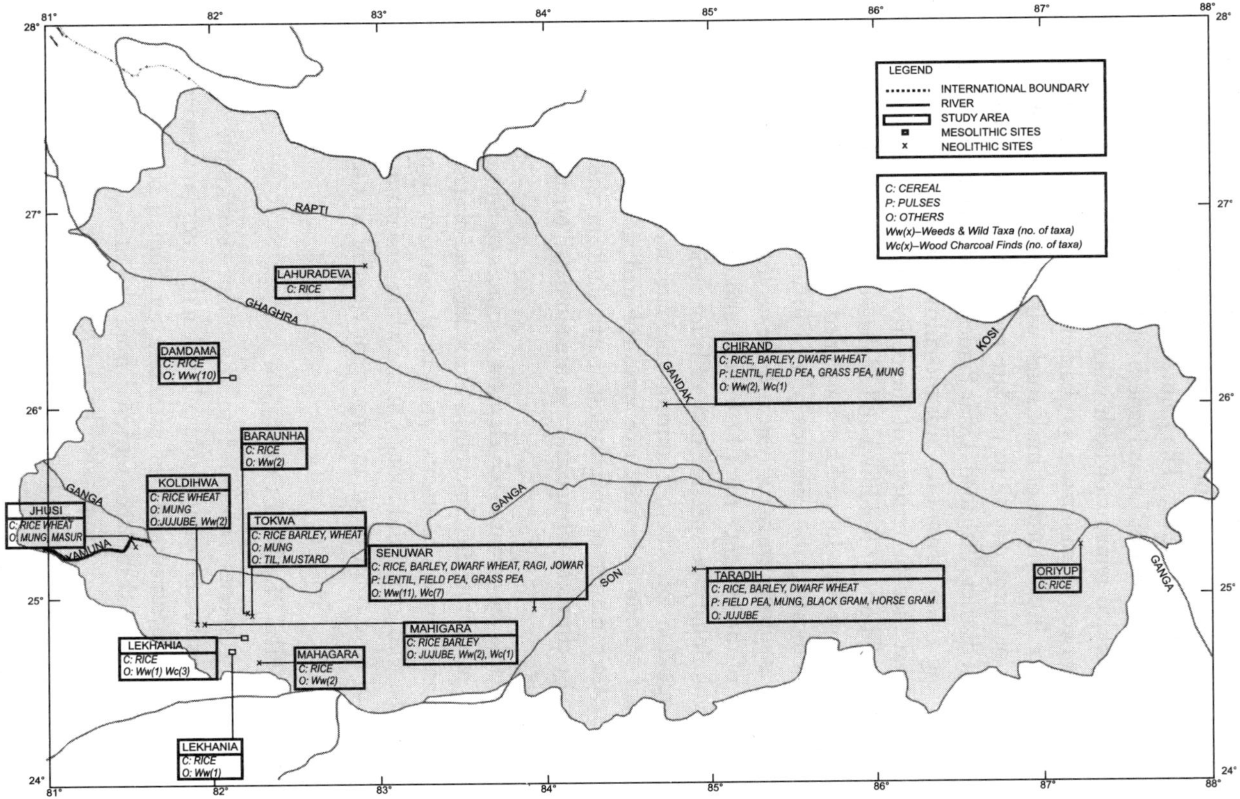

FIGURE 3.6: Botanical taxa from mesolithic and neolithic sites

pendula is postulated to have been a local tree, while the timbers of *Lagerstroemia speciosa* and *Callicarpa arborea* were possibly obtained from the forests of Pilibhit, Gonda, and Gorakhpur regions in northern Uttar Pradesh.[21] The painted rock shelter site of Lekhania in Mirzapur district of Uttar Pradesh, dated to *c.* third millennium BC, also yielded remains of both wild (*Oryza rufipogon* Griff.) and cultivated rice (*Oryza sativa* L.).[22] Earlier, on a similar note, the find of wild rice in the form of husk stuck with pottery and embedded in lumps of burnt clay from the late mesolithic phase at Chopani Mando in district Allahabad, Uttar Pradesh, had been emphasized as suggesting a step forward towards the cultivation of grains. It was in this context that the retrieval of the cultivated variety of rice along with the wild one at Koldihwa and Mahagara, at a distance of 3 km from Chopani Mando, had been assigned considerable significance as well, indicating the presence of rice in wild form in the area, which was subsequently cultivated in the neolithic period. However, in view of the evidence from Damdama and other mesolithic sites, this evolutionary perspective now calls for serious reconsideration. The question of whether during the late mesolithic phase at Chopani Mando cultivated rice was exploited along with its wild variety, is a matter of speculation, particularly in the absence of systematic efforts to salvage and examine in detail botanical remains from there.

As regards the extent to which plant resources could have served as items of mesolithic diet, microliths like sickles and blades, ringstones, quern, and muller fragments attest to the dietary significance of gathered wild grains and roots. On the whole, the plant component seems to have constituted an important element in the mesolithic diet.

NEOLITHIC PLANT ECONOMY

Wild plant species continued to contribute significantly to the subsistence structure of neolithic cultures in the study area, providing irrefutable documentation of gathering for human consumption. The botanical assemblages retrieved from the sites of this cultural period are, however, dominated by the remains of cultivated crops. The major domesticated crop was rice, which formed the mainstay of the neolithic diet. Both winter and summer crops were cultivated. Rice was the staple food grain, supplemented by wheat (*Triticum sphaerococcum*) and barley (*Hordeum vulgare*).

Archaeobotanical evidence illustrating patterns of plant resource exploitation in this period comes mainly from the sites of Koldihwa, Mahagara, Manigara, Baraunha Tokwa, Jhusi, and Lahuradeva in Uttar Pradesh, and Oriyup, Chirand, Taradih and Senuwar in Bihar. At sites of the Vindhyan neolithic culture complex including Koldihwa,[23,] Mahagara,[24] and Manigara[25] dating to *c.* second millennium BC, and Baraunha,[26] the emphasis was primarily on the utilization of cultivated rice along with its wild varieties like the perennial *Oryza rufipogon* and the annual *Oryza nivara*. The presence of a wild variety of rice along with the domesticated one clearly hints at the practice of gathering wild rice along with its cultivation. Evidence of cultivated rice in an early context has also recently come forth from the site of Lahuradeva in district Sant Nagar, Uttar Pradesh.[27] While wheat and *mung* (*Phaseolus radiatous*) supplemented the diet at Koldihwa,[28] and barley at Mahagara,[29] which also yielded a wild grass fruit of *Ischaemum rugosum*, a common weed growing in marshy paddy fields,[30] Tokwa is the only neolithic site to have yielded evidence for the exploitation of oleiferous crops like *til* and mustard, in addition to domesticated rice, barley, wheat, mung, and some fruits and beans.[31] Similarly at Jhusi, located on the left bank of the Ganga–Yamuna confluence at a distance of about 7 km to the east of Allahabad, recent excavations have yielded evidence for the exploitation of rice, wheat, mung, and *masur* (*Lens culnaris*) in the neolithic phase.[32.]

The eastern neolithic culture complex with sites like Chirand, Taradih, and Senuwar attested to the exploitation of a wider array of cultivated crops. While the rice record at Oriyup, in district Bhagalpur, Bihar, compared with that of the cultivated variety (*Oryza sativa*),[33] botanical investigations at neolithic Chirand showed the plant economy as consisting of wheat, barley *(Hordeum* sp.), rice, lentil (*Lens culinaris*), field pea (*Pisum arvense*), and grass pea *(Lathyrus sativus*). The rice grains belonged to both the cultivated *Oryza sativa*, and wild *Oryza perennis* and *Oryza rufipogon*.[34] Later, mung was also identified.[35] Charcoal in samples radiocarbon-dated to 2590 ± 105 BC (2665 ± 105), were identified as sal (*Shorea robusta*).[36] The evidence of wheat, barley, lentil, and field pea were considered by Vishnu Mittre[37] as suggestive of the contemporaneity of neolithic Chirand with the Harappan cultures. The site, estimated to date from *c.* 2500 BC by him, is now suggested to have been earlier than the middle of the third millennium BC.[38] Similarly, convincing evidence for indigenously domesticated crops like rice, black gram, green gram, and common bean during the second millennium BC, has also been retrieved from Taradih in district Gaya, Bihar, which revealed uninterrupted evidence for plant husbandry from neolithic, chalcolithic, and early historical and historical cultures covering a time span from *c.* 2000 BC to AD 500.[39]

The retrieval and analysis of botanical remains from the site of Senuwar in district Rohtas, Bihar, by K.S. Saraswat has helped in establishing a complete sequence of crop cultivation practices during different cultural periods at the site. The results of the investigations are based on the typed manuscript kindly provided by him during my visit to the Birbal Sahni Institute of Palaeobotany, Lucknow. The earliest and metal-free neolithic period, represented as Period IA (*c.* 2200–1950 BC), yielded evidence for the gradual addition of new types of food grains from the bottom to upper levels in the stratigraphical continuum. The lower half of the neolithic deposits suggested that initially the Senuwarians were cultivating only rice, which along with foxtail grass (*Setaria glauca*) was encountered in the bottom layers, just above the natural soil. Subsequently, the inclusion of job's-tear (*Coix lachryma jobi*) was marked. The earliest sign of a major shift in agriculture as reflected in the dietary chart of neolithic people at the site was noticeable in almost the middle levels of the deposits of Period IA, when the Senuwarians also started cultivating barley, followed by wheat, and, finally, millets and pulses as well. Rice continued to be cropped side by side with new cereals like barley, dwarf wheat, *jowar* millet (*Sorghum bicolor*), finger/*ragi* millet (*Eleusine coracana*), lentil, field pea, and grass pea/*khesari*. The species of these new cereals and pulses were found to have been similar to those cultivated by the Harappans.

In association, the weeds and wild taxa identified included *Setaria glauca* and *Coix lachryma jobi*, both considered to be wholesome by virtue of their higher fat and protein content, tiny vetch (*Vicia hirsuta*), common vetch (*Vicia sativa*), *chaulai* (*Amaranthus* sp.), wild rice, panic grass (*Panicum* sp.), brome grass (*Bromus* sp.), dock nut (*Rumex dentatus*), morning glory (*Ipomea pestigridis*), and jujube (*Ziziphus nummularia*). The exploitation of woods by ancient settlers for fuel and other requirements was testified by the wood charcoal remains of *babul/khair* (*Acacia nilotica/catechu*), bamboo (*Bambusa* sp.), *heens* (*Capparis sepiaria*), *mahua* (*Madhuca indica*), sal, *dahia* (*Streblus asper*), and *bhillaur* (*Trewia phudiflora*) (Fig. 3.6).

NEOLITHIC–CHALCOLITHIC AND CHALCOLITHIC CULTURES

This agricultural tradition witnessed further diversification in the subsequent neolithic–chalcolithic cultures of the region. Rice continued as the staple diet, dominating cereal remains at all sites. The botanical evidence retrieved from the neolithic–chalcolithic sub-period IB at Senuwar (*c.* 1950–1300 BC) suffices to demonstrate the establishment of a full-blown agricultural economy in the Middle Ganga Valley as early as the beginning of the second millennium BC. While crops like barley, dwarf wheat, and jowar millet were a legacy of the neolithic period at the site, bread wheat (*Triticum aestivum*) and *kodon* millet (*Paspalum scrobiculatum*) were added to the diet. Ragi, however, seemed to have lost its importance.[40] A similar range of cereals constituted the diet at pre-Narhan Imlidih Khurd, in district Gorakhpur, Uttar Pradesh, where in Period I, which has been assigned a pre-1300 BC date and was characterized by Cord Impressed Ware and the use of copper, settlers exploited pearl millet/*bajra* (*Pennisetum typhoides*) instead of kodon millet (*Paspalum scrobiculatum*).[41] The high protein content of pulses appears to have been realized, as is evident from a wide variety comprising a significant proportion of the diet. At Senuwar, while masur/lentil, field pea and grass pea/khesari continued from the earlier neolithic period, the introduction of mung/green gram (*Vigna radiata*), chick pea (*Cicer arietinum*), and horse gram (*Dolichos biflorus*) indicated further enrichment of the diet.[42] Evidence of the exploitation of the same varieties, with the exception of horse gram and chick pea, are preserved in the archaeological records of Imlidih Khurd, which also confirmed the utilization of oleiferous crops like field brassica (*Brassica juncea*) and sesame/til (*Sesamum indicum*). The remains of wild jujube (*Ziziphus nummularia*) and *anwala* (*Emblica officinalis*) attested to the common exploitation of local fruits at the site, while the retrieval of raisin (*Vitis vinifera*) was considered suggestive of the region's cultural contacts with contemporaneous communities in the north-west.[43] Additionally, the remains of weeds and wild taxa support the assumption that wild species continued to play an important role in the diet of the populations at both sites. The repertoire at Imlidih Khurd comprised of *Brachiaria* sp., *Chenopodium album*, *Eleusine indica*, *Poa* sp., and Setaria (cf. *S. glauca*),[44] while at Senuwar the associated seeds and fruits of weeds and wild taxa belonged to foxtail grass, wild rice, kander grass (*Ischaemum*), common vetch, *jangali matar* (*Lathyrus aphaca*), clover (*Melilotus* sp.), jujube, *kundroo* (*Coccinia cordifolia*), *panibel* (*Vitis tomentosa*), *dhatura* (*Datura* sp.), *bhang* (*Cannabis sativa*), and milk bush (*Euphorbia* sp.). The retrieval of the seeds of hemp/bhang (*Cannabis sativa*) and dhatura (*Datura* sp.) deserve particular mention in view of their known narcotic effects. The wood charcoal remains, included, besides taxa from the preceding period, *bel* (*Aegle marmelos*), *siras* (*Albizia* cf. *procera*), bhang (*Cannabis sativa*), *amaltass* (*Cassia fistula*), *dhaura* (*Lagerstroemia parviflora*), *nagkesar*/ironwood (*Mesua ferrea*), and jujube (*Ziziphus* sp.).[45] Interestingly, *Mesua ferrea* is known to be one of the hardest, heaviest, and strongest timbers of India. The nearest source exploited by the inhabitants of Senuwar were probably the evergreen forests of Bengal and Assam, signifying the knowledge of forest products of far-eastern regions by ancient settlers in the Kaimur foothills of southern Bihar.[46] Suitable as a substitute for metal, ironwood is postulated to have been utilized in the making of some tools like the hand hoe for tilling the soil to aid agricultural operations.[47]

The diet during the Black and Red Ware phases at Imlidih Khurd (*c.* 1300–800 BC), Narhan (*c.* 1300–800 BC), and Khairadih continued to have the traditional composition of cereals and legumes flavoured with fruits. A few additions, suggesting dependence on a better and larger spectrum of field crops and other plant resources, however, deserve attention. Period II at Imlidih Khurd featured an extension of the stable crop economy recorded in Period I/the pre-Narhan phase at the site, with archaeobotanical evidence, attesting to the remains of rice, bread wheat, dwarf wheat (*Triticum sphaerococcum*), barley, and pulses like lentil and green gram (*Vigna radiata*). A fragmented seed of chick pea was reported from the Black and Red Ware phase, while in Period I there was no trace of this legume. Similarly, kodon millet, which found representation in Period II, was a new element in the subsistence economy of the people at the site. Among the weeds, bathua and setaria (cf. *S. glauca*) are postulated to have been used for food because of their large nutritious seeds. The seeds of *Eleusine indica, Indigofera*, and *Amaranthus* species were also represented in Period II. The leaves of some of the *Amaranthus* species, locally known as *chaulai*, are eaten as a vegetable, while *Indigofera* plants are herbs or shrubs, having several species in the region and occurring in overgrazed pastures, grasslands, banks, and waste places.[48]

The discovery of the 'Narhan culture' dating from *c.* 1300 to 800 BC at Narhan in district Gorakhpur, Uttar Pradesh, on the left bank of the Ghaghra river yielded the greatest variety of crop plants, weeds, and other wild taxa and fruits. The cereals encountered in Period I at Narhan included rice, barley, three forms of wheat, that is, bread wheat, club wheat (*Triticum compactum*), and dwarf wheat, pearl millet/bajra, and kodon millet. Pulses, which figure prominently in the crop plants represented at the site, seem to have constituted a more conspicuous proportion of vegetable food available to the settlers, including chick pea/gram, horse gram, grass pea/khesari, lentil, field pea, moth bean (*Vigna aconitifolia*), and green gram/mung. The exploitation of oleiferous sesame/til, field-brassica, and linseed (*Linum usitatissimum*) has also been confirmed. As far as fruits are concerned, dates (*Phoenix dactylifera*), significant for their high sugar content, and jackfruit (*Artocarpus heterophyllus*) are noteworthy in having supplemented the diet along with wild jujube and grapes (*Vitis vinifera*). Both grapes and dates are postulated to have been acquired through cultural contacts with contemporaneous communities in the north-western region. The wood charcoal remains of trees like mango (*Mangifera indica)*, mahua, tamarind (*Tamarindus indica*), and *shahtoot*/mulberry (*Morus alba*) made apparent the utilization of their fruits and floral parts in the food economy. Investigations also confirmed the exploitation of babul/khair (*Acacia* sp.), siras (*Albizia* sp.), bamboo, *dhak* (*Butea monosperma*), *karanj* (*Pongamia pinnata*), *dhera* (*Diospyros montana*), *tulsi* (*Ocimum sanctum*), *arni* (*Premna mucronata*), sal, *kuchla* (*Strychnos nux-vomica*), *jhau* (*Tamarix dioica*), teak (*Tectona grandis*), and *gurch* (*Tinospora cordifolia*). Additionally, the presence of 33 species of weeds and wild taxa, including *Andropogon* sp., *Cenchrus ciliaris, Dactyloctenium aegyptium, Echinochloa crusgalli, Lolium temulentum, Panicum* sp., *Poa* sp., *Fimbristylis tetragona, Fimbristylis dichotoma, Fimbristylis tenuicula, Cyperus* sp., *Elaecharis* sp., *Rhynchospora hookeri, Desmodium* sp., *Indigofera enneaphylla, I. linifolia, Lathyrus aphaca, Rhynchosia minima, Trigonella occulta, Vicia sativa, Amaranthus* sp., *Chenopodium album, Polygonum barbatum, Rumex dentatus, Cucumis* sp., *Commelina benghalensis, Cleome viscosa, Malvastrum coromandelianum, Sida* sp., *Trianthema portulacastrum, Ipomoea pestigridis, Oldenlandia dichotoma*, and *Argemone mexicana*, furnish evidence of their gathering for food and other purposes, and strongly support the proposition of the direct output of plant husbandry being supplemented by starch and protein derived from wild plants. A significant find from the upper levels of the Black and Red Ware phase (900–800 BC) was that of the fibre remains of ramie (*Boehmeria* sp.), the knowledge and subsequent selection of which for fishing lines by the Narhan people is remarkable in view of the strength and durability of the fibre, together with its high resistance to water action.[49]

At Sohgaura in district Gorakhpur, Uttar Pradesh, dated *c.* second millennia BC, remains of barley have been identified,[50] while the imprints of wild and cultivated rice have been reported on the pottery.[51] Khairadih, on the right bank of the Ghaghra river in district Ballia, Uttar Pradesh, revealed a similar cultural chronology as well as crop economy as at Narhan. In addition to the field brassica already known of, finds of yellow mustard (*Brassica campestris*) and castor (*Ricinus communis*) suggested diversification in the knowledge of oleiferous crops and were new additions to the chalcolithic culture of the Middle Ganga Valley.[52]

The site of Waina in district Ballia, Uttar Pradesh, also yielded a good quantity of archaeobotanical remains from sub-Period IB, marked by the pottery assemblage of Narhan culture and Period II, characterized by iron objects and some Northern Black Polished-associated Wares. Sub-Period IA characterized by pottery assemblage comparable with pre-Narhan pottery at Imlidih Khurd, has been tentatively dated between *c.* 1600 and 1300 BC. The retrieval of crop remains by flotation technique from samples from different horizons of cultural deposits from *c.* 1300 to 600 BC by Saraswat revealed the presence of cultivated rice, barley, bread wheat, mung, lentil, field pea, grass pea/khesari, gram (*Cicer arietinum*), field brassica, and sesame/til, suggesting an advanced agriculture at Waina, where the settlers were familiar with the rotation of crops, and grew cereals, pulses, and oilseeds in the summer and winter seasons.[53]

The Ochre Coloured Pottery culture at Sringaverapura on the left bank of the Ganges in district Allahabad, Uttar Pradesh, dating to *c.* 1050–1000 BC, is notable for providing, in addition to the food grains of rice, barley, and sesame/til, the first evidence of cotton (*Gossypium arboreum/herbaceum*) cultivation in the Gangetic plains of north India. Wood remains of *Pinus roxburghii, Ziziphus* sp., *Acacia nilotica/catechu, Mangifera indica, Madhuca indica*, and bamboo were also retrieved.[54]

At Senuwar, with the exception of moth bean (*Vigna aconitifolia*), which was an addition, cereals, millets, and pulse crops encountered in chalcolithic Period II (*c.* 1300–600 BC) were continuations of the kind exploited in the earlier period at the site. The cultivation of til *(Sesamum indicum)* field brassica, safflower (*Carthamus tinctorius),* linseed, and castor (*Ricinus communis),* postulated to have been used by the Senuwarians in cooking, medicine, toiletry, illumination, rituals, and other purposes, hints at a significant advancement in the crop economy. In this context, evidence for the cultivation of watermelon/*tarbuza (Citrullus lanatus)*, reported for the first time in the archaeological context of India, is particularly remarkable.[55] A native of South Africa, its introduction in the Indian subcontinent is postulated to have been through the maritime intercourse of Harappans from Western coasts.[56] The introduction of mango and jackfruit/*katahal* tree cultivation at the site in this period suggests their inclusion in the food economy, which continued as before to derive substantially from wild plant species as well. Associated weeds and wild taxa belonged to foxtail grass, *mandla* grass (*Eleusine indica*), *anjan* grass (*Cenchrus ciliaris*), dock nut (*Rumex dentatus*), common vetch, indigo (*Indigofera* sp.), *siah kanta* (*Mimosa* sp.), jujube, bathua, bhang (*Cannabis sativa*), *bhanjira* (*Perilla frutescens*), and *ban-piazi* (*Asphodelus tenuifolius*). In addition, the wood charcoal remains of babul/khair, siras (*Albizia* cf. *procera*), bamboo, bhang (*Cannabis sativa*), heens/*jhiri*, amaltass (*Cassia fistula*), *sheesham* (*Dalbergia sissoo*), mahua, sal, dahia (*Streblus asper*), teak (*Tectona grandis*), *bhillaur* (*Trewia phudiflora*), and jujube (*Ziziphus* sp.) were also recorded. The remains of *akol* (*Alangium salvifolium*), katahal (*Artocarpus heterophyllus*)), *deodar* (*Cedrus deodara*), mango, and castor (*Ricinus communis*) were new elements in this phase.[57] Deodar is postulated to have been exploited from the Himalayan forests.[58] On the basis of the tree taxa identified, a dry deciduous forest surrounding the site has been postulated.[59]

As regards chalcolithic sites in the Vindhyas, excavation accounts provide scanty evidence pertaining to agriculture. However, evidence of the cultivation of rice has been obtained from a number of sites in the form of grain as well as husk impressions in potsherds and burnt clay lumps.[60] The chalcolithic settlement at Kakoria located on the Chandraprabha in Chakia sub-division of Varanasi district, Uttar Pradesh, yielded samples rich in rice husk remains, among which the wild perennial *Oryza rufipogon* and the cultivated *Oryza sativa* have been identified.[61] Imprints of wild perennial and cultivated strains of *Oryza rufipogon* and *Oryza sativa* were also identified from the chalcolithic site of Magha in the Adwa valley, district Mirzapur, Uttar Pradesh. Imprints of kodon millet, two well-preserved grains of *sawan* (*Echinochloa crusgalli*), and imprints of fruits of *Ischaemum rugosum*, a wild grass in paddy fields, have also been identified from burnt clay lumps.[62] At Koldihwa carbonized remains of rice and rice husk, wheat, and mung of cultivated variety have been recovered, suggesting the practice of a mixed economy (Fig. 3.7).[63]

IRON AGE AND EARLY HISTORIC CULTURES

A glance at the botanical remains retrieved from Iron Age and early historic sites (Fig. 3.8) reveals that the crops utilized, broadly appear to have been the same as in the preceding period—rice, barley, wheat, kodon millet, ragi millet, jowar, bajra, chick pea, field pea, grass pea/khesari, lentil, horse gram, mung, field brassica, safflower, and sesame/til. Significant glimpses into the Iron Age plant economy in the Middle Ganga Valley are now available in view of a number of sites having yielded crucial evidence.

Period I (*c.* 1700–1300 BC) at Raja Nala Ka Tila in district Sonbhadra, Uttar Pradesh, in the northern Vindhyas, was a pre-iron phase, where the settlers appeared to have relied on the cultivation of rice, barley, lentil, field pea, ragi (*Eleusine coracana*), and foxtail millet (*Setaria italica*) of Harappan nutritional traits in north-western and western regions in India. A few seeds of khesari and mung are also reported. The predominance of ragi and foxtail millet in the collection has been emphasized in view of the ability of these to thrive in poor soil and with little water, suggesting thereby that the inhabitants of Raja Nala Ka Tila, on the flats of a plateau region, gave due consideration to their ecological surroundings. Double cropping of rice in the rainy season, and lentil and pea in winter was probably practised in the inundated areas of river Karmanasa. Period II, dated between *c.* 1300 and 700 BC, and representing an iron-using culture, yielded similar crop remains as in Period I, with the addition of dwarf wheat, horse gram, and common millet (*Panicum* cf. *miliaceum*). Among the weed species, seeds, and fruits of wild taxa, reported from Period I and II, *jharberi* (*Ziziphus nummularia*), and *harra*/*haritaki* (*Terminalia chebula*) were important ones. Grains of the grass family belonging to *ban-kangani* (*Setaria* cf. *glauca*) and job's tear (*Coix lachryma jobi*) were suggested to have been important in the food economy of settlers at the site.[64]

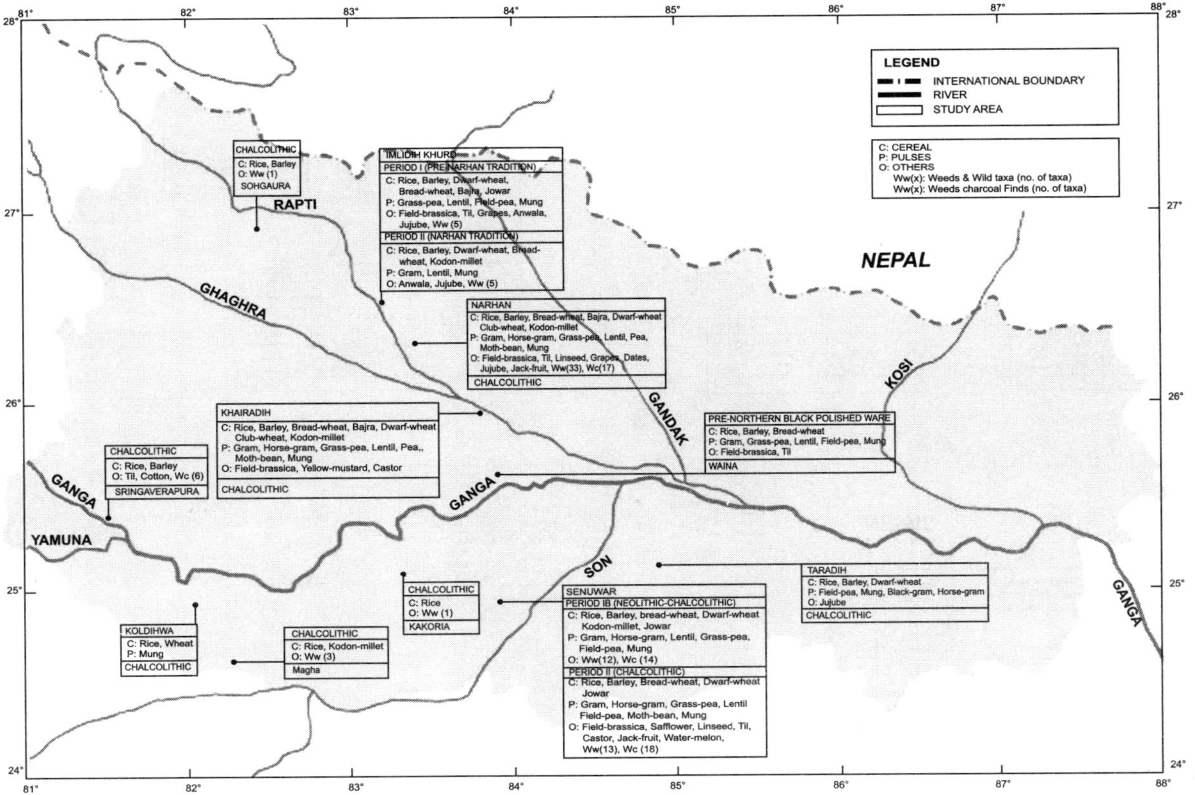

FIGURE 3.7: Botanical taxa from neolithic–chalcolithic and chalcolithic sites

FIGURE 3.8: Botanical taxa from Iron Age and early historic sites

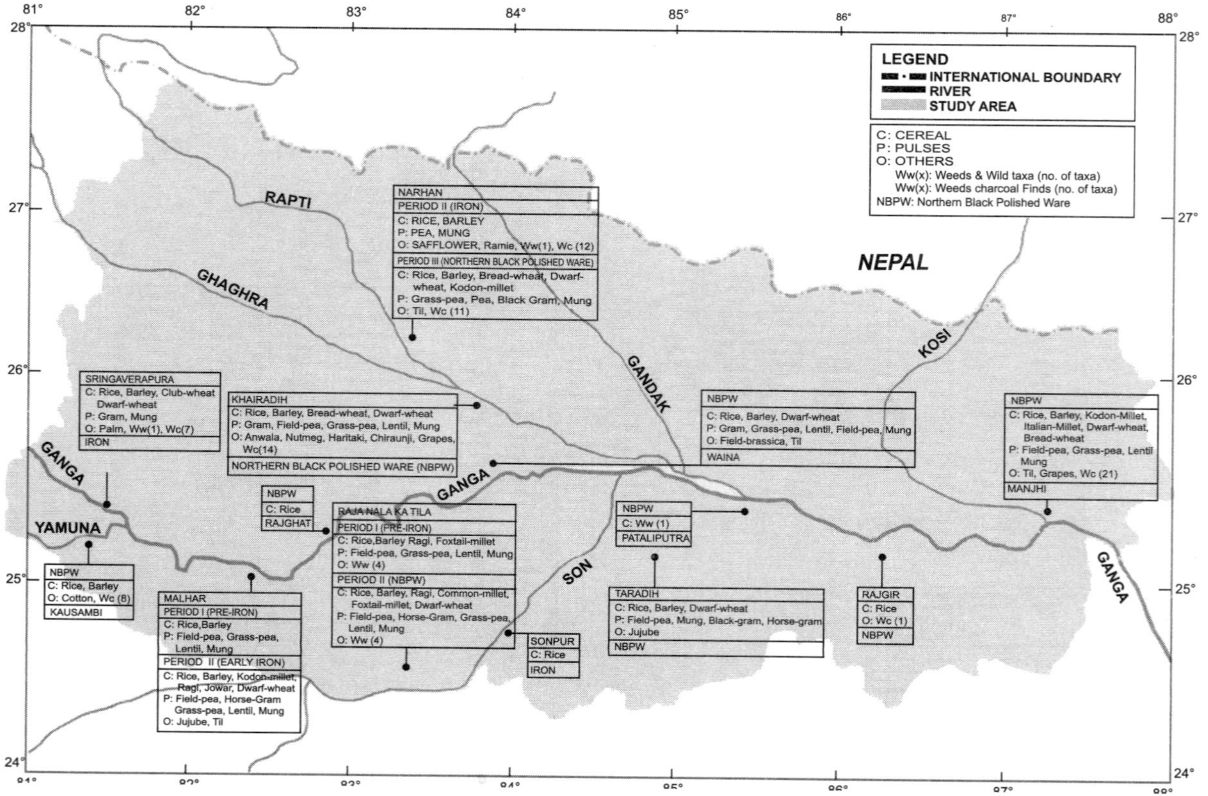

LEGEND
INTERNATIONAL BOUNDARY
RIVER
STUDY AREA
C: CEREAL
P: PULSES
O: OTHERS
Ww(x): Weeds & Wild taxa (no. of taxa)
Ww(x): Weeds charcoal Finds (no. of taxa)
NBPW: Northern Black Polished Ware
NEPAL
RAPTI
GHAGHRA
GANDAK
KOSI
GANGA
YAMUNA
SON
NARHAN
PERIOD II (IRON)
C: RICE, BARLEY
P: PEA, MUNG
O: SAFFLOWER, Ramie, Ww(1), Wc (12)
PERIOD III (NORTHERN BLACK POLISHED WARE)
C: Rice, Barley, Bread-wheat, Dwarf-wheat, Kodon-millet
P: Grass-pea, Pea, Black Gram, Mung
O: Til, Wc (11)
SRINGAVERAPURA
C: Rice, Barley, Club-wheat Dwarf-wheat
P: Gram, Mung
O: Palm, Ww(1), Wc(7)
IRON
KHAIRADIH
C: Rice, Barley, Bread-wheat, Dwarf-wheat
P: Gram, Field-pea, Grass-pea, Lentil, Mung
O: Anwala, Nutmeg, Haritaki, Chiraunji, Grapes, Wc(14)
NORTHERN BLACK POLISHED WARE (NBPW)
NBPW
C: Rice, Barley, Dwarf-wheat
P: Gram, Grass-pea, Lentil, Field-pea, Mung
O: Field-brassica, Til
WAINA
NBPW
C: Rice, Barley, Kodon-Millet, Italian-Millet, Dwarf-wheat, Bread-wheat
P: Field-pea, Grass-pea, Lentil Mung
O: Til, Grapes, Wc (21)
MANJHI
NBPW
C: Rice
RAJGHAT
RAJA NALA KA TILA
PERIOD I (PRE-IRON)
C: Rice,Barley Ragi, Foxtail-millet
P: Field-pea, Grass-pea, Lentil, Mung
O: Ww (4)
PERIOD II (NBPW)
C: Rice, Barley, Ragi, Common-millet, Foxtail-millet, Dwarf-wheat
P: Field-pea, Horse-Gram, Grass-pea, Lentil, Mung
O: Ww (4)
NBPW
C: Ww (1)
PATALIPUTRA
NBPW
C: Rice, Barley
O: Cotton, Wc (8)
KAUSAMBI
MALHAR
PERIOD I (PRE-IRON)
C: Rice,Barley
P: Field-pea, Grass-pea, Lentil, Mung
PERIOD II (EARLY IRON)
C: Rice, Barley, Kodon-millet, Ragi, Jowar, Dwarf-wheat
P: Field-pea, Horse-Gram Grass-pea, Lentil, Mung
O: Jujube, Til
SONPUR
C: Rice
IRON
TARADIH
C: Rice, Barley, Dwarf-wheat
P: Field-pea, Mung, Black-gram, Horse-gram
O: Jujube
NBPW
RAJGIR
C: Rice
O: Wc (1)
NBPW
81°
82°
83°
84°
85°
86°
87°
88°
28°
27°
26°
25°
24°

A pre-iron horizon was also identified at Malhar in district Chandauli, southern Uttar Pradesh, where evidence has taken the antiquity of Iron Age culture back by 300 years, dated to *c.* 1600 BC. Information derived from imprints in potsherds and burnt mud clods revealed rice as the most important cereal. Though not as numerous, the other grains and seeds belonged to barley, mung, field pea, lentil, grass pea/khesari, and so on. These remains of crop plants were found in association with the remains of wild plants, though a complete analysis of these remains is yet unavailable. Period I at Malhar was proposed to be placed between c. 1900 BC and *c.* 1700–1600 BC (calibrated 2283–1639 BC). During the early iron phase, represented by Period II at Malhar, rice continued to dominate the assemblage of food grains. The grain samples of rice, barley, mung, lentil, field pea, and khesari were observed to be of the same kind as in the preceding pre-iron phase. New cereals and pulses included dwarf wheat, kodon millet, jowar millet, ragi millet, and horse gram/kulthi.[65]

A few seeds in a highly mutilated stage were considered to be of oil-yielding til (*Sesamum indicum*). Carbonized stones and fruit pieces of wild jujube/jharberi were also retrieved. The samples were found to be mixed with a large number of small pieces of wood charcoal, along with seeds of weeds and other wild flora. The lower limit of Period II at Malhar was suggested to be *c.* 1600 BC on the basis of radiocarbon dating. Due to the absence of Northern Black Polished Ware potsherds in layer 2 or 1, Period II was considered to have been earlier than the Northern Black Polished Ware.[66]

From the Northern Black Polished Ware culture (*c.* 600–200 BC) at Kausambi in district Allahabad, Uttar Pradesh, barley, cotton (*Gossypium arboreum/herbaceum*) and the timbers of *Soymida febrifuga, Holarrhena antidysenterica, Adina cordifolia, Ziziphus, Terminalia, Lagerstroemia, Anogeissus,* and *Dalbergia* species have been reported.[67] Among food grains the remains of rice (*Oryza* sp.) were also reported.[68]

The phases of iron using cultures at Sringaverapura in district Allahabad, Uttar Pradesh, were characterized by Black Slipped, Black and Red, Burnished Grey, and associated Red Wares, dating from *c.* 950 to 700 BC. The botanical remains retrieved from the site included rice, barley, wheat (*Triticum sphaerococcum* and *Triticum compactum*), chick pea, green gram (*Vigna radiata*), cuticles of barley husk and leaf epidermal remains of rice, palm (*Phoenix* sp.), and *khus* grass (*Vetiveria zizanoides*). Wood charcoals belonged to *Madhuca indica,*

Mangifera indica, Mesua ferrea, Ziziphus sp., *Albizia* sp., *Betula utilis*, and *Bombax malabarica.* Interestingly, it has been pointed out that *Pinus roxburghii*, recorded from the preceding chalcolithic period at the site, occurs in the outer Himalaya and Siwalik range, and also in the valleys of some Himalayan rivers at an elevation of about 450 m to 2,290 m. In this connection, the presence of *bhojpatra* (*Betula utilis*) at the site during the iron-using phase confirmed the exploitation of still higher ranges of the Himalayas, since the trees are found in the Kurram valley in the western Himalayas at an elevation of 3,350 m to Bhutan, ascending to about 4,265 m, and they rarely descend below 3,050 m. In view of this information, the nearest possible source of bhojpatra known to the inhabitants of Sringaverapura is suggested to have been the Garhwal Himalayas, implying that Iron Age people in the Ganga valley were familiar with upper Himalayan forest wealth. In view of the use of its papery bark for writing since ancient times, it can be speculated that the evidence of bhojpatra material at Sringaverapura during *c.* 950–700 BC could be an indication of its utilization for writing.. Further, the evidence of iron-wood (*Mesua ferrea*) at the site, also earlier documented at Senuwar in the neolithic–chalcolithic phase, suggested a well-knit trade system facilitating the exploitation of this valuable raw material of the far-flung eastern localities.[69]

The use of iron at Narhan was attested to towards the close of the Black and Red Ware period by the remains of iron rust particles found adhered on the surface of a fishing hook impression, indicating that the hook was made of iron. Investigations[70] revealed that the subsequent Black Slipped Ware (*c.* 800–600 BC), which formed Period II at the site, and Period III characterized by Northern Black Polished Ware (600–200 BC) exploited the same grains as the preceding period, with the exception of a few new types. Carbonized grains from Period II included rice, barley, field pea, green gram, and safflower (*Carthamus tinctorius*), which was a new element in the diet. Among weeds, the remains of *Vicia* sp. were retrieved. Taxa represented in wood charcoal remains included babul/khair (*Acacia* sp.), bamboo, dhera (*Diospyros montana*), mahua, mango, sal, imli, and teak (*Tectona grandis*), all of which were in continuation of Period I. However, the wood charcoals of sheesham (*Dalbergia sissoo*), anwala, *keim* (*Mitragyna parviflora*), and *jamun* (*Syzygium cumini*) were new entrants in this period.

Crop plants from Period III, marked by the Northern Black Polished Ware, were represented by the remains of rice, barley, kodon millet, bread wheat, dwarf wheat, grass pea/khesari, field pea, green gram/mung, and sesame/til. Exploitation of black gram/*urd* (*Vigna mungo*) in this period is significant, particularly in view of its high calcium content in addition to protein. The deposits of this culture have also yielded fruit remains including a jujube stone and the endocarp fragments along with seeds of anwala. Jujube (ber) from this phase belonged to *Ziziphus mauritiana*, a tree species grown in orchards and yielding fleshy, large, and egg-shaped fruits, indicating advancement in the food economy of this period as against the use of wild fruits of jharberi (*Ziziphus nummularia*) in Period I. Among taxa represented in wood charcoal remains recovered from Period III, bamboo, anwala, mahua, mango, tulsi (*Ocimum sanctum*), and imli were continuations from the earlier periods. *Punarnava* (*Boerhavia diffusa*), dhaura (*Lagerstroemia parviflora*), chirwood (*Pinus roxburghii*), and, most notably, sandalwood (*Santalum album*), featured for the first time during Period III. Whether sandalwood had some ritualistic significance can be speculated. An evergreen semi-parasitic tree in the dry regions of Mysore and Tamil Nadu, the occurrence of sandalwood at Narhan has been perceived as an indication of ingenuity in commercial activities. The evidence of the majority of locally occurring trees envisaged the predominance of deciduous elements. Similarly, analysis of the environmental characteristics and consequent climatic orientation peculiar to some of the species identified at the site suggested the formation of riparian type forest in the region. The climate was postulated to have been similar to that of today or possibly a little more humid at that time.[71]

Khairadih in district Ballia, Uttar Pradesh, yielded a good quantity of botanical remains belonging to the Northern Black Polished Ware culture (*c*. 600–200 BC). Food grains of rice, barley, wheat (*Triticum sphaerococcum* and *Triticum aestivum*), green gram/mung, chick pea, field pea, grass pea, lentil, and so on. have been recorded. Wood charcoal remains belonged to mahua, babul/khair, mango, kandi (*Flacourtia indica*), sal, *neem* (*Azadirachta indica*), teak (*Tectona grandis*), sheesham (*Dalbergia sissoo*), dhak (*Butea monosperma*), *maharukh* (*Ailanthus excelsa*), *bistendu* (*Diospyros montana*), tamarind, *chilbil* (*Holoptelia integrifolia*), and *dhela* (*Alangium salvifolium*).[72]

The remains of some drug-yielding plants and dry fruits from this period at the site are of particular interest. The Khairadih finds included the remains of haritaki /chebulic myrobalan (*Terminalia chebula*), emblic myrobalan (*Emblica officinalis*), nutmeg/*jaiphal* (*Myristica fragrans*), currants or sweet raisin, *draksha* (*Vitis vinifera*), and *chiraunji* (*Buchanania lanzan*).[73]

Though the botanical retrievals from Waina in district Ballia, Uttar Pradesh, have not been delved into period-wise, observations on the state of crop husbandry within the broad time span of c. 1300–600 BC, suggested that Period II, characterized by iron objects and some Northern Black Polished associated wares (as in the case of sub-Period IB discussed earlier), also rested on an advanced agricultural economy marked by the cultivation of rice, barley, bread wheat, mung, lentil, field pea, grass pea, gram, field brassica, and til/sesame.[74]

Further eastward, a study[75] of seed and fruit remains from Manjhi in district Saran of Bihar during the Northern Black Polished Ware phase dating from *c.* 600–50 BC revealed an agriculture-based subsistence economy of settlers at the site. A rich plant economy was recorded comprising cereals, namely, bread wheat, dwarf wheat, rice, and barley; pulses like green gram/mung, field pea, lentil, grass pea; oil seed crops including sesame; and millets grown as a summer crop like kodon millet and Italian millet (*Setaria* sp.). The agricultural economy was found to be in continuation from much earlier neolithic times in Bihar and the neolithic–chalcolithic phase at Senuwar in southern Bihar. Edible fruits like grape pips (*Vitis vinifera*) also formed part of the food economy; edible young shoots of weeds like *Amaranthus* sp. *Chenopodium album, Medicago sativa*, and of wild taxa like *Commelina benghalensis, Trianthema portulacastrum*, and *Rumex dentatus* were used as vegetables. The seeds of *Cleome viscosa*, a weed, are used as a condiment, while the grains of wild grasses like *Eleusine indica* are eaten in times of scarcity. The utilization of *Argemone mexicana* as a medicinal plant in India was postulated in view of its mention in an ancient medical treatise, the *Bhava Prakash* of fifteenth century AD. Other weeds and wild taxa, which found representation in the archaeological record at the site, included *Lathyrus aphaca, L. sphaericus, Trigonella* sp., *Vicia sativa, Jaquemontia* sp., *Echinochloa crusgalli, Indigofera* sp., *Melilotus indica, Cyperus* sp., *Elaeocharis* sp., *Fimbristylis* sp., and *Solanum* sp. These are postulated to have come through direct or indirect human activities along with the cultural produce. The seeds of *Argemone mexicana*, earlier recorded at Narhan in its Black and Red Ware phase, were perceived as evidence of diffusion of this plant of American origin. Grape pips were a new element from Bihar, and in the light of contemporaneous records from sites like Narhan and Khairadih in eastern Uttar Pradesh, suggest that more than one settlement imported them from a western or north-western direction.

During the early historic period, the piles of wooden palisade at Pataliputra were made of sal.[76] Similarly, at Rajgir, district Patna, Bihar, *Madhuca longifolia* var. *latifolia* associated with the Northern Black Polished Ware culture at the site, was a common local tree. The wood was used in house building, for furniture, country vessels, etc., while its flowers were possibly used for the distillation of spirit. The outer coat of the fruit was eaten and the oil extracted from the seeds, possibly utilized for cooking and burning.[77] Rice (*Oryza* sp.) has also been reported from the site. Rice remains (*Oryza* sp.) were also attested to at the sites of Rajghat (*c.* 500 BC) and Sonepur (*c.* 800–600 BC).[78]

IMPLICATIONS

The emergent picture calls for understanding certain nuances of human interactions with the vegetational environment in the prehistoric and proto-historic past. The first relates to the issue of the much-speculated antiquity of rice cultivation in the region. In this context, the identification of rice grains, wild at Chopani-Mando (ninth–eighth millennium BC) and domesticated (*Oryza sativa*) in the neolithic context at Koldihwa and Mahagara (seventh–fifth millennia BC), were perceived as the most crucial archaeological records of rice in India, and the chronological contexts in which rice occurred at these sites was thought to be of considerable importance. The evidence from Chopani-Mando, though of a wild variety was considered significant as it proved the use of rice in the advanced mesolithic or proto-neolithic context, thus tracing back the history of its exploitation to the last phase of the mesolithic.

Based on evidence from these sites and the early dates from Koldihwa, 6570± 210 BC, 5440±240 CBC, and 4530± 185 CBC, and even a pre-neolithic date of 8080±115 BC from Mahagara itself, an argument was built up by G.R. Sharma and his colleagues for the Belan valley in the Vindhyas being 'an original, primary and nuclear center of neolithic transformation, for the beginnings of agriculture, of rice and of domestication of animals'.[79]

Subsequent historiography, however, expressed reservations against the postulated early dates, which, instead, Pal believed to have been placed within the second millennium BC. On a similar note, based on the similarities of these sites with Kunjhun II in the Son valley and a number of calibrated ranges of C14 dates, came Possehl and Rissman's observations (mentioned by Saraswat in a manuscript on botanical investigation at Senuwar), placing the Vindhyan neolithic culture within the time bracket of about 4000–1200 BC.

Later reviews of the evidence also drew attention to the lack of a clear temporal sequence, suggesting a move from wild to domesticated rice. With reference to the Koldihwa material that was offered as evidence of both the wild and domestic kinds occurring together, it was argued that though initially wild rice was reported, the stratigraphic sequence of rice finds as summarized later had only *Oryza sativa* in the lower stratum (level 10), while *Oryza sativa* co-occurred with *Oryza rufipogon* and *Oryza nivara* in levels 8 and 9 above it. Thus, in this sequence, wild finds actually post-dated the earliest reported domesticate.[80]

These arguments notwithstanding, in view of the presence of wild rice in the 'proto-neolithic' context at Chopani-Mando, which according to D.K. Chakrabarti[81] can be 'justifiably placed in the 9th–8th millennia BC... the presence of domesticated rice in the neolithic level of Koldihawa in the same area may not be fortuitous'. He further contends that from the radiocarbon dates applicable to the Koldihawa neolithic, showing the calibrated ranges 7505–7033 BC, 6190–5764 BC, and 5432–5051 BC, a date from the eighth to the sixth millennia BC seems to be in order.

Moreover, the early dates of Koldihwa are no more in isolation. The presence of early rice in the eastern Vindhyas is also attested to by the evidence from Kunjhun. Radiometric determination for the Kunjhun neolithic complex of the Son valley in the Vindhyas, which shares many characteristics with the Koldihwa–Mahagara neolithic culture, yielded dates spread between the mid-fourth and mid-second millennium BC. Rice husks and other plants were found embedded in the clay of the pottery, and rice was both wild and domesticated.[82]

There is also at least one radiocarbon date of 4620±110 BC (calibrated date 5475–5262 BC) from a sample yielding evidence for cultivated rice from Malhar in district Chandauli, Uttar Pradesh.[83]

Moreover, the identification of cultivated rice in the mesolithic context at Damdama by K.S. Saraswat, in a personal communication with the author, has also undoubtedly pushed back the tradition of rice cultivation to much earlier times. New AMS C14 dates for Damdama and Lekhahia, both having yielded evidence for rice cultivation, have suggested a greater degree of contemporaneity between mesolithic sites of the Kaimur hills and the Gangetic plains. The temporal sequence of these two sites makes the presence of cultivated rice at Damdama more plausible. The dates for Damdama 8865±65 BP and 8640±65 BP place it in the first half of the seventh millennium CBC, while those for Lekhahia, 8000±75 BP and 8370±75 BP, place it towards the end of the seventh millennium BC.[84] D.K. Chakrabarti[85] subsequently pointed out that the calibrated chronology for Damdama is the eighth millennium BC according to one series of AMS dates, and the late fourth–third millennium BC according to another set of of AMS dates. This, he asserted, was a crucial development in view of the total occupational deposit at Damdama being divided into 10 layers, which may have incorporated different phases of hunting-gathering and domestication.

Recent and more specific evidence for the presence of cultivated rice in an early context at Lahuradeva also synchronizes well with the early dates proposed for the cultivation of rice at Koldihwa. Carbonized material from Period IA containing grains of cultivated rice along with a few wild grasses have been documented. Husk marks of rice are also embedded in the core of a number of potsherds of this sub-period. Two radiocarbon dates, available for the charcoal samples collected from the trench are 5320±90 BP (calibrated 4220, 4196, 4161 BC) and 6290±160 BP (calibrated 5298 BC), indicating an antiquity as early as late sixth and fifth millennium BC.[86] In fact, domesticated rice found in the lowest archaeological deposit of the site has been dated 8259 BP (calibrated) or 6309 BC, with phytoliths and cerealia pollens indicating well-developed agriculture in the area in the seventh–sixth millennia BC. Fully domesticated rice in this level was found in association with both wild rice and foxtail millet (*Setaria* sp.). Excavations at the site have, thus, been of fundamental importance in proving that the Central Ganga Plain was an independent early centre of rice cultivation.[87]

Though metal technology has been considered instrumental in accelerating forest clearance for obtaining arable tracts of land and thereby aiding cultural development, the rich data on crop remains retrieved from the neolithic levels of sites like Chirand, Taradih, and Senuwar do not support this view as far as agriculture is concerned.

It has not been possible to observe any pattern related to botanical variability that could be associated with the introduction of metal technology. There is ample evidence to demonstrate the successful exploitation of land resources for purposes of crop husbandry by neolithic farmers, even prior to the introduction of metal technology which at best provided what Saraswat refers to as 'an additional techno-environmental efficiency'. In the case of Senuwar, for instance, Saraswat observes:

> Traditionally, they were having wet-field cultivation system and grew rice in swampy or inundated habitats. Only by creation of artificial habitats, it would have been possible for them to raise crops of various types.... Certain technological innovations even in the neolithic times made it possible to transfer cultivation systems of highly advanced Harappan and other chalcolithic cultures to diverse environmental zones, where they would otherwise not be found. Very fundamental ways of manipulating the environment would have involved attempts to regulate the water supply by draining water, by retaining it through bunds. Conversely, artificial drainage could have permitted the transformation of swampy environment into dry land habitats.... Through this sort of creation of land habitats, it would have been possible for settlers to raise crops of wheat and barley, cereals, pulses and even drought resistant millets of *jowar* and *ragi*, in their natural environment suitable for rice cultivation.[88]

The exploitation of the vegetational environment for medicinal purposes is another aspect of plant resource utilization that deserves particular mention. The remains of some medicinal plants retrieved from different cultures at the sites of Imlidih Khurd, Narhan, and Khairadih in the Ghaghra valley of eastern Uttar Pradesh provide indubitable evidence of the use of herbal medicines in the archaeology of the Middle Ganga Plains. The finds, summarized by Saraswat,[89] suggest the utilization at Imlidih Khurd of grapes/draksha and date/khajoor (*Phoenix officinalis*) in the Cord Impressed Red Ware culture (*c*. 1700–1300 BC), nux vomica/kuchla (*Strychnos nuxvomica*) in the overlapping phase of Cord Impressed Red Ware and Narhan cultures (*c*. 1400–1300 BC), and grapes/draksha, beleric myrobalan/*bahera* (*Terminalia belerica*), anwala, chebulic myrobalan/harra (*Terminalia chebula*), gurch (*Tinospora cordifolia*), and ginger (*Zinziber officinola*) during the Black and Red Ware/Narhan culture (c. 1300–800 BC). At Narhan, the Black and Red Ware culture testified to the exploitation of grapes, dates, nux vomica, gurch, and tulsi/holy basil (*Ocimum sanctum*), while the Northern Black Polished Ware phase (*c*. 600–200 BC) yielded the remains of anwala, tulsi, punarnava (*Boerhavia diffusa*), and sandalwood/*chandan* (*Santalum album*). Similarly, the Northern

Black Polished Ware culture at Khairadih (*c.* 600–200 BC) attested to the knowledge of the medicinal value of chiraunji (*Buchanania lanzan*), jaiphal/nutmeg (*Myristica fragrans*), in addition to grapes, anwala, punarnava, harra, and bahera. Such evidences considerably aid the recognition in the proto-historic past of the drug-yielding value of these plants.

The trends of plant resource utilization in the chalcolithic and Iron Age cultures of the Ganga valley are also indicative of growing cultural contacts and ingenuity in commercial activities between diverse cultural regions. In this context, 'the assimilative power of the farming community' at Senuwar, right from neolithic times, needs to be taken particular cognizance of. Saraswat observes:

> Innovation waves of the diffusion of the crops of Harappan nutritional traits from cultural settlements, brought the drastic changes in the economy of the rice growing neolithic people. Further contemplated developments in the agricultural economy and the exploitation of varied plant material indicate that multi-directional avenues of cultural contacts fetched the material prosperity of Senuwar.[90]

Pant has argued in favour of 'a two way acculturation' [91] resulting from long-lasting first-hand contact between the two cultures, whereby both borrowed culture patterns from each other. While the cultivation of barley, wheat, millet, and pulses was evidently the consequence of Harappan influence, the Indus people learnt the cultivation of rice from these people. In this context, recent evidence of cultivated rice from some of the Harappan sites of Punjab and Haryana is noteworthy, since the regions are not rice-cultivating areas. Saraswat[92] cites the evidence of rice cultivation in the remains of grains and husk impressions in pottery and mud clods from the early Harappan settlement at Kunal in Hisar district from the levels dated between 2850 and 2600 BC. Seeds of watermelon (*Citrullus lanatus*) found at Senuwar from the chalcolithic period (1300–600 BC) were also represented in the deposits of mature Harappan levels at the site. Botanical evidence from Narhan, Imlidih Khurd, Chirand, and Senuwar have thrown considerable light on the adoption of the cultivation of crops of Harappan nutritional traits by communities in the Middle Gangetic Plains.

The finds of medicinal plants also support this proposition about the interaction between cultures. Sandalwood was brought from south India, chiraunji from central India, and draksha/grapes and dates from north-western India, while nutmeg/jaiphal, is a native of Moluccas,

Celebes, and the Sumatra islands.[93] The use of the quality woods of *Cedrus deodora* at chalcolithic Senuwar and *Pinus roxburghii*, *Mesua ferrea*, and *Betula utilis* in the chalcolithic and Iron Age cultures at Sringaverapura lend further support to this contention.

Finally, an evaluation of the rich body of archaeobotanical data reveals elements of continuity in the agricultural milieu, whereby the fundamental practices of growing cereal and pulse crops can be presumed to have been the same as in present times. Points of departure have surfaced with subsequent sophistication in agricultural techniques, but practices like the rotation of crops and the mixed cultivation of cereals and pulses certainly go back to much ancient times.

ACKNOWLEDGEMENTS

I would like to express my gratitude to K.S. Saraswat of the Birbal Sahni Institute of Palaeobotany, Lucknow, and the faculty of the University of Allahabad for sparing time and helping me with their expertise in the course of my fieldtrips to Lucknow and Allahabad. My sincere thanks go out to Nayanjot Lahiri for her invaluable suggestions in the writing of this paper.

NOTES

1. J.N. Pandey, 'Mesolithic in the Middle Ganga Valley', *Bulletin of the Deccan College Post-Graduate and Research Institute*, vol. 49, 1990, p. 311.
2. R.L. Singh, *India: A Regional Geography*, Varanasi: National Geographical Society of India, 1971, p. 184.
3. O.H.K. Spate and A.T.A. Learmonth, *India and Pakistan: A General and Regional Geography*, London: Methuen, 1972, pp. 563–64.
4. Singh, *India*, p. 190.
5. G.R. Sharma, 'Mesolithic Lake Cultures in the Ganga Valley, India', *Proceedings of the Prehistoric Society*, vol. 39, 1973, p. 129.
6. V.D. Misra, *Some Aspects of Indian Archaeology*, Allahabad: Prabhat Prakashan, 1977, p. 24.
7. Pandey, 'Mesolithic in the Middle Ganga Valley', p. 311 and G.R. Sharma, V.D. Misra, D. Mandal, B.B. Misra, and J.N. Pal, *Beginnings of Agriculture*, Allahabad: Abinash Prakashan, 1980, p. 6.
8. Sharma *et al.*, *Beginnings of Agriculture*, 1980, p. 4.
9. R.K. Varma, 'Pre-Agricultural Mesolithic Society of the Ganga Valley', in J.M. Kenoyer (ed.), *Old Problems and New Perspectives in the Archaeology of India*, Madison: University of Wisconsin, 1989, p. 55.
10. G.R. Sharma, 'Seasonal Migrations and Mesolithic Lake Cultures of the Ganga Valley', in *K.C. Chattopadhyaya Memorial Volume*, Allahabad: University of Allahabad, 1975, p. 13; J.N. Pal, 'The Mesolithic Phase in the Ganga Valley',

in K. Padayya (ed.), *Recent Studies in Indian Archaeology*, New Delhi: Munshiram Manoharlal, 2002, p. 66.

11. Indra Bir Singh, 'Geological Evolution of the Ganga Plain: An Overview', *Journal of the Palaeontological Society of India*, vol. 41, 1996, pp. 99–137; Indra Bir Singh, 'Late Quaternary Evolution of Ganga Plain and Proxy Records of Climate Change, Neotectonics and Anthropogenic Activity', *Pragdhara*, vol. 12, 2002, pp. 1–25.
12. H.P. Gupta, 'Holocene Palynology from Meander Lake in the Ganga Valley, District Pratapgarh, UP', *The Palaeobotanist*, vol. 25, 1976, pp. 109–19.
13. C. Sharma, M.S. Chauhan, S. Sharma, M. Sharma, and I.B. Singh, 'Proxy Records of Holocene Vegetation and Climate Change from Sanai Tal, Central Ganga Plain, Uttar Pradesh', *National Symposium Role of Environmental Sciences Integrated Development and Related Societal Issues*, vol. 65 (GSI Special Publication), 2001, pp. 199–202; S. Sharma, M. Joachimski, M. Sharma, H.J. Tobschall, I.B. Singh, C. Sharma, M.S. Chauhan, and G. Morgenroth, 'Lateglacial and Holocene Environmental Changes in Ganga Plain, Northern India', *Quaternary Science Review*, vol. 23, 2004, pp. 145–59.
14. Indra Bir Singh, 'Quaternary Palaeoenvironments of the Ganga Plain and Anthropogenic Activity', *Man and Environment*, 30 (1), 2005, pp. 1–35.
15. J.N. Pal, 'Mesolithic Settlements in the Ganga Plain', *Man and Environment*, 19 (1–2), 1994, p. 95.
16. Singh, 'Late Quaternary Evolution of Ganga Plain', pp. 15–17.
17. I.B. Singh, Shikha Sharma, Maneesh Sharma, Pradeep Srivastava, and Govindaraja Rajagopalan, 'Evidence of Human Occupation and Humid Climate of 30 Ka in the Alluvium of Southern Ganga Plain', *Current Science*, 76 (7), 1999, pp. 1022–6.
18. J.R. Lukacs and J.N. Pal, 'Mesolithic Subsistence in North India: Inferences from Dental Attributes', *Current Anthropology*, 34 (5), 1993, p. 750.
19. M.D. Kajale, 'Some Initial Observations on Palaeobotanical Evidence for Mesolithic Plant Economy from Excavations at Damdama, Pratapgarh, Uttar Pradesh', in N.C. Ghosh and S.C. Chakrabarti (eds), *Adaptation and Other Essays*, Shantiniketan: Visva Bharati, 1990, pp. 98–102.
20. P.C. Pant, 'Indus Civilisation versus Mahagara Neolithic Culture: A Note on Acculturation', *Puravritta*, vol.1, 2001, p. 69.
21. *Indian Archaeology: A Review, 1983–4*, p. 178.
22. M.D. Kajale, 'Current Status of Indian Palaeoethnobotany: Introduced and Indigenous Food Plants with a Discussion of the Historical and Evolutionary Development of Indian Agriculture and Agricultural Systems in General', in Jane Renfrew (ed.), *New Light on Early Farming: Recent Developments in Palaeoethnobotany*, Edinburgh: University Press, 1991, p. 164.
23. *Indian Archaeology: A Review, 1974–5*, p. 80; *Indian Archaeology: A Review, 1975–6*, p. 88.
24. G.R. Sharma, D. Mandal, and G.K. Rai (eds), *History to Prehistory*, Allahabad: University of Allahabad, Department of Ancient History Culture and Archaeology, 1980; *Indian Archaeology: A Review, 1981–2*, p. 106; *Indian Archaeology: A Review, 1982–3*, p. 149.

25. *Indian Archaeology: A Review, 1981–2*, p. 106; *Indian Archaeology: A Review, 1982–3*, p. 149; *Indian Archaeology: A Review, 1983–4*, p. 178.
26. *Indian Archaeology: A Review, 1981–2*, p. 106; *Indian Archaeology: A Review, 1982–3*, p. 149; *Indian Archaeology: A Review, 1983–4*, p. 177.
27. R. Tewari, R.K. Srivastava, and K.K. Singh, 'Excavation at Lahuradeva, District Sant Nagar, Uttar Pradesh', *Puratattva*, vol. 32, 2001–2, pp. 55–6.
28. Sharma et al., *History to Prehistory*, p. 184.
29. *Indian Archaeology: A Review, 1980–1*, p. 110.
30. *Indian Archaeology: A Review, 1981–2*, p. 106.
31. V.D. Misra, J.N. Pal, and M.C. Gupta, 'Excavation at Tokwa: A Neolithic-Chalcolithic Settlement', *Pragdhara*, vol. 11, 2001, pp. 65, 68.
32. J.N. Pal, 'The Beginning of Agriculture in the Middle Ganga Plain with Special Reference to the Evidence of Recent Excavations at Jhusi', in *Agriculture in South Asia's History: Issues and Paradigms*, New Delhi: Indian Council of Historical Research, 2005, p. 4.
33. Kajale, 'Current Status of Indian Palaeoethnobotany', p. 160.
34. Vishnu-Mittre, 'Neolithic Plant Economy at Chirand, Bihar', *The Palaeobotanist*, vol. 21, 1972, pp. 18–22.
35. *Indian Archaeology: A Review, 1974–5*, p. 78.
36. *Indian Archaeology: A Review, 1975–6*, p. 86.
37. Vishnu-Mittre, 'Neolithic Plant Economy', 1972.
38. D.K. Chakrabarti, *India: An Archaeological History*, New Delhi: Oxford University Press, 1999, p. 244.
39. Kajale, 'Current Status of Indian Palaeoethnobotany', p. 172.
40. K.S. Saraswat, 'Plant Economy of Early Farming Communities at Senuwar' unpublished. The typed manuscript was kindly provided by him during my visit to the Birbal Sahni Institute of Palaeobotany.
41. K.S. Saraswat, 'Seed and Fruit Remains at Ancient Imlidih Khurd, Gorakhpur: A Preliminary Report', *Pragdhara*, vol. 3, 1993, pp. 37–41.
42. Saraswat, 'Plant Economy of Early Farming Communities'.
43. Saraswat, 'Seed and Fruit Remains'.
44. Ibid.
45. Saraswat, 'Plant Economy of Early Farming Communities'.
46. *Indian Archaeology: A Review, 1991–2*, p. 139.
47. Birendra Pratap Singh, 'Transformation of Cultures in the Middle Ganga Plains: A Case Study of Senuwar', *Pragdhara*, vol. 6, 1996, p. 91.
48. Saraswat, 'Seed and Fruit Remains'.
49. K.S. Saraswat, N.K. Sharma, and D.C. Saini, 'Plant Economy at Ancient Narhan (*c.* 1300 BC–300/400 AD)', in Purushottam Singh (ed.), *Excavations at Narhan (1984–1989)*, Varanasi: Banaras Hindu University, 1994, pp. 255–342.
50. Kajale, 'Current Status of Indian Palaeoethnobotany', p. 160.
51. K.S. Saraswat, 'Archaeobotanical Remains in Ancient Cultural and Socio-economical Dynamics of the Indian Subcontinent', *The Palaeobotanist*, vol. 40, 1992, p. 533.
52. Ibid.

53. Purushottam Singh and Ashok Kumar Singh, 'Trial Excavations at Waina, District Ballia (UP)', *Pragdhara*, vol. 6, 1996, pp. 51–3.
54. K.S. Saraswat, 'Ancient Crop Plant Remains from Sringaverapura, Allahabad (*c.* 1050–1000 BC)', *Geophytology*, 16 (1), 1986, pp. 97–106; K.S. Saraswat, 'Archaeobotanical Remains', p. 532.
55. Saraswat, 'Plant Economy of Early Farming Communities'.
56. Birendra Pratap Singh, 'Transformation of Cultures in the Middle Ganga Plains: A Case Study of Senuwar', *Pragdhara*, vol. 6, 1996, p. 92.
57. Saraswat, 'Plant Economy of Early Farming Communities'.
58. *Indian Archaeology: A Review, 1991–2*, p. 139.
59. Saraswat, 'Plant Economy of Early Farming Communities'.
60. J.N. Pal, 'Chalcolithic Vindhyas', *Pragdhara*, vol. 5, 1995, pp. 13–18.
61. *Indian Archaeology: A Review, 1981–2*, p. 106.
62. Ibid.
63. B.B. Misra, 'Chalcolithic Cultures of the Vindhyas and the Central Ganga Valley', in J.N. Pal and V.D. Misra (eds), *Indian Prehistory 1980*, Allahabad: University of Allahabad, 1997, p. 291.
64. R. Tewari, and R.K. Srivastava, 'Excavations at Raja Nala Ka Tila (1995–96), District Sonbhadra (UP): Preliminary Observations', *Pragdhara*, vol. 7, 1997, p. 92.
65. R. Tewari, R.K. Srivastava, K.S. Saraswat, and K.K. Singh, 'Excavations at Malhar, District Chandauli (UP) 1999: A Preliminary Report', *Pragdhara*, vol.10, 2000, p. 76.
66. Ibid, p. 86.
67. Saraswat, 'Archaeobotanical Remains', p. 535.
68. Kajale, 'Current Status of Indian Palaeoethnobotany', p. 160.
69. Saraswat, 'Archaeobotanical Remains', pp. 535–6.
70. Saraswat, 'Plant Economy at Ancient Narhan', pp. 255–342.
71. Ibid., p. 341.
72. Saraswat, 'Archaeobotanical Remains', p. 536.
73. Ibid., p. 537; *Indian Archaeology: A Review, 1985–6*, p. 123.
74. Singh and Singh, 'Trial Excavation at Waina', pp. 51–3.
75. Chanchala Srivastava, 'Seed and Fruit Remains from Ancient Manjhi, District Saran, Bihar', *Pragdhara*, vol. 11, 2001, p. 152.
76. Saraswat, 'Archaeobotanical Remains', p. 537.
77. *Indian Archaeology: A Review, 1983–4*, p. 175.
78. Kajale, 'Current Status of Indian Palaeoethnobotany', p. 160.
79. Sharma *et al.*, *Beginnings of Agriculture*, p. 113.
80. D.Q. Fuller, 'Fifty Years of Archaeobotanical Studies in India', in S. Settar and R. Korisettar (eds), *Indian Archaeology in Retrospect: Archaeology and Interactive Disciplines*, vol. III, New Delhi: Manohar, 2002, pp. 299–300.
81. D.K. Chakrabarti, *The Oxford Companion to Indian Archaeology: The Archaeological Foundations of Ancient India*, New Delhi: Oxford University Press, 2006, p. 216.
82. Ibid.
83. Pant, 'Indus Civilisation', p. 69.

84. J.R. Lukacs, V.D. Mishra, and J.N. Pal, 'Chronology and Diet in Mesolithic North India: A Preliminary Report of New AMS C14 Dates, δ 13C Isotope Values, and their Significance', in G.E. Afanas'ev, S. Cleuziou, J.R. Lukacs, and M. Tosi (eds), *Bioarchaeology of Mesolithic India: An Integrated Approach*, Colloquium XXXII of the International Union of Prehistoric and Protohistoric Sciences, Forli: ABACO Edizioni, 1996, p. 303.
85. Chakrabarti, *The Oxford Companion to Indian Archaeology*, p. 216.
86. Tewari, 'Excavation at Lahuradeva', pp. 55–6.
87. Chakrabarti, *The Oxford Companion to Indian Archaeology*, p. 217.
88. Saraswat, 'Plant Economy of Early Farming Communities'.
89. K.S. Saraswat, 'Archaeological Evidence of Some Herbal Drug Yielding Plants from Eastern Uttar Pradesh (Summary)', in K.M. Shrimali (ed.), *Reason and Archaeology*, Delhi: University of Delhi, 1998, pp. 63–6.
90. Saraswat, 'Plant Economy of Early Farming Communities'.
91. Pant, 'Indus Civilisation versus Mahagara Neolithic Culture', p. 67.
92. Saraswat, 'Plant Economy of Early Farming Communities'.
93. Saraswat, ' Archaeobotanical Remains', p. 541.

REFERENCES

Chakrabarti, D.K., *India: An Archaeological History*, New Delhi: Oxford University Press, 1999.

——, *The Oxford Companion to Indian Archaeology: The Archaeological Foundations of Ancient India,* New Delhi: Oxford University Press, 2006.

Fuller, D.Q., 'Fifty Years of Archaeobotanical Studies in India', in S. Settar and R. Korisettar (eds), *Indian Archaeology in Retrospect: Archaeology and Interactive Disciplines*, vol. III, New Delhi: Manohar, 2002, pp. 247–364.

Gupta, H.P., 'Holocene Palynology from Meander Lake in the Ganga Valley, District Pratapgarh, U.P.', *The Palaeobotanist*, vol. 25, 1976, pp. 109–19.

Kajale, M.D. 'Some Initial Observations on Palaeobotanical Evidence for Mesolithic Plant Economy from Excavations at Damdama, Pratapgarh, Uttar Pradesh', in N.C. Ghosh and S.C. Chakrabarti (eds), *Adaptation and Other Essays*, Shantiniketan: Visva Bharati, 1990, pp. 98–102.

——, 'Current Status of Indian Palaeoethnobotany: Introduced and Indigenous Food Plants with a Discussion of the Historical and Evolutionary Development of Indian Agriculture and Agricultural Systems in General', in Jane Renfrew (ed.), *New Light on Early Farming: Recent Developments in Palaeoethnobotany*, Edinburgh: University Press, 1991, pp. 155–89.

——, 'Plant Resources and Diet Among the Mesolithic Hunters and Foragers', in G.E. Afanas'ev, S. Cleuziou, J.R. Lukacs, and M. Tosi (eds), *Bioarchaeology of Mesolithic India: An Integrated Approach, Colloquium XXXII of the International Union of Prehistoric and Protohistoric Sciences,* Forli: ABACO Edizioni, 1996, pp. 251–3.

Lukacs, J.R. and J.N. Pal, 'Mesolithic Subsistence in North India: Inferences from Dental Attributes', *Current Anthropology*, 34 (5), 1993, pp. 745–65.

Lukacs, J.R., V.D. Mishra, and J.N. Pal, 'Chronology and Diet in Mesolithic North India: A Preliminary Report of New AMS C14 Dates, δ 13C Isotope Values, and their Significance', in G.E. Afanas'ev, S. Cleuziou, J.R. Lukacs, and M. Tosi (eds), *Bioarchaeology of Mesolithic India: An Integrated Approach, Colloquium XXXII of the International Union of Prehistoric and Protohistoric Sciences,*. Forli: ABACO Edizioni, 1996, pp. 301–11.

Misra, B.B., 'Chalcolithic Cultures of the Vindhyas and the Central Ganga Valley', in J.N. Pal and V.D. Misra (eds), *Indian Prehistory 1980*, Allahabad: University of Allahabad, 1997, pp. 286–92.

Misra, V.D., *Some Aspects of Indian Archaeology*, Allahabad: Prabhat Prakashan, 1977.

Misra, V.D., J.N. Pal, and M.C. Gupta, 'Excavation at Tokwa: A Neolithic–Chalcolithic Settlement', *Pragdhara*, vol. 11, 2001, pp. 59–72.

Pal, J.N., 'Mesolithic Settlements in the Ganga Plain', *Man and Environment*, 19 (1–2), 1994, pp. 91–101.

——, 'Chalcolithic Vindhyas', *Pragdhara*, vol. 5, 1995, pp. 13–19.

——, 'The Mesolithic Phase in the Ganga Valley', in K. Padayya (ed.), *Recent Studies in Indian Archaeology*, New Delhi: Munshiram Manoharlal, 2002, pp. 60–80.

——, 'The Beginning of Agriculture in the Middle Ganga Plain with Special Reference to the Evidence of Recent Excavations at Jhusi', in *Agriculture in South Asia's History: Issues and Paradigms*, New Delhi: Indian Council of Historical Research, 2005, pp. 1–7.

Pandey, J.N., 'Mesolithic in the Middle Ganga Valley', *Bulletin of the Deccan College Post-graduate and Research Institute*, vol. 49, 1990, pp. 311–16.

Pant, P.C., 'Indus Civilisation versus Mahagara Neolithic Culture: A Note on Acculturation', *Puravritta*, vol. 1, 2001, pp. 65–70.

Saraswat, K.S., 'Plant Economy in Ancient Sringaverapura Phase I (*c.* 1050–1000 BC)', *Puratattva*, vol. 12, 1980–1, pp. 79–89.

——, 'Ancient Crop Plant Remains from Sringaverapura, Allahabad (*c.* 1050–1000 BC)', *Geophytology*, 16 (1), 1986, pp. 97–106.

——, 'Archaeobotanical Remains in Ancient Cultural and Socio-economical Dynamics of the Indian Subcontinent', *The Palaeobotanist*, vol. 40, 1992, pp. 514–45.

——, 'Seed and Fruit Remains at Ancient Imlidih Khurd, Gorakhpur: A Preliminary Report', *Pragdhara*, vol. 3, 1993, pp. 37–41.

——, 'Archaeological Evidence of Some Herbal Drug Yielding Plants from Eastern Uttar Pradesh (Summary)', in K.M. Shrimali (ed.), *Reason and Archaeology*, Delhi : University of Delhi, 1998, pp. 63–6.

——, 'Plant Economy of Early Farming Communities at Senuwar', unpublished manuscript (to be published in B.P. Singh, *Report of Archaeological Excavations at Senuwar*).

Saraswat, K.S. and Chanchala Srivastava, 'Palaeobotanical and Pollen Analytical Investigations', *Indian Archaeology: A Review, 1991–2,* 1996, pp. 139–40.

Saraswat, K.S., D.C. Saini, M.K. Sharma, and Chanchala Srivastava, 'Palaeobotanical and Pollen Analytical Investigations', *Indian Archaeology A Review, 1985–6*, 1990, pp. 122–5.

Saraswat, K.S., N.K. Sharma, and D.C. Saini. 'Plant Economy at Ancient Narhan (*c.* 1300 BC–300/400 AD)', in Purushottam Singh (ed.), *Excavations at Narhan (1984–1989),* Varanasi: Banaras Hindu University, 1994, pp. 255–346.

Sharma, C., M.S. Chauhan, S. Sharma, M. Sharma, and I.B. Singh, 'Proxy Records of Holocene Vegetation and Climate Change from Sanai *Tal*, Central Ganga Plain, Uttar Pradesh', *National Symposium Role of Environmental Sciences Integrated Development and Related Societed Issues* 65 (GSI Spl. Publ.), 2001, pp. 199–202.

Sharma, G.R., 'Mesolithic Lake Cultures in the Ganga Valley, India', *Proceedings of the Prehistoric Society*, vol. 39, 1973, pp. 129–46.

——, 'Seasonal Migrations and Mesolithic Lake Cultures of the Ganga Valley', in *K.C. Chattopadhyaya Memorial Volume,* Allahabad: University of Allahabad, 1975.

——, 'Palaeobotanical and Pollen Analytical Investigations', *Indian Archaeology: A Review, 1980–1,* 1983, p. 110.

Sharma G.R., V.D. Misra, D. Mandal, B.B. Misra, and J.N. Pal, *Beginnings of Agriculture.* Allahabad: Abinash Prakashan, 1980.

Sharma G.R., D. Mandal, and G.K. Rai (eds), *History to Prehistory*, Allahabad: University of Allahabad, Department of Ancient History Culture and Archaeology, 1980.

Sharma, S., M. Joachimski, M. Sharma, H.J. Tobschall, I.B. Singh, C. Sharma, M.S. Chauhan, and G. Morgenroth, 'Lateglacial and Holocene Environmental Changes in Ganga Plain, Northern India', *Quaternary Science Review,* vol. 23, 2004, pp. 145–59.

Singh, Birendra Pratap, 'Transformation of Cultures in the Middle Ganga Plains: A Case Study of Senuwar', *Pragdhara,* vol. 6, 1996, pp. 75–93.

——, 'Stages of Culture Development in the Middle Ganga Plains: A Case Study of Senuwar', *Pragdhara*, vol. 11, 2001, pp. 109–18.

Singh, Indra Bir, 'Geological Evolution of the Ganga Plain: An Overview', *Journal of the Palaeontological Society of India*, vol. 41, 1996, pp. 99–137.

——, 'Late Quaternary Evolution of Ganga Plain and Proxy Records of Climate Change, Neotectonics and Anthropogenic Activity', *Pragdhara,* vol. 12, 2002, pp. 1–25.

——, 'Quaternary Palaeoenvironments of the Ganga Plain and Anthropogenic Activity', *Man and Environment,* 30 (1), 2005, pp. 1–35.

Singh I.B., Shikha Sharma, Maneesh Sharma, Pradeep Srivastava, and Govindaraja Rajagopalan. 'Evidence of Human Occupation and Humid Climate of 30 Ka in the Alluvium of Southern Ganga Plain', *Current Science*, 76 (7), 1999, pp. 1022–6.

Singh, Purushottam, 'Archaeological Excavations at Imlidih Khurd, 1992', *Pragdhara*, vol. 3, 1993, pp. 21–35.

Singh, Purushottam and Ashok Kumar Singh, 'Trial Excavations at Waina, District Ballia (UP)', *Pragdhara*, vol. 6, 1996, pp. 41–61.

Singh, R.L., *India: A Regional Geography*, Varanasi: National Geographical Society of India, 1971.

Spate, O.H.K. and A.T.A. Learmonth, *India and Pakistan: A General and Regional Geography*, London: Methuen, 1972.

Srivastava, Chanchala, 'Seed and Fruit Remains from Ancient Manjhi, District Saran, Bihar', *Pragdhara*, vol. 11, 2001, pp. 143–53.

Tewari, R. and R.K. Srivastava, 'Excavations at Raja Nala Ka Tila (1995–96), District Sonbhadra (UP): Preliminary Observations', *Pragdhara*, vol. 7, 1997, pp. 77–95.

Tewari, R., R.K. Srivastava, and K.K. Singh, 'Excavation at Lahuradeva, District Sant Nagar, Uttar Pradesh', *Puratattva*, vol. 32, 2001–2, pp. 54–9.

Tewari R., R.K. Srivastava, K.S. Saraswat, and K.K. Singh, 'Excavations at Malhar, District Chandauli (UP) 1999: A Preliminary Report', *Pragdhara*, vol. 10, 2000, pp. 69–98.

Varma, R.K., 'Pre-Agricultural Mesolithic Society of the Ganga Valley', in J.M. Kenoyer (ed.), *Old Problems and New Perspectives in the Archaeology of India*, Madison: University of Wisconsin, 1989, pp. 55–8.

Vishnu-Mittre. 'Neolithic Plant Economy at Chirand, Bihar', *The Palaeobotanist*, vol. 21, 1972, pp. 18–22.

Vishnu-Mittre and R. Savithri, 'Palaeobotanical and Pollen Analytical Investigations', *Indian Archaeology: A Review, 1974–5*, 1979, pp. 78–81.

——, 'Palaeobotanical and Pollen Analytical Investigations', *Indian Archaeology: A Review, 1975–6*, 1979, pp. 86–8.

Vishnu-Mittre, A. Sharma, and Chanchala Srivastava, 'Palaeobotanical and Pollen Analytical Investigations', *Indian Archaeology: A Review, 1981–2*, 1984, pp. 105–6.

——, 'Palaeobotanical and Pollen Analytical Investigations', *Indian Archaeology: A Review, 1982–3*, 1985, pp. 146–50.

——, 'Palaeobotanical and Pollen Analytical Investigations', *Indian Archaeology: A Review, 1983–4*, 1986, pp. 174–8.

Whitcombe, Elizabeth, *Agrarian Conditions in Northern India: The United Provinces Under British Rule, 1860–1900*, vol. 1, New Delhi: Thomson Press (India) Limited, 1971.

APPENDIX 3.1: A Database of Botanical Retrievals in the Middle Ganga Plains

Site	Cultural Context / Date	Archaeobotanical Evidence	Reference
Damdama, Dist. Pratapgarh, Uttar Pradesh	Mesolithic	The assemblage comprised three taxa identified to species: wild grasses (*Heteropogon contortus* and several of indeterminate type), goosefoot (*Chenopodium album*), and purslane (*Portulaca oleracea*). Seeds belonging to plant groups identified to family included buckwheat (*Polygonaceae*), nightshade (*Solanaceae*), and mint *Labiatae* Recent findings by K.S. Saraswat also indicate the exploitation of both cultivated and wild rice	Kajale 1990: 98–102. Pant 2001: 69
Lekhahia, Dist Mirzapur, Uttar Pradesh	Mesolithic	**Cereals:** Wild rice (*Oryza rufipogon*) and cultivated rice (*Oryza sativa*) **Others:** Wood charcoal remains of *Anogeissus pendula, Lagerstroemia speciosa*, and *Callicarpa arborea*	*Indian Archaeology: A Review, 1983–4*, 178
Lekhania, Dist Mirzapur, Uttar Pradesh	Mesolithic (c. 3rd mil. BC)	**Cereals:** Wild rice (*Oryza rufipogon* Griff.) and cultivated rice (*Oryza sativa* L.)	Kajale 1991: 164.
Chopani Mando, Dist Allahabad, Uttar Pradesh	Advanced Mesolithic	**Cereals:** Remains of wild rice in the form of husk stuck with pottery and embedded in lumps of burnt clay **Others:** Bamboo	Sharma *et al.* 1980
Koldihwa, Dist Allahabad, Uttar Pradesh	Neolithic (7th–5th mil. BC)	**Cereals:** Perennial wild rice (*Oryza rufipogon*), annual wild rice (*Oryza nivara*) and cultivated rice (*Oryza sativa*), and wheat **Pulses:** Mung	*Indian Archaeology: A Review, 1974–5*, 80 *Indian Archaeology: A Review, 1975–6*, 88 Sharma *et al.* 1980: 184

Site	Cultural Context / Date	Archaeobotanical Evidence	Reference
Lahuradeva, Dist Sant Nagar, Uttar Pradesh	Neolithic (Late 6th–5th mil. BC)	**Cereals:** Cultivated rice (*Oryza sativa*)	Tewari *et al.* 2001–2: 55–6
Chirand, Dist Saran, Bihar	Neolithic	**Cereals:** Wheat (*Triticum sphaerococcum*), barley (*Hordeum* sp.), rice, both cultivated (*Oryza sativa*) and wild (*Oryza perennis* and *Oryza rufipogon*) **Pulses:** Lentil (*Lens culinaris*), field pea (*Pisum arvense*), grass pea/khesari (*Lathyrus sativus*), and mung (*Phaseolus radiatous*) **Others:** Some leguminous weeds also recognized. Charcoal in samples identified as sal (*Shorea robusta*)	Vishnu-Mittre 1972: 18–22 *Indian Archaeology: A Review, 1974–5:* 78 *Indian Archaeology: A Review, 1975–6:* 86
Senuwar, Dist Rohtas, Bihar	Neolithic (Period 1A *c.* 2200–1950 BC)	**Cereals:** Rice (*Oryza sativa*) and wild rice (*Oryza-rufipogon*), foxtail grass (*Setaria glauca*), job's tear (*Coix lachryma jobi*), barley (*Hordeum vulgare*), dwarf wheat (*Triticum sphaerococcum*), jowar millet (*Sorghum bicolor*), and finger/ragi millet (*Eleusine coracana*) **Pulses:** Lentil (*Lens culinaris*), field pea (*Pisum arvense*), and grass pea/khesari (*Lathyrus sativus*) **Others:** Weeds and wild taxa identified included other than *Setaria glauca* and *Coix lachryma jobi*, tiny vetch (*Vicia hirsuta*), common vetch (*Vicia sativa*), chaulai (*Amaranthus* sp.), panic grass (*Panicum* sp.), brome grass (*Bromus* sp.),	Saraswat, typed manuscript

Contd...

Appendix 3.1 *Contd...*

Site	Cultural Context / Date	Archaeobotanical Evidence	Reference
		dock nut (*Rumex dentatus*), morning glory (*Ipomea pestigridis*), and jujube (*Ziziphus nummularia*) Wood charcoal remains included babul/khair (*Acacia nilotica/catechu*), bamboo (*Bambusa* sp.), heens (*Capparis sepiaria*), mahua (*Madhuca indica*), sal (*Shorea robusta*), dahia (*Streblus asper*), and bhillaur (*Trewia phudiflora*)	
Mahagara, Dist Allahabad, Uttar Pradesh	Neolithic	**Cereals:** Wild rice (*Oryza rufipogon*) and cultivated rice (*Oryza sativa*), and two carbonized grains of barley (*Hordeum vulgare*) **Others:** Bamboo, jujube, and a wild grass fruit of *Ischaemum rugosum* also identified	Sharma et al. 1980. *Indian Archaeology: A Review, 1980–1:* 110 *Indian Archaeology: A Review, 1981–2:* 106 *Indian Archaeology: A Review, 1982–3:* 149
Taradih, Dist Gaya, Bihar	Neolithic – Late Historical (*c.* 2000 BC–AD 500)	**Cereals:** Rice Pulses: Black gram, green gram / mung and common bean	Kajale 1991: 172
Manigara, Dist Mirzapur, Uttar Pradesh	Neolithic (2nd mil. BC)	**Cereals:** Rice husk remains referred to the wild perennial (*Oryza rufipogon*), wild annual (*Oryza nivara*), and cultivated (*Oryza sativa*)	*Indian Archaeology: A Review, 1981–2:* 106 *Indian Archaeology: A Review, 1982–3:* 199 *Indian Archaeology: A Review, 1983–4:* 178

Site	Cultural Context / Date	Archaeobotanical Evidence	Reference
Baraunha, Dist Mirzapur, Uttar Pradesh	Neolithic	**Cereals:** Wild annual rice (*Oryza nivara*), wild perennial (*Oryza rufipogon*) and cultivated rice (*Oryza sativa*)	*Indian Archaeology: A Review, 1981–2:* 106 *Indian Archaeology: A Review, 1982–3:* 149 *Indian Archaeology: A Review, 1983–4:* 177
Tokwa, Dist Mirzapur, Uttar Pradesh	Neolithic	**Cereals:** Rice, barley, and wheat **Pulses:** Mung **Others:** Til and mustard along with some fruits and beans	Misra *et al.* 2001: 65, 68
Jhusi, Dist Allahabad, Uttar Pradesh	Neolithic	**Cereals:** Rice and wheat Pulses: Mung and masur	Pal 2005: 4
Oriyup, Dist Bhagalpur, Bihar	Neolithic	**Cereals:** Cultivated rice (*Oryza sativa*)	Kajale 1991: 160
Senuwar, Dist Rohtas, Bihar	Neolithic–Chalcolithic (Period 1B *c.* 1950–1300 BC)	**Cereals:** Rice (*Oryza sativa*), barley (*Hordeum vulgare*), dwarf wheat (*Triticum sphaerococcum*), bread wheat (*Triticum aestivum*), kodon-millet (*Paspalum scrobiculatum*), and jowar millet (*Pennisetum typhoides*) **Pulses:** Lentil (*Lens* culinaris), field pea (*Pisum* arvense), grass pea/khesari (*Lathyrus sativus*), mung/green gram (*Vigna radiata*), chick pea (*cicer arietinum*), and horse-gram (*Dolichos biflorus*) **Others:** Seeds and fruits of weeds and wild taxa belonged	Saraswat, typed manuscript

Contd...

Appendix 3.1 *Contd...*

Site	Cultural Context / Date	Archaeobotanical Evidence	Reference
		to foxtail grass (*Setaria glauca*), wild rice (*Oryza rufipogon*), kander grass (*Ischaemum*), common vetch (*Vicia sativa*), jangali matar (*Lathyrus aphaca*), clover (*Melilotus* sp.), jujube (*Ziziphus oenoplia*), kundroo (*Coccinia cordifolia*), panibel (*Vitis tomentosa*), dhatura (*Datura* sp.) bhang (*Cannabis sativa*), and milk bush (*Euphorbia* sp.) Wood charcoal remains included besides taxa from the preceding period, bel (*Aegle marmelos*), siras (*Albizia* cf. *procera*), bhang (*Cannabis sativa*), amaltass (*Cassia fistula*), dhaura (*Lagerstroemia parviflora*), nagkesar/ironwood (*Mesua ferrea*), and jujube (*Ziziphus* sp.)	
Imlidih Khurd, Dist Gorakhpur, Uttar Pradesh	Pre-Narhan / pre-1300 BC	**Cereals:** Rice (*Oryza sativa*), bread wheat (*Triticum aestivum*), dwarf wheat (*Triticum sphaerococcum*), barley (*Hordeum vulgare*), jowar (*Sorghum bicolor*) and pearl millet/bajra (*Pennisetum typhoides*) **Pulses:** Lentil (*Lens culinaris*), green gram/mung (*Vigna radiata*), field pea (*Pisum arvense*) and grass pea/khesari (*Lathyrus sativus*) **Others:** Oleiferous crops included field brassica (*Brassica juncea*) and sesame/til	Saraswat 1993: 37–41

Site	Cultural Context / Date	Archaeobotanical Evidence	Reference
		(*Sesamum indicum*) Fruit remains of jujube (*Ziziphus nummularia*), anwala (*Emblica officinalis*), and a seed of grape (*Vitis vinifera*) 5 species of weeds including *bathua* (*Chenopodium album*), foxtail grass (*Setaria* cf. *S. glauca*), *Eleusine indica, Brachiaria* sp., and *Poa* sp.	
Imlidih Khurd, Dist Gorakhpur, Uttar Pradesh	Chalcolithic (*c.*1300–800 BC)	**Cereals:** Rice (*Oryza sativa*), bread wheat (*Triticum aestivum*), dwarf wheat (*Triticum sphaerococcum*), barley (*Hordeum vulgare*), and kodon-millet (*Paspalum scrobiculatum*). **Pulses:** Lentil (*Lens culinaris*), green gram/mung (*Vigna radiata*), and gram (*Cicer arietinum*) **Others:** Fruits of jujube (*Ziziphus nummularia*) and anwala (*Emblica officinalis*) 5 species of weeds including *Chenopodium album, Setaria* (cf. *S. glauca*), *Eleusine indica, Indigofera* sp., and *Amaranthus* sp.	Saraswat 1993: 37–41
Narhan, Dist Gorakhpur, Uttar Pradesh	Chalcolithic Black and Red Ware (Period I *c.* 1300–800 BC)	**Cereals:** Rice (*Oryza sativa*), barley (*Hordeum vulgare*), three forms of wheat, i.e., bread wheat (*Triticum aestivum*), club wheat (*Triticum compactum*), and dwarf wheat (*Triticum sphaerococcum*), pearl millet/ bajra (*Pennisetum typhoides*), and kodon millet (*Paspalum scrobiculatum*)	Saraswat *et al.* 1994: 255–342

Contd...

Appendix 3.1 *Contd...*

Site	Cultural Context / Date	Archaeobotanical Evidence	Reference
		Pulses: Gram (*Cicer arietinum*), horse gram (*Dolichos biflorus*), grass pea/khesari (*Lathyrus sativus*), lentil (*Lens culinaris*), field pea (*Pisum sativum*), moth bean (*Vigna aconitifolia*), and green gram/mung (*Vigna radiata*) **Others:** Oil seed remains of sesame (*Sesamum indicum*), field brassica (*Brassica juncea*), and linseed (*Linum usitatissimum*) Fruits of wild jujube/ber (*Ziziphus nummularia*), grapes (*Vitis vinifera*), dates (*Phoenix dactylifera*), and jackfruit/katahal (*Artocarpus heterophyllus*) 33 species of weeds and wild plants recovered including *Andropogon* sp., *Cenchrus ciliaris, Dactyloctenium aegyptium, Echinochloa crusgalli, Lolium temulentum, Panicum* sp., *Poa* sp., *Fimbristylis tetragona, Fimbristylis dichotoma, Fimbristylis tenuicula, Cyperus* sp., *Elaecharis* sp., *Rhynchospora hookeri, Desmodium* sp., *Indigofera enneaphylla, I. linifolia, Lathyrus aphaca, Rhynchosia minima, Trigonella occulta, Vicia sativa, Amaranthus* sp., *Chenopodium album, Polygonum barbatum, Rumex dentatus, Cucumis* sp., *Commelina benghalensis, Cleome viscosa, Malvastrum*	

Site	Cultural Context / Date	Archaeobotanical Evidence	Reference
		coromandelianum, Sida sp., *Trianthema portulacastrum, Ipomoea pestigridis, Oldenlandia dichotoma*, and *Argemone mexicana.* Wood charcoal remains including mango (*Mangifera indica*), mahua (*Madhuca indica*), tamarind (*Tamarindus indica*), mulberry/shahtoot (*Morus alba*), babul/khair (*Acacia* sp.), siras (*Albizia* sp.), bamboo (*Bambusa* sp.), dhak (*Butea monosperma*), karanj (*Pongamia pinnata*), dhera (*Diospyros montana*), tulsi (*Ocimum sanctum*), arni (*Premna mucronata*), sal (*Shorea robusta*), kuchla (*Strychnos nux-vomica*), jhau (*Tamarix dioica*), teak (*Tectona grandis*), and gurch (*Tinospora cordifolia*)	
Khairadih, Dist Ballia, Uttar Pradesh	Chalcolithic Black and Red Ware	Crop economy similar to that of Narhan revealed additional evidence of the exploitation of field brassica (*Brassica juncea*), yellow mustard (*Brassica campestris*), and castor (*Ricinus communis*)	Saraswat 1992: 533
Waina, Dist Ballia, Uttar Pradesh	Chalco-lithic–Iron Age (*c.* 1300–600 BC)	**Cereals:** Rice (*Oryza sativa*), barley (*Hordeum vulgare*), and wheat (*Triticum aestivum*) **Pulses:** Green gram/mung (*Vigna radiata*), lentil (*Lens culnaris*), grass pea/khesari (*Lathyrus sativus*), field pea (*Pisum arvense*), and gram (*Cicer arietinum*)	Singh and Singh 1996: 51–3

Contd...

Appendix 3.1 *Contd...*

Site	Cultural Context / Date	Archaeobotanical Evidence	Reference
		Others: Field brassica (*Brassica juncea*) and til/sesame (*Sesamum indicum*)	
Senuwar Dist Rohtas, Bihar	Chalcolithic (Period II *c.*1300–600 BC)	Cereals, millets, and pulse crops were of the same kinds as exploited in the earlier periods, with the exception of moth bean (*Vigna aconitifolia*) which was an addition **Others:** Oleiferous crop remains of til/sesame (*Sesamum indicum*), field brassica/brown mustard (*Brassica juncea*), safflower/kusum (*Carthamus tinctorius*), linseed/alsi (*Linum usitatissimum*), and castor (*Ricinus communis*) Seeds of watermelon/tarbuza (*Citrullus lanatus*) recorded for the first time in the archaeological context of India. Associated weeds and wild taxa belonged to foxtail grass (*Setaria glauca*), mandla grass (*Eleusine indica*), anjan grass (*Cenchrus ciliaris*), dock nut (*Rumex dentatus*), common vetch (*Vicia sativa*), indigo (*Indigofera* sp.), siah kanta (*Mimosa* sp.), jujube (*Ziziphus nummularia* and *Ziziphus mauritiana*), bathua (*Chenopodium album*), bhang (*Cannabis sativa*), bhanjira (*Perilla frutescens*), and ban piazi (*Asphodelus tenuifolius*) Wood charcoal remains of babul/khair (*Acacia nilotica/catechu*), siras (*Albizia* cf.	Saraswat, typed manuscript

Site	Cultural Context / Date	Archaeobotanical Evidence	Reference
		procera), bamboo (*Bambusa* sp.), bhang (*Cannabis sativa*), heens/jhiri (*Capparis sepiaria*), amaltass (*Cassia fistula*), sheesham (*Dalbergia sissoo*), mahua (*Madhuca indica*), sal (*Shorea robusta*), dahia (*Streblus asper*), teak (*Tectona grandis*), bhillaur (*Trewia phudiflora*), jujube (*Ziziphus* sp.), akol (*Alangium salvifolium*), katahal (*Artocarpus heterophyllus*), deodar (*Cedrus deodara*), mango (*Mangifera indica*), and castor (*Ricinus communis*) recorded from this phase	
Magha, Dist Mirzapur, Uttar Pradesh	Chalcolithic Black and Red Ware (*c*. 1200–600 BC)	**Cereals:** Wild perennial (*Oryza rufipogon*) and cultivated rice (*Oryza sativa*), and kodon millet (*Paspalum scrobiculatum*) **Others:** Two well-preserved grains of Sawan (*Echinochloa crusgalli*) and imprints of fruits of *Ischaemum rugosum* retrieved	*Indian Archaeology: A Review, 1981–2:* 106
Sringaverapura, Dist Allahabad, Uttar Pradesh	Chalcolithic Ochre coloured pottery (*c*. 1050–1000 BC)	**Cereals:** Rice (*Oryza sativa*) and barley (*Hordeum vulgare*) **Others:** Sesame/til (*Sesamum indicum*) and cotton (*Gossypium arboreum/herbaceum*), together with wood remains of *Pinus roxburghii, Ziziphus* sp., *Acacia nilotica/catechu, Mangifera indica, Madhuca indica*, and bamboo	Saraswat 1986: 97–106 Saraswat 1992: 532
Sohgaura, Dist Gorakhpur, Uttar Pradesh	Chalcolithic (*c*. 2nd mil. BC)	**Cereals:** Wild (*Oryza rufipogon*) and cultivated rice (*Oryza sativa*), and barley (*Hordeum vulgare*)	Kajale 1991: 160 Saraswat 1992: 533

Contd...

Appendix 3.1 *Contd...*

Site	Cultural Context / Date	Archaeobotanical Evidence	Reference
Koldihwa, Dist Allahabad, Uttar Pradesh	Chalcolithic	**Cereals:** Rice and wheat **Pulses:** Mung	Misra 1997: 291
Kakoria, Dist Varanasi, Uttar Pradesh	Chalcolithic	**Cereals:** Wild perennial (*Oryza rufipogon*) and cultivated rice (*Oryza sativa*)	*Indian Archaeology: A Review, 1981–2*, 106
Malhar, Dist Chandauli, Uttar Pradesh	Pre-Iron (Period I *c.* 1900 BC– *c.* 1700–1600 BC)	**Cereals:** Rice (*Oryza sativa*) and barley (*Hordeum vulgare*) **Pulses:** Mung (*Vigna radiata*), field pea (*Pisum arvense*), lentil (*Lens culinaris*), and grass pea/khesari (*Lathyrus sativus*)	Tewari *et al.* 2000: 76
Raja Nala Ka Tila, Dist Sonbhadra, Uttar Pradesh	Pre-Iron (Period I *c.* 1700–1300 BC)	**Cereals:** Rice (*Oryza sativa*), barley (*Hordeum vulgare*), foxtail millet (*Setaria italica*), and ragi millet (*Eleusine coracana*) **Pulses:** Lentil (*Lens culinaris*), field pea (*Pisum arvense*), grass pea/khesari (*Lathyrus sativus*), and mung (*Vigna radiata)*	Tewari and Srivastava 1997: 92
Malhar, Dist Chandauli, Uttar Pradesh	Early Iron (Period II *c.* 1600 BC)	**Cereals:** Rice (*Oryza sativa*), barley (*Hordeum vulgare*), dwarf wheat (*Triticum sphaeroccocum*), kodon millet (*Paspalum scrobiculatum*), jowar millet (*Sorghum bicolor*), and ragi millet (*Eleusine coracana*) **Pulses:** Lentil (*Lens culinaris*), field pea (*Pisum arvense*), grass pea/khesari (*Lathyrus sativus*), and horse gram/kulthi (*Dolichos biflorus*) **Others:** Til (*Sesamum indicum*) and carbonized stones and fruit pieces of wild jujube/jharberi (*Ziziphus nummularia*)	Tewari *et al.* 2000: 86

Site	Cultural Context / Date	Archaeobotanical Evidence	Reference
Raja Nala Ka Tila, Dist Sonbhadra, Uttar Pradesh	Iron Age (Period II *c.* 1300–700 BC)	**Cereals:** Crop remains mostly of similar kinds as in Period I, with the addition of dwarf wheat (*Triticum sphaerococcum*) and common millet (*Panicum* cf. *miliaceum*) **Pulses:** Horse gram (*Dolichos biflorus*) added to the dietary chart **Others:** Weed species and wild taxa from Period I and II including jujube/jharberi (*Ziziphus nummularia*), harra/haritaki (*Terminalia chebula*), ban kangani (*Setaria* cf. *Glauca*), and job's tear (*Coix lachryma jobi*)	Tewari and Srivastava 1997: 92
Sringaverapura, Dist Allahabad, Uttar Pradesh	Iron-Age (*c.* 950–700 BC)	**Cereals:** Rice (*Oryza sativa*), barley (*Hordeum vulgare*), and wheat (*Triticum sphaerococcum* and *Triticum compactum*) **Pulses:** Chick pea (*Cicer arietinum*) and green gram/mung (*Vigna radiata*). **Others:** Palm (*Phoenix* sp.), khus grass (*Vetiveria zizanoides*), and wood charcoal remains of *Madhuca indica, Mangifera indica, Mesua ferrea, Ziziphus* sp., *Albizia* sp., *Betula utilis*, and *Bombax malabarica*	Saraswat 1992: 536
Narhan, Dist Gorakhpur, Uttar Pradesh	Iron Age Black Slipped Ware (Period II *c.* 800–600 BC)	**Cereals:** Rice (*Oryza sativa*) and barley (*Hordeum vulgare*) **Pulses:** Field pea (*Pisum sativum*) and green gram/mung (*Vigna radiata*) **Others:** Safflower (*Carthamus tinctorius*) and weeds of *Vicia* sp.	Saraswat *et al.* 1994: 255–342

Contd...

Appendix 3.1 *Contd...*

Site	Cultural Context / Date	Archaeobotanical Evidence	Reference
		Wood taxa including babul/ khair (*Acacia* sp.), bamboo (*Bambusa* sp.), dhera (*Diospyros montana*), mahua (*Madhuca indica*), mango (*Mangifera indica*), sal (*Shorea robusta*), imli (*Tamarindus indica*), teak (*Tectona grandis*), sheesham (*Dalbergia sissoo*), anwala (*Emblica officinalis*), keim (*Mitragyna parviflora*), and jamun (*Syzygium cumini*)	
Sonpur, Dist Gaya, Bihar	Iron (*c.* 800–600 BC)	**Cereals:** Rice (*Oryza* sp.)	Kajale 1991: 160
Narhan, Dist Gorakhpur, Uttar Pradesh	Northern Black Polished Ware (Period III *c.* 600–200 BC)	**Cereals:** Rice (*Oryza sativa*), barley (*Hordeum vulgare*), bread wheat (*Triticum aestivum*), dwarf wheat (*Triticum sphaerococcum*), and kodon millet (*Paspalum scrobiculatum*)	
		Pulses: Grass pea/khesari (*Lathyrus sativus*), field pea (*Pisum sativum*), green gram/ mung (*Vigna radiata*), and black gram/urd (*Vigna mungo*) **Others:** Sesame/til (*Sesamum indicum*) and fruit remains of *anwala* (*Emblica officinalis*) and jujube/ber (*Ziziphus mauritiana*) Taxa represented in wood charcoal remains including bamboo (*Bambusa* sp.), anwala (*Emblica officinalis*), mahua (*Madhuca indica*), mango (*Mangifera indica*), tulsi (*Ocimum sanctum*), imli (*Tamarindus indica*), punarnava	Saraswat *et al.* 1994: 255–342

Site	Cultural Context / Date	Archaeobotanical Evidence	Reference
		(*Boerhavia diffusa*), dhaura (*Lagerstroemia parviflora*), chirwood (*Pinus roxburghii*), and sandalwood (*Santalum album*)	
Khairadih, Dist Ballia, Uttar Pradesh	Northern Black Polished Ware (*c.* 600–200 BC)	**Cereals:** Rice (*Oryza sativa*), barley (*Hordeum vulgare*), wheat (*Triticum sphaerococcum* and *Triticum aestivum*). **Pulses:** Green gram/mung (*Vigna radiata*), chick pea (*Cicer arietinum*), field pea (*Pisum arvense*), grass pea (*Lathyrus sativus*), and lentil (*Lens culinaris*)	Saraswat 1992: 536
		Others: Wood charcoal remains of mahua (*Madhuca indica*), babul/khair (*Acacia nilotica/A. catechu*), mango (*Mangifera indica*), kandi (*Flacourtia indica*), sal (*Shorea robusta*), neem (*Azadirachta indica*), teak (*Tectona grandis*), sheesham (*Dalbergia sissoo*), dhak (*Butea monosperma*), maha-rukh (*Ailanthus excelsa*), bistendu (*Diospyros montana*), tamarind (*Tamarindus indica*), chilbil (*Holoptelia integrifolia*), and dhela (*Alangium salvifolium*) Finds included remains of herbal drug-yielding plants/ dry fruits like haritaki or chebulic myrobalan (*Terminalia chebula*), emblic myrobalan (*Emblica officinalis*), nutmeg or jaiphal (*Myristica fragrans*), currants or sweet raisin, draksha	*Indian Archaeology: A Review, 1985–6*, 123 Saraswat 1992: 537

Contd...

Appendix 3.1 *Contd...*

Site	Cultural Context / Date	Archaeobotanical Evidence	Reference
		(*Vitis vinifera*), and chiraunji (*Buchanania lanzan*)	
Kausambi, Dist Allahabad, Uttar Pradesh	Northern Black Polished Ware (*c.* 600–200 BC)	**Cereals:** Rice (*Oryza* sp.) and barley (*Hordeum vulgare*) **Others:** Cotton seeds (*Gossypium arboreum/ herbaceum*), timbers including *Soymida febrifuga, Holarrhena antidysenterica, Adina cordifolia, Ziziphus, Terminalia, Lagerstroemia, Anogeissus*, and *Dalbergia sissoo*	Kajale 1991: 160 Saraswat 1992: 535
Manjhi, Dist Saran, Bihar	Northern Black Polished Ware (*c.* 600–50 BC)	**Cereals:** Rice (*Oryza sativa*), bread wheat (*Triticum aestivum*), dwarf wheat (*Triticum sphaerococcum*), barley (*Hordeum vulgare*), kodon millet (*Paspalum scrobiculatum*), and Italian millet (*Setaria* sp.) **Pulses:** Green gram/mung (*Vigna radiata*), field pea (*Pisum arvense*), lentil (*Lens culinaris*), and grass pea/khesari (*Lathyrus sativus*) **Others:** Oil seed remains of til (*Sesamum indicum*) and grape pips (*Vitis vinifera*); wild taxa like *Amaranthus* sp., *Chenopodium album, Medicago sativa, Commelina benghalensis, Trianthema portulacastrum, Rumex dentatus, Cleome viscosa, Eleusine indica, Argemone mexicana, Lathyrus aphaca, L. sphaericus, Trigonella* sp., *Vicia sativa, Jaquemontia* sp., *Echinochloa crusgalli, Indigofera* sp., *Melitotus indica, Cyperus* sp., *Elaeocharis* sp., *Fimbristylis*	Srivastava 2001: 143–53

Site	Cultural Context / Date	Archaeobotanical Evidence	Reference
		sp., and *Solanum* sp. also identified	
Rajghat, Dist Varanasi, Uttar Pradesh	Northern Black Polished Ware (*c*. 500 BC)	**Cereals:** Rice (*Oryza* sp.)	Kajale 1991: 160
Pataliputra, Dist Patna, Bihar	Northern Black Polished Ware (*c*. 400 BC)	**Cereals:** Rice (*Oryza* sp.) **Others:** Sal (*Shorea robusta*)	Kajale 1991: 160 Saraswat 1992: 537
Rajgir, Dist Patna, Bihar	Northern Black Polished Ware (*c*. 200 BC)	**Cereals:** Rice (*Oryza* sp.) **Others:** *Madhuca longifolia* var. *latifolia*	Kajale 1991: 160 *Indian Archaeology: A Review, 1983–4*, 175

4. Landscapes of Life and Death
Considering the Region of Vidarbha

UTHARA SUVRATHAN

THE LANDSCAPE: LOOKING AT THE 'REGION'

Regions do not have an objective existence, but are artefacts and can be defined as a 'perceived segment of the time space continuum differentiated from others on the basis of one or more defining characteristics'.[1]

The definition of any region varies according to the variables chosen to study it, and also upon its particular location in time and space. Therefore, the study of any region needs to look at a variety of variables (and sources), take into consideration the element of time *and* space, and do all this without representing the region as a 'given' by incorporating the elements of human thought and action. I consider the idea of the 'landscape' a conceptual tool for retrieving past patterns of history and providing a coherent theoretical framework to take into account the complex and multifaceted nature of any region.

The 'landscape' has been variously defined[2] and the variety of perspectives in defining this concept adds to the appeal of studying landscapes as a medium that draws upon diverse approaches. Landscapes may be defined as a collection of natural, semi-natural, and constructed features that form the physical framework within which human societies exist.[3] However, the landscape is not merely the background or determinant of human action, or simply the outcome of social structure or practice. Landscapes are shaped by, and also shape history, in a complex and reciprocal relationship. Not only do we have 'constructed' landscapes formed by the alteration of the earth's surface by human activity, but also 'landscapes of the mind' where the physical surroundings need not be altered, but can hold a variety of meanings for contemporary society. These interlinked and not easily separable facets of the landscape will be the focus of this essay.

I am interested in the landscape as a 'text' that can be 'read', encoding a variety of themes, be they belief systems or socio-political and economic patterns. The shaping, (re)use, and (re)interpretation of the landscape not only illustrates crucial ideologies, beliefs, and values and specific ecological adaptations, but also sheds light on historical processes. The term 'text' has been used to underline an approach to the study of the landscape as a palimpset representing a complex tapestry of numerous changes, continuities, (re)interpretations, and historical processes over time. The aim is not to draw attention away from the materiality of the landscape by extending the literary analogy too far. I will study some of the facets of meaning inherent in the landscape, representing as it does a variety of meanings and spatial and temporal scales. From among the innumerable strands that go into the making of this web, the emphasis will be on tradition and memory, socio-political identities, and processes of change and continuity. These three themes bring out a small part of the diversity of meanings a landscape holds for the various groups that inhabit it.

Vidarbha has been defined according to present-day administrative boundaries, that is, eastern Maharashtra, bounded by the rivers Tapti and Penganga in the north and the south respectively, and comprising the modern districts of Chandrapur, Bhandara, Nagpur, Wardha, Yavatmal, Amaravati, Akola, and Gadchiroli. The period under consideration is approximately 1000 BC to AD 300. This includes the megalithic phase (Eighth/Seventh–Fourth/Third century BC) and the early historic (Third century BC–Third century AD). I will move backwards in time looking at some of the innumerable 'landscapes' of which this region was constituted in order to bring out the variety of processes that went into its making through time and in space.

Beginning with the mortuary landscapes of the megaliths (Fig. 4.1), I will trace the variety of spatial and temporal contexts within which the megaliths were implicated, highlighting the various processes of continuity and change in the definition of this region. Based on a limited database[4] culled from published reports, I study the megaliths from two perspectives: spatial variations in archaeological geography (horizontal) and temporal changes in the archaeological landscape (vertical). At one level, I will look at the spatial organization of the

Figure 4.1: Megalithic sites in Vidarbha

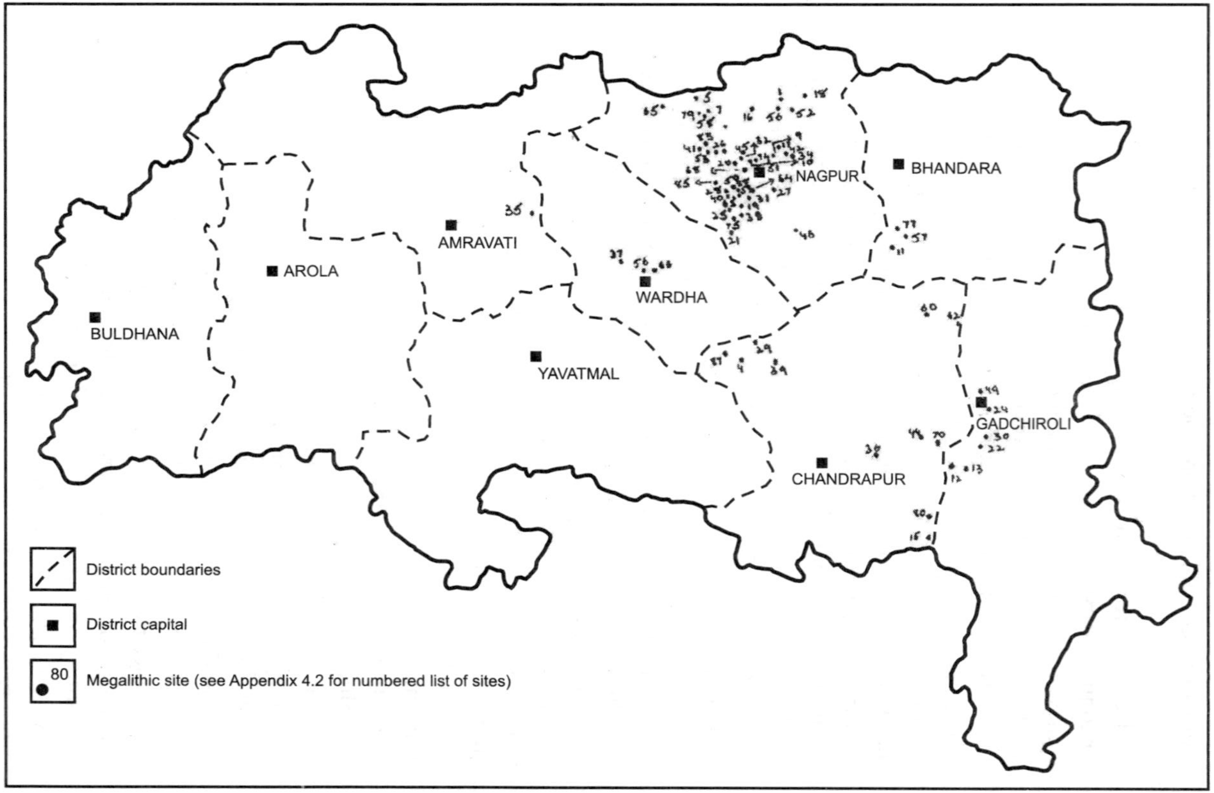

megaliths to derive regional patterns in the use of the landscape. Second, I will analyse the changes in and the reuse of the megalithic landscape over time. This approach will highlight the internal dynamics of historical development in the region of Vidarbha, as reflected in the archaeological landscape, instead of merely looking at external factors.

LANDSCAPES OF LIFE: CONSIDERING SPACE

The relief of Vidarbha comprises the residual hill ranges of the Satpuras, enclosing between them undulating black soil valleys. Most of the topography is Deccan Trap with flat-topped and terraced features, low buttressed sides, and isolated knolls. This plateau is drained by the Wardha and Wainganga rivers and their tributaries. Early scholarly work on the megaliths had emphasized the nomadic and pastoral nature of their subsistence base. Based on recent research, however, the emerging picture is that of a complex economy with a multifaceted pattern including agriculture, pastoralism, hunting,[5] fishing, and a variety of artisanal activities. Some habitation-cum-burial sites have also been identified, for instance, at Takalghat-Khapa, Raipur-Hingna, Naikund, Bhawar, Pachkheri, Khairwara, and Bhagimahari (Appendices 4.1 and 4.2). These sites are fairly extensive with thick habitational deposits indicating settled habitation over a considerable period of time. There is also the possibility of habitation sites without associated burials, megalithic levels having been identified at Kaundinyapur, Arni, Paunar, Tharsa, Arambha, and Adam.[6]

Some of the burial-cum-habitation sites seem to have been important symbolic centres to which the dead were brought, and several were centres of production. For instance, an iron smelting workshop has been identified at Naikund.[7] There is also some pattern in the location of these important sites. Not only are the major sites located in the hilly and forested Nagpur–Wardha region, but there is a settlement hierarchy within the four major habitation sites, indicating the existence of a complex socio-political organization.[8] Moreover, all these sites are located in areas with fertile soil[9] and on the banks of perennial rivers (Table 4.1). Was this proximity to rivers due to the advantages it provided in terms of habitation and movement (of people and materials? It is interesting that Khairwada is located on the route that later came to be known as the *Dakṣiṇāpatha*. There is some evidence of interregional exchange of goods as is indicated by the presence of carnelian (not found in the region) and other beads at sites like Takalghat-Khapa and Mahurjhari.[10]

The megalithic people also seem to have preferred locations with other advantages. The megaliths are concentrated in the Bhandara, Nagpur, and Chandrapur districts, which are known for their abundant mineral deposits, especially raw iron, coal, and manganese.[11] However, while the habitation-cum-burial sites were mainly located in ideal areas, many of the burial sites were located in hilly, forested regions or in wastelands.[12]

At first glance, the megaliths of Vidarbha seem to represent a homogeneous group, with the majority consisting of stone circles with cairn fillings. However, great variation between sites can be identified. Not only do some sites have dolmens (for example, at Pimpalgaon, Chamorsi, and Kelzar), but there are constructional differences among the various sites with stone circles (see Appendices 4.1 and 4.2). The stone circles at Bhagimahari contain a huge block of Gondwana formation placed in a slanting position within the circle, and Megalith 3 at Boregaon was marked by a huge trough cutout of a boulder placed in the centre of the circle.[13]

Moreover, there seems to be some variation between sites in terms of burial practice. At Khapa, for instance, many circles have a central pit in the *murum* and some funerary items (often including a Black and Red Ware [henceforth BRW] or Micaceous Red Ware [henceforth MRW] pot containing bones) are either placed in the pit or in the centre of the circle. Mahurjhari is characterized by the presence of numerous primary extended burials and the human skeletal remains recovered from this site are relatively large. At Junapani, artefacts are placed in the rubble packing, while at Raipur they are placed only in the black clay filling. Finally, there is some amount of variability within each site. The megaliths are generally grouped in two or more locations even within each site, for instance, at Raipur–Hingna. Did each group belong to a particular family or clan? If burials are a reflection of social status in life, then it can be noted that there does seem to be some amount of inequality in the distribution of wealth and/or in social status.[14] For instance, Megalith I (Locality I) at Mahurjhari contains very few funerary items, while Megalith 3 (Locality III) has a rich artefactual deposit. However, the contents of each burial vary. There is no clear pattern visible that would enable us to make many generalizations regarding burial practice.[15] A variety of items were enclosed in the megaliths along with the human remains.

TABLE 4.1: Sites, Locations, Sequence of Cultures

Site	Location	Character of Site	Sequence of Cultures
Arambha	Right flood plain of R. Pothra, tributary of the Wardha	Habitation	Chalcolithic/Iron Age Northern Black Polished Ware (NBPW) Satavahana Gupta/Vakataka Early medieval
Arni	On the banks of R. Arunavati	Habitation	Megalithic Mauryan Post Mauryan/Satavahana Vakataka
Bhagimohari	Bank of R. Kolar	Burial and habitation	Single culture megalithic site
Bhawar	Left flood plain of the Wainganga. Close to local stream	Burial and habitation	Microlithic Iron free horizon Iron using horizon Mauryan Satavahana
Boregaon	---	Burial	Single culture megalithic site
Gangapur	On the fringes of the southern slopes of the Kalari hills	Burial	Single culture megalithic site
Junapani	---	Burial	Single culture megalithic site
Kaundiyapur	Northern bank of the Wardha	Habitation	Megalithic (Black and Red Ware) NBPW Satavahana Late Satavahana Late medieval
Khairwada	Right bank of R. Dham	Burial and habitation	Megalithic Early historic/Satavahana Late Satavahana Medieval
Khapa	Left bank of R. Krishna. Close to seasonal *nala* and spur of Kalari hills	Burial	Single culture megalithic site

Contd...

Table 4.1 *Contd...*

Site	Location	Character of Site	Sequence of Cultures
Mahurjhari	Series of low hills on the north-east and a seasonal nala on the west and south-west	Burial	Single culture megalithic site with early Historic remains to the north-west of the present day village
Naikund	Left bank of R. Pench.	Burial and habitation	Single culture megalithic site with modern day village
Pachkeri	Close to a local nala, the Tembra nala and the R. Amb	Burial and habitation	Mesolithic Iron Age Mauryan Satavahana Medieval
Paunar	Right bank of Dham	Habitation	Chalcolithic Iron Age Early Historic Early Medieval
Pimpalgaon	Left flood plains of Wainganga system	Burial	Single culture megalithic?
Raipur-Hingna	Either side of R. Wenna	Burial	Single culture megalithic site next to modern day village
Shirkanda	Left bank of the R. Sur	Habitation	Chalcolithic–megalithic
Takalghat	Right bank of river Krishna	Habitation	Single culture megalithic site
Takli	Left bank Wenna	Burial	
Tharsa	Left bank of a river (?)	Habitation and burials (urn)	Chalcolithic/Megalithic Pre-Satavahana/Satavahana Vakataka Medieval Modern

Source: Various secondary sources and excavation reports

These range from items of copper (dishes, bangles), gold (primarily ornaments), beads (of carnelian, agate, jasper, and so on), and stone (pounders) to even the skeletal remains of a horse, hinting at the complex symbolic associations of the megalithic structures. Megaliths with skeletal remains generally give evidence of a rich assemblage of funerary items,[16] but there is no correlation between the presence of skeletal remains and the size of the megalith.[17] Unusual items, however (like items made of two metals and sandstone pounders), are generally found in megaliths with skeletal remains.

It is clear that each item included had some meaning, which is now lost. The presence of items like copper bangles (found in nearly all the excavated burials) or iron lamps indicate that they could have had some ritual significance. There have been attempts to classify the funerary items into various categories in order to derive meaning from them.[18] However, most of the funerary items could be, and were, combined with each other, which suggests that instead of forming a rigid system for expressing rank or gender, the burial of artefacts with the dead was a flexible means of displaying socio-political and economic status. It could also be suggested that the range of artefacts found in the megaliths represents an attempt to replicate the range of items used in daily life—tools (chisels, adzes), weapons (spearheads, arrowheads, daggers), items of daily use (nail parers), ornaments, pottery, and symbolic items (lamps).

TIME AND THE LANDSCAPE

Not only does the landscape represent the product of specific historical conditions, but it is continuously refashioned and reinterpreted through time. One way of approaching this is by recognizing that landscapes embody time at different scales. It is the continued use, modification, or abandonment of a material landscape *over time* that archaeologists study, often dividing this continuum into chronological units correlated with particular archaeological periods. Historians too attempt to trace the movement of human society and the forms it takes *through time*, as well as to conceptualize the diversity of human thought and perceptions. It is here, in landscape as time, that the convergence of history and archaeology can be located. The landscape can, therefore, be approached by analysing material changes on the earth's surface, as well as by studying the changing perceptions of the landscape over time. Reference can be made specifically to the fact that the landscape reflects both cyclical and linear time, concepts that have often been seen as contradictory. At one level the landscape is used and reused, reflecting a cyclical movement. Simultaneously, this movement is through time, reflecting a variety of processes located not just in that particular space, but also at various points in time. Therefore, we are talking about a 'spiral' movement of time—an interesting concept, since it takes into account traditional Indian conceptualizations of time and not a linear, western one.

In the study of the megalithic culture in India, time has mainly been considered in terms of chronology or periodization, and the focus has been on deriving patterns of society/polity/economy. However, instead of merely considering static patterns, some of the numerous scales of time embodied in the landscape can be studied.[19]

I will look at the meanings surrounding the megaliths with respect to two temporal scales: short and long term. No distinct values (of time) are assigned to these two scales. The short term is taken to refer to that span of time when the specific meanings of the megaliths and the set of practices associated with them are immediate and very much part of the cultural ethos, that is, the so-called 'megalithic period'. The long term takes into account a much longer span of time, stretching both before and after the period of the megalith builders, when the meanings and symbolic connotations of the megaliths were lost, with new values being assigned to them[20] and when the archaeological landscape was altered.

The Short Term: Memory and Material Culture

The biographies of artefacts and structures are closely linked to those of humans. The megaliths were built to commemorate death and can be considered to mark the passage of a human life or lives (if the burial contained the remains of more than one person). Moreover, not just the megaliths, but a specific point in time was sought to be commemorated. In certain cases, this point in time was immediately after the death of the individual, as is seen by the presence of primary burials at some of the sites.[21] In the case of secondary burials,[22] clearly some time had elapsed after the point of death and the burials merely marked the final resting place of the remains. Could there have been a period of mourning before the dead were interred? Or were there a series of other rituals (cremation, exposure) before the remains were finally placed in the megalith?

It was not just a particular point in time that was rendered significant but time was constructed as cyclical by the repetition of activities. Not only was the same site used for the construction of megaliths over a long period of time, but individual graves too seem to have been reused. Apart from multiple burials, there is some evidence that burials were reopened and reused.[23] It also seems that the megaliths were maintained over a period of time. Megalith 8 at Raipur, erected on a north-south slope and in danger of flooding, was protected by an arrangement of peripheral stones, with two layers of biggish stones laid one over the other on the northern periphery.[24] Such evidence of small variations made in the constructional plan so as to strengthen the structure or compensate for weaknesses[25] indicates that the megaliths were meant to have significance over a longer period of time, maintaining a place of importance in future physical landscapes. In fact, at Raipur, five circles with no filling were built for future use, placed on the fringes of the site with only the boulders aligned.[26] This also raises the possibility that the megaliths were constructed such that they were placed around a central location (an earlier megalith?) containing older structures that possibly held some meaning for the builders.

What is important is not just the continuity in the use and ideas about the landscape, but its role in the construction of history. It has been recently argued by certain scholars that the past/history mattered to people in prehistory.[27] Historical consciousness could have taken many forms, and a search for this consciousness need not be restricted to textual sources, but could extend to material structures, which, as discussed earlier, could hold meaning for a people over time. The pattern of reuse seen in Vidarbha could be termed the creation of 'genealogical history',[28] where the history of a group was constructed around links to (real or mythical) ancestors. It has been argued that such a form of constructing history relied not merely on human memory, but also worked with a series of mnemonics, with the biggest memory prompt of all coming from the constructed landscape, the megaliths.[29]

Considering the Long Term: Continuity and Change

Frequently linear, deterministic models, which assume an evolution towards increasing complexity, have been used in historical (and archaeological) explanation. However, the landscape reflects a variety of non-linear processes.

Questions concerning the origin and spread of the megalithic tradition and associated cultural elements (iron, the BRW) have attracted a lot of interest. The origin of megalithic cultural practices is frequently seen in terms of the migration of people (or ideas) from outside the region.[30] An analysis of long-term developments provides a different and much more complex perspective. Vidarbha had been an important region of human settlement from very early times. Numerous Stone Age sites have been identified, most situated in the major river basins.[31] Earlier it was believed that the chalcolithic

(Jorwe) culture of western Maharashtra extended only as far east as Tuljapur Garhi (district Amaravati).[32] However, recent excavations at Adam[33] have thrown light on the chalcolithic cultures of Vidarbha, termed the 'Vidarbha Chalcolithic', as the ceramic industry does not correspond to that of any of the contemporary chalcolithic cultures.[34]

The number of inhabited sites does seem to increase from the chalcolithic to the megalithic. This, of course, might be a function of the importance given to the megaliths and the lack of detailed studies of the chalcolithic in Vidarbha (till relatively recently). While several of the megalithic (mainly burial) sites are single culture sites, there is evidence of chalcolithic-megalithic overlap/continuity at some sites, and even of a mesolithic-megalithic continuity (Table 4.2).[35]

The external imposition of the megalithic culture is further problematized when we look at the associated cultural elements of the megalithic. After all, the construction of the megaliths was but one element of contemporary material culture. The BRW, often considered a 'necessary cultural adjunct' of the megalithic burials, is not peculiar to the megalithic period, but is found in a variety of spatial and temporal contexts. This widespread ceramic category, likely produced through inverted firing techniques that generate a black interior and a red exterior, has a long history in South Asia (as in other regions of the world, where it is not an uncommon technological strategy). In South Asia, black and red ceramics have antecedents in pre-Iron Age contexts. This ware appears from Harappan times in Saurashtra, and is characteristic of the Ahar culture of Mewar, which later spread to central India.[36] It also makes an appearance in the western Indian chalcolithic (that is, Jorwe), as well as in early historic contexts along with the Northern Black Painted Ware (henceforth NBPW). In Vidarbha too, no distinguishing feature could be noticed to differentiate the BRW of the chalcolithic and that of the megalithic. This overlap has been noticed at several sites like Arambha, Adam, and Bhawar.[37] Moreover, even in the megalithic habitation sites, numerous other wares were present, and the MRW was predominant.[38]

The BRW is so widely found in numerous sites and from a wide range of chronological contexts that it seems to have been locally produced. It might even be suggested that BRW ceramics might not constitute a distinct type, but refer to a method of ceramic manufacture. This,

TABLE 4.2: Radiocarbon Dates

Site	Context	Radiocarbon Dates
Adam	Megalithic Levels	2710 ± 110 = 760 ± 110 BC
		2010 ± 60 = 160 ± 60 BC
		2390 ± 60 = 440 ± 60 BC
		2410 ± 70 = 460 ± 70 BC
	Habitation:	
	Layer 9	750±100 BC
	Layer 9	690±100 BC
Khairwada	Layer 8	600±100 BC
	Layer 7	450±90 BC
	Layer 6	500±100 BC
	Layer 4	490±100 BC
	Layer 2	570±100 BC
Naikund	*Habitation*:	
	Mound I, Layer 6	2470 ± 100 = 520 ± 100 BC
	Mound I, Layer 5	2480 ± 120 = 530 ± 120 BC
	Mound I Layer 4	2110 ± 100 = 160 ± 110 BC
	Mound II, Layer 8	2360 ± 100 = 410 ± 100 BC
	Mound II, Layer 6	2470 ± 90 = 520 ± 90 BC
	Mound II, Layer 5	2250 ± 100 = 300 ± 100 BC
	Mound II, Layer 5	2280 ± 110 = 330 ± 110 BC
	Mound II, Layer 5	2320 ± 120 = 370 ± 120 BC
	Mound II, Layer 4	2400 ± 100 = 450 ± 100 BC
	Mound II, Layer 4	2640 ± 110 = 690 ± 110 BC
	Mound II, Layer 3	2440 ± 110 = 490 ± 110 BC
	Mound II, Layer 2	2450 ± 100 = 500 ± 100 BC
	Mound II, Layer 2	2460 ± 120 = 570 ± 120 BC
	Mound II, Layer 2	2450 ± 120 = 500 ± 120 BC
	Stone Circles:	
	Megalith 7 (50 cm below surface)	2455 ± 100 = 505 ± 100 BC
	Megalith 7 (80 cm below surface)	2495 ± 105 = 545 ± 105 BC
Takalghat	*Habitation*:	
	Layer 7A (3.03 m below surface)	2505 ± 100 = 555 ± 100 BC
	Layer 9A (4.78 m below surface)	2565 ± 105 = 615 ± 105 BC

Source: Deo 1970; Deo, Jamkhedkar 1982; Nath 1999; *IAR* 1988–9, 1989–90, 1991–2

however, does not preclude the movement of ceramic technologies and forms. However, the issue remains inconclusive. The BRW, therefore, cannot be attributed to a particular group of people. Perhaps it can be seen as composed of forms that remained stable over time and space, but with different meanings at the local level, open to reinterpretation at different spatial or temporal contexts.

The origins of iron, a much debated topic, and megalithism are two separate issues. While all megalithic sites have iron artefacts, all Iron Age sites are not necessarily megalithic.[39] Apart from iron, the other important element of change was, of course, the introduction of a new structural form of commemorating death. This practice marked a distinct change from previous (and later) forms of memorialization,[40] but there probably was the coexistence of other practices relating to death during the megalithic period. At chalcolithic-megalithic Tharsa, for instance, were found two urn burials of infants.[41]

This complex picture is further complicated by the megalithic-early historic continuity that is noticed at several habitation sites. While the megalithic culture was in evidence in Vidarbha, the middle Ganga valley of the mid-first millennium BC witnessed the beginning of the early historic. The rise of urban centres and associated economic changes; the introduction of metallic coinage and writing; the increasing use of iron and baked brick; the development of more complex forms of political organization; and the appearance of distinct early historic ceramics (especially the NBPW)[42] are considered some of the most important features of this period. These cultural traits are seen as spreading to Vidarbha and other regions of peninsular India as a result of a variety of external processes, including the role of the Mauryan Empire. We can briefly carry the narrative further and look at the changing historical landscape in early historic Vidarbha.

Towards Increasing Complexity: Third/Second Centuries BC to Third Century AD

To move away from dynastic labels while considering historical development, the chronological span of third/second centuries BC to third century AD will be discussed here. In any case, the lack of extensive horizontal excavations and the use of general time brackets (like the 'early historic') make it difficult to clearly identify the changes in settlement patterns during the period when the Sātavāhanas were politically dominant in the region or at the end of their rule. However, at a very general level it could be noted that there was a spread of settlement in Vidarbha in the early historic period.[43] Some sites could even be classed as urban centres,[44] and there is evidence of fortification at several sites like Adam, Arni, and Ramtek (Appendix 4.3).[45]

Early historic sites in Vidarbha seem to have been based on an expanding agricultural economy[46] with a corresponding shift of settlement from hilly/forested regions (Nagpur district) to the fertile river valleys of the Wainganga and its tributaries, the Kanhan and the Dham (Fig. 4.2, Appendix 4.1).[47] There is evidence for the existence of an artisanal class,[48] and a monetized economy was well established, as seen in the extensive coin finds. Studies have shown that the Sātavāhana coinage drew on preceding coin-making traditions, incorporating regional symbolism, shapes, metals, and techniques (punch marked).[49] Inter- and intra-regional trade connections were probably well established.[50] There is even evidence of trade in Roman goods, which could reflect the forging of links between Vidarbha and the western coast of the subcontinent.[51]

It can be argued that the foundations of this socio-political and economic complexity so apparent in the early historic had been laid

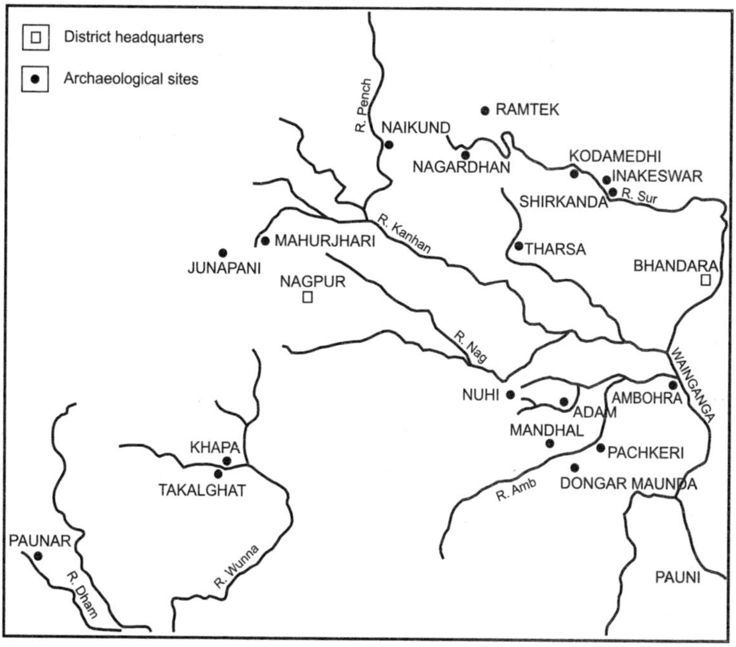

Figure 4.2: Archaeological sites in the Wainganga Valley

in the megalithic period which witnessed some social differentiation and complexity, hierarchization of settlement size,[52] exchange, craft specialization, and varied subsistence base.

Moreover, not only is Vidarbha well endowed in terms of natural resources,[53] but the region (especially the Wainganga valley) lies on an important route connecting north India with the Deccan (that is, the *dakṣiṇāpatha*). Among the cultural traits which might have been spread via these routes, NBPW, associated primarily with the Gangetic sites, makes an appearance in Vidarbha in cultural levels dating to the second half of the first millennium BC.[54] However, the dates for the NBPW cover a broad range and the implications of their occurrence are difficult to assess. The probability that a single set of cultural characteristics could be associated with such a long-lived pottery type is minimal. At the most, they aid us in theorizing about possible linkages between the north and the south. The presence of early Buddhism in the region further highlights the establishment of links with the Ganga valley.

Another evidence of such links is the use of the Brahmi script and the Prakrit language in inscriptions and sealings found in Vidarbha, dated between the second/third centuries BC and first/second centuries AD.[55] The earliest indigenous currency are the silver and copper punch-marked coins (which continue into the early centuries AD) followed by uninscribed cast and die-struck coins,[56] and it is possible that some of the coins found in Vidarbha bear evidence of northern influence.[57] It has also been argued that the uninscribed coins reflect the emergence of 'localities' and indicate a network of contact within the Deccan in a period removed from that of the high incidence of punch-marked and uninscribed cast coins in north India alone.[58]

The emergence of local elite (if not of localities)[59] becomes much clearer with the finds of inscribed coins. Before the rise of the Sātavāhanas, the Vidarbha region has yielded coins of the Mitra and Bhadra rulers.[60] The fact that many of the megalithic sites continue right into the early historic period seem to indicate that there was no major disruption of settlement. In fact, the level of direct Mauryan involvement in the region can be questioned. Archaeologically, all we have is the presence in late century BC stratigraphic levels of artefacts showing some similarity to items from the same chronological context in the Ganga valley;[61] the use of Brahmi; the location in Vidarbha of stūpas dating from the late Mauryan period (at Pauni);

and the presence of two questionable Mauryan inscriptions within the region.[62]

Perhaps this early phase can be understood not in terms of the integration of the region within the Mauryan Empire,[63] but in terms of the establishment of linkages with the north (as well as the continuing linkages with the rest of the Deccan), leading to the introduction of new features. A variety of processes led to the changes so apparent in the early historic. At one level, the internal dynamics included the preceding long history of settlement in the region—an agricultural subsistence base, the rise of local elite groups, and so on. At another level, we have the processes that might have been initiated due to external factors. These include the establishment of links with different parts of the subcontinent, the use of NBPW, of a currency system, and of the Brahmi script, as well as the introduction of Buddhism.

The rise of the Sātavāhanas in the early historic Deccan definitely represented the introduction of a new element in the historical development of the region. While Sātavāhana rule is known to have terminated early in third century AD, the period of the emergence of the Sātavāhanas and the span of their rule is still debated and remains unresolved. The precise dating of the rise of the Sātavāhanas is not the subject of this essay. It will suffice to state that the Sātavāhanas emerged only after the so-called Mauryan phase in the Deccan and the emergence of local elite groups.

What is important to this study is the place of Vidarbha in the Sātavāhana Empire. What new features, if any, did the rise of the Sātavāhanas introduce in Vidarbha? What really was their role in Vidarbha? The fact that the Sātavāhanas claimed to have ruled Vidarbha is clear from the reference in Gautamī Balaśrī's donative inscription to the region' being part of the empire of Gautamīputra Sātakarṇi. But what does the archaeological evidence show?

Several sites yield early Sātavāhana coins.[64] However, on the basis of these limited coin finds, the single reference to the region in the Sātavāhana inscriptions and the absence of any royal inscription located in the region, the position of Vidarbha in the Sātavāhana Empire is not clear. The preceding period was probably characterized by the rise of local elite groups, a development perhaps based on the incipient differentiation that was already present in the earlier megalithic phase, and there is evidence that local groups were not completely 'exterminated' or incorporated, but were still present and active as evident from their coin issues found in Sātavāhana levels. Mahārathi coins both precede and overlap with those of the Sātavāhanas in stratigraphical contexts as at Adam.[65] Moreover, Vidarbha might have come under Mahāmeghavāhana[66] rule and Kṣatrapa influence (if not rule).[67] What emerges, therefore, is the possibility that this phase saw the amorphous and diffuse control of the region by a variety of powers. We have the emergence of Vidarbha as a core area of dynastic rule, with a distinct territorial identity, only in the third century AD with the rise of the Vākāṭakas. The changing political affiliations of the region reflect the processes of continuity (of local power groups) and change (that is, the rise of new powers) that are so apparent in the history of the region.

In a move away from focusing on politics or administration, I demonstrate how internal developments and external linkages were formed and played a role in the definition of the region. It is these processes that go into the creation of a historical region, and therein lies the importance of their study, not as isolated factors. There are no clear-cut answers, but it can be suggested that there is a necessity to move away from looking at culture change as either external or internal, autonomous or introduced. This brief survey of cultural developments in Vidarbha, shows that the reality was much more complex. At one level, there is continuity from the Stone Age and the chalcolithic up to the megalithic, and even beyond, into the early historic. Certain cultural elements (like BRW) also continue. On the other hand, the use of iron represents a distinct change in material cultural practices, as does the construction of the megaliths. The point being made here is that there is no linear development of culture from the past to the present. Continuity and change occurred simultaneously, and both need to be considered in any historical explanation. Perhaps long-term history can be conceptualized as a series of parallel processes through time. These multiple trajectories/cultural elements did not simply flow into one another, and did not necessarily have any teleological implication, but at a particular historical moment, particular groups of people drew on a number of different traditions in order to create something new. For instance, in Vidarbha, people drew on the earlier tradition of settlement, on certain cultural elements (BRW) as well as on new technologies (iron) and forms of symbolic commemoration (the megaliths) in order to create a distinctive culture located in a particular time and space. The practice of constructing megaliths might very well have originated elsewhere. I am not against the idea of external influence, but against any explanation based on only one factor, be it external *or* internal.

Interpretation and Reinterpretation

In a sense, the life history of the megaliths came to an end after the early historic, since megaliths were no longer constructed. There was also no later reuse of the megalithic structures, as evidenced by the scarcity of temporally later artefacts in and around the megaliths. We can only speculate whether megalithic practices of commemorating the dead continued in different forms, as represented in stūpas or satī stones, for instance. However, later generations did engage with the megalithic landscape, attributing new meanings to these ancient structures, within an altered contemporary set-up. Megaliths would then have featured as an element of 'mythical history',[68] deriving meaning from its age and obscure origin. For instance, a variety of mythical stories and characters have been associated with the megaliths. At Naikund, the stone circles are considered the final resting place of either an ancient king or a horse.[69] The Madia Gonds of Bhamragarh, district Garhchiroli, still erect megaliths.[70] While their religious and sepulchral practices have been studied, it is difficult to draw any direct parallels with the ancient megalithic culture of Vidarbha. This is in fact related to the argument made previously about how groups at specific points in time draw upon existing and new cultural traditions in order to create something unique. There need not necessarily be any direct links between these past and present communities. Their cultural/historical context and even subsistence patterns need not coincide. To assume that a particular material basis necessarily implies a particular belief system or vice versa is merely a form of determinism.

At another level, the archaeologist and historian too seek to reinterpret the landscape. The archaeologist engages with and interprets the landscape, although the methods of this engagement would differ from those of the people who build and use megaliths. Starting with the early antiquarians who saw the megaliths as druidical monuments, the megaliths have been interpreted in a variety of ways. A crucial issue concerning them was identifying the race of the megalith builders. Therefore, the megalithic landscape, seen from this point of view, represented a particular people. Later, the landscape was incorporated into the toils of a scientific, measurable, and linear time. Through radiocarbon dating and a variety of other scientific tools, the megalithic culture of Vidarbha has been securely dated to between the eighth/seventh centuries BC to the third/fourth centuries BC (Table 4.2).

Therefore, the megaliths are implicated in numerous narratives and conceptions of time. A complex life history of the megaliths emerges where they are linked to the past and the present in numerous ways, some of which have been considered here.

LANDSCAPES OF THE MIND: FROM THE OUTSIDE, LOOKING IN

After looking at some of the constructed landscapes that went into the making of the region, I consider the landscapes of the mind—the ways in which Vidarbha has been conceptualized in texts and inscriptions.[71] While these conceptualizations might not reflect 'reality', they reflect ways of dealing with the landscape, since perceptions are a part of lived historical experience.

Apart from a few references to the Vedic texts (*Ṛg Veda*, *Śatapatha Brāhmaṇa*), the discussion will centre on the epics and the Purāṇas,[72] particularly the *Agni*, *Varāha*, *Śiva*, *Vāyu*, *Matsya*, and *Mārkaṇḍeya Purāṇas*. These and the few non-religious texts (Kālidāsa's *Mālavikāgnimitram*) referred to are mostly located in north India, the perspective on our region, therefore, being one from the 'outside'.

Instead of a purely chronological focus, which would tend to imply that the region of Vidarbha is a given, a well-defined unit through time, my interest is in the *construction* of Vidarbha as a region in these texts and the various characteristics considered crucial to the definition of this constructed region.

Not considered part of the Brahmanical heartland, Vidarbha and Dakṣiṇāpatha[73] find mention in certain Brāhmaṇa texts,[74] and the first description of its location is furnished by the Mahābhārata and the *Harivaṁśa*. While the location of the region within Dakṣiṇāpatha[75] and its broad outlines can be identified, it is not possible to precisely define its limits.

This implicit distancing of the region is further borne out by a possible association between Vidarbha and the Daṇḍakāraṇya forest, probably comprising all the forests from Bundelkhand to the Krishna river.[76] While this region has generally been viewed, especially in the epics, in terms of a lack of civilization, it is not very clear whether Vidarbha was considered an essential part of this negatively defined area.[77] Moreover, there is a certain acceptance and incorporation of the region in the textual tradition. This discourse of acceptance can be dismembered to reveal four major themes that went into the definition of the region.

The Purāṇas enumerate Vidarbha as one of the *janapada*s of the Deccan, and a certain importance seems to have been given to this region as in the *Nalopākhyāna*, the king of Vidarbha is styled lord of Dakṣiṇāṭya.[78] Kālidāsa in the *Mālavikāgnimitram* tells us that the Śuṅga dynasty was founded along with the establishment of a new kingdom at Vidarbha.[79] Not only did the term Vidarbha denote a territory, but also a people, perhaps a tribal unit.[80] A prince of Vidarbha named Rukmi is not allowed to take part in the battle of Kurukṣetra, but his people figure in the 'Battle Books' as do other tribes like the Kaliṅgas, Mekalas, and Traipuras, coming under the general designation of *Dakṣiṇāṭyas*.[81] Each janapada and its people were often depicted as possessing distinct customs and languages, and the *Agni Purāṇa* lists Vaidarbhī as one of the four kinds of diction.[82]

The people, or possibly the ruling clan, of Vidarbha have also been identified with the Bhojas. The Bhojas were one of the five branches of the Haihayas, who were in turn a branch of the Yādavas/Yadu *vaṁśa*.[83] This name seems to have had more than one application and it is difficult to isolate the region of their residence,[84] but as early as the time of the later Vedic texts, the Bhojas have been associated with the southern region.[85]

Vidarbha also plays a central role in important mythical episodes. Damayantī, the wife of Nala, was born to Bhīṣmaka, king of Vidarbha. Rukminī too was a daughter of a king of Vidarbha, and it is from here that she was carried away by Kṛṣṇa.[86]

Finally, the texts also reflect a more detailed and specific knowledge of the region. This comes across in the references to some of the cities located in Vidarbha. Of the cities traditionally associated with Vidarbha, the earliest, according to the testimony of the *Harivaṁśa* was Vidarbhapura on the southern slopes of the Vindhyas;[87] Kundina (identified with Kaundinyapura) is mentioned as the metropolis (*Vidarbha-nagarī*) in the Mahābhārata; and Bhojakaṭa, which finds mention in the epics, as well as in early Brahmi inscriptions from Bharhut has been identified with Bhatkuli in the Amaravati district.[88] Other places referred to include Padmapura (Bhavabhūti's *Mālatimādhavam*, *Padma Purāṇa*) and Vatsagulma (Rājaśekhara's *Kāvyamīmāṁsā*).[89]

TEXT AND ARCHAEOLOGY

How can these images be correlated to what we have discussed regarding the archaeological landscapes of the region? Can and need they be so? The earliest concern in Indian archaeology has been the identification of ancient places mentioned in literature. Several sites in Vidarbha (Bhojakaṭa, Kauṇḍinyapura, Vatsagulma, and Pravarapura) have been sought to be identified both by archaeological exploration and by drawing linguistic parallels with modern places having similar names.

Such attempts at direct correlation have proved to be valuable, and several ancient sites have been so identified.[90] However, it needs to be noted that such text–archaeology correlation may not always produce conclusive answers. In some cases, there is a tendency to let the textual tradition direct archaeological approaches. The excavations at Paunar, for instance, were undertaken in order to ascertain if the site was indeed ancient Pravarapura of the land grants.[91] No such evidence was forthcoming. It could be suggested that there is a need to move away from identifying and excavating important sites referred to in texts and to look at region-wide surveys that might aid us in identifying the dynamics of historical development.[92]

Apart from attempting such one-to-one correlations, the coming together of text and archaeology is also seen in attempts to discuss the political history of the region. Important studies have been conducted to correlate archaeological, epigraphic, and textual sources to work out a feasible chronology for the Sātavāhana kings.[93] However, the issue remains unresolved. One of the main reasons for the lack of consensus may lie in the difficulty of correlating divergent traditions. Different Purāṇas provide conflicting statements regarding the number of kings and the period of their rule. Palaeographic evidence too has been interpreted differently by different scholars and at best can only help in fixing a broad chronological framework. Archaeological evidence also produces no exact dates and yet at the same time provides interesting insights into chronology.[94]

The problem of correlation seems to be a central one in historical analysis. Perhaps the value of using both text and archaeology does not lie in providing exact chronologies, but in providing insights into broad processes of historical development. For example, the *Mālavikāgnimitram* can be considered of value not because it provides the name of the post-Mauryan ruler of Vidarbha, but because it indicates the possibility of northern influence in the region, which is also borne out by archaeological evidence. And great caution needs to be exercised while attempting this sort of correlation. There can be no easy equation of archaeological cultures and textual lineages. Pottery traditions, for instance (and especially not the BRW, as we have seen), cannot be considered homogeneous or as representing any one 'people'/cultural tradition. The argument that BRW, associated with the Yādava lineage, moved via the west coast and into Vidarbha is not borne out by archaeological evidence, which shows an early (megalithic) origin for it. Nevertheless, it remains interesting that the Purāṇas seem to show a spread of people into Vidarbha. Specifically, the five groups of the Haihayas (a branch of the Yādavas) are said to have moved along the Narmada into central India.[95] Vidarbha, the son of a Yādava prince, is said to have established a kingdom of the same name. If this tradition is taken to record an early pattern of movement, the difficulty lies in associating this movement with that of archaeological artefacts—in identifying the material traits of specific (textually known) groups.

While the correlation between text and archaeology has led to some interesting insights in the case of early historic India, such correlation is problematic when it comes to considering pre- and proto-historic cultures, characterized by the absence of contemporaneous texts. For instance, in the case of the megaliths of Vidarbha, the main source of information remains archaeological data. Whether later texts could provide information on this period remains open to question.[96]

The need to highlight the value of *both* kinds of sources, text and archaeology, has been amply discussed. However, we cannot simplistically conflate the textual and the archaeological tradition, while having to use both in order to produce a well-rounded historical analysis. Do we, then, need to correlate the two? Perhaps their value lies in the fact that they provide different perspectives (which might be contradictory or which might at times overlap) on the same historical process(es). The very fascination of the study of history, lies in the diversity of patterns and perspectives that one has to deal with.

The focus of this essay was to draw the contours of Vidarbha in its varied spatial *and* temporal complexity, recognizing that the delineation of the region could vary depending on the variables or sources chosen to define it. Moreover, the region also presents a different picture at different points in time. So how then was one to study this multifaceted and multi-layered entity that was the region of Vidarbha?

The conceptual tool of the 'landscape' provided a broad framework within which this variability could be studied. The value of this approach lay in that it allowed for the consideration not only of a variety of sources, but of both the material and the mental, without creating any artificial dichotomy. I sought to understand the region of Vidarbha by studying some of the numerous landscapes of which it was constituted through time: the mortuary landscape of the megaliths, the changing landscapes in the early historic, and textual conceptualizations of the land and the people.

The main focus of this essay has been on discussing the historical development of Vidarbha. It traced the patterns of continuity and change that linked each landscape to the ones before and after it. Certain lines of enquiry have run through the entire discussion, and the patterns identified reveal that certain processes played a role in the delineation of the region. This is not to suggest that they structured the region, but these processes, put together in a unique configuration, formed the distinct personality of the region.

The first of these processes is the geographical. As seen, Vidarbha is a distinct geographic unit comprising the Wardha–Wainganga valleys and the hills surrounding them, and this played a role in the creation of a separate identity. The second process that was considered is the dynamic of various social, economic, and political groups as they interacted with each other and with their environment. The landscape was created due to people living within, experiencing, altering, and in turn being influenced by their surroundings. Therefore, I studied the web of social, political, and economic ties and relationships that were embedded in these landscapes. Last, religion and ideology, and the associated constructed and ideational landscapes, also lent definition to the region through time.

In conclusion, this essay represents a preliminary attempt to consider the historical development of the region of Vidarbha from a holistic perspective—through a study of the various landscapes that embodied it, drawing upon different approaches and examining differing domains of human action, experience, and thought. The landscape provides a meaningful context for the joint consideration of different classes of evidence, drawing from different methodological/theoretical traditions. While we will get no easy answers nor a complete picture, we can infer several contours of the past and enrich our study of specific historic contexts and longer historical processes.

NOTES

1. J.E. Schwartzberg, 'Prologmena to the Study of South Asia in Regions and Regionalism', in R.I. Crane (ed.), *Regions and Regionalism in South Asian Studies,* Durham, NC: Duke University, 1966, p. 93.
2. As pointed out by Crumley and Knapp (Wendy Ashmore and B.A. Knapp, *Archaeologies of Landscape: Contemporary Perspectives,* Oxford, MA: Blackwell, 1999. pp. 3–5), several fields besides archaeology have grappled with landscape issues. For instance, American geographer Carl Sauer formulated the concept of a 'cultural' landscape as fashioned from the 'natural' one. Human geographers now seek meaning in the landscape as a 'repository of human striving', and post-modernist perspectives visualize the landscape as a 'cultural image' whose verbal or written representations provide images, or 'texts' of its 'reading'. Similarly, for social and cultural anthropologists, the landscape is a 'process' yielding a foregrounded, everyday human life from a background range of potential social existence.
3. B.K. Roberts, 'Landscape Archaeology', in J.M. Wagstaff (ed.), *Landscape and Culture: Geographical and Archaeological Perspectives,* Oxford: Basil Blackwell, 1987, p. 79.
4. The data on the megaliths have been gathered from various short reports in *Indian Archaeology: A Review* (henceforth *IAR*) volumes and other journals (*Man and Environment,* etc.), and longer discussions in published excavation reports. This data was then tabulated in my MPhil Thesis, 'Archaeology and Text: A Study of the Landscape in Vidarbha', completed in 2004 as part of the requirements for that course at the Jawaharlal Nehru University, New Delhi. For this article I only include the final results, as given in Appendix 4.1. The burial sites that have been excavated are: Junapani (*IAR* 1961–2), Naikund (S.B. Deo and A.P. Jamkhedkar, *Excavations at Naikund,* Bombay: Department of Archaeology and Museums, Govt. of Maharashtra, 1982), Takalghat-Khapa (S.B. Deo, *Excavations at Takalghat and Khapa,* Nagpur: Nagpur Vidyapeeth Mudranalaya, 1970), Gangapur (ibid.), Raipur-Hingna (G.B. Deglurkar and Gouri P. Lad, *Megalithic Raipur,* Pune: Deccan College, 1992), Mahurjhari (S.B. Deo, *Mahurjhari Excavation,* Nagpur: Nagpur Vidyapeeth Mudranalaya, 1973), Khairwada (*IAR* 1981–2), Boregaon (*IAR* 1980–1), Bhagimohari (*IAR* 1982–3, 1983–4, 1992–3), Bhawar (*IAR* 1987–8, 1992–3), and Pachkeri.
5. There are several instances of animal bones with cut marks on them. Once again, arguments in this section are based on data tabulated in Suvrathan, 'Archaeology and Text', Tables III and IV.
6. It is difficult to attribute, without the possibility of any doubt, these settlements to the megalithic people. This is largely because there are no associated burials, which are considered the most important characteristic of the megalithic period. However, at Kaundinyapur, Arni, and Paunar there is the occurrence of adzes and other iron objects that are very similar to types found at firmly identified

megalithic sites (S.B. Deo, 'The Megaliths: Their Culture, Ecology, Economy and Technology', in S.B. Deo and K. Paddayya (eds), *Recent Advances in Indian Archaeology*, Poona: Deccan College, 1985, p. 94). This similarity is also found between the pottery types at the megalithic levels of these sites and those found at the other burial cum habitation sites. For instance, at Kaundinyapur, Black and Red Ware was found along with etched beads with megalithic decorative patterns (S.B. Deo, 'A New Painted Pottery from Vidarbha', *Purattatva*, vol. 1, 1967–8, p. 36).

7. Deo and Jamkhedkar, *Excavations at Naikund*, p. 11.
8. The sizes of these sites are: Khairwada (107,000 m^2), Bhagimahari (82,000 m^2), Naikund (100,000 m^2), and Takalghat (22,500 m^2).
9. Bhagimahari is located in a region with black-brown soil on trap. Borgaon, Mahurjhari, and Junapani are located on ferriginous loamy soil, and Raipur, Kamptee, and Takalghat on dark clay soil on alluvium (U.S.S. Moorti, *Megalithic Cultures of South India: Socio-economic Perspectives,* Varanasi: Ganga Kaveri Publishing House, 1994, pp. 21–2).
10. Ibid., pp. 16–17.
11. Naikund, for instance, is located close to a manganeferrous belt, and an exploration of the area around the site has revealed that iron ore was located in the form of rubble in a nala 1 km south-east of the smelting site (Deo and Jamkhedkar, *Excavations at Naikund*, pp. 52–6). Raipur is located near a source of constructional material for the megaliths—deep fissures in an extensive pebbly vein contained beds of Deccan trap, which represented an easy source of raw material (Deglurkar and Lad, *Megalithic Raipur*, pp. 2–3).
12. S.R. Walimbe, 'Human Skeletal Remains from Megalithic Vidarbha', *Purattatva*, vol. 18, 1987–8, p. 11.
13. *IAR*, 1982–3, p. 62; 1980–1, p. 40.
14. An interesting experiment in megalith building was conducted at Bhagimahari. A megalith of 13.5 m diameter was constructed and it was noted that the whole enterprise took 130 to 150 man-days. The expenditure of this much time and labour, it is argued, suggests that the megalithic community was agricultural and not nomadic (R.K. Mohanty and S.R. Walimbe, 'An Investigation into the Mortuary Practices of Vidarbha Megalithic Cultures', in C. Margabandhu and K.S. Ramachandran (eds), *Spectrum of Indian Culture*, Delhi: Agam Kala Prakashan, 1996, pp. 136-49).
15. Most of the identifiable skeletal remains in Vidarbha are of adults (13), but young individuals (four) and aged people (one) are also represented (Suvrathan, 'Archaeology and Text', Table III). The fragmentary nature of most of the remains makes any generalization difficult.
16. There are, of course, graves which have skeletal remains, but are relatively poor in artefacts, for example, Megalith 6 at Khapa.
17. For example, the full length burials at Mahurjhari are not in the larger circles.
18. Moorti (*Megalithic Cultures*) classified the artefacts found in megaliths into technomic (those that deal with the physical environment), ideotechnic (those that reflect/symbolize ideology), and sociotechnic (those that signify social status).

19. In this context, it can be noted that Tim Ingold makes a very interesting argument emphasizing the temporality of the landscape. He argues that the landscape may be understood by way of a 'dwelling perspective' (denoted by the term 'taskscape'), considering the way in which the world is constituted by the totality of organism (human and animal)—environment relations. Central to such a consideration would be the element of time, which is then seen as an essential component of the landscape (Tim Ingold, 'The Temporality of the Landscape', *World Archaeology*, 25 (2), 1993, pp. 152–74).
20. A clarification is required here. I do not subscribe to a Braudelian view where the long term is considered to structure historical development. This term as used here does not refer to elements like climate or geography that have been considered to influence history over the long term, but is used merely to indicate that processes of historical development will be considered over a long span of time.
21. Primary burials, with the skeleton(s) placed in an extended position have been reported from Mahurjhari, Megaliths 3, 6, 8, 9 in Locality III (Deo, *Mahurjhari Excavation*, pp. 15–18).
22. Most sites provide some evidence about the post crematory nature of the interred human remains. Not only are some bones charred (Khapa, Megalith 9; Gangapur, Megalith 1), but some even bear cut marks (Mahurjhari, Locality II, Megalith 1). All data taken from my MPhil Thesis, 'Archaeology and Text', Tables III and IV, pp. 72–86.
23. The stratigraphy at Megalith 3 at Gangapur points to the possibility of the reopening of an earlier burial containing brown clay and pebbles, the redepositing of black clay and pebbles, and the capping of this second deposit with pebbles (Deo, *Excavations at Takalghat and Khapa*, 12).
24. Deglurkar and Lad, *Megalithic Raipur*, p. 8.
25. For example, Megalith 3 at Junapani had smaller boulders retaining the rubble packing along the fall of the clay heap (*IAR*, 1961–2).
26. Deglurkar and Lad, *Megalithic Raipur*, p. 3.
27. Chris Gosden and Gary Lock, 'Prehistoric Histories', *World Archaeology*, 30 (1), 1998, pp. 2–12; Richard Bradley, *The Past in Prehistoric Societies*, London and New York: Routledge, 2002.
28. That is, the main device employed through which to recount history (especially in non-literate societies) is that of genealogy, in which relations of blood and kin are specified and become the basis for recounting stories about these known individuals. One could speculate that the Vidarbha megaliths played a similar role (Gosden and Lock, 'Prehistoric Histories', p. 5).
29. Gosden and Lock, 'Prehistoric Histories'.
30. R.K. Mohanty and V. Selvakumar, 'The Archaeology of the Megaliths in India: 1947–1997', in S. Settar and R. Korisettar (eds), *Indian Archaeology in Retrospect*, vol. I, Delhi: Indian Council of Historical Research and Manohar, 2001, pp. 313–481; S.B. Deo, 'Ancient History of Maharashtra', in A.K. Bhagwat (ed.), *Maharashtra: A Profile*, Kolhapur: Visnu Sakharam Khandekar Amrit Mahotsav Satkar Samiti, 1977, pp. 15–64.
31. From Suvrathan, 'Archaeology and Text', Appendix I, pp. 142–51. This

impression may be a factor of the surveys that seem to have been mainly conducted in river valleys. See also Appendix 4.1 in this essay.

32. M.K. Dhavalikar, 'Development and Decline of the Deccan Chalcolithic', in D.P. Agrawal and A. Ghosh (eds), *Radiocarbon and Indian Archaeology*, Bombay: Tata Institute of Fundamental Research, 1973, p. 138.
33. The excavations at Adam yielded a fivefold cultural sequence, the first (Period I), represented by a microlithic industry and dated between the third and second millennium BC. Period II has been termed the 'Vidarbha Chalcolithic', and Period III was characterized by the occurrence of iron (dated to between 1000 and 500 BC); Period IV has been termed Mauryan and post-Mauryan, and Period V has been attributed to the Sātavāhanas, and extended right up to the Maratha age (*IAR*, 1988–9). Other chalcolithic sites in Vidarbha include Marda (*IAR*, 1959–60, 1963–4) (Chanda district), and Parsoda (*IAR*, 1987–8) (district Amaravati). See Appendix 4.1.
34. There were six pottery types: Red Ware with chocolate slip and painted in white; Red Ware with red slip painted in white; Red Ware with red slip and painted in black; unslipped Red Ware with black painting; unslipped Red Ware with white painting; and Black and Red Ware with red slip and painted in black (*IAR*, 1988–9, pp. 50–3).
35. At Tharsa, for instance, the limited excavation conducted revealed that Period I (subdivided into four layers) could be attributed to the megalithic culture, but it also betrayed some affinities with the chalcolithic. The house plans with associated circular bin platforms found at this site are among the features of the chalcolithic as are the presence of urn burials (*IAR*, 1985–6, pp. 58–60; *IAR*, 1989–90, pp. 66–8). Similarly, at the habitation area at Pachkeri there is a continuous sequence of cultures from the mesolithic to the megalithic, and right up to the medieval (*IAR*, 1992–3, pp. 62–7), and Bhawar shows an iron-free horizon preceding the megalithic. Habitation at this latter site continued up to the Sātavāhana period.
36. Mohanty and Selvakumar, 'The Archaeology of the Megaliths in India', p. 330.
37. *IAR*, 1991–2; *IAR*, 1992–3, p. 61. At Bhawar there was no marked change between the ceramic industry of the chalcolithic and that of the Iron Age. The demarcation between the levels was made because of the occurrence of iron artefacts. However, as at Adam (see earlier), some chalcolithic sites in Vidarbha were characterized by distinctive wares, apart from the occurrence of BRW.
38. At Takalghat, for instance, the ceramic assemblage included painted Black on Red Ware, Black Burnished Ware, Black and Red Ware, Tan Slipped Ware, Matt Red Ware, Coarse Red Ware and Micaceous Red Ware (Deo, *Excavations at Takalghat and Khapa*, pp. 15–40).
39. Even in Vidarbha, there are habitation sites with iron artefacts but no megaliths, for example, Adam. Are these the habitation sites corresponding to the burial ones?
40. In the chalcolithic context at Tuljapur Garhi, there was a secondary burial of a child in a small oval shallow pit. The bones were arranged in an east-west orientation and were found in association with carnelian beads and a bowl of

the ubiquitous BRW (*IAR*, 1984–5, p. 50). In early historic Adam were found a variety of different types of burials including pot burials, terracotta ring burials, and pit burials (*IAR*, 1988–9, p. 59).

41. Both the urns (Red Ware) were buried in pits dug into the natural soil and contained post-excarnated skeletal remains of infants. In one of the urns, the remains were kept in a BRW bowl along with a thin copper ring. One of the urns was kept horizontally and the other vertically, and they were covered by a thick Red Ware basin and a Black Slipped Ware dish, respectively (*IAR*, 1985–6, pp. 59–60).
42. This ware is dated to the fifth and fourth centuries BC in the north, but is found in a later stratigraphical context in the Deccan. A few other important early historic ceramics that are found after the decline of the NBPW in north India in about the second century BC include the Śuṅga-Kuṣāṇa assemblage (located in north India), Red Polished Ware (Gujarat, northern Deccan), Rang Mahal Ware (Rajasthan), and the Russet Coated Painted Ware in the lower Deccan (A. Ghosh [ed.], *An Encyclopaedia of Indian Archaeology*, vol. I, New Delhi: Munshiram Manoharlal, 1989, pp. 131–2).
43. Perhaps it would be better to say that there was extensive settlement in this period. As seen (Appendix 4.2), there are several megalithic burial sites, and it is increasingly being realized that the lack of megalithic habitation sites have been overstated. All data from Suvrathan, 'Archaeology and Text', Appendix III, pp. 155–7.
44. Once again, the urban centres are difficult to identify in the light of the absence of extensive archaeological surveys and excavations. The presence of urban centres in Vidarbha has been noted in the early textual tradition. Important cities referred to in this context include Kaundinyapura and Bhojakatapura.
45. Fortifications dating possibly from Sātavāhana times have been identified at Adam and Arni (*IAR*, 1984–5; *IAR*, 1989–90; *IAR*, 1992–3). Vākāṭaka fortifications have been found at Ramtek and Mansar (*IAR*, 1989–90).
46. The excavation at Paunar reflects the cultivation of sorghum and rice. It can be noted that there seems to have been an increase in the cultivation of rice in the Vākāṭaka period, as is seen by the larger amounts of rice grains (as compared to sorghum) in the Vākāṭaka levels. The implication of this is not clear (Vishnu Mittre and H.P. Gupta, 'Ancient Plant Economy at Paunar, Maharashtra', in S.B. Deo and M.K. Dhavalikar (eds), *Paunar Excavation (1967)*, Nagpur: Nagpur Vidyapeeth Mudranalaya, 1968, pp. 128–31). The Bhandara region is still known as the rice bowl of Maharashtra.
47. The sites include Pauni, Paunar, Shirkanda, Ramtek, Nagardhan, Adam, Pachkeri, and Kuhi.
48. A wide range of metal, stone, and other finely crafted artefacts were found at sites like Adam, Kaundinyapur, and Paunar.
49. I.K. Sarma, 'New Evidences on the Early Sātavāhana Coinage, Culture and Commerce', in A.M. Shastri (ed.), *The Age of the Satavahanas*, vol. II, New Delhi: Aryan Books International, 1999, p. 342.
50. This can be deduced from the finds of NBP at various sites, the similarity of certain artefacts with those found in north India and the numerous finds

of coins and seals (including one with the legend '*Asaka Janapada*' from Adam).

51. This is borne out by the occurrence of Red Polished Ware and Roman coins from Adam (*IAR*, 1991–2), clay bullae from Kholapur, Amaravati district (Deo and Dhavalikar, *Paunar Excavation,* p. 3), and amphorae sherds and Red Polished Ware from Paunar (Deo and Dhavalikar, *Paunar Excavation,* pp. 3, 41, 48, 115). The issue of RPW is a vexed one. This ware has been found along the routes of the so-called Roman trade, and it has been argued that it is a foreign import. This view has been questioned.
52. Erdosy's work (*Urbanisation in Early Historic India.* BAR International Series 430, Oxford: BAR International, 1988) on the Ganga valley sees a crucial indicator for the rise of urban centres in the development of a hierarchy of settlement types on a regional scale and, therefore, regards the socio-cultural transformations accompanying the rise of cities as the central issue.
53. The western hill ranges near Ramtek are important for their mineral deposits. The main Wainganga valley is a fertile belt for agriculture. Places like Bhandara and Pauni are fording points across the Wainganaga (C.D. Deshpande, *Geography of Maharashtra*, New Delhi: National Book Trust, 1971, pp. 204–5). It has also been argued that the establishment of favourable climatic conditions in the latter half of the first millennium BC, as inferred from data reflecting an increase in the Nile floods (and, therefore, monsoons in India), was a causative factor in the period of prosperity and cultural efflorescence under the Sātavāhanas (M.K. Dhavalikar, 'The Satavahana Epoch: An Ecological Perspective', in A.M. Shastri (ed.), *The Age of the Satavahanas*, vol. I, New Delhi: Aryan Books International, 1999. pp. 102–14).
54. Sites like Kaundinyapura, Paunar, and Pauni have reported some NBP sherds. A variety of Red Wares (including the Red Painted Ware) characterize the next phase of the early historic, overlapping with the NBP and continuing beyond it.
55. For instance, votive inscriptions found at the stupa site at Pauni range between the late Mauryan/early Sātavāhana period (third to second centuries BC), up to the early centuries AD (S.B. Deo and J.P. Joshi, *Pauni Excavation: 1969–70*, Nagpur: Nagpur Vidyapeeth Mudranalaya, 1972, pp. 37–43). Similar early Prakrit inscriptions were found at Chandala (*IAR*, 1970–1, p. 24) and Mansar (J.P. Joshi and A.K. Sharma. 'Excavations at Mansar, Distt Nagpur, Maharashtra—1997–2000', *Puratattva*, vol. 30, 1999–2000, p. 130), and seals and coins with Brahmi characters at Adam (*IAR*, 1990–91: 50), Kaundinyapur (*IAR*, 1961–2, p. 29), and Paunar (Deo and Dhavalikar, *Paunar Excavation* [1967], p. 15).
56. A.M. Shastri, 'Closing Phase of the Satavahana Power and Allied Issues', in A.M. Shastri, *Early History of the Deccan: Problems and Perspectives*, Delhi: Sundeep Prakashan, 1987, p. 15.
57. Several hoards of silver punch-marked coins are reported from Vidarbha. They have been found at Bhandara, Malegaon, Mangrul, Umrer, and Nevari (Deo and Joshi, *Pauni Excavation*, p. 97). Copper punch-marked coins are rarer, but have been found at Kaundinyapur, Pauni (Deo and Joshi, *Pauni Excavation*), and

Adam (*IAR*, 1990–1, p. 49). Whether the practice of using coins in exchange originated in the north, and spread to the rest of the subcontinent from there is an issue that we are not getting into. Nevertheless, many similarities to northern issues have been noted. For instance, we have the find of an uninscribed cast copper coin at Pauni which is identical with coins found at sites like Kanauj and Hastinapur (Deo and Joshi, *Pauni Excavation*, p. 32). Similarly, the cast coins of Taxila have been found at Adam (*IAR*, 1991–2, p. 68).

At the same time, it can be noted that some coins are not identical to northern issues, implying that all coins need not have been carried into Vidarbha directly from the north. For example, a new variety of punch-marked copper coins at Pauni contains five symbols not known to occur together elsewhere in the north (ibid., p. 97).

58. B.D. Chattopadhyaya, *Studying Early India: Archaeology, Texts and Historical Issues*, Delhi: Permanent Black, 2003, p. 42.
59. At least in the case of Vidarbha it is not very clear whether the distribution of these coins reflect the existence of distinct localities with a well-defined boundary. At most they seem to show the rise of local elite groups (H.P. Ray, 'Early Historical Settlement in the Deccan: An Ecological Perspective', *Man and Environment*, 14 (1), 1989, pp. 103–8). It can also be noted here that a hoard of uninscribed sealings found at Adam bear an hourglass motif (*bhadrapeetha*) and have been identified as representing the 'token of Adam' (A. Nath, 'Satavahana Antiquities from Adam', in Shastri (ed.), *The Age of the Satavahanas*, vol. II, p. 462). H.P. Ray notes the importance of the *nigama* in the early historic Kṛṣṇa valley.
60. There were at least three Mitra rulers (Bhūmimitra, Kanhamitra, and Sūryamitra) and four Bhadra kings (Dhamabhadra, Dharmabhadra, Sarvabhadra, and Satyabhadra) who ruled almost contemporaneously in the pre-Sātavāhana period. There is a unique coin of Sūryamitra restruck by Sātakarṇi that establishes that the Mitra kings at least ruled prior to the Sātavāhanas (A.M. Shastri, 'Puranas on the Satavahanas: An Archaeological-Historical Perspective', in Shastri (ed.), *The Age of the Satavahanas*, vol. I, p. 15). Mitra and Bhadra coins have been reported from pre-Sātavāhana levels at Adam. The coin yielding strata belonged to Period V, dated to *c.* 150 BC to AD 250 (*IAR*, 1989–90, p. 67; *IAR*, 1991–2, p. 63). Similar coins have also been reported from Kaundinyapura.
61. For instance, Nath ('Satavahana Antiquities from Adam') notes the occurrence of stone querns with a typical Mauryan polish in the pre-Sātavāhana levels at Adam.
62. One is a fragmentary inscription (on the same slab of which is a later Vākāṭaka inscription) recording the command of some lord (Sami) prohibiting the capture and slaughter (of animals?) (V.V. Mirashi, *Corpus Inscriptionum Indicarum: Inscriptions of the Vakatakas*, vol. V, Ootacamund: Archaeological Survey of India, 1963. pp.1–2). The second is supposedly a copy of the Bairat stone slab inscription, found (and since untraceable) near the Ghuggus in Chandrapur (A.M. Shastri, 'A Lost (?) Asokan Edict from Vidarbha', *Puratattva*, vol. 28, 1997–8. pp. 55–7).

63. It has been suggested that the interests of the Mauryan state were of an economic nature, that is, in the exploitation of local resources, and not in territorial annexation and control. Seneviratne has suggested that the Mauryan state provided the functional apparatus and an external stimulus to the already existing megalithic societies. This would then bring us back to a consideration of the internal dynamics of change in Vidarbha. S. Seneviratne, *The Mauryan State in The Early State*, edited by H.J.M. Claasen and P. Skalnik, The Hague: Mouton, 1978, pp. 381–402. See also his 'Kalinga and Andhra: The Process of Secondary State Formation in Early India', *The Indian Historical Review*, 7(1–2), 1981, pp. 54–69.
64. Two potin coins attributed to Sātakarṇi I on typological grounds have been reported from Pauni, one of which is a surface find, while the other was recovered in a stratigraphical context. The latter coin contains the Brahmi legend '*Rāṁño-Siri-Sātakaṁni-sa*', probably referring either to Sātakarṇi I or to Sātakarṇi II, both early Sātavāhana kings (Deo and Joshi, *Pauni Excavation*, pp. 99–100). A number of Sātakarṇi I coins of the Pauni type have been found at the lower Sātavāhana levels at Adam (Nath, 'Satavahana Antiquities from Adam', p. 461). The elephant type coins of King Sātavāhana from Akola and Paunar and four copper coins from Kaundinyapura are also significant examples of early Sātavāhana coins. These latter coins are a copper coin with the legend '*Satisa*' (Sakti Sri), a Lakṣmī type, and two more attributed to Sātakarṇi II (I.K. Sarma, *Coinage of the Satavahana Empire,* Delhi: Agam Kala Prakashan, 1980, p. 38). Coins of the later Sātavāhana kings have been found in hoards at Chanda and Tarhala (Sarma, *Coinage of the Satavahana Empire,* pp. 37–8). In fact, it has been argued that with the decline of the imperial line of the Sātavāhanas after Pulumāvi IV, a subsidiary branch of the family ruled over Vidarbha even after their sway had come to an end in the other parts of the empire. This has been argued by A.M. Shastri ('Closing Phase of the Satavahana Power', pp. 38–44) on the basis of recent coin finds of Kumbha Sātakarṇi, Karṇa Sātakarṇi, and Śaka Sātakarṇi, three kings who are not mentioned in the Purāṇas. It can be noted here that the gap between the Sātavāhanas and the Vākāṭakas was thought to have been filled by the rule of the Muṇḍa-Putra chiefs.
65. *IAR*, 1989–90, pp. 61–8. Also found at this site were terracotta sealings of Sālankāyaṇa and Mahāsenāpati. It is interesting to note that these two groups are referred to in the Sātavāhana inscriptions and there are indications that there were matrimonial relations between them and the Sātavāhanas.
66. Khāravela's Hathigumpha inscription records that without thinking about Sātakarṇi, he sent an army to Kanhabemna (identified with a tributary of the Wainganga, past Takalghat and Khapa) and terrorized the city of the Musikas. In his fourth regnal year, he caused the Rathikas and Bhojakas (held to inhabit the Vidarbha region) to pay obeisance (*Epigraphia Indica*, vol. XX, p. 79). Moreover, it can be noted that Mahāmeghavāhana (the dynasty of Khāravela) coins and inscriptions have been found in the Andhra region during the reign of the Sātavāhanas (S.J. Mangalam, 'Coins of the Feudatories and Contemporaries of the Satavahanas', in Shastri (ed.), *The Age of the Satavahanas*, p. 371).

67. Several Kṣatrapa coins have been found at sites in Vidarbha, for example, at Pauni, Adam, and Paunar. At Pauni was found a *chāyā stambha* of Mahākṣatrapa Rupiamma. In the early centuries of the Christian Era there was a temporary collapse of Sātavāhana power due to the rising importance of the Kṣatrapa families of Scythian origin in the western part of the country. The Kṣaharāta family of Nahapāṇa is said to have ousted the Sātavāhanas from the western regions. However, Gautamīputra seems to have ousted the Śakas and won back large parts of his empire, including Vidarbha (as mentioned in the Nasik cave inscription of Queen Balaśrī). Several coins of Nahapāṇa restruck by Gautamīputra have also been found. The Sātavāhanas continued to be threatened by these western rulers. The Kardamakas under Rudradāman seem to have defeated the Sātavāhanas at least twice, but refrained from annihilating him due to a marriage alliance between the two families. A coin of Rudradāman I has been found at Arambha (*IAR*, 1991–2, p. 73).
68. Gosden and Lock, 'Prehistoric Histories', p. 5. Myths have been opposed to history as fact. However, myths too represent a way of conceptualizing and dealing with the past. From this perspective, they are involved in the creation of 'history'.
69. K.P. Rao, *Deccan Megaliths*, Delhi: Sundeep Prakashan, 1988, p. 8. There are a variety of other myths connected with the megaliths. Some of the more popular ones link them to the Pāṇḍavas, or to an ancient race who built these 'stone houses' in order to escape the wrath of the gods, etc.
70. This group, whose subsistence economy is based on cultivation as well as hunting, fishing, and the gathering of forest produce, erect a variety of sepulchral monuments including menhirs, circle, and dolmens (Anuja Geetali, 'Living Megalithic Practices Amongst the Madia Gonds of Bhamragad, Dist Gadchiroli, Maharashtra', *Purattatva,* vol. 32, 2001–2, p. 92; S.S. Kulkarni, 'Megalithic Culture of the Madias of Maharashtra', *Man and Environment*, 27 (2), pp. 107–11, 2002).
71. However, this does not necessarily mean that texts only provide information on ideas or perceptions/'landscapes of the mind', and archaeology on material reality. We can derive thoughts from a study of archaeological landscapes and discuss the material aspects of historical process through an analysis of texts.
72. The epics refer to events that took place during the early part of the first millennium BC. However, the versions that survive date to the first half of the first millennium AD and have seen several alterations over the centuries. The Purāṇas were compiled between 500 BC and AD 500.
73. D.C. Sircar, *Studies in the Geography of Ancient and Medieval India*, New Delhi: Motilal Banarsidass, 1971, p. 29.
74. The *Aitareya Brāhmaṇa* mentions the *dakṣiṇa diś*, southern region, beyond the Kuru-Pañcāla country, that is, beyond the Chambal. The Vidarbhas are also referred to and seem to be associated with the region south of the Vindhyas. It is likely that initially, in the Vedic texts, the term 'Vidarbha' referred to a people or tribe, but they were so much associated with a particular region that land and people became synonymous. The country in question is, in the *Jaiminīya*

Brāhmaṇa, noted for its dogs, which were even capable of killing tigers (M.R. Singh, *Geographical Data in the Early Puranas: A Critical Study*, Calcutta: Punthi Pustak, 1972, pp. 43–4; S.M. Ali, *The Geography of the Puranas*, 1966, New Delhi: People's Publishing House, 1983, p. 20; G. Yazdani, *The Early History of the Deccan,* New Delhi: Oriental Books, 1982, pp. 14–15).

75. According to the Purāṇas, the people of Vidarbha were the dwellers of the Deccan (*Dakṣiṇāpathavasinah*) (F.E. Pargiter trans. and annotated), *The Markandeya Purāṇa* (Bibliotheca Indica: A Collection of Oriental Works published by the Asiatic Society of Bengal), Varanasi: Indological Book House, 1969, p. 335). The territory is placed on the northern fringe of Dakṣiṇāpatha in the *Nalopākhyāna* (Yazdani, *The Early History of the Deccan*, p. 24).
76. B.C. Law, *Historical Geography of Ancient India*, New Delhi: Oriental Books, 1984, p. 41.
77. In certain sections of the Rāmayāṇa and the Purāṇas, the Vidarbha is considered to be distinct from Daṇḍakāraṇya/ the region called Daṇḍaka. In the Rāmayāṇa, Sugrīva directs the monkeys to go to the Vidarbhas, Richikas, Mahiśākas, and also to Daṇḍakāraṇya (Singh, *Geographical Data in the Early Puranas*, p. 283). In the Purāṇas, the region of Daṇḍaka is mentioned separately from that of Vidarbha (Pargiter, *The Mārkaṇḍeya Purāṇa*, pp. 335–6). It has in fact, been argued on the basis of references to Vidarbha in the *Jaiminīya* and *Bṛhadāraṇyaka Upaniṣad* that it was the oldest Aryan colony in the south (Pargiter, *The Mārkaṇḍeya Purāṇa*, p. 283.) It can also be noted that in the *Aitareya Brāhmaṇa*, unlike groups like the Āndhras, Puṇḍras, Śavaras, Pulindas, and Mutibas, the Vidarbhas are not styled as *udantya* or 'beyond the borders [of Aryandom]' (Yazdani, *The Early History of the Deccan*, p. 15).
78. Sircar, *Studies in the Geography of Ancient and Medieval India*, p. 38; Pargiter, *The Markandeya Purana*, pp. 335–6. For the *Nalopakhyana,* Yazdani, *The Early History of the Deccan*, p. 24. The kingdom of Vidarbha was said to have been founded by Jyamagha or his son Vidarbha. The Mahābhārata refers to Bhīṣmaka and his son Rukmin who ruled over Vidarbha. Sahadeva, in the course of his southern conquest, made Bhīṣmaka, ruling in Bhojakata, acknowledge his suzerainty.
79. Law, *The Historical Geography of Ancient India*, p. 341. Kālidāsa's play seems to indicate that Vidarbha was part of the Mauryan sphere of influence. Agnimitra's minister refers to the kingdom as one established not long ago (*aciradhiṣṭhita*) and compares its king, who was related to the Mauryas, to a newly planted tree (*navasamropaṇasithilastaru*). The story also refers to the defeat of the ruler of Vidarbha Yajñasena, a near relation of the last Mauryan king's minister by Agnimitra, son of Puṣyamitra Śuṅga. This was because the former had imprisoned the latter's friend Mādhavasena. Ultimately, the territory was divided between Yajñasena and Mādhavasena.
80. V.R.R. Dikshitar, *The Purāṇa Index,* vols I and II, Madras: University of Madras, 1951, p. 329.
81. Yazdani, *The Early History of the Deccan*, p. 17.
82. N. Gangadharan, (trans. and annotated), *The Agni Purāṇa: Ancient Indian Tradition and Mythology Series,* vols 27–30, Delhi and Paris: Motilal

Banarsidass-UNESCO, 1984–7. The other types of diction were the Pancali, the Gaudadesiya, and the Lataja.

83. N. Gangadharan, (trans. and annotated), *The Agni Purāṇa* (Ancient Indian Tradition and Mythology Series), Delhi and Paris: Motilal Banarsidass and UNESCO, 1986, p. 275. The five families were: the Bhojas, Vītihotras, Śāryātas, Avantis, and Tuṇḍikeras. The Bhojas are said to be descendants of Sātvata, the son of Mahābhoja (Law, *Historical Geography of Ancient India*, p. 145). The exact lines of descent are very difficult to unravel and vary from Purāṇa to Purāṇa. The Bhojas seem also to be closely linked to the Vṛṣṇis and Andhakas, since they are very often mentioned together as being residents of Dwārakā (S.V. Iyer (trans. and ed.), *The Varāha Purāṇa* (Ancient Indian Tradition and Mythology Series), vol. 32, Delhi and Paris: Motilal Banarsidass and UNESCO, 1985).
84. The term applied to all *kṣatriyas* descending from Yayāti. Along with the Sātvatas, they dwelt on the banks of the Yamuna, and were a Yādava tribe who dwelt in Saurashtra. They also inhabited Mṛttikavatī, situated somewhere on the north-eastern limits of modern Gujarat (Law, *Historical Geography of Ancient India*, p. 145; Pargiter, *The Markandeya Purāṇa*, pp. 335, 342).
85. We read in the *Aitareya Brāhmaṇa*: 'In the southern region whatever kings there are of the Sātvatas, they are anointed for Bhaujya; "O Bhoja" they style them when consecrated in accordance with the action of the deities' (Singh, *Geographical Data in the Early Puranas*, p. 342).
86. J.L. Shastri (trans. and ed.), *The Śivapurāṇa* (Ancient Indian Tradition and Mythology Series), vol. 3, Delhi and Paris: Motilal Banarsidass and UNESCO, 1970; Vettam Mani, *Puranic Encyclopaedia*, Delhi: Motilal Banarsidass, 1993, p. 847.
87. Yazdani, *The Early History of the Deccan*, p. 14.
88. N.L. Dey, *The Geographical Dictionary of Ancient and Medieval India*, New Delhi: Munshiram Manoharlal, 1971, p. 234.
89. Yazdani, *The Early History of the Deccan*, pp. 14–15.
90. For instance, we have the widely accepted identification of Kauṇḍinyapura with the archaeological site of the same name.
91. Deo and Dhavalikar, *Paunar Excavation (1967)*, pp. 114–15.
92. Adam is one important site that has not been identified because of references to it in texts.
93. Shastri (ed.), *The Age of the Satavahanas*, 1999.
94. For instance, there are some Sātavāhana kings known from inscriptions and coins, and not from any textual references, for instance, Vediśrī, Śaktiśrī, Kumbha, Karṇa, and Śaka Sātakarṇi of the Vidarbha branch.
95. Romila, Thapar, 'Puranic Lineages and Archaeological Cultures', *Puratattva*, vol. 8, 1975–6, pp. 92–3.
96. Scholars have looked at the Tamil Sangam texts in order to throw some light on the megalithic in Tamil Nadu (K.R. Srinivasan, 'The Megalithic Burials and Urn-fields of South India in the Light of Tamil Literature and Tradition', *Ancient India*, vol. 2, 1946–7, pp. 3–72). However, one would need to look at a text located in the region of Vidarbha in order to attempt a similar study. It

could be suggested that instead of trying to look for references to megalithic practice in later texts, perhaps ethnographic and ethno-archaeological studies might have more value.

REFERENCES

Agrawal, D.P. and A. Ghosh (eds), *Radiocarbon and Indian Archaeology*, Bombay: Tata Institute of Fundamental Research, 1973.

Akhtar, J.D. (ed.), *The Matsya Puranam* (S.V. Shastri, general editor, The Sacred Books of the Aryans), vol. I, New Delhi: Oriental Publishers, 1972.

Ali, S.M., *The Geography of the Puranas*, New Delhi: People's Publishing House, 1983 (1966).

Ashmore, Wendy and B. Knapp, *Archaeologies of Landscape: Contemporary Perspectives*, Oxford, Massachusetts: Blackwell, 1999.

Baker, Alan R.H. and Mark Billinge (eds), *Period and Place: Research Methods in Historical Geography*, Cambridge Studies in Historical Geography, 1, Cambridge: Cambridge University Press, 1982.

Baker, Alan R.H. and Derek Gregory (eds), *Explorations in Historical Geography: Interpretative Essays*, Cambridge: Cambridge University Press, 1984.

Bakker, Hans T., 'Ramtek: An Ancient Centre of Visnu Devotion in Maharashtra', in Hans T. Bakker (ed.). *The History of Sacred Places in India as Reflected in Traditional Literature: Panels of the VIII World Sanskrit Conference*. Leiden: E.J. Brill, 1990, pp. 62–86.

——, *The Vakatakas: An Essay in Hindu Iconology*, Groningen: Egbert Forsten, 1997.

Barker, Graeme (ed.), *Companion Encyclopedia of Archaeology*, vol. I, London and New York: Routledge, 1999.

Bhagwat, A.K. (ed.), *Maharashtra: A Profile*, Kolhapur: Padmabhushan Vishnu Sakharam Khandekar Amrit Mahotsava Satkar Samiti, no date.

Bhandarkar, R.G., *Early History of the Deccan*, Calcutta: Susil Gupta, 1928.

Binford, Lewis R., 'Archaeology as Anthropology', *American Antiquity*, 28 (2), 1962, pp. 217–25.

Boado, Felipe Criado and Rafael Penedo Romero, 'Art, Time and Thought: A Formal Study Comparing Palaeolithic and Postglacial Art', *World Archaeology*, (25) 2, 1993, pp. 187–203.

Boivin, Nicole, 'Life Rhythms and Floor Sequences: Excavating Time in Rural Rajasthan and Neolithic Catalhoyuk', *World Archaeology*, 31 (3), 2000, pp. 367–88.

Bond, George C. and Angela Gilliam (eds), *Social Construction of the Past: Representation as power*, (One World Archaeology), vol. 24, London and New York: Routledge, 1994.

Bradley, Richard, *The Past in Prehistoric Societies*, London and New York: Routledge, 2002.

Bradley, Richard, Felipe Criado Boado, and Ramon F. Valcarce, 'Rock Art Research as Landscape Archaeology: A Pilot Study in Galicia, North-west Spain', *World Archaeology*, 25 (3), 1994, pp. 374–90.

Bunkse, Edmunds V., 'Commentary on "The Lowenthal Papers": Environment, the Humanities and Landscape', *Annals of the Association of American Geographers*, 93 (4), 2003, pp. 882–4.

Carmichael, D.L., J. Hubert, and B. Reeves (eds), *Sacred Sites, Sacred Places*, London: Routledge, 1994.

Carter, Paul, *The Road to Botany Bay: An Essay in Spatial History*, London: Faber and Faber, 1987.

Chakrabarti, D.K., *Theoretical Issues in Indian Archaeology*, New Delhi: Munshiram Manoharlal, 1988.

——, *The Archaeology of Ancient Indian Cities*, New Delhi: Oxford University Press, 1995.

——, *Archaeological Geography of the Ganga Plain: The Lower and Middle Ganga*, Delhi: Permanent Black, 2001.

Champion, T.C. (ed.), *Centre and Periphery: Comparative Studies in Archaeology* (One World Archaeology), vol. 11, London: Unwin Hyman, 1989.

Chattopadhyaya, B.D., *A Survey of Historical Geography of Ancient India*, Calcutta: Manisha Granthalaya, 1984.

——, *Studying Early India: Archaeology, Texts and Historical Issues*, Delhi: Permanent Black, 2003.

Cooper, Zarine, 'Perceptions of time in the Andaman Islands', *World Archaeology*, 25 (2), 1993, pp. 261–7.

Crane, R.I. (ed.), *Regions and Regionalism in South Asian Studies: An Exploratory Study*, Durham, NC: Duke University, 1967.

Dallapicola A.L. and Z-A. Lallemant (eds), *The Stupa: Its Religious, Historical and Architectural Significance*, Weisbaden: Südostasien Institut Universität Heidelberg, 1980.

Deglurkar, G.B., *Temple Architecture and Sculpture of Maharashtra*, Nagpur: Nagpur University, 1974.

Deglurkar, G.B. and Gouri P. Lad, *Megalithic Raipur*, Pune: Deccan College, 1992.

Deo, S.B., 'A New Painted Pottery from Vidarbha', *Purattatva*, vol. I, 1967–8, pp. 89–99.

——, *Paunar Excavation (1067)*, Nagpur: Nagpur Vidyapeeth Mudranalaya, 1968.

——, *Excavations at Takalghat and Khapa*, Nagpur: Nagpur Vidyapeeth Mudranalaya, 1970.

——, *Mahurjhari Excavation*, Nagpur: Nagpur Vidyapeeth Mudranalaya, 1973.

——, 'The Megaliths: Their Culture, Ecology, Economy and Technology', in S.B. Deo and K. Paddayya (eds), *Recent Advances in Indian Archaeology*, Poona: Deccan College, 1985, pp. 89–99.

Deo, S.B., 'Technology of the Vidarbha Megalithians', in I.K. Sarma D.V. Devaraj, and R. Gopal (eds), *Narasimhapriya: Essays on Indian Archaeology, Epigraphy, Numismatics, Art, Architecture, Iconography and Cultural History*, vol. I, New Delhi: Sundeep Prakashan, 2000, pp. 23–8.

——, 'Ancient History of Maharashtra', in A.K. Bhagwat (ed.), *Maharashtra: A Profile*, Kolhapur: Visnu Sakharam Khandekar Amrit Mahotsav Satkar Samiti, 1977, pp. 15–68.

Deo, S.B. and M.K. Dhavalikar, *Paunar Excavation (1967)*, Nagpur: Nagpur Vidyapeeth Mudranalaya, 1968.

Deo, S.B. and J.P. Joshi, *Pauni Excavation: 1969–70*, Nagpur: Nagpur Vidyapeeth Mudranalaya, 1972.

Deo, S.B. and A.P. Jamkhedkar, *Excavations at Naikund*, Bombay: Department of Archaeology and Museums, Government of Maharashtra, 1982.

Deshpande, C.D., *Geography of Maharashtra*, New Delhi: National Book Trust, 1971.

Dey, N.L., *The Geographical Dictionary of Ancient and Medieval India*, New Delhi: Munshiram Manoharlal, 1971 (1927).

Dhavalikar, M.K., 'Development and Decline of the Deccan Chalcolithic', in D.P. Agrawal and A. Ghosh (eds), *Radiocarbon and Indian Archaeology*, Bombay: Tata Institute of Fundamental Research, 1973, pp. 138–47.

——, 'The Satavahana Epoch: An Ecological Perspective', in A.M. Shastri (ed.), *The Age of the Satavahanas*, vol. I, New Delhi: Aryan Books International, 1999, pp. 102–14.

Dikshitar, V.R.R., *The Purana Index*, vols I and II. Madras: University of Madras, 1951.

Doniger, W. and B.K. Smith (trans. and annotated), *The Laws of Manu*, New Delhi: Penguin, 1991.

Ehrich, Robert. 'Further Reflections on Archaeological Interpretation', *American Anthropologist*, 65 (1), 1963, pp. 16–31.

Epigraphia Indica, vol. 20.

Erdosy, G., *Urbanisation in Early Historic India* (BAR International Series 430), Oxford: BAR International, 1988.

Feldhaus, Anne, 'The Image of the Forest in the *Mahatmyas* of the Rivers of the Deccan', in Hans T. Bakker (ed.), *The History of Sacred Places in India as Reflected in Traditional Literature: Panels of the VIII World Sanskrit Conference*, Leiden: E.J. Brill, 1990, pp. 90–102.

Foxhall, Lin, 'The Running Sands of Time: Archaeology and the Short-term', *World Archaeology*, 31 (3), 2000, pp. 484–98.

Gangadharan, N. (trans. and annotated), *The Agni Purāṇa* (Ancient Indian Tradition and Mythology Series), vols 27–30, Delhi and Paris: Motilal Banarsidass and UNESCO, 1984–7.

Gazin-Schwartz, Amy and Cornelius Holtorf (eds), *Archaeology and Folklore*, London and New York: Routledge, 1999.

Geetali, Anuja, 'Living Megalithic Practices Amongst the Madia Gonds of Bhamragad, Dist. Gadchiroli, Maharashtra', *Purattatva*, vol. 32, 2001–2, pp. 89–92.

Ghosh, A., *The City in Early Historical India*, Simla: Indian Institute of Advanced Studies, 1973.

—— (ed.), *An Encyclopaedia of Indian Archaeology*, vol. I, New Delhi: Munshiram Manoharlal, 1989.

Gledhill, J., B. Bender, and M.T. Larsen (eds), *State and Society: The Emergence and Development of Social Hierarchy and Political Centralization* (One World Archaeology), vol. 4, London: Unwin Hyman, 1988.

Gokhale-Turner, Jayashree, 'Region and Regionalism in the Study of Indian Politics', in N. K. Wagle (ed.), *Images of Maharashtra: A Regional Profile of India*, London and Dublin: Curzon Press, 1980, pp. 88–101.

Goodsell, Charles T., *The Social Meaning of Civic Space: Studying Political Authority through Architecture*, Kansas: University Press of Kansas, 1988.

Gosden, Chris and Gary Lock, 'Prehistoric Histories', *World Archaeology*, 30 (1), 1998, pp. 2–12.

Gururaja Rao B.K., *The Megalithic Culture in South India*, Mysore: University of Mysore Prasaranga, 1972.

Heitzman, J., 'Early Buddhism, Trade and Empire', in K.A.R. Kennedy and G.L Possehl (eds), *Studies in the Archaeology and Palaeoanthropology of South Asia*, New Delhi: Oxford University Press, 1984, pp. 121–37.

Hodder, I. (ed.), *Archaeology as Long-term History*, Cambridge: Cambridge University Press, 1987.

Hodder, I., 'The Narrative and Rhetoric of Material Culture Sequences', *World Archaeology*, 25 (2), 1993, pp. 268–82.

Holtorf, Cornelius J., 'The Life-histories of Megaliths in Mecklenburg-Vorpommern (Germany)', *World Archaeology*, 30 (1), 1998, pp. 23–38.

Indian Archaeology: A Review, 1954–97.

Ingold, Tim, 'The Temporality of the Landscape', *World Archaeology*, 25 (2), 1993, pp. 152–74.

Iyer, S.V. (trans. and ed.), *The Varaha Purāṇa* (Ancient Indian Tradition and Mythology Series), vol. 32, Delhi and Paris: Motilal Banarsidass and UNESCO, 1985.

Johnson, Gregory A., 'Aspects of Regional Analysis in Archaeology', *Annual Review of Anthropology*, vol. 6, 1977, pp. 479–508.

Joshi, J.P. and A.K. Sharma, 'Excavations at Mansar, Distt. Nagpur, Maharashtra: 1997–2000', *Puratattva*, vol. 30, 1999–2000, pp. 127-31.

Kennedy, K.A.R., *Physical Anthropology of Megalith Builders* (Oriental Monograph Series), no. 17, Canberra: Australian National University Press, 1975.

Kong, Lily, 'Geography and Religion: Trends and Prospects', *Progress in Human Geography*, 14 (3), 1990, pp. 355–71.

Kulkarni, S.S., 'Megalithic Culture of the Madias of Maharashtra', *Man and Environment*, 27 (2), 2002, pp. 107–11.

Lahiri, Nayanjot, *The Archaeology of Indian Trade Routes Up to c. 200 BC: Resource Use, Resource Access, and Lines of Communication*, New Delhi: Oxford University Press, 1992.

——, 'Archaeological Landscapes and Textual Images: A Study of the Sacred Geography of Late Medieval Ballabgarh', *World Archaeology*, 28 (2), 1996, pp. 244–64.

Law, B.C., *Historical Geography of Ancient India*, New Delhi: Oriental Books Reprint Corporation, 1984 (1954 reprint).

Layton, Robert (ed.), *Who Needs the Past: Indigenous Values and Archaeology* (One World Archaeology), London: Unwin Hyman, 1989.

Mangalam, S.J., 'Coins of the Feudatories and Contemporaries of the Satavahanas', in A.M. Shastri (ed.), *The Age of the Satavahanas*, vol. II, New Delhi: Aryan Books International, 1999, pp. 360–90.

Mani, Vettam, *Puranic Encyclopaedia*, Delhi: Motilal Banarsidass, 1993 (1964 reprint).

McDonald, Ellen E., 'The Growth of Regional Consciousness in Maharashtra', *Indian Economic and Social History Review*, vol. 5, 1968, pp. 223–43.

McIntosh, J.R., 'The Megalith Builders of South India: A Historical Survey', in I.K. Sarma and B.V. Rao (eds), *Sri Subrahmanya Smrti* (Dr R. Subrahmanyam Commemoration Volume), vol. I, New Delhi: Sundeep Prakashan, 2001, pp. 203–10.

Menin, Sarah (ed.), *Constructing Place: Mind and Matter*, London and New York: Routledge, 2003.

Meskell, Lynn, 'Cycles of Life and Death: Narrative Homology and Archaeological Realities', *World Archaeology*, 31 (3), 2000, pp. 423–41.

Metcalf, Peter and R. Huntington, *Celebrations of Death: The Anthropology of Mortuary Ritual*. Cambridge: Cambridge University Press, 1991 (1979 reprint).

Miller, D., M. Rowlands, and C. Tilley (eds), *Domination and Resistance* (One World Archaeology), vol. 3, London: Unwin Hyman, 1989.

Mirashi, V.V., *Corpus Inscriptionum Indicarum: Inscriptions of the Vakatakas*, vol. V, Ootacamund: Archaeological Survey of India, 1963.

Mizoguchi, Koji, 'Time in the Reproduction of Mortuary Practices', *World Archaeology*, 25 (2), 1993, pp. 223–35.

Mittre, Vishnu and H.P. Gupta, 'Ancient Plant Economy at Paunar, Maharashtra', in S.B. Deo and M.K. Dhavalikar, *Paunar Excavation (1967)*, Nagpur: Nagpur Vidyapeeth Mudranalaya, 1968, pp. 128–31.

Mohanty, R.K. and S.R. Walimbe, 'An Investigation into the Mortuary Practices of Vidarbha Megalithic Cultures', in C. Margabandhu and K.S. Ramachandran (eds), *Spectrum of Indian Culture*, Delhi: Agam Kala Prakashan, 1996, pp. 136–49.

Mohanty, R.K. and V. Selvakumar, 'The Archaeology of the Megaliths in India: 1947–1997', in S. Settar and R. Korisettar (eds), *Indian Archaeology in Retrospect*, vol. I, Delhi: Indian Council of Historical Research and Manohar, 2001, pp. 313–481.

Moorti, U.S.S., *Megalithic Cultures of South India: Socio-economic Perspectives*, Varanasi: Ganga Kaveri Publishing House, 1994.

Moreland, John, *Archaeology and Text*, London: Duckworth, 2001.

Muir, Richard, *Approaches to Landscape*, London: Macmillan, 1999.

Murray, Tim, 'Archaeology and the Threat of the Past: Sir Henry Rider Haggard and the Acquisition of Time', *World Archaeology*, 25 (2), 1993, pp. 175–86.

___ (ed.), *Time and Archaeology* (One World Archaeology), vol. 37, London and New York: Routledge, 1999.

Murthy, P.R., *Megalithic Culture of the Godavari Basin*, Delhi: Sharada Publishing House, 2000.

Nath, A., 'Satavahana Antiquities from Adam', in A.M. Shastri (ed.), *The Age of the Satavahanas*, vol. II, New Delhi: Aryan Books International, 1999, pp. 460–6.

Nuttgens, Patrick, *The Landscape of Ideas*, London: Faber and Faber, 1972.

Olwig, Kenneth, 'Landscape: The Lowenthal Legacy', *Annals of the Association of American Geographers*, 93 (4), 2003, pp. 871–7.

Oubina, Cesar Parcero, Felipe Criado Boado, and Manuel Santos Estevez, 'Rewriting Landscape: Incorporating Sacred Landscapes into Cultural Traditions', *World Archaeology*, 30 (1), 1998, pp. 159–76.

Parasher-Sen, Aloka, *Social and Economic History of Early Deccan: Some Interpretations*, New Delhi: Manohar, 1993.

Pargiter F.E. (trans. and annotated) *The Markaṇdeya Purāṇa* (Bibliotheca Indica: A Collection of Oriental Works published by the Asiatic Society of Bengal), Varanasi: Indological Book House, 1969 (reprint).

Parsons, Jeffrey R., 'Archaeological Settlement Patterns', *Annual Review of Anthropology*, vol. 1, 1972, pp. 127–50.

Philips, C.H. (ed.), *Historians of India, Pakistan and Ceylon*, London: Oxford University Press, 1961.

Preston, James J., 'Sacred Centres and Symbolic Networks in India', in S. Mahapatra (ed.), *The Realm of the Sacred*, Calcutta: Oxford University Press, 1992, pp. 79–112.

Rao, B.K. Gururaja, *The Megalithic Culture in South India*, Mysore: University of Mysore Prasaranga, 1972.

Rao, K.P., *Deccan Megaliths*, Delhi: Sundeep Prakashan, 1988.

Ray, H.P., 'Early Historical Settlement in the Deccan: An Ecological Perspective', *Man and Environment*, 14 (1), 1989, pp. 103–208.

Ray, H.P. and Carla Sinopoli (eds), *Archaeology as History in Early South Asia*, New Delhi: Indian Council of Historical Research and Aryan Books International, 2004.

Richards, Colin, 'Monuments as Landscape: Creating the Center of the World in Late Neolithic Orkney', *World Archaeology*, 28 (2), 1996, pp. 190–208.

Roberts, B.K., 'Landscape Archaeology', in J.M. Wagstaff (ed.), *Landscape and Culture: Geographical and Archaeological Perspectives*, Oxford: Basil Blackwell, 1987, pp. 77–95.

Rowlands, Michael, 'The Role of Memory in the Transmission of Culture', *World Archaeology*, 25 (2), 1993, pp. 141–51.

Salomon, Richard, *Indian Epigraphy: A Guide to the Study of Inscriptions in Sanskrit, Prakrit and the Other Indo-Aryan languages*, New York and Austin: Oxford University Press and Centre for Asian Studies, University of Texas, 1998.

Sarma, I.K., *Coinage of the Satavahana Empire*, Delhi: Agam Kala Prakashan, 1980.

——, 'New Evidences on the Early Satavahana Coinage, Culture and Commerce', in A.M. Shastri (ed.), *The Age of the Satavahanas*, vol. II, New Delhi: Aryan Books International, 1999, 341–8.

Schwartzberg, J.E., 'Prologmena to the Study of South Asian Regions and Regionalism', in R.I. Crane (ed.), *Regions and Regionalism in South Asian Studies*, Durham, NC: Duke University, 1966, pp. 89–107.

——, 'The Evolution of Regional Power Configurations in the Indian Subcontinent', in R.G. Fox (ed.), *Realm and Region in Traditional India*, New Delhi: Vikas Publishing House, 1977, pp. 197–233.

Schwartzberg, J.E., 'Folk Regions in Northwestern India', in A.B. Mukerji and A. Ahmad (eds), *India: Culture, Society and Economy*, New Delhi: Inter-India Publications, 1985, pp. 205–35.

Settar, S. and G.D. Sontheimer (eds), *Memorial Stones: A Study of Their Origin, Significance and Variety*, Dharwad and Heidelberg: Institute of Indian Art History, Karnatak University and University of Heidelberg, 1982.

Settar, S. and R. Korisettar (eds), *Indian Archaeology in Retrospect*, vols I–IV, New Delhi: Indian Council of Historical Research and Manohar, 2001.

Shastri, A.M., *Early History of the Deccan: Problems and Perspectives*, Delhi: Sundeep Prakashan, 1987.

——, 'Closing Phase of the Satavahana Power and Allied Issues', in A.M. Shastri, *Early History of the Deccan: Problems and Perspectives*, Delhi: Sundeep Prakashan, 1987, pp. 38–44.

——, 'Early Satavahanas and Vidarbha', in Bhaskar Chatterjee (ed.), *History and Archaeology: Prof. H. D. Sankalia Felicitation Volume*, Delhi: Ramanand Vidya Bhavan, 1989, pp. 329–35.

——, 'A Lost (?) Asokan Edict from Vidarbha'. *Puratattva*, vol. 28, 1997–8, pp. 55–8.

——, *The Satavahanas and the Western Kshatrapas: A Historical Framework*, Nagpur: Dattsons, 1998.

—— (ed.), *The Age of the Satavahanas*, vols I and II, New Delhi: Aryan Books International, 1999.

——, 'Puranas on the Satavahanas: An Archaeological-historical Perspective', in A.M. Shastri (ed.), *The Age of the Satavahanas*, vol. I, New Delhi: Aryan Books International, 1999, pp. 3–72.

Shastri, J.L. (trans. and ed.) *The Sivapurana*(Ancient Indian Tradition and Mythology Series), vol. 3. Delhi and Paris: Motilal Banarsidass and UNESCO, 1970.

Shennan, S.J. (ed.), *Archaeological Approaches to Cultural Identity* (One World Archaeology), vol. 10. London: Unwin Hyman, 1989.

Singh, M.R., *Geographical Data in the Early Puranas: A Critical Study*, Calcutta: Punthi Pustak, 1972.

Sircar, D.C., *Studies in the Geography of Ancient and Medieval India*, New Delhi: Motilal Banarsidass, 1971 (revised).

Sopher, David E.(ed.), *An Exploration of India: Geographical Perspectives on Society and Culture*, London: Longman, 1980.

Srinivasan, K.R., 'The Megalithic Burials and Urn-fields of South India in the Light of Tamil Literature and Tradition', *Ancient India*, vol. 2, 1946–7, pp. 9–16.

Subbarao, B., 'Regions and Regionalism', in *Widening Horizons: Some Recent Studies in Early Indian History* (Anthology for the Workshop on History of India [Up to c. AD 1200], 31 March–11 April 1997), Delhi: University of Delhi, 1997.

Sundara, A., *The Early Chamber Tombs of South India: A Study of the Megalithic Monuments of Northern Karnataka*, Delhi: University Publishers, 1975.

Suryavanshi, Bhagwan Singh, 'Geography of Dakshinapatha as Depicted in Valmiki Ramayana', in Bhaskar Chatterjee (ed.), *History and Archaeology: Prof. H. D. Sankalia Felicitation Volume*, Delhi: Ramanand Vidya Bhavan, 1989, pp. 5–19.

Suvrathan, Uthara, 'Archaeology and Text: A Study of the Landscape in Vidarbha', MPhil Thesis, New Delhi: Jawaharlal Nehru University, 2004.

Thapar, Romila, 'Puranic Lineages and Archaeological Cultures', *Puratattva*, vol. 8, 1975–6, pp. 86–98.

——, 'Society and Historical Consciousness', in S. Bhattacharya and R. Thapar (eds), *Situating Indian History*, New Delhi: Oxford University Press, 1986, pp. 353–83.

——, *Time as a Metaphor of History: Early India (The Krishna Bharadwaj Memorial Lecture)*, New Delhi: Oxford University Press, 1996.

Thomas, Julian, *Time, Culture and Identity: An Interpretive Archaeology*, London and New York: Routledge, 1996.

Trautmann, T. and Carla M. Sinopoli, 'In the Beginning was the Word: Excavating the Relations Between History and Archaeology in South Asia', *Journal of the Economic and Social History of the Orient*, 45 (4), 2002, pp. 492–523.

Vatsyayan, K. (ed.), *Concepts of Time: Ancient and Modern*, New Delhi: IGNCA and Sterling, 1996.

Wagstaff, J.M. (ed.). *Landscape and Culture: Geographical and Archaeological Perspectives*. Oxford: Basil Blackwell, 1987.

Walimbe, S.R. 'Human Skeletal Remains from Megalithic Vidarbha', *Purattatva*, vol. 18, 1987–8, pp. 61–71.

Wheeler, R.E.M. 'Brahmagiri and Chandravalli', *Ancient India*, vol. 4, 1948, pp. 181–308.

World Archaeology (Buddhist Archaeology), 27 (2), 1995.

Yazdani, G. (ed.). *The Early History of the Deccan*. New Delhi: Oriental Books, 1982 (1960, reprint).

Appendix 4.1: Additional Information

Number of Stone Age Sites in Vidarbha: 227

District-wise Breakup of Stone Age Sites

District	Number of Sites	Location
Akola	9	Mainly Purna Basin
Amaravati	10	Mainly on banks of Pedhi nala, tributary of Purna
Bhandara	27	
Chandrapur	121	Mainly in Wardha-Wainganga Basin
Garhchiroli	1	
Nagpur	24	
Wardha	8	Confluence of Wuna and Wardha
Yavatmal ((including Nanded and Parbhani)	27	

Number of (identified) Chalcolithic Sites: 9

Number of Megalithic Sites in Vidarbha: 89

District-wise Breakup of Megalithic Sites

District	Number of Sites	Percentage of Total
Amaravati	1	1.12
Bhandara	5	5.62
Chandrapur	20	22.47
Garhchiroli	6	6.74
Nagpur	51	57.30
Wardha	2	2.25
Yavatmal	1	1.12
Unidentified	3	3.37

Nature of Megalithic Sites

Nature of Site	Number	Percentage of Total
Only Burial	56	62.92
Habitation	8	8.99
Habitation and Burial	7	7.87
Unknown	18	20.22

Type of Burials

Type of Burials	Number of Sites
Stone/Cairn Circles	54
Dolmens	4
Dolmens and stone circles	1

Number of Early Historic Sites: 95

APPENDIX 4.2: Megalithic Sites

Site	District	Details	Reference (*IAR*)
Amgaon/Angaon	Nagpur	Stone circles	1970–1
Arsoda	Garhchiroli	Possible habitation	1984–5
Arni	Yavatmal	Possible habitation	1978–9, 1984–5
Aturdi	Chanda	Stone circles	1967–8
Badegaon	Nagpur	Stone circles	1970–1
Bandegaon	Chandrapur	Stone circles	1978–9
Bhagimohari	Nagpur	Habitation cum burial	1982–3, 83–4, 1992–3
Bhawar	Bhandara	Habitation cum burial	1992–3
Bhilgaon	Nagpur		
Boregaon	Nagpur	48 Stone circles	1980–1
Brambi	Bhandara	Stone circles	
Chakalpet	Gadchiroli		
Chamurshi	Gadchiroli	Dolmen	
Chak Kosambi	Chanda	Stone circles	1973–4
Chak-Vithalwada	Chanda	Stone circles	1960–1
Chicholi	Nagpur	Stone circles	1970–1
Chakki-Khapa	Nagpur	Stone circles	1968–9
Deoli	Nagpur	Stone circles	1970–1
Devlipet/Deolimet	Nagpur		1968–9
Drugdhamna	Nagpur	Stone circle, small tumuli without lithic appendage	1959–60
Dudh	Nagpur	Stone circles	1968–9
Dongargaon	Gadchiroli	Stone circles	1960–1
Dongarmounda	Nagpur	Stone circles, cairn circle	1977–8, 88–9, 75–6
Garhchiroli	Gadchiroli		
Gangapur	Nagpur	Stone circles	
Ghorad	Nagpur		
Gondi	Nagpur	Stone circles	
Hingna-Kinhi	Nagpur	Stone circles	1970–1
Hirapur	Chanda		1963–4
Jambhali			
Jodholi	Chandrapur	Stone circles	
Junapani	Nagpur	Over 150 Stone circles	1961–2
Kahali	Chandrapur	Around 100 Stone circles, possible habitation	1978–9, 1979–80
Kamptee	Nagpur		
Kaundinyapura	Amaravati	habitation	1960–1
Kelzar	Chandrapur	Dolmen	

Contd...

Appendix 4.2 *Contd...*

Site	District	Details	Reference (*IAR*)
Khairwada	Wardha	1400 Stone circles, habitation	1981–2
Khapa	Nagpur	Stone circles, pit burials	
Khemjai	Chanda	Stone circles	1967–8
Kinhi	Nagpur		
Kohli	Nagpur	Stone circles	
Koradih	Nagpur	Stone circles	
Kuhi	Nagpur	Stone circles	1975–6, 1977–8
Kukad Chimda	Chanda	Stone circles	1960–1
Mahurjhari	Nagpur	Stone circles	
Makar Dhokara	Nagpur		
Mandhal	Nagpur	Stone circles	1969–70, 75–6, 77–8
Masala Tukum	Chandrapur	Stone circles	1970–1
Mohzari	Gadchiroli		
Nagalwadi	Nagpur	Stone circles 1970–1	
Nagpur/Aathva Milestone	Nagpur	Stone circle, cairn circle	1994–5
Naikund	Nagpur	Habitation cum burial	
Neeldhoa	Nagpur	Stone circles	
Panchkhedi	Nagpur	Burial cum Habitation	1987–8, 1992–3
Parseon	Nagpur		
Paunar	Wardha	Possible habitation	1966–7
Pimpalgaon	Bhandara	Stone circle and dolmens	1992–3
Pipla	Nagpur		
Raipur-Hingna	Nagpur	Habitation cum burial site with over 262 stone circles	1970–1, 84–5, 89–90
Ramparsodi	Chandrapur	Stone circles	
Ranjala		Possible habitation	
Ravi	Chanda	Dolmen	1960–1
Sangam	Nagpur	Stone circles	
Sonegaon	Nagpur		
Sawargaon	Nagpur	Stone circles	
Selu Road	Chanda		
Selur	Chanda	Stone circles	1973–4
Seminary Hills	Nagpur	Stone circles enclosing cairns	1961–2
Shirkanda	Nagpur	Possible chalcolithic-megalithic habitation site	1991–2, 1993–4
Sindhla	Chanda	2 Stone circles	1959–60
Sirsala	Bhandara	Dolmens	1992–3

Site	District	Details	Reference (*IAR*)
Sonegaon	Nagpur	Stone circles	1970–1
Sukali Takali	Nagpur	Stone circles	1970–1
Takli	Nagpur	Stone circles	
Takalghat	Nagpur	Habitation	
Tharsa		Habitation	1985–6, 89–90
Tilantakhairi/ Tilota Khairi	Bhandara	Stone circles	
Udasa	Nagpur	Stone circles	1977–8
Umrer	Nagpur	Stone circles	1977–8
Umri	Chandrapur	Stone circles	
Vadgaon	Nagpur	Stone circles	
Vagnak	Chandrapur	Stone circles	
Vathora	Nagpur	Stone circles	
Veltur	Nagpur		1984–5
Vyad	Nagpur	Around 20 cairn circles	1968–9
Wag	Nagpur		1977–8
Waganakh	Chandrapur		
Wanadongri	Nagpur	Stone circles	
Warora	Chandrapur	Stone circles	1979–80

Appendix 4.3: Early Historic Sites

Site	District	Cultural Periods	Details
Adam	Nagpur	Chalcolithic to medieval	Habitation, stupa, fort
Adyal	Bhandara	Historical	Mound and stray sculptures (Nandi, Gaṇeśa, Sūrya, Śiva–Pārvatī, Hanumān)
Akot	Akola	Early Historic (?)	Kṣatrapa coins
Ambhora Khurd	Nagpur	Early Historic mound	
Antar Dodo	Wardha	Early Historic, medieval	R, Dull R, BW, GW
Arambha	Wardha	Chalcolithic to medieval	NBP, habitation
Arni	Yavatmal	Megalithic, Sātavāhana, Vākāṭaka	Fort, habitation
Ashti	Chanda	Chalcolithic, Early Historic	BRW,[1] handmade GW[2]
Assnegaon	Akola/ Amaravati	Early Historic	Red Slipped, BRW with graffiti
Bahadarpur	Akola/ Amaravati	Early Historic	Red Slipped, BRW with graffiti
Belgaon	Bhandara	Historical mound	
Belora	Akola/ Amaravati	Early Historic	Red Slipped, BRW with graffiti
Bhamiwara	Nagpur	Early Historic	
Bhandak	Chandrapur	Early Historic	BRW, Buddhist caves
Bhatkuli	Amaravati	Early Historic	BRW
Bhawar	Bhandara	Chalcolithic to Sātavāhana	
Borgaon	Amaravati	Early Historic	R, R Slipped, MRW, CRW, BBW,[3] B Painted RW
Brahmi Budruk Man	Akola/ Amaravati	Early Historic	Red Slipped, BRW with graffiti
Chakara	Bhandara	Historical mound	
Chamak	Amaravati	Early Historic	BRW
Chandala forest	Nagpur		Buddhist rock cut caves, second century BC inscription
Chenduk	Akola/ Amaravati	Early Historic	Red Slipped, BRW with graffiti

Site	District	Cultural Periods	Details
Chinchpur	Amaravati	Early Historic, medieval	R, CRW, MRW, GW
Chowa	Bhandara	Historical mound	
Dhamak	Amravati	Early Historic	
Dhamantri	Amaravati	Early Historic, medieval	
Dhanora	Wardha	Early Historic, medieval	R slipped, GW
Digikhanapur	Yavatmal	Early Historic	
Ganeshpur	Bhandara	Historical mound	
Gavali Tekadi	Nagpur	Early Historic	BRW, R slipped W, Narasiṁha sculpture
Gavha Nipani	Amaravati	Early Historic, medieval	
Ghota	Amaravati	Early historic, medieval	
Golewari	Bhandara	Historical mound	
Guikhed	Amaravati	Early Historic	
Hamlapuri	Nagpur		Vākāṭaka sculptures (Gaṇapati, Lajjā Gaurī)
Hasapur	Bhandara	Historical mound	
Jalgaon	Amravati	Early Historic	B, MRW
Juna Dhamangaon	Amaravati	Early Historic, medieval	
Kardha	Bhandara	Historical mound	
Kaundinyapur	Amaravati	Megalithic to medieval	Habitation, NBP
Kavli	Amaravati	Early Historic, medieval	Dull BW, MRW
Kawadsi	Bhandara	Early Historic	Iron slag
Khairi	Bhandara	Historical mound	
Khapri	Bhandara	Historical site	
Kholapur	Amaravati		
Kopra	Yavatmal	Chalcolithic, Early Historic	
Kuraigaon	Yavatmal	Early Historic	
Lohara	Bhandara	Microliths, Historical mound	
Mandhal	Nagpur		Vākāṭaka temples
Mansar	Nagpur		Monastery, temples, stūpa, *caitya*, Vākāṭaka fortification
Mangrul	Amaravati	Early Historic, medieval	R Slipped, CRW, MRW

Contd...

Appendix 4.3 *Contd...*

Site	District	Cultural Periods	Details
Mendha	Bhandara	Historical mound	
Morad	Amaravati	Early Historic	
Mulchera	Gadchiroli		Late Sātavāhana temple, stūpa?
Nagara	Bhandara		stūpa
Nagardhan	Nagpur	Early Historic	
Nagra	Bhandara		Vākāṭaka temple
Nandori	Chandrapur	Early Historic	RW, GW (Slipped and Unslipped)
Nandpur	Nagpur	Early Historic	Brick structure
Nimboli	Amaravati	Early Historic, medieval	Red Slipped, Black Burnished, MRW, GW
Pahur	Yavatmal	Early Historic	
Paloti	Yavatmal	Chalcolithic, Early Historic	
Panchkedi	Nagpur	Megalithic, Early Historic	
Pandhi	Bhandara	Historical mound	
Parsoda	Amaravati	Chalcolithic, Early Historic	BuRW,[4] CRW,[5] MRW[6]
Parsori	Nagpur	Historical mound	
Paunar	Wardha	Chalcolithic, Iron Age, Early Historic, early medieval	Habitation, NBP
Pauni	Bhandara		Stūpas, possible *vihara*, NBP
Pendhri	Bhandara	Early Historic mound	NBP
Pimpalgaon	Chandrapur	Early Historic, medieval	
Site	District	Cultural Periods	Details
Pimpalkhuta	Yavatmal	Early Historic	
Ramgarh	Nagpur		Four rock shelters
Ramtek	Nagpur		Vākāṭaka fortifications, temples
Ramtola	Nagpur	Early Historic	RPW,[7] stone images of mother goddess on rectangular plates
Rohna	Wardha	Early Historic, medieval	Brick structure
Salbardi	Amaravati		Buddhist rock-cut caves
Salebhatti	Nagpur	Historical mound	
Savanga	Yavatmal	Early Historic	
Sawargaon	Bhandara	Historical mound	

Site	District	Cultural Periods	Details
Sawudar	Bhandara	Historical mound	
Seldoh	Wardha		Stūpa
Sindola Rith	Hinganghat Tlk.	Early Historic	
Sirkanda	Nagpur	Early Historic	BRW, B slipped, plain and painted RW, MRW
Sitepar	Bhandara	Historical	
Takri	Bhandara	Historical	Mound and stray sculptures (Nandi, Hanumān)
Tharsa	Nagpur	Proto to modern	Pottery, Narasiṁha sculpture
Udapur	Chandrapur		BRW, legged querns, B Slipped W
Vadhon	Wardha	Early Historic, medieval	CRW, GW, rubble foundations
Vaigaon/ Ashoknagar	Amaravati	Early Historic, medieval	CRW, MRW, BRW, B Painted RW, R Slipped W
Varud	Amaravati	Early Historic	Brick structure, R, CRW, BRW, GW
Vasad	Amaravati	Early Historic	Brick structure, R, R Slipped, MRW, BRW
Vathoda	Amaravati	Early Historic, medieval	
Virul	Wardha	Early Historic	Rubble foundation, R Slipped, CRW, GW
Wadgaon	Amaravati	Early Historic	CRW, BuRslW,[8] CGW,[9] BRW
Washim	Akola	Early Historic (?)	Kṣatrapa coins

Notes:

1. Black and red Ware
2. Grey Ware
3. Black Burnished Ware
4. Burnished Red Ware
5. Coarse Red Ware
6. Micaceous Red Ware
7. Red Painted Ware
8. Burnished Red Slipped Ware
9. Coarse Grey Ware

5. Of Death and Fertility
Landscapes of Heroism in Ancient South India

MEERA VISVANATHAN

IN THE POEMS of the Tamil anthologies, utterances of love and war meet unexpectedly, like strangers. Conventionally, these poems have been divided into two categories—*akam* (or interior) and *puṟam* (or exterior)—differing in style, substance, and technique. The akam poems use imagery and complex suggestion to transform a single event into an intensity of experience. In the puṟam poems we find a more straightforward account of the honour and tragedy of men's lives, arising from the demands of a warrior society. Yet as A.K. Ramanujan argues in a brilliant essay, 'The two genres define each other mutually; what one is, the other is not,' so that 'every poem resonates with the absent presence of others like it... [and] we respond to a system of presences and absences.'[1] Within this unstable dialectic lies the question I wish to raise: In what manner is it possible to locate the *experience* of martial heroism within the larger structures of early historic south India? To do so, however, one must first address the questions of methodology which arise. Of particular concern is correlating the information provided by literature and archaeology for the study of this period.

INTRODUCTION AND ISSUES OF METHODOLOGY

For the poets, Tamiḷagam was 'the beautiful land where Tamil is spoken', extending from Venkatam in the north to Kumari in the south, and bounded by the eastern and western seas. Tradition assigns the composition of the Eight Anthologies, or *Eṭṭutogai*[2] to the Third Sangam, an academy of gods, saints, and poets said to have met at Madurai; hence, they are often called the 'Sangam anthologies'. Yet

George Hart argues convincingly that this is the stuff of legend, lacking historical veracity.[3]

Other equally important sources exist in general contemporaneity to the period of the anthologies (third century BC to third century AD).[4] Excavations at sites such as Uraiyur, Kaveripattinam, Karur, and Arikamedu have shown the existence of a megalithic cultural level, identified by iron implements and Black and Red Ware (BRW) pottery. The evidence of epigraphy—some eighty-three short cave inscriptions and over 300 inscribed potsherds—indicates the adaptation of the northern Brahmi script to the Tamil phonetic system from around the third century BC. Inscribed copper coins bearing legends of the Cōḷa, Cēra, and Pāṇḍya dynasties have also been found. Finally, Roman coins, the accounts of Pliny and Ptolemy, and the anonymous *Periplus of the Erythraean Sea* bear witness to this period when Yavaṇas came as merchants to the southern ports, and Tamiḻagam found itself drawn to the rhythms of Indian Ocean trade.

While there exist detailed studies of individual source categories, the work of M.G.S. Narayanan, R. Champakalakshmi, and Rajan Gurukkal stands out for its integrated analysis of the dynamics of this period. Sharing a common orientation, their analyses provide the currently accepted model of history; I shall refer to this as 'the chiefdom hypothesis'.

The 'chiefdom hypothesis' holds that the early Tamil poems are oral compositions, belonging to the period marking the transition from the late megalithic to the early historic period. Here, the state had not yet evolved, and polities lacked well-defined boundaries, standing armies, bureaucracies, and taxation systems. There existed, instead, a hierarchy of chiefs, and the emphasis on plundering raids meant that economic advancement, whether in commerce or agriculture, was severely retarded. Local involvement in maritime trade was limited since the social milieu lacked surplus production, economic specialization, and the profit motive. Basic transactions are identified in terms of the gift economy, as resources acquired through plunder circulated through redistributive networks. From these conditions sprang a martial ethic, an ideology of patronage and heroism, which came to define this period.[5]

But a growing body of data, especially from archaeology, suggests a greater degree of cultural complexity than hitherto allowed for. We see this in the Tamil Brahmi inscriptions that refer to a number of specialized merchants, and in coins issued by the ruling dynasties of the age. Surveys and explorations have revealed a widespread distribution of settlements, comprising both burial and habitation sites. Excavations at Arikamedu and Kodumanal have provided sufficient evidence for local influence and involvement in trade. Although this is not the central concern of this essay, using certain issues as a vantage point, it *will* argue for the need to interrogate, re-examine, and reconsider certain key elements of the 'chiefdom hypothesis' mentioned earlier.

With regard to methodology, K.R. Srinivasan's study of burial practices, surveying textual, epigraphic, and folk sources paved the way for viable correlations between literature and the southern megalithic sites.[6] Many succeeding exercises, however, became mired in questions of 'Aryan' and 'Dravidian' and associated issues of race, language, and migration. In this context, R. Champakalakshmi's 'Archaeology and Tamil Textual Tradition' stands out for its attempt to systematically collate the archaeological and literary information available for a number of sites.[7] Recently, K. Darsana's study situates the megaliths of the Palar basin as markers of territory, using both categories of sources to support her claim.[8]

Undoubtedly, the archaeological record has its share of problems. While many sites remain unexplored, the continuous occupation of a site such as Uraiyur limits what is available for the archaeologist to study. Even more troubling is the ambiguity that remains over the effectiveness of literary–archaeological correlations, and Champakalakshmi herself holds that 'the results of such an investigation seem neither too promising nor too discouraging to be utterly discarded'.[9] I would like to use this essay to argue that where archaeology and literary texts exist alongside each other, depending on the questions we ask, their correlation can prove to be an exercise both cogent and necessary. Such an approach begets the issue of what kinds of correlations are actually feasible.

Champakalakshmi's work calls for a systematic 'indexing of names, places, people and regions',[10] and an ambitious project has now begun to undertake such a mapping.[11] But a 'gazetteer approach' by itself, is not enough. Also, historians tend to privilege the poetic texts as a body of information, often using them as an index against which to measure archaeological data. Such an approach is clearly flawed, for as John Moreland argues, there is a need to recognize that people in the past constructed their identities through texts and artefacts alike.[12] Both categories draw from a common social reality, and what is required is an analytical approach that will bring them together to shed light upon the past.

The poems exalt the deeds of heroes, and the ideology of heroism has been studied in some detail.[13] This essay, however, locates itself around the category of 'experience' in order to discuss a variety of perspectives—everyday, complex, and palpable—that mark the period at hand. To do so, I will draw upon the concept of 'landscape', using it to refer to both a physical and conceptual category. As a physical entity, the landscape marks an environment shaped by human activity; conceptually, it refers to the ways in which people view the world around them.[14] Gabriel Cooney advances the idea of a 'social landscape', bringing together text and archaeology, environment and ideology, to reconstruct the worlds of people in the past.[15] This is a perspective this study will adopt to understand how literary and archaeological landscapes cohere to shed light on the early historic south.

LANDSCAPES AS LANGUAGE: QUESTIONING UNIFORMITY, EMPHASIZING DIVERSITY

Among other things, landscapes constitute powerful ways of viewing the world. As John C. Barrett argues, 'To inhabit a landscape is to look at, observe and to make sense of what one sees.'[16] Yet to reconstruct such a perspective for the distant past, one needs to locate what Cooney, drawing on the work of Clifford Geertz, refers to as 'experience-near' concepts. These relate to how cultures perceive and define their worlds, allowing us to place such an understanding within a more generalized analysis.[17] In this regard, the Tamil poems contain the concept of *akam aiñtiṇai*, but attempts at interpretation have shown the complexities involved in such an analysis.

The akam poems bear no names. Their subject is the inner world, the love of man and woman in all its myriad forms. The characters involved are very few: the hero, heroine, friends and messengers, foster-mother, concubine, and passers-by. These are the people whose voices we hear; the poet's own voice never intrudes. No references exist to political events or to specific names and places. Instead, there is a highly specific grammar of meaning and conventions that determine the enactment of love.[18]

One such poetic convention is 'the *tiṇai* concept', where the Lexicon defines 'tiṇai' as 'place, region or site'.[19] The *Tolkāppiyam*, an early treatise on grammar and poetics, speaks of five tiṇais, five regions, each of which is presided over by a deity and named after a characteristic flower or tree. Kamil Zvelibil argues, however, that the tiṇais are more than mere regions where events take place. Rather, they constitute complex systems of association that link human behaviour to an appropriate landscape. To each tiṇai, poets assign a mode of behaviour characterizing a particular phase of love.[20] These are listed in the following Table 5.1.

TABLE 5.1: The Link between Tiṇais, Landscapes, and Behaviours

Tiṇai		Behaviour	
kuṟiñci	Mountains	*puṇartal*	The sudden meeting of lovers, falling in love, the immediate union
pālai	Arid desert	*pirital*	Anxiety before marriage, the symptoms of love, elopement, and possible marriage
marutam	Riverine country	*ūṭal*	The lover's infidelity and reconciliation
neytal	Seashore	*iraṅkal*	The lover leaves in search of wealth and fame, the pining anxiety of the wife or beloved
mullai	Pastoral	*iruttal*	Patient waiting and the return of the hero

A further nexus of categories includes *mutal* and *karu*. Mutal provides each poem an appropriate season and time of day, while karu refers to certain 'inborn elements' such as deity, food, beast, bird, and tree that provide clues to the setting of the poem. Alongside a 'tiṇai' or 'setting', the poems are also assigned a *tuṟai* or situation and a *koḷu* or theme, all of which are interrelated categories.[21]

From a system so complex and conventionalized, the bards fashioned poems still resonant with their spare and haunting images. But can one use this poetry with all its symbols, 'complex, manifold and conventional', to write *history*? In this regard, I find interesting an argument put forward by the anthropologist Clifford Geertz. He argued that rather than shielding reality, the symbols people use function both as 'models of' their social and ideological world and as 'models for' what they think this world should be.[22] It follows that symbols are linked to experience and bear upon the realities of the world. The tiṇai landscapes, though highly formalized, were understood by people because they saw these images reflected in their lives. In turn, this enabled the poets to create a repertoire of images, readily understandable to their audience of listeners.[23]

The real and symbolic worlds did not stand apart; instead, they were implicated in the act of poetry. The work of botanist B.L. Swami shows how in their references to over 200 plants, the poems are tremendously accurate. Thus, the *kuṟiñci* plant, belonging to the *Strobilanthus* genus grows in the mountains, 6,000 feet above sea level, flowering only nine to twelve years after it is planted.[24] As a poetic metaphor, kuṟiñci describes the suddenness of first love blossoming when the heroine comes of age. Ramanujan argued that such conventions make of landscapes a kind of language: 'The poet's language is not only Tamil; the landscapes, the personae, the appropriate moods all become a language within a language... [enabling him to] say with familiar words what has never been said before.'[25]

Yet the question at hand also relates to how such a system may be used as a tool of historical analysis. K. Sivathamby made a pioneering attempt, arguing that the tiṇai categories could be used to reconstruct the society and economy of the age.[26] Following him, Champakalakshmi, Seneviratne, and Gurukkal identify the distinctive forms of production within these five 'eco-situations.'[27] As Gurukkal argues, 'the poetic delineation of human behaviour patterns' is of no concern; 'to us the classification of land and nature involved in the concept alone matters'.[28] Thus, kuṟiñci is associated with hunting-gathering; *mullai* with stock rearing and shifting cultivation; *pālai* with plundering and cattle lifting; *marutam* with plough cultivation and commodity production; and *neytal* with fishing and the sale of salt. Against the poetic conventions of mood, time, and emotion, we are provided with a segmentation of peoples, activities, and economies within the wider Tamil region.

But the tiṇais are not mere exercises in description. Instead, they represent a highly formalized ecology. Further, the seven tiṇais listed by the Tolkāppiyam for the puṟam poems are similar but not identical to the akam tinai, and are used to a rather different effect. George Hart points out that the tiṇais of the Tolkāppiyam do not find reflection within a text such as the *Puranāṉūṟu* where reference is made to eleven different tiṇais. Of the sixty-seven tuṟais listed in the same text, only forty-two agree with the 158 enumerated in the Tolkāppiyam.[29] There is also the issue of the 'overlap of tiṇais' (*tiṇaimayakkam),* which goes against straightforward attempts at classification. Attempts to connect the concept with archaeology, it would seem, end up perpetuating a binary of pastoralism and agriculture quite distinct from the complexity of the five landscapes.[30]

This is not to deny the validity of the tiṇai concept as a category for analysing socio-economic history. But it is fair to argue that the fluidity of tiṇais as poetic categories is transformed in the work of some historians into a forced correlation of landscapes, peoples, and economic activities. The tiṇais are complex literary devices. They cannot be seen as standardized, unquestionable categories to be simply 'read-off' by historians into neat associations of communities, occupations, and localities. The tiṇai concept offers us a glimpse into how people understood their landscape, but we must be cautious about using it as *the* single framework for reconstructing social complexity. We need to recognize that other categories of sources and classifications exist, and that there could have been different ways of demarcating landscapes and regions.

But where the tiṇai concept projects an image of diversity, it is common for historians to speak of archaeological uniformity and even to adopt a single framework for megalithic cultures in all the southern states. It is this picture that Robert Brubaker deconstructs in an important article that stresses the need to recognize variability and diversity in the archaeological record.[31] The causes for such diversity may vary: chronology, local geology, or distinctive cultural traditions. More extensive mapping is clearly a necessity, and Mohanty and Selvakumar call for a shift from a site-based approach to extensive surface surveys that study a site within its wider region.[32]

Ideas of uniformity—whether linguistic, archaeological, or cultural—must be subject to close scrutiny. Although linkages exist within the peninsula, the fact remains that as the later Iron Age shaded into the historical period, the southern region as a whole did not experience a uniform trajectory. In seeking to correlate the Tamil anthologies with the evidence of archaeology, it is essential to distinguish between those characteristics specific to Tamiḻagam and those that mark south India as a whole.

KODUMANAL: THE MANY LOCATIONS OF A MEGALITHIC SITE

The experience of landscape is not a unitary one. Differences exist in the ways people view town and country, field and forest, and these perceptions are influenced by their own locations in society. A single landscape often encompasses settlements, cemeteries, and sacred sites, as well as the pathways traversed each day.[33] Timothy Ingold advances the concept of 'task space' to describe such a lived reality. He tries to situate human engagement with the land, recognizing that just as the environment shapes human action, so also human activity affects the terrain, both processes extending over periods of time.[34]

Thus, landscapes constitute acts of dwelling, complex systems within which people live out their lives. Studies of megalithic archaeology draw from such an understanding, seeking to correlate 'the settlement landscape of the living' with the 'funerary landscape of the dead'.[35] Often cemeteries were deliberately aligned in a landscape as markers of territory or collective memory. K. Rajan's meticulous analysis of the site of Kodumanal and the larger Kongu region can be used to study such associations in greater detail.

The issue of burial and habitation is still a pivotal one. When early excavations found no trace of habitations associated with burials, it was assumed that the 'megalithic people' must have been non-sedentary, wandering pastoralists. Where habitation sites *did* exist, it was argued that these deposits were 'flimsy' and of little worth. Yet, while there exist burials without associated habitation and vice versa, recent evidence overturns the impressions provided by the earlier studies: it indicates, quite clearly, the existence of 'burial-and-habitation sites'. Of these, Kodumanal is an important example.

The village of Kodumanal lies on the banks of the Noyyal, a tributary of the Kaveri, in the Periyar district of Tamil Nadu. Here, excavations were begun in 1985 by Tamil University together with Madras University and the State Department of Archaeology. Subsequent seasons of work took place in 1986, 1989, 1990, and 1997. Excavations have yielded remains of house floors, iron objects, rouletted ware, potsherds inscribed with Brahmi, and semi-precious beads. Square and rectangular dwellings were uncovered in the central zone, and evidence of gemstone manufacturing and iron smelting provide indications of industrial activity.[36] As Rajan argues, 'The volume of trade, the use of a script, the nature of industries, and the size of megalithic remains clearly proves that ...[these] people were not nomads.' Two periods of occupation have been identified: megalithic (250 BC to AD 100) and early historic (AD 100 to 250). Alongside these dates, the cultural deposit at the site gives us good grounds to associate Kodumanal with the period reflected in the poetic anthologies.[37]

To the east and north-east of the habitation, there is an extensive burial complex. Over 150 burials are spread over 100 acres, with the cairn circle as the dominant type. Urn burials occur rarely. The cairn circle comprises a single or double circle of stones, within which was the actual burial in a cist.[38]

The act of burial is a deliberate one, involving the allocation of time, labour, and resources. Thus, at the site of Bhagimohari in Vidarbha, excavators carried out an experiment to calculate the 'energy expenditure' required to construct a medium-sized cairn circle surrounded with boulders. Their analysis suggests a figure of 200 to 230 man-days, a function that could be accomplished by seventy to eighty young adults in three to four days.[39] As is the case at Kodumanal, grave goods such as pottery, iron objects, and beads were made especially for the occasion. Additionally, there would also be the time taken in the ceremonies and rituals that followed. What this means is that the traditions of burial observed in megalithic cemeteries like Kodumanal could be the preserve of a very few, usually those who could command and marshal resources on such a large scale. As for the rest, when they died, their bodies were disposed of in alternative ways, and these are absences we need to account for. Mike Parker Pearson speaks of burials as 'acts of representation', engineered to reflect the dead person's position in society. Where the actual ceremony was often a site of chaos and debate, what remains for examination is a carefully prepared deposit.[40] Even the choice of grave goods was made by the living, reflecting what was appropriate for the context of death and the social status of the next-of-kin.

At Kodumanal, the evidence suggests that artefacts interred in the graves were prestige items and markers of identity. Offerings in the earlier burials were made inside the cist, but later, as rituals grew complex, they were placed in the passage and all around the cist. Most graves yielded carnelian beads, and in an exceptional discovery, 2,220 beads were found from Megalith V. However, in burials possessing objects of gold, silver, and copper, carnelian beads are proportionately fewer.[41] A copper tiger inlaid with alternating pieces of carnelian and sapphire is a remarkable find; interestingly, its form bears similarities to the tiger depicted on the Coḷa coins.[42] Iron objects include long and short swords, a battle-axe, knife, and tanged and barbed arrowheads. These were laid out in directions and arrangements that appear to have been symbolically significant.[43] Horse bits and stirrups were found in Megaliths VIII, X, and XI.

Many types of pottery occur among the grave goods—bowls, plates, ring stands, four-legged jars, and miniature pots. Interestingly, each burial has a distinctive graffiti symbol engraved upon its pottery, and such symbols occur in the habitation area as well. The presence of a symbol specific to a grave suggests its importance to the individual buried therein. Within the burial complex, certain symbols recur, and Megaliths III, VII, VIII, X, XII, and XIII possess a common symbol of four vertical lines hanging from a horizontal line. Rajan's conclusion is that these symbols represent clan marks, constituting a form of social identity.[44] Similar evidence comes from explorations at the urn burial sites of Kalapatti, Idaikadu, and Sivagiri, and the recent excavations at Adichanallur will reinforce these conclusions.[45]

Yet burial and habitation are not separate spheres, but interlinked horizons of cultural production. At Kodumanal the excavations show that the 'graffiti marks, Brahmi letters, Russet Coasted Painted Ware, carnelian and agate beads ... pottery types like ring stands, plates and bowls, iron slag and arrowheads unearthed in the burials have their counterparts in the habitation trenches'.[46] This is not to suggest that the evidence can be paralleled, but rather, to stress the relationship between funerary activity and the practices of dwelling, subsistence, and trade.

Burial sites were used by communities over long periods of time; hence, they tend to reflect processes of social continuity and change. Repetitive patterns of siting and orientation indicate their strategic location, standing as impressive structures visible from miles around.[47] Tombs were built from local material, usually available within a couple of kilometres. Boulders were used for stone circles, and slabs for cists and capstones. As Rajan argues, such a movement of materials necessitates an understanding of petrology and technology. U.S. Moorti, in an interesting analysis, examines the choices involved in constructing such tombs. He argues that while the *location* of a burial site was determined by proximity to resources, the *choice* of burial practice was determined by cultural preference, not local geology.[48]

There is also the larger matrix to which Kodumanal belongs. This is the Kongu region, comprising the Coimbatore, Periyar, and Salem districts of Tamil Nadu.[49] Here, explorations have recorded over 150 megalithic sites, enabling us to construct wider frameworks of analysis. A regular pattern seems absent from the layout of graves in cemeteries of this region. Large and small cairn circles lie scattered in various parts of a burial complex. However, when a cemetery contains more than one kind of burial, these tend to occupy different areas of the site.[50] In each case, the attempt seems to have been to keep the burial site at a distance from the habitation, and to demarcate the difference between them.

In the neolithic-chalcolithic period, burials were commonly placed within the habitation. In the Iron Age, however, a shift occurs: a fact well established from the earliest excavations is the location of megalithic burials in hilly, waste, or rocky ground. In the Kongu region, Rajan's survey reveals that when a particular cemetery was exhausted, funerary activity would shift to the nearest elevated ground rather than utilize the nearby plains; this phenomenon was noticed at a number of sites.[51] At sites located on riverbanks, burial and habitation occupy different sides.

There appears to have been a clear symbolic association with the east in the orientation of burials. A common practice in the Noyyal valley was the location of the burial ground to the east of the habitation. In cists, portholes were constructed on the eastern slab or orthostat. The skeletal remains at Kodumanal were placed in an east-west orientation, with the head to the east, an arrangement replicated in Megalith XIV, where swords were laid out with their tips to the east.[52] In contrast, trenches laid in the site's habitation zone yielded house floors oriented in a north-south direction, with arrangements to support the storage of grain.[53] What this indicates is a relationship of difference: the house stood at the core of settlement and life, while the cemetery, important but less familiar, was arranged in ways removed from the ordinary.

The relationship between burial and habitation, death and fertility can be seen as a pervasive one. It is well accepted by now that the early Tamil anthologies refer to practices such as urn burials, cairn circles, inhumation, excarnation, and cremation, many of which find reflection in megalithic sites.[54] The poems indicate (as we shall discuss further) that the *kāṭu* or burial ground was a site of polluting power from which most people kept away. In a dramatic image from the *Kuṟuntokai*, a woman pining for her lover says:

Even though he lives in my village
he does not come to my street.
And even if he does come
he does not hold me close.
He sees me and passes me by
as if I were a burning ground for strangers.[55]

But these mortuary landscapes also encompass many varied kinds of activity. Kodumanal, for instance, is a bead-manufacturing centre, located in an area rich in semi-precious stones. It stands on an ancient trade route connecting the Malabar coast, via the Palaghat gap, with the Kaveri delta on the eastern coast. The occurrence of many sites along this route, some of which are rather large, indicates not only its commercial importance, but also a measure of economic prosperity.[56] A major concentration of Roman coin hoards occurs in the Coimbatore region, with the issues of Augustus and Tiberius predominating. Given this background, the evidence from Kodumanal acquires greater significance; for it shows the involvement of megalithic sites in the trading world of the early centuries AD. Further evidence of trading activity comes from a set of label inscriptions dated between the third and first centuries BC, with an important concentration occurring on a route linking Madurai with Tiruchirapalli. These record donations, mainly to Jaina monks and nuns, and the donors mentioned include the *pānitavāṇikan* (toddy merchant), *koḻuvāṇikan* (iron ploughshare merchant), *ponvāṇikan* (gold merchant), *aṟuvaivāṇikan* (textile merchant), and *uppuvāṇikan* (salt merchant).[57] Interestingly, these individuals deal in commodities whose importance is well attested in the poetic texts.

THE POLITICAL LANDSCAPES OF AGRICULTURE

What slips from the archaeological record is the voice of the poet, poignant and questioning, when he asks:

Does this life of a bard in search of favour harm anyone else
as he grows lean in search of a reward, thinks about patrons,
moves along like a bird, crosses many rugged wastelands
and does not think them long, sings the best that he can
with his tongue that isn't perfect, and is happy with whatever
he receives…

…. holding nothing back?[58]

Wandering across the Tamil country, the bards sang of lovers' meetings and the praises of kings. They sought the patronage of those in power, kings and chieftains alike, and were rewarded for their efforts with food and valuables. Yet the relationship did not lack for reciprocal advantages, as kings depended on bards for friendship and advice, and for the poems which legitimized their rule.

It was an age that made great demands of its heroes and kings. Conflict could erupt suddenly, 'a time of terrible battle/come one day like the world/torn out of place'.[59] In the puṟam poems we see a clear hierarchy of political power, though the poets were quick to point out that those most powerful were not always the most generous.[60] At the apex, stood the Mūvēntar, the 'three crowned kings' made superior by the political clout they wielded and their economic power. Below them ranged a variety of small rulers (*kuṟunilamaṉṉar*),[61] of whom, the *vēḷir* have been described as hill chieftains and the *kiḻār* as village headmen.[62]

The Vēntar began to gather power in the rice growing plains, with the Cōḷas in the Kaveri valley, the Cēras in the Periyar valley, and the Pāṇḍyas in the Vaigai and Tamraparni valleys. Each dynasty had its own insignia: the Cōḷas, the tiger; the Pāṇḍyas, the carp; and the Cēras, the bow. Importantly, these symbols find reflection in the coins of these rulers, dated by numismatists between the second century BC and first century AD.[63] Each dynasty also possessed its floral emblem and tutelary tree. Other indicators of royal status were the sceptre, the white umbrella, and the royal drum.

As the Vēntar fought each other, the poems describe how their forces poured over the earth, 'the finest of men in armies dense with spears'.[64] Force was also used to quell the lesser chieftains, a process Gurukkal argues, which involved three methods—tributary obligations, expulsion, and marital alliances.[65] Those who accepted an overlord would come to receive some part of the spoils of war and occasionally even the grant of a village.[66] A poem in the *Puṟanāṉūṟu* describes one such subordinate, a warrior, 'sword raised in his right hand', who stands facing the enemy though he is only 'the ruler of a village which other than always/feeding those who come to it singing/does not even create enough income to merit being taxed by a king'.[67]

For a heroic society, acts of plunder were vital to war. Gurukkal attaches central importance to the spoils of war, describing plunder as 'an essential economic function'[68] of the age. He stresses the devastation of fields and the burning of settlements, a 'scorched earth policy... utterly incongenial to the development of wetland agriculture'.[69]

But though plunder raids were common, differences exist in the methods adopted by the Mūvēntar and the chieftains of the hills. The Vēntar fought each other in the riverine tracts, venting their fury on the cultivated fields. A poet says to the Pāṇḍya king, 'Let your men plunder the fields where/the heavy stalks of paddy bend low, and let fire eat/great, vast cities'.[70] But in forested lands, conflicts broke out in defence of cattle,[71] and bands of men returning from a raid filled the city squares with herds and feasted on toddy and meat. Champakalakshmi emphasizes the economic nature of these conflicts, arguing that the Vēntar in particular clashed in pursuit of wealth and power, seeking access to areas rich in resources and a coastline rich in the profits of trade.[72]

Did ceaseless plunder hinder the development of agriculture? We cannot doubt that these raids occurred, but it is possible to question the nature of the consequences attributed to them by historians. Perhaps, a one-sided emphasis on the puṟam poems has led historians to construct a picture of endemic warfare,[73] untrue to the reality of the period itself. While many puṟam poems present an overwhelming emphasis on conquest and war, one could argue that these were characteristics that the poets had to emphasize to acquire the favour of their patrons. Emanating from a society where heroism was eulogized, this does not mean that the poems are a simple reflection of reality.

The poems differentiate between *meṉpulam*, or fertile paddy land, and *vaṉpulam*, or forested terrain where only dry land grains are grown. Where most chieftains controlled one kind of land, the different tracts held by a great monarch symbolized his strength and power.[74] It has been argued that the area under wetland agriculture was small, lacking optimum conditions, and restricted to the riverine plains.[75] This position, while not invalid, needs to be set alongside other studies that show that early agriculture was never widespread, and elsewhere, as in Tamiḻagam, the forest continued to be an area both familiar and menacing.[76]

In the megalithic burials, a high proportion of weapons over tools leads some to argue that this was a culture of pastoralists and subsistence farmers. But assuming that burials well stocked with grave goods belonged to the ruling elite, isn't it more likely that weaponry would be found? Also, while metal implements might survive, others, such as wooden ploughs, would not occur as easily in the archaeological record. A second century BC inscription from Mankulam refers to a *koḻuvāṇikan* or a dealer in ploughs.[77] As a practice, plough agriculture is well documented in the texts, and in a remarkable poem Ōrēruḻavaṉār says:

Her round arms are as lovely as swaying bamboo,
her large eyes are angry
The town she lives in is far away
and my heart rushes towards her
like a farmer with one plough
when his field is wet and ready.[78]

But plough cultivation per se is not agriculture, and a variety of practices, beginning from the neolithic, existed alongside each other for centuries. The importance of millet and pulses in the agricultural regime can be seen in the context of earlier developments of the southern neolithic, where the local domestication of millet grasses went alongside the introduction of crops and livestock from other regions.[79] The proponents of the 'chiefdom hypothesis' regard paddy cultivation and plough agriculture as an index of progress. Consequently, the 'failure' of these elements to develop to their 'full potential' is seen as resulting in a measure of stagnancy. Yet agricultural intensification is not a teleology but a process, and the changes occurring even in this period—sedentism, plough agriculture, tank irrigation, and the production of a surplus—were of importance for the subsequent development of agriculture in this region.

The texts refer to the peasantry as *uḻavar* or ploughmen. They are also called *veḷḷāḷar*, 'masters of the soil'. For decades, the exploitation of the peasantry has been a dominant theme in the work of historians. M.G.S. Narayanan, for instance, speaks of 'the defenceless plight of the peasants', forced to choose between the marauding attacks of tribal spearmen and the extravagant demands of a royal court.[80] There is, however, a need to question this idea of continuous and total subjugation. For ancient Tamiḻagam in particular, these discussions need to be more convincingly rooted with regard to two issues: the extent of differentiation within peasant communities and the degree of invasive power actually wielded by the state.

For all the ravages of war, evidence exists as well for the settled life of the peasantry. Then, as now, the images are familiar: of dry heat and hard labour, waiting for the rain.[81] It was common for poets to extol the fertility of their patrons' lands. Though these descriptions are often formulaic, they give us a glimpse of a peopled reality. In Cōḷa territory, for instance, poets speak of fields murmuring with water, where birds alighting on ripe paddy have to be chased away. Here,

in the watery fields where the eels go flashing and the women
weed out the small and lovely patches of blue and white waterlillies
where the harrow has passed and has killed and cut up scabbard fish
so that the fat pieces can be taken and eaten right from the pools
by the labourers with strong arms, fathers of children too young
to dress their hair who after getting tired of the taste of great coconuts
climb up on the growing stacks of grain their fathers are raising and
leap into the air trying to bring down fruit from the palmyra palms—
in that good land prosperity is born again each day.[82]

Agricultural operations described in the texts include ploughing, sowing, weeding, husking, and winnowing. Remarkably, we have evidence for women's participation as well. Vijaya Ramaswamy has shown that women were involved in a variety of other occupations—dairy farming, basket weaving, fishing, and the sale of salt.[83]

A recurring theme in historiography suggests that Tamiḻagam's warrior-kings failed to respond to the needs of agriculture.[84] But the poems of the *Puṟanāṉūṟu* seem to suggest that for vēḷir and vēntar alike, agriculture was clearly an issue of worth. A powerful monarch alone could protect the peasantry and his land; for this, force was necessary. A poet addressing a Cēra king says: 'Those who live under your shade/know nothing at all of burning other than the fire/that cooks their rice or the burning of the red sun.'[85]

The vēntar are addressed as *kāvalar*, protectors of the settlers (*kuṭimākkal*), and bards provide instruction in the ethics of rule. To the Pāṇḍya king Neṭuñcēḻiyaṉ, the poet says: 'Those who construct dams so that water collects/in low grounds in the fields are assured, in this world of glory/Those who build none will have no renown enduring in this world'.[86] Elsewhere, a monarch is exhorted to tax justly, 'aware of what is right', for a selfish king is like an elephant that enters a cane field to destroy more than it can possibly eat.[87]

But the ideological moorings of authority run deeper. The poems emphasize metaphors of fertility: where the just king rules, disorder turns to order, the rains fall, there is victory in battle.[88] For this reason, Mōcikīraṉār sings:

Rice is not the life of the world nor is water the life.
The king is the life of the world with its vast expanses.
And so it is imminent upon a king who maintains an army
Wielding many spears to know of himself: 'I am this world's life.'[89]

On the battlefield, arrows fall like rain; spears flash suddenly, like lightning; the corpses bend like grain.[90] This is the field of the warrior-king, 'where a dust of dried blood swirls'.[91] When a ruler dies, death becomes, in this symbolic territory, the figure of the grim reaper, swallowing up kings and their retinues. Saddened by his patron's death, a poet cries out:

Death! You who have
no virtues …
… like a farmer whose family has fallen
into hard times and so he forgets the good of the fields
which are the source of his life and eats his own seeds, if you
had not eaten up this man, how you would have grown
fat wolfing down the lives of his many enemies in the killing fields![92]

In this landscape of sacred power, the Tamils marked the difference between kāṭu, the forest or burial ground, and *nāṭu* or agricultural land. Hart argues that the kāṭu represented a zone of chaos and dangerous power, to be kept separate from the ordered prosperity of the cultivated lands.[93] Strangely, this disjuncture of death and fertility is contested or else ignored by historians. For Narayanan, the poems reflect a deep-rooted and irreconcilable opposition between the 'cult of peace', so necessary for the peasantry and the chieftains' nihilistic 'cult of war'.[94] Similarly, while emphasizing the importance of the aiñtiṇai concept in the physiographic reality of Tamiḻagam, Gurukkal argues, 'It is clear that people seldom conceived of the forest land [kāṭu] in contradiction to human inhabited land [nāṭu]. The kāṭu–nāṭu opposition as it existed in the consciousness of later agriculturalists is not known to them.'[95] Taking into account the evidence of archaeology as well as the metaphors of the poetic texts, one has tried to show that these arguments of the 'chiefdom hypothesis' are especially worthy of reconsideration.

THE KING OF THE HILLS

With wars came death and destruction, an inescapable reality of which the poets were aware.[96] In an age where generosity was held paramount, the death of a patron meant the end of celebration, of feasting, of security. It meant not only the death of the individual, but of the structures that surrounded him.[97] For some historians, the act of giving acquires importance in the circulation of resources, where it provided 'the main means of redistribution'.[98] While gift giving *is* an economic transaction, it is not an impersonal one, and we need to examine the ties that were involved: of obligation, friendship, reciprocity, and a loyalty so deep it could extend beyond death.

Such loyalty is the subject of a cycle of poems that tell the story of Kapilar and his patron, Vēḷ Pāri. Kapilar was a *Pulavāṉ*, a Brahmin, one of the foremost poets of the age. Clearly, he did not lack for patrons, but his poems addressed to the Cēra king Vāḻiyātaṉ and the chieftains Pēkaṉ and Kāri[99] lack the intimacy that characterizes his poems to Pāri. Above all things it is Pāri's generosity that is praised:

Again and again they call out his name:
Pāri! Pāri!
Thus do poets with skilled tongues all praise one man.
Yet Pāri is not alone:
there is also the rain to nourish the earth.[100]

Food is a source of grace, and Pāri provided to those who came singing: rice, fried meat, curry with tamarind, toddy, and sweet buttermilk.[101] The poems imply that Paṟampu's fertility was a consequence of Pāri's generosity and strength. So long as Pāri was alive, Kapilar never wandered far. Even his *akam* poems are set in *kuṟiñci tiṇai*, the mountainous terrain.[102] Images spring forth of a 'mountain dense with vines where the rains poured down', filled with ripening jackfruit and sugarcane, the thundering sound of the waterfall.

It is interesting that the Vēntar unite against Pāri, an indication, perhaps of the chieftain's power. Eventually, they prevail due to the treachery of some of Pāri's men. Pāri is killed and Paṟampu ransacked, its reservoirs destroyed so that it could never resist the kings again.[103] That Pāri's death was not an isolated incident may be inferred from poem 158 of the Puṟanāṉūru, which speaks of 'those seven dead'—Pāri, Ōri, Malaiyaṉ, Eḻiṉi, Pēkaṉ, Āy, and Naḷḷi—chieftains famous for their wealth and generosity. It was, in many ways, the passing of an age.

Kapilar is left shattered. 'I am bewildered and there is nothing I can do.' Yet duty demands that he find husbands for Pāri's daughters. Some of the most beautiful descriptions of Paṟampu are those Kapilar sings while leaving—of a remembered land where Pāri ruled, 'he who was like a single tree on a long shadowless road'.[104] At the court of the chieftain Viccikōṉ, Kapilar identifies himself as a Pulavaṉ, a sage who would have preserved the girls' chastity. 'Accept these gifts I am offering you,/O Lord who overcomes any recalcitrant/opponents, ruler of a country where the harvests never fail'.[105] In the context of its time, it is the strangest of gifts: a bard offering to a ruler the daughters of his former patron. It is said that he finally married the girls to Brahmins, and this being done, sat facing north, starving himself to death in the rite of *vaṭakiruttal.*

It is noteworthy that Kapilar, a Brahmin and poet par excellence, seeks the patronage of the hill chieftain Pāri. It is, I think, an interesting comment on the hierarchies of power. We must be cautious about the degree to which we presume the supremacy of the Mūvēntar. For all their strength, their absolute authority remained confined to the heartland of their domains, and towards the peripheries the vēḷir ruled, almost unbidden, the lords of their realm. Rather than locating the vēḷir on a hierarchical scale alone, we must consider the variability between them, their ideologies of self-perception, as well as their involvement in networks of exchange.

The wealth of the lesser chieftains could not compare to the Mūvēntar, and Gurukkal argues 'the range of redistributive relationships of the hill chief was limited, though a few bards from distant places also met him occasionally'.[106] The poems, however, tend to overemphasize the rhetoric of generosity, using it to legitimate the chieftain's power.[107] They extol the greatness of men who, even when they had only a little toddy, rice, or meat, would give it all so as to appease the hunger of a wandering bard.

Mahadevan identifies Arikamedu with ancient Viṛai, the capital of the vēḷir chieftain Viṛai Vēḷiyan Vēnman.[108] This suggests that at least some of the chieftains had a stake in long-distance trade. Even small rulers issued coins in this period, and the Andipatti coin hoards bear the names of local chieftains inscribed in the Tamil Brahmi script.[109] From megalithic graves in the Nilgiri hills, finds of 'prestige items' have included a Roman gold coin, gold and silver jewellery, bronze vessels, and a number of beads. While some of the jewellery pieces are unique, others, such as gold chains made of circular links and a necklace of small gold beads are strikingly similar to artefacts found from sites in coastal Tamil Nadu.[110]

There is also the larger question of the involvement of so-called 'peripheral regions' in networks of trade. In a recent article, Kathleen

Morrison points to references in Latin and Tamil texts that speak of forest products like pepper, honey, and aromatic woods as commodities involved in the Indo-Roman trade. She argues that although these could have been collected by lowland farmers and traders, their seasonal availability and the specialized knowledge required would suggest they were collected by forager-traders from the hills.[111] Similar indications occur in Rajan's discussion of bead-making techniques where he cites references describing the *kōvalar*s (cattle herders) and *kanava*s (hill people) collecting semi-precious stones in their regions. That these were processed and then traded is evident from archaeology, and an inscription from Archchalur speaks of a *maṇivaṇakkan* or a trader in gems.[112]

This is not to suggest the widespread involvement of these regions in market exchange, but to argue that the relationship between hunter-gatherer groups and those involved in settled agriculture, urban commerce, and trade was a complex and variable one.[113] While it could involve hostility and plunder, it was also oriented towards interaction and exchange.

The poems show that the hill chieftains shared certain cultural norms with the rulers of agrarian lands. Themes of heroism and generosity recur, indicating a common praxis, but the differences in material reality are also etched as sharply. A whole hierarchy of patrons exists, yet even in the smallest courts and in the houses of 'strong men', generosity stands paramount despite their poverty.[114] Whatever exists is apportioned out and still the poets sing, although what is provided by way of food is 'a stew cooked of a lizard with its short legs', and the prize is only a forehead ornament of gold worn by an elephant in battle.[115]

The practice of erecting hero-stones to fallen warriors is considered a distinctive tradition of these regions, although we do not know how widespread this practice actually was. The poems refer to *naḍukal*s and *virakkal*s, but though archaeology provides evidence for a later hero-stone tradition, no such finds are dated to this period. Attempts made to correlate the poetic references with megalithic dolmens, although interesting, have yet to be conclusively accepted or proved.[116]

Such stones were raised in memory of warriors who fell defending village cattle from the marauding attacks of raiders.[117] They were set up outside villages, on barren and rocky ground. A poem says that although the hero's body lies in an inaccessible place, his memorial stands within a pavilion, 'on a small site no one else can fill'.[118]

Ceremonies held to worship these naḍukal decorated them with peacock feathers and flowers, and presented offerings of paddy and bark wine.[119] Such worship, it is argued, arose from a sense of respect and fear, and the desire to placate the dead spirits and use their power to bring benefit to the land.[120]

These are songs written in retrospect, recalling past glory. Along with the rituals of worship, they would have been the focus of community gatherings, of importance for historical memory.[121] Remembering a hero's greatness, the poet sings: 'Ignorant of the death of that noble man who brought in/cows and calves and drove off/his enemies, will the families of bards come here still?'[122]

SONGS FOR AN ABSENT LOVER

Linked to death are the structures of grieving. Alongside poets' lamentations for kings and chieftains, there are the lamentations of women. A poem in the *Puṟanāṉūṟu* has the earth goddess weep that she does not pass away like former kings have done, but remains like a whore, consorting with rulers who come and go.[123] A wife standing over the body of her dead husband laments:

> If I start to scream, I fear that tigers may come for you
> If I hug you and try to lift you up, I cannot raise
> your broad chest. May unjust Death, who brought you pain
> shiver till he is exhausted, just as I do. Take my hand
> which is still dense with bangles and we
> will go into the shadow of the mountain—only walk a little while![124]

In a parallel akam universe, we hear a woman's lament for an absent lover. Often, the poems tell us of how the hero would leave in search of wealth and fame. In his absence, the heroine grieves. Like the widow, she no longer fits the conventional pattern: her husband is not at home, and while he is away she cannot wear any jewellery.[125] The poems describe a variety of absences, separating hero from heroine, and in one poem a girlfriend says to the hero: 'You say that the wasteland/you have to pass through/is absence itself… But tell me really, do you think home will be sweet/for the ones you leave behind?'[126] Lament exists within a gendered ideology of power; it locates itself within many cultural meanings, combining personal anguish and public display.[127]

The *Puṟanāṉūṟu* provides no simple answers to the questions of life and death. Some verses speak of an afterlife, but it is not an unquestionable certainty. Instead, there is life, in all its strange complexities, and the realization that death is but a footfall away. Where in one house a funeral drum rattles, another reverberates to a concert drum.[128] Poetic elegies stand as acts of memory, remembering a life of generosity and justice. The tombs enshrine community memory, standing in their monumentality, visible from miles around. Just as the elegy does not stand alone, but exists in the context of the life that preceded it, so also is the case with monumental tombs. Ways of remembrance are vital to society; they are part of its working and its sense of continuity. Whether expressed through words or through material culture, they make of memory a corporeal and enduring thing.

ACKNOWLEDGEMENTS

I would like to thank Upinder Singh and Uma Chakravarti for their detailed comments and suggestions on earlier versions of this essay.

NOTES

1. A.K. Ramanujan, 'Where Mirrors are Windows: Towards an Anthology of Reflections', in Vinay Dharwadker (ed.), *The Collected Essays of A.K. Ramanujan*, New Delhi: Oxford University Press, 1999, p.10.
2. These are— the *Naṟṟiṇai, Kuṟuntogai, Aiṅguṟunūṟu, Padiṟupāṭṭu, Paripāḍal, Kalittogai, Akanāṉūṟu*, and *Puṟanāṉūṟu*. The *Pattupāṭṭu* as a collection dates to slightly later.
3. George L. Hart, *The Poems of Ancient Tamil: Their Milieu and Their Sanskritic Counterparts*, New Delhi: Oxford University Press, 1999, p. 9.
4. Questions of textual chronology remain open to debate. This framework has been accepted by Gurukkal, Mahadevan, Krishnamurthy, Srinivasan, etc. Hart attributes the poems to the second and third centuries AD. The work of Herman Tieken ('Old Tamil Literature and the so-called Cankam Period', *The Indian Economic and Social History Review*, 40 [3], 2003, pp. 247–78) has received attention for his argument challenging the accepted chronology of the Tamil anthologies. While this essay is not in a position to review his work in detail, his hypothesis remains unconvincing because of its lack of incorporation of archaeological data and its inversion of the relationship between the poetry of the Tamil anthologies and Prakrit and Sanskrit poetry.
5. For an outline of this hypothesis see: R. Champakalakshmi, *Trade, Ideology and Urbanization: South India 300 BC to AD 300*, New Delhi: Oxford University Press, 1999; Rajan Gurukkal, 'Aspects of Early Iron Age Economy: Problems of Agrarian Expansion in Tamilakam', in B.D. Chattopadhyaya (ed.), *Essays in Ancient Indian Economic History*, Delhi: Munshiram Manoharlal, 1987, pp. 46–57; Rajan Gurukkal, 'Forms of Production and Forces of Change in Ancient Tamil Society', *Studies in History*, 5 (2), 1989, pp. 159–75; Rajan Gurukkal,

'The Beginnings of the Historic Period: The Tamil South', in Romila Thapar (ed.), *Recent Perspectives of Early Indian History*, Bombay: Popular Prakashan, 1995, pp. 246–75; Rajan Gurukkal, 'Antecedents of State Formation in South India', in R. Champakalakshmi, Kesavan Veluthat, and Venugopalan (eds), *State and Society in Pre-Modern South India*, Thrissur: Cosmo Books, 2002, pp. 39–59.

6. K.R. Srinivasan, 'The Megalithic Burials and Urn Fields of South India in the Light of Tamil literature and Tradition', *Ancient India*, vol. 2, 1946, pp. 9–16.
7. R. Champakalakshmi, 'Archaeology and Tamil Literary Tradition', *Puratattva*, vol. 8, 1975–6, pp. 110–22.
8. S.B. Darsana, 'Megaliths in the Upper Palar Basin, Tamil Nadu: A New Perspective', *Man and Environment*, XXIII (2), 1998, pp. 51–64.
9. Similarly, see B.D. Chattopadhyaya, 'Indian Archaeology and the Epic Traditions', in B.D. Chattopadhyaya, *Studying Early India: Archaeology, Texts and Historical Issues*, Delhi: Permanent Black, 2003, pp. 22–3, footnote 31.
10. Champakalakshmi, 'Archaeology and Tamil Literary Tradition', p. 110.
11. See the *Historical Atlas of South India* at http://www.ifpindia.org/histatlas/ (under preparation).
12. John Moreland, *Archaeology and Text*, London: Duckworth, 2001, pp. 82–3.
13. See K. Kailasapathy, *Tamil Heroic Poetry*, Chennai: Kumaran Book House, 2002; and Hart, *The Poems of Ancient Tamil*.
14. Robert Layton and Peter J. Ucko, 'Introduction: Gazing on the Landscape and Encountering the Environment', in Peter J. Ucko and Robert Layton (eds), *The Archaeology and Anthropology of Landscape*, London: Routledge, 1999, p. 1.
15. Gabriel Cooney, 'Social Landscapes in Irish Prehistory', in Ucko and Layton (eds), *The Archaeology and Anthropology of Landscape*, p. 47.
16. John C. Barrett, 'Chronologies of Landscape', in Ucko and Layton (eds), *The Archaeology and Anthropology of Landscape*, p. 26.
17. Cooney, 'Social Landscapes in Irish Prehistory', p. 47.
18. A.K. Ramanujan (trans.), *The Interior Landscape: Love Poems from a Classical Anthology*, London: Peter Owen, 1970, p. 112; A.K. Ramanujan, 'Form in Classical Tamil Poetry', in Vinay Dharwadker (ed.), *The Collected Essays of A.K. Ramanujan*, New Delhi: Oxford University Press, 1999, p. 199.
19. George L. Hart, 'Introduction', in George Hart and Hank Heifetz (trans.), *The Puṟanāṉūṟu*, Delhi: Penguin, 2002, p. xxvii.
20. Kamil Veith Zvelibil, *Tamil Literature* (A History of Indian Literature Series), vol. X, Wisebaden: Otto Harrassowitz, 1974, pp. 36–7.
21. For a detailed discussion of these concepts see Zvelebil, *Tamil Literature*; and Ramanujan, *The Interior Landscape*.
22. Clifford Geertz, *The Interpretation of Cultures*, New York: Basic Books Inc, 1973, pp. 87–125, cited in Kathryn R. Blackstone, *Women in the Footsteps of the Buddha: Struggle for Liberation in the Therigatha*, Delhi: Motilal Banarsidass, 2000, p. 6.
23. The debate on the oral character (and, consequently, the audience) of the early Tamil poems is a continuing one. Kailasapathy (*Tamil Heroic Poetry*, Chennai: Kumaran Book House, 2002) argued that the early Tamil poems were

oral compositions, marked by 'formulaic diction, stock phrases and the use of symbols for unconscious meaning'. Yet epigraphy indicates the presence of literacy, and George Hart argues that the metrical forms and literary conventions of the poems are more complex that oral poetry. He says that the Pulavaṉs, high-status, literate bards, in drawing upon the poems of the Kiṇaiyaṉs, Tuṭiyaṉs, and Pāṇaṇs, the low-status tribal bards who preceded them, engaged in an act of mimicry (*The Poems of Ancient Tamil*, pp. 152–8). The problem is a complex one, for the transformations of a text depend on conventions of narrative and society—on relationships spelt out between performer, audience and ideology—that enable a poem to survive, to be remembered, across generations.

24. Swami's work (in Tamil) is cited by Ramanujan, 'Form in Classical Tamil Poetry', p. 210, but no reference is provided.
25. Ramanujan, 'Form in Classical Tamil Poetry', p. 210.
26. K. Sivathamby, 'Early South Indian Economy: The *Tinai* Concept', *Social Scientist*, 3 (5), 1974, pp. 20–37.
27. See Gurukkal, 'The Beginnings of the Historical Period', p. 252; Champakalakshmi, *Trade, Ideology and Urbanization*, pp. 25–6, 95–6.
28. Gurukkal, 'Aspects of Early Iron Age Economy', p. 47.
29. Hart, 'Introduction', pp. xxix–xxx.
30. Darsana , 'Megaliths in the Upper Palar Basin', pp. 53–5.
31. Robert Brubaker, 'Aspects of Mortuary Variability in the South Indian Iron Age', *Bulletin of the Deccan College Research Institute*, vols 60–1, 2001, p. 279.
32. R.K. Mohanty and V. Selvakumar, 'The Archaeology of the Megaliths in India, 1947–1997', in S. Settar and Ravi Korisettar (eds), *Indian Archaeology in Retrospect: Vol. I*, Delhi: Manohar, 2003, p. 316.
33. Cooney, 'Social Landscapes in Irish Prehistory', pp. 49–51; Layton and Ucko, 'Introduction', p.1.
34. Barrett, 'Chronologies of Landscape', p. 23.
35. U.S. Moorti, *Megalithic Culture of South India: Socio-Economic Perspectives*, Varanasi: Ganga-Kaveri Publishing House, 1994, p. 6.
36. K. Rajan, 'New Light on the Megalithic Culture of the Kongu Region, Tamil Nadu', *Man and Environment*, XV (1), 1990, p. 97.
37. K. Rajan, 'Further Excavations at Kodumanal, Tamil Nadu', *Man and Environment*, XIII (6), 1998, p. 65.
38. Rajan, 'New Light on the Megalithic Culture for Kongu Region', p. 99.
39. Mohanty and Selvakumar, 'The Archaeology of the Megaliths in India', p. 328.
40. Mike Parker Pearson, *The Archaeology of Death and Burial*, Gloustershire: Sutton Publishing, 1999, pp. 3–5.
41. Rajan, 'New Light on the Megalithic Culture for Kongu Region', p. 99.
42. R. Krishnamurthy, 'Tamil Coins of the Sangam Age', in Ajay Mitra Sastri and Manmohan Kumar (eds), *Numismatic Studies*, vol. 4, Delhi: Harman Publishing House, 1996, pp. 53–4.
43. Thus, it appears to have been customary to place a sword in front of the passage. In Megalith XIV we see the symbolic placement of arrowheads near other weapons such as swords.

44. K. Rajan, *Archaeology of Tamilnadu: Kongu Country*, Delhi: Book India Publishing, 1994, pp. 118–20.
45. T.S. Subramanian, 'Motifs on Urn found at Iron Age Burial', *The Hindu*, 25 June 2004.
46. Rajan, 'New Light on the Megalithic Culture for the Kongu Region', p. 102.
47. Cooney, 'Social Landscapes in Irish Prehistory', pp. 52–4; Darsana, 'Megaliths in the Upper Palar Basin', p. 59.
48. Moorti, *Megalithic Culture of South India*, p. 15.
49. Rajan, *Archaeology of Tamilnadu*, p. 4.
50. Ibid., p. 29.
51. Ibid., pp. 27–9. He refers to Kodumanal, Vannathuraipudur, Pattakaranur, Kaliyapuṟam, etc. as sites in this regard.
52. Ibid., pp. 27, 36.
53. Rajan, 'New Light on the Megalithic Culture for the Kongu Region', p. 97.
54. Champakalakshmi, 'Archaeology and Tamil Literary Tradition', p. 119.
55. George L. Hart (trans.), *Kuṟuntokai*, 231, *Poets of the Tamil Anthologies*, Princeton, NJ: Princeton University Press, 1979, p. 73.
56. Moorti, *Megalithic Culture of South India*, p. 16; Rajan, *Archaeology of Tamilnadu*, p.109.
57. Iravatham Mahadevan, 'From Orality to Literacy: The Case of Early Tamil Society', *Studies in History*, 11 (2), new series, 1995, p. 176; Rajan Gurukkal, 'Writing and its Uses in the Ancient Tamil Country', *Studies in History*; 12 (1), new series, 1996, p. 70.
58. *Puṟanāṉūṟu* (henceforth *Pur.*) 47 . Unless otherwise cited, all translations from the *Puṟanāṉūṟu* are from George L. Hart and Hank Heifetz (trans.), *The Puṟanāṉūṟu*, Delhi: Penguin, 2002.
59. *Pur.* 139.
60. See *Pur.* 127 where the poet contrasts the generosity of the Ay chieftain to 'those kings with their war drums who give nothing away to others'. Also *Pur.* 127, *Pur.* 137.
61. George L. Hart, 'Ancient Tamil Literature: Its Scholarly Past and Future', in Burton Stein (ed.), in *Essays on South India,* Delhi: Vikas Publications, 1978, p. 51.
62. Rajan Gurukkal, 'Tribes, Forest and Social Formation in Early South India', in S.B. Chaudhri and Arun Bandopadhyaya (eds), *Tribes, Forest and Social Formation in Indian History*, Delhi: Manohar, 2004, p. 68.
63. Krishnamurthy, 'Tamil Coins of the Sangam Age', pp. 45–5.
64. *Pur.* 41.
65. Gurukkal, 'Tribes, Forest and Social Formation', p. 72.
66. M.G.S. Narayanan, 'The Role of Peasants in the Early History of Tamilakam in South India', in B.P. Sahu (ed.), *Land System and Rural Society in Early India*, Delhi: Manohar, 1997, p. 239. Also see *Pur.* 314, *Pur.* 319, *Pur.* 320.
67. *Pur.* 330.
68. Gurukkal, 'The Beginnings of the Historic Period', p. 260.
69. Ibid., pp. 261–2.
70. *Pur.* 47. Also see *Pur.* 16, *Pur.* 23.

71. *Pur.* 258, *Pur.* 259, *Pur.* 262.
72. Champakalakshmi, *Trade, Ideology and Urbanization*, pp. 94–5.
73. See Narayanan, 'The Role of Peasants', p. 242: 'A picture of continuous warfare is presented by the poems composed by hundreds of poets and collected in the akam and puṟam types.'
74. Hart, 'Ancient Tamil Literature', p. 51.
75. Gurukkal, 'Aspects of Early Iron Age Economy', p. 54; Gurukkal, 'The Beginnings of the Historic Period', pp. 261–2.
76. For north India, the iron and urbanism debate shows that a large-scale clearing of forests was not necessary for agricultural expansion, and that the resources of forest and pasture continued to hold importance, forming a series of symbiotic relationships that overlapped in the agricultural domain. See Makkhan Lal, 'Iron Tools, Forest Clearance and Urbanization in the Gangetic Plains', *Man and Environment*, vol. XX, 1986, pp. 83–90; and Shereen Ratnagar, *The Other Indians: Essays on Pastoralists and Prehistoric Tribal People*, Delhi: Three Essays Press, 2004.
77. Gurukkal 'The Beginnings of the Historic Period', p. 252.
78. *Kuṟuntokai* 131, from Hart, *Poets of the Tamil Anthologies*; Also see *Pur.* 391, *Pur.* 390.
79. Ravi Korisettar, 'Origins of Plant Agriculture in South India', in H.P. Ray and C. Sinopoli (eds), *Archaeology as History in Early South Asia*, Delhi: Aryan Books International, 2004, pp. 174–9.
80. Narayanan, 'The Role of Peasants in the Early History of Tamilakam', p. 244. For a similar argument, Gurukkal, 'Aspects of Early Iron Age Economy', p. 53.
81. See *Pur.* 391.
82. *Pur.* 61. Also see *Pur.* 13, *Pur.* 29, *Pur.* 212, *Pur.* 399.
83. See Vijaya Ramaswamy, 'Aspects of Women and Work in Early South India', in Kumkum Roy (ed.), *Women in Early Indian Societies*, Delhi: Manohar, 1999, pp. 150–71.
84. Gurukkal, 'Aspects of Early Iron Age Economy', p. 55; Narayanan, 'The Role of Peasants in the Early History of Tamilakam', p. 242; Gurukkal, 'The Beginnings of the Historic Period', pp. 261–2.
85. *Pur.* 20.
86. *Pur.* 18.
87. *Pur.* 184. Also see *Pur.* 35.
88. Hart, 'Introduction', pp. xviii–xix.
89. *Pur.* 186.
90. Hart, 'Introduction', p. xix. Also see *Pur.* 342, *Pur.* 369, *Pur.* 370.
91. *Pur.* 371.
92. *Pur.* 230.
93. Hart, 'Introduction', p. xviii.
94. Narayanan, 'The Role of Peasants in the Early History of Tamilakam', p. 242. He also says that poetic comparisons between harvest and war are propaganda attempts by the bards who, as upholders of the values of martial heroism, would naturally justify the cult of war.

95. Gurukkal, 'Tribes, Forest and Social Formation in Early South India', p. 68. I would argue that there is a tendency to misread this metaphor, as in Gurukkal, 'Aspects of Early Iron Age Economy', p. 53 where he says: 'The undeniable significance of agriculture in life was influencing poets to make use of agrarian imagery even for describing war.... However, the ideology of peace which had relevance to the agrarian regions could not dominate since the general material milieu nurtured war as an economic necessity.'
96. *Pur.* 62, *Pur.* 63.
97. See *Pur.* 261, where the poet compares the mansion of his lord to his widow stripped of ornaments. Also *Pur.* 265.
98. Gurukkal, 'The Beginnings of the Historic Period', p. 260; Champakalakshmi, *Trade, Ideology, and Urbanization*, p. 92.
99. *Pur.* 8, *Pur.* 14, *Pur.* 143, *Pur.* 121–4.
100. *Pur.* 107, from Hart, *Poets of the Tamil Anthologies.*
101. *Pur.* 113, *Pur.* 119.
102. See *Aiṅguṉunūṟu* 203, 206, 208, 295, 299; *Kuṟuntokai* 42, 95, 355, from Hart, *Poets of the Tamil Anthologies.*
103. *Pur.* 118.
104. *Pur.* 119.
105. *Pur.* 200.
106. Gurukkal, 'Tribes, Forest and Social Formation in Early South India', pp. 68–70.
107. For example, see *Pur.* 235, *Pur.* 127, *Pur.* 180.
108. Iravatham Mahadevan, 'The Ancient Name of Arikamedu', in *Surya Narayan Sastri Centenary Volume*, Madurai: Publisher?, 1970, cited by Champakalakshmi, 'Archaeology and Tamil Literary Tradition', p. 117.
109. K.V. Soundara Rajan, 'Origin and Spread of Memorial Stones in Tamil Nadu', in S. Settar and G. Sontheimer (eds), *Memorial Stones: A Study of their Origin, Significance and Variety*, Dharwad: Indian Institute of Art History, 1982, p. 73.
110. H.P. Ray, 'A Resurvey of "Roman" Contacts with the East', in M. Francoise-Boussac and J.F. Salles (eds), *Athens, Aden, Arikamedu*, Delhi: Manohar, 1994, p. 110.
111. Kathleen D. Morrison, 'Pepper in the Hills: Upland–Lowland Exchange and the Intensification of the Spice Trade', in Kathleen D. Morrison and Laura L. Junker (eds), *Forager-traders in South and South East Asia*, Cambridge: Cambridge University Press, 2002, p. 109.
112. K. Rajan, 'Traditional Bead Making Industry in Tamilnadu', *Purattatva*, vol. 28, 1997–8, p. 59.
113. Morrison, 'Pepper in the Hills', p.105.
114. *Pur.* 327, *Pur.* 328, *Pur.* 329, *Pur.* 331,
115. *Pur.* 326.
116. See Darsana, 'Megaliths in the Upper Palar Basin'.
117. *Pur.* 260, *Pur.* 261, *Pur.* 263, *Pur.* 264.
118. *Pur.* 260, *Pur.* 265, *Pur.* 329, *Pur.* 314.

119. *Pur.* 232, *Pur.* 263, *Pur.* 264, *Pur.* 306.
120. Vijaya Ramaswamy, '*Walking Naked; Women, Society and Spirituality in South India*', Shimla: Indian Institute of Advanced Study, 1997, pp. 44, 51.
121. See N. Vanamamalai, 'Herostone Worship in Ancient South India', *Social Scientist*, 3 (10), 1975, pp. 40–6; Romila Thapar, 'Death and the Hero', in Romila Thapar, *Cultural Pasts*, New Delhi: Oxford University Press, 2004, pp. 680–95.
122. *Pur.* 264.
123. *Pur.* 365.
124. *Pur.* 255.
125. Hart, *Poets of the Tamil Anthologies*, p.11.
126. *Kuruntokai* 124 from Ramanujan, *The Interior Landscape.*
127. See Parita Mukta, 'Lament and Power: The Subversion and Appropriation of Grief', *Studies in History*, 13 (2), 1997, p. 209.
128. *Pur. 194.*

REFERENCES

Barrett, John C., 'Chronologies of Landscape', in Peter J. Ucko and Robert Layton (eds), *The Archaeology and Anthropology of Landscape*, London: Routledge, 1999, pp. 21–50.

Blackstone, Kathryn R., *Women in the Footsteps of the Buddha: Struggle for Liberation in the Therigatha*, Delhi: Motilal Banarsidass, 2000.

Brubaker, Robert, 'Aspects of Mortuary Variability in the South Indian Iron Age', *Bulletin of the Deccan College Research Institute*, vols 60–1, 2001, pp. 253–302.

Champakalakshmi, R., 'Archaeology and Tamil Literary Tradition', *Puratattva,* vol. 8, 1975–6, pp. 110–22.

———, *Trade, Ideology and Urbanization: South India 300 BC to AD 300*, New Delhi: Oxford University Press, 1999.

Chattopadhyaya, B.D., *Studying Early India: Archaeology, Texts and Historical Issues*, New Delhi: Permanent Black, 2003.

Cooney, Gabriel, 'Social Landscapes in Irish Prehistory', in Ucko and Layton (eds), *The Archaeology and Anthropology of Landscape*, pp. 46–64.

Darsana, S.B., 'Megaliths in the Upper Palar Basin, Tamil Nadu: A New Perspective', *Man and Environment*, XXIII (2), 1998, pp. 51–64.

Dharwadker, Vinay (ed.), *The Collected Essays of A.K. Ramanujan,* New Delhi: Oxford University Press, 1999.

Gurukkal, Rajan, 'Aspects of Early Iron Age Economy: Problems of Agrarian Expansion in Tamilakam', in B.D. Chattopadhyaya (ed.), *Essays in Ancient Indian Economic History*, Delhi: Munshiram Manoharlal, 1987, pp. 46–57.

——, 'Forms of Production and Forces of Change in Ancient Tamil Society', *Studies in History*, 5 (2), new series, 1989, pp. 159–75.

——, 'The Beginnings of the Historic Period: The Tamil South', in Romila Thapar (ed.), *Recent Perspectives of Early Indian History*, Bombay: Popular Prakashan, 1995, pp. 246–75.

Gurukkal, Rajan, 'Writing and its Uses in the Ancient Tamil Country', *Studies in History*, 12 (1), new series, 1996, pp. 67–81.

——, 'Antecedents of State Formation in South India', in R. Champakalakshmi, Kesavan Veluthat, and Venugopalan (eds), *State and Society in Pre-Modern South India*, Thrissur: Cosmo Books, 2002, pp. 39–59.

——, 'Tribes, Forest and Social Formation in Early South India', in S.B. Chaudhri and Arun Bandopadhyaya (eds), *Tribes, Forest and Social Formation in Indian History*, Delhi: Manohar, 2004, pp. 65–80.

Hart, George L., 'Ancient Tamil Literature: Its Scholarly Past and Future', in Burton Stein (ed.), *Essays on South India*, Delhi: Vikas Publications, 1978, pp. 41–64.

—— (trans.), *Poets of the Tamil Anthologies*, Princeton, NJ: Princeton University Press, 1979.

——, *The Poems of Ancient Tamil: Their Milieu and Their Sanskritic Counterparts*, New Delhi: Oxford University Press, 1999.

——, 'Introduction', in George Hart and Hank Heifetz (trans.), *The Purananuru*, Delhi: Penguin, 2002, pp. v–xxxvii.

Hart, George L., and Hank Heifetz (trans.), *The Purananuru*, Delhi: Penguin, 2002.

Kailasapathy, K., *Tamil Heroic Poetry*, Chennai: Kumaran Book House, 2002.

Korisettar, Ravi, 'Origins of Plant Agriculture in South India', in H.P. Ray and C. Sinopoli (eds), *Archaeology as History in Early South Asia*, Delhi: Aryan Books International, 2004, pp. 162–84.

Krishnamurthy, R., 'Tamil Coins of the Sangam Age', in Ajay Mitra Sastri and Manmohan Kumar (eds), *Numismatic Studies*, vol. 4, Delhi: Harman Publishing House, 1996, pp. 45–55.

Lal, Makkhan, 'Iron Tools, Forest Clearance and Urbanization in the Gangetic Plains', *Man and Environment*, vol. X, 1986, pp. 83–90.

Layton, Robert and Peter J. Ucko, 'Introduction: Gazing on the Landscape and Encountering the Environment', in Ucko and Layton (eds), *The Archaeology and Anthropology of Landscape*, 1999, pp. 1–20.

Mahadevan, Iravantham, 'From Orality to Literacy: The Case of Early Tamil Society', *Studies in History*, 11 (2), new series, 1995, pp.173–88.

Maloney, Clarence, 'Archaeology in South India: Accomplishments and Prospects', in Burton Stein (ed.), *Essays on South India*, Delhi: Vikas Publications, 1978, pp. 1–40.

Mohanty, R.K. and V. Selvakumar, 'The Archaeology of the Megaliths in India, 1947–1997', in S. Settar and Ravi Korisettar (eds), *Indian Archaeology in Retrospect: Vol. I*, Delhi: Manohar, 2003, pp. 313–51.

Moorti, U.S., *Megalithic Culture of South India: Socio-economic Perspectives*, Varanasi: Ganga-Kaveri Publishing House, 1994.

Moreland, John, *Archaeology and Text*, London: Duckworth, 2001.

Morrison, Kathleen D., 'Pepper in the Hills: Upland–Lowland Exchange and the Intensification of the Spice Trade', in Kathleen D. Morrison and Laura L. Junker (eds), *Forager-Traders in South and Southeast Asia*, Cambridge: Cambridge University Press, 2002, pp. 105–28.

Mukta, Parita, 'Lament and Power: The Subversion and Appropriation of Grief', *Studies in History*, 13 (2), 1997, pp. 209–46.

Narayanan, M.G.S., 'The Role of Peasants in the Early History of Tamilakam in South India', in B.P. Sahu (ed.), *Land System and Rural Society in Early India*, Delhi: Manohar, 1997, pp. 237–60.

Pearson, Mike Parker, *The Archaeology of Death and Burial*, Gloustershire: Sutton Publishing, 1999.

Rajan, K., 'New Light on the Megalithic Culture of the Kongu Region, Tamil Nadu', *Man and Environment*, XV (1), 1990, pp. 93–102.

——, *Archaeology of Tamilnadu: Kongu Country*, Delhi: Book India Publishing, 1994.

——, 'Kodumanal Excavations: A Report', in K.V. Ramesh, V. Shivananda, M. Sampath, and L.N. Swamy (eds), *Gauravam: Prof. B.K. Gururaja Rao Felicitation Volume*, Delhi: Harman Publishing House, 1996.

——, 'Traditional Bead Making Industry in Tamilnadu', *Purattatva*, vol. 28, 1997–8, pp. 59–63.

——, 'Further Excavations at Kodumanal, Tamil Nadu', *Man and Environment*, XXIII (6), 1998, pp. 65–76.

——, 'Archaeology of the South Arcot Region with Special Reference to Megalithic Burial Complexes', *Man and Environment*, XXIII (1), 1998, pp. 93–105.

Ramanujan, A.K. (trans.), *The Interior Landscape: Love Poems from a Classical Anthology*, London: Peter Owen, 1970.

——, 'Where Mirrors are Windows: Towards an Anthology of Reflections', in Vinay Dharwadker (ed.), *The Collected Essays of A.K. Ramanujan*, New Delhi: Oxford University Press, 1999, pp. 6–33.

———, 'Form in Classical Tamil Poetry', in Vinay Dharwadker (ed.), *The Collected Essays of A.K. Ramanujan*, New Delhi: Oxford University Press, 1999, pp. 197–218.

Ramaswamy, Vijaya, *Walking Naked: Women, Society and Spirituality in South India*, Shimla: Indian Institute of Advanced Study, 1997.

——, 'Aspects of Women and Work in Early South India', in Kumkum Roy (ed.), *Women in Early Indian Societies*, Delhi: Manohar, 1999, pp. 150–71.

Ratnagar, Shereen, *The Other Indians: Essays on Pastoralists and Prehistoric Tribal People*, Delhi: Three Essays Press, 2004.

Ray, H.P., 'A Resurvey of "Roman" Contacts with the East', in M. Francoise-Boussac and J.F. Salles (eds), *Athens, Aden, Arikamedu*, Delhi: Manohar, 1994, pp. 97–114.

Selvakumar, V., 'Archaeological Investigations in the Upper Gundar Basin, Madurai District, Tamil Nadu', *Man and Environment*, XXI (2), 1996, pp. 27–42.

Seneviratne, Sudarshan, 'Kalinga and Andhra: The Process of Secondary State Formation in Early India', *Indian Historical Review*, VII (1–2), 1980–1, pp. 54–69.

Sivathamby, K., 'Early South Indian Economy: The *Tinai* Concept', *Social Scientist*, 3 (5), 1974, pp. 20–37.

Soundara Rajan, K.V., 'Origin and Spread of Memorial Stones in Tamil Nadu', in S. Settar and G. Sontheimer (eds), *Memorial Stones: A Study of their Origin,*

Significance and Variety, Dharwad: Indian Institute of Art History, 1982, pp. 59–76.

Srinivasan, K.R., 'The Megalithic Burials and Urn Fields of South India in the Light of Tamil literature and Tradition', *Ancient India*, vol. 2, 1946, pp. 9–16.

Subramanian, T.S., 'Motifs on Urn found at Iron Age Burial', *The Hindu*, 25 June 2004.

Thapar, Romila. *Cultural Pasts*, New Delhi: Oxford University Press, 2004.

Tieken, Herman. 'Old Tamil Literature and the So-called Cankam Period', *Indian Economic and Social History Review*, 40 (3), 2003, pp. 247–78.

Ucko, Peter J. and Robert Layton (eds), *The Archaeology and Anthropology of Landscape*, London: Routledge, 1999.

Vanamamalai, N., 'Herostone Worship in Ancient South India', *Social Scientist*, 3 (10), 1975, pp. 40–6.

Zvelebil, Kamil Veith, *Tamil Literature* (A History of Indian Literature Series), vol. X, Wisebaden: Otto Harrassowitz, 1974.

6. Religious Coexistence in Gujarat
Second/Third Century to Eighth Century AD

SUSAN VERMA MISHRA

THIS ESSAY aims at bringing out the coexistence of different religions in the region of Gujarat in the period covering the early historical and continuing up to the early medieval. It addresses the issue of multiple affiliations at sites and religious coexistence in the region of Gujarat. Most studies on religion fail to address the varied religious practices and beliefs within a region. The multiple traditions inherent in Hinduism fail to appear in most of the studies on religion. As has been pointed out by Gavin Flood, 'The formation of Hinduism as the world religion we know today has occurred since the nineteenth century, when the term started being used by Hindu reformers and Western Orientalists.'[1] Hinduism has been viewed within the same parameters as Christianity and, as has been pointed out by Gauri Viswanathan, 'An inability to view Hinduism in its own terms has shaped the study of comparative religion, whether to prove the superiority of Christianity or to show that Hinduism is a part of Christian teleology.'[2] The comparative approach to studying religions invariably implies studying them in terms of distinguishing one from the other and identifying traits within a religion that makes its stand apart from others. To view Hinduism and study it within the same framework as Christianity is not without problems, as unlike Christianity, there is neither a single text nor a religious leader or religious site that is equally important to all Hindus. On the other hand, nationalists also used the term Hinduism to create an overarching cultural unity,[3] and in the process contributed to the systemization of disparate traditions for their own purposes.[4] This Sanskritic Hinduism was located in a combination of oral and written texts,[5] and was far from representative of the worship of diverse peoples and their lived religious experience.[6] Gerard Colas, in a study on Vaiṣṇava traditions, rightly points out that they had to cater to a variety of human needs in terms of devotion, rituals, and doctrine, and that trends such as asceticism, devotion, and image worship probably coexisted at the same time, although the texts do not give them equal importance.[7] As has been rightly observed by Gavin Flood, 'There is a wide body of ritual practices, forms of behaviour, doctrines, stories, texts and deeply felt experiences and testimonies to which the term Hinduism refers.'[8] Thus, rather than defining multiple traditions by a single term, it is necessary to look for manifestations of various traditions and cultural practices that define this religion.

The foregoing discussion makes it apparent that rather than concentrating on textual traditions, it is equally important to incorporate evidence pertaining to religious practice. Also, it is important to diverge from studying religion in a simplistic comparative manner and look for varied traditions that constitute a religion. It is important to focus not only on contestations, but also on the coexistence of various religious beliefs and practices, as religion develops to cater to varied human needs, and it 'needs to be located squarely within human society and culture'.[9] This essay is thus an attempt to bring forth the coexistence of diverse streams of religious thought and practices with the aid of data such as temples and images that provide clues to religious practices in society.

This essay also aims to highlight the coexistence of different religions in the region of Gujarat covering the period ranging from the earliest appearance of shrines, around second/third century AD up to the eighth century AD. The sites that demonstrate coexistence are not limited to one particular area of Gujarat, but are located in Saurashtra (Amreli), northern Gujarat (Devnimori and Shamalaji), and east Gujarat (Akota and Vadodara). Though located in different ecological zones, most of the sites demonstrate continuity over a period covering fourth to eighth centuries AD. These sites have revealed Brahmanical remains as well as those of the Buddhist or the Jaina religious community.

One does come across a vast pool of data—archaeological, sculptural, and inscriptional—but it has not been put together to bring forth the religious diversity and coexistence of religions in the region. The essay will demonstrate that within the region, there is diversity in the database of the sites as well as their religious affiliation. The sites that I will discuss exist in different niches, along the coast, in valleys, and at the foot of hill ranges, and data from sites vary considerably. While at Devnimori, one encounters an entire Buddhist complex (the only one in the region so far), for the site of Valabhi, our main source for the existence of Buddhism are land grants, and at Amreli, archaeological excavations have brought to light a number of potsherds and possibly the structural remains of a *vihāra*. The essay also highlights the coexistence of Jainism with Hinduism in the region.

HISTORIOGRAPHY

Historical studies have normally associated Buddhism with trade and urbanism, and have focused on the causes of the rise and decline of this religion in the subcontinent. They have also tried to establish the patronage of the extant religious architecture of the Buddhists that would have required a vast amount of resources. The increase in the number of Buddhist lay followers has been attributed to the increase in trade and trading activities resulting from an increase in agricultural production, and conversely a decline of the religion has been attributed to a decline of trading activities resulting from the growth of feudalism. According to R.S. Sharma, 'Ordinary people were certainly attracted to it [Buddhism] because of its successful response to the challenge posed by the social developments generated by the material conditions created by the use of iron, plough agriculture and coins and by the rise of towns in eastern U.P. and Bihar.'[10] As for its decline, D.D. Kosambi opines that Brahmanism, divested of expensive rituals, strengthened its hold on the newly colonized areas and their aboriginal population, and Buddhism and its vast unproductive monastic foundations served no useful purpose after the decline of trade and emergence of closed village economic units when it 'had become a drain upon the economy instead of stimulus'.[11] Kulke's view is that religion was used by rulers to strengthen their position, since 'it is most likely that through the construction of these temples the rajas tried to create a new and centralized ritual structure, focused on the new state temple and its royal cult'.[12] In his study of early medieval India, B.D. Chattopadhyaya cites various examples to stress the role of important religious centres in cultic assimilation.

According to him, the Brāhmaṇas came to control the major cults and cult centres, and this mechanism transformed the character of earlier local and tribal cults.[13] In this formulation, temples are stated to have provided cultic integration. According to Chattopadhyaya, 'In the religious atmosphere in the early medieval period the trend was of integration of local cults, rituals and sacred centres into a pantheistic supra local structure and this was done by affiliating to a deity or a sacred centre that had supra local significance.'[14]

Following the theory of Sanskritization, Vijay Nath suggests that it was economic expediency that pushed the Sanskritic culture into the peripheral zones and acted as a catalyst to the forces of acculturation.[15]Along with the economic factor were the political forces unleashed by state formations. The ruling elite and the priestly groups played a crucial role.[16] In this phase, it was the ruling aboriginal chiefs and their priests who provided the initiative for acculturation since they were keen to enter the cultural mainstream. Further, only certain cultural traits were accepted by the acculturated groups. Nath stresses on the role played by tribal chieftains, who staked their claim to political power and turned collaborators with the migrant Brāhmaṇas. The process of acculturation was peaceful and through religious indoctrination.

There has been a general association of temple construction with royalty. For instance, in southern India, many of the temple sites were constructed by ruling dynasties and were also the constant recipients of land grants. The temples that exist in Gujarat, dating between the sixth to the eighth century AD, do not provide any direct or indirect reference regarding their patron or maintenance by either rulers or members of the royal family. These temples are modest in size and shape, and bear no evidence of being statements of royal power, of any role in either legitimizing the rule of a dynasty, or spreading a state-sponsored religion. Their modest size further hints at the involvement of communities or individuals, and their importance in the continuity of worship at the sites rather than links with royalty. An inscription mentioning the movement of a group of silk weavers to Mandasor where they constructed a temple dedicated to Sūrya reflects the construction of a temple by a community. It is also interesting to note that the spurt in temple construction activities occurs away from the capital of the then ruling Maitraka dynasty. The capital city of Valabhi and its surrounding environs were not selected as sacred sites for temple construction activities. Rather, the focus of the activity lay at a distance from Valabhi, with the majority of sites being located between Dwarka and Somanath.

Historical studies also seem to present a picture of linear development of religion, wherein one religion was followed by the other, not analysing their coexistence. Also, the theory of Sanskritization negates the separate existence of the worship of the local deities, such as *Lajjāgaurī* at the site of Valabhi, and does not account for the diversity in the forms of worship either. It is also noticed that Jainism as a religion is not discussed in these studies even though it existed along with Buddhism and Brahmanism, and had a following that was to attain significance in the medieval period.

The sites that I have chosen to examine are those that contain archaeological evidence for the existence of both Buddhism and the Brahmanical religion, as well as of the Brahmanical religion and Jainism. These sites demonstrate that it is difficult to connect a particular economic activity with a particular religion. Rather, most of these sites demonstrate their involvement in more than one activity. One economic activity absent from most discussions is manufacturing and craft activities, which existed at most of the major sites in Gujarat. These sites demonstrate religious coexistence, and were involved in one or the other manufacturing activity such as bead manufacturing, shell working, or iron extraction. As for trade, the sites contain evidence of their being a part of a trading network that connected sites within the region, or lay on routes that led towards Rajasthan or Ujjain. The Buddhist site of Devnimori, for instance, was on a route that connected parts of Gujarat with Rajasthan and beyond, and the site demonstrates continuity from the third/fourth century AD to seventh/eighth century AD. The essay attempts to identify the economic activities that supported these sites in order to locate their resource base. It does not attempt to identify the sites as either urban or rural based on these activities.

In order to carry out a comparative analysis of the sites' importance, I shall consider the following factors: structural remains; sculptural remains, in which the number of images and the number of Brahmanical deities found will also be considered; continuity of the site; resources that sustained the religious site and the location; and inscriptional data pertaining to the site, which will also incorporate patronage.

MULTIPLE RELIGIOUS AFFILIATIONS

Buddhist and Brahmanical Remains

The sites (Fig. 6.1) I find the most important, and therefore discuss first, are Devnimori and Shamalaji. They are located in close proximity to each other and contain the maximum number of archaeological and sculptural data pertaining to Buddhism as well as the Brahmanical religion. They are located on either side of the river Meshvo in the northern region of Gujarat. Devnimori is the only Buddhist site in Gujarat, where archaeological excavation brought to light a large Buddhist establishment. In addition, a total of forty-six Brahmanical images[17] belong to the sites of Devnimori and Shamalaji, and the site of Devnimori has the maximum number of *Śivaliṅgas* in the region of Gujarat. The Buddhist site of Devnimori had only a vihāra in its initial phase, and over time it developed into a full-fledged Buddhist complex, enclosed by a wall.

Devnimori is situated on the eastern side of the bend of River Meshvo, on a commanding elevated position overlooking the gorge, the river, and the whole valley.[18] Excavations at the site brought to light

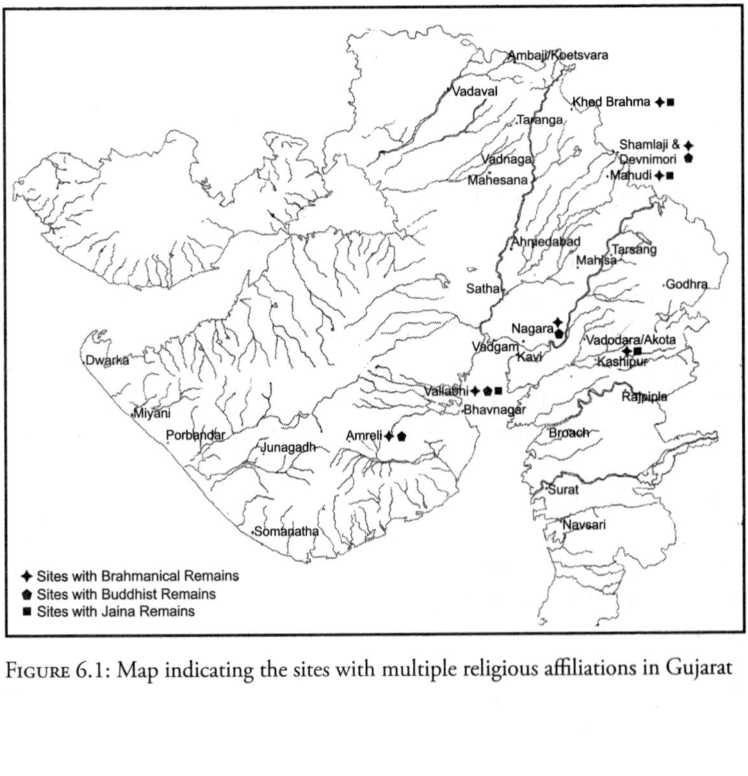

Figure 6.1: Map indicating the sites with multiple religious affiliations in Gujarat

FIGURE 6.2: Model of the Devnimori Buddhist complex in the museum at Shamalaji

a large *śārīrika* stūpa, four *uddeśika* stūpas, a rectangular structure, an apsidal temple, and a protecting wall (Fig. 6.2). The Buddhist settlement at the site began with the construction of a large vihāra, which has been dated to before the third quarter of the fourth century AD.[19] Near this vihāra, Sādhu Agnivarman and Sudarṣaṇa built the *śārīrika* stūpa. Along with it, the votive stūpas, the apsidal temple, and the protecting wall were built in the fourth century AD.[20] On the basis of the antiquities found at the site, it has been pointed out that the settlement flourished till the seventh/eighth century AD.[21]

Two caskets were obtained from the *mahāstūpa*—the lower one, which contained only ashes, was made of schist, was cylindrical, and measured 12 cm high and 1.8 cm thick at the top. The other casket is of greater interest as it is inscribed and contained a cylindrical copper box with silk bags, a gold bottle, and what appeared to be organic material.[22] As for the architecture of the site, to the south of the stūpa was a large four-sided *catuśālā* vihāra with a northern entrance, containing an inner verandah and a courtyard.[23] The vihāra contained thirty rooms, a shrine room in its southern side and at the main entrance at its northern side, and a flight of steps near its entrance.[24] A second vihāra contained two rooms, 8 × 8–9 feet each, an inner and outer verandah, drains in the south-western corner of the courtyard, parts of steps, and a west-facing main entrance was towards the main stūpa.[25] The rooms of the vihāra were divided into four categories—residential quarters, shrine rooms, entrance room, and storeroom.[26] The mahāstūpa was located to the north-east of Vihāra I. The apsidal ended structure, which is probably a caitya hall, was located to the south-west of the main stūpa, and was also of brick. The hall is divided into three parts—the apse, the rectangular approach chamber, and the side aisle.[27] A total of twenty-six terracotta images of the Buddha in *Dhyānamudrā* were brought to light, all of which are three-dimensional, with the backs hidden from view as they were meant for fixing on the face of the stūpa.[28]

The excavation report also informs us that the excavations on other mounds within an area of about 4 km^2 at Devnimori indicate that the Śaivas also built their temples here,[29] and that some of them were contemporary to the Buddhist settlement, as the size of the bricks used in the temples was the same as those used in the Buddhist structures. It further states that the discovery of numerous images of Hindu deities from this area points to the fact that worshippers of these deities also occupied the valley.[30] When the site was visited by Goetz in 1947, he reported, 'In the midst of the jungle, along a small brooklet coming down the hillside, quite a number of small brick temples have been erected, with the usual simple moulded Gupta plinths and a rectangular cella, the walls of which are still standing to a height of 46 feet above the floor level.'[31] I shall now turn to a few of the images recovered from in and around the area. Found from the site were two *Mānuṣaliṅgas* of the Kṣatrapa period (Fig. 6.3) [32] and another liṅga of antiquity is to be seen at the village site of Devnimori, which is worshipped by the local inhabitants.[33] Also found from the site were four images of *Mātṛkās*, the head of a Mātṛkā, and the torso of another, dating to the fifth century AD.[34] The sculptural evidence points to the earlier presence of Śaivites at the site as well. A number of Brahmanical images have been recovered from Shamalaji, the earliest being a two-armed figure of Gaṇeśa (Fig. 6.4) dating to the third/fourth century AD. Belonging to the fourth/fifth century AD is a two-armed image of Kārttikeya (Fig. 6.5),[35] and ascribed to AD 500 are figures that seem to represent *gaṇas*.[36] A Śivaliṅga currently in the museum dates to fourth century AD. Recovered from the area of Shamalaji are a seated and a standing image dating to the sixth century AD of Vīṇādhara Vīrabhadra where Śiva is seen holding a *vīṇā*.[37] Also recovered from the site are three sets of Mātṛkā images dated to between AD 520 and 530. While the first set dating to AD 520

FIGURE 6.3: Devnimori: Śivaliṅga under worship

FIGURE 6.4: Devnimori: Gaṇeśa image in the museum at Shamalaji

FIGURE 6.5: Devnimori: Kārttikeya image in the museum at Shamalaji

contains images of Brāhmaṇī and Cāmuṇḍā, the second set dating to AD 525 includes images of Agneyī, Maheśvarī, Aindrī, Vaiṣṇavī, Vārāhī, and Cāmuṇḍā. The third set consists of mother and child images and is dated AD 525–30. According to Scahstok, the second and third set of Mātṛkā images as well as the image of Vīrabhadra Śiva (Fig. 6.6) measuring about 1.1 m in height can be attributed to a temple dedicated to Śiva.[38] The images of two *dvārapālas*, an image of Gaṅgā, two *Nandi* images, and the throne back suggest the earlier existence of a temple at the site. An *Ekamukhaliṅga* of schist currently in the Kāśīviśvesara temple dates from the Gupta period.[39] In the Khak Chowk area of Shamalaji is a temple of Trilokanātha, which contains a beautiful sixth century AD image of Śiva.[40] The image is noted as not belonging originally to the temple, and it may have come from one of the earlier Śaiva temples at Devnimori. The size of the liṅgas again suggests that there were temples earlier, since these liṅgas seemed worthy of being installed in some religious structure. Of the seventh century AD is an image of Śiva and Pārvatī[41] and an Ekamukhaliṅga[42] as well. These finds show the continued Śaivite association of the site. Also seen here are images of Bhadrā

FIGURE 6.6: Shamalaji: Vīrabhadra Śiva, AD 525

or Yasodā (fifth century AD),[43] the head of one Mātṛkā, the figure of another, Pārvatī as Bhilan, and an image of Lajjāgaurī,[44] as well as a *Saptamātṛkā* panel of the seventh century AD .[45] In and around the area, Viśvarūpa Viṣṇu images have also been found (Fig 6.7),[46] one of which is currently being worshipped at Shamalaji. Thus, there is evidence of Śiva, Mātṛkā, as well as Viṣṇu worship at the site. A look at the size of the images will demonstrate that these were crafted either for being the central images of worship, in a shrine or in the open, or were meant to adorn the walls of some religious structure.

The site has structural remains of both the Buddhist and the Brahmanical religions, and has the maximum number of images for both as well. It also has a long period of continuity, beginning from the third/fourth century AD and continuing up to the seventh/eighth century AD, the longest period for a site in the region. The site may be one of the major Buddhist sites of the region as it is the only one in Gujarat from where there is clear evidence of the existence of the Buddha's relics in a casket, and could have been part of a wider Buddhist religious network. The fifth stanza of the inscription on the casket reads that it was a receptacle for the relics of Daśabala (the Buddha).

The finds from the site of Amreli date from the Kṣatrapa to the Gupta period. It has been pointed out that 'Amreli appears to have been an important centre for various religious sects, especially for Brahmanism and Buddhism.... Besides worship of Vishnu the cults of Śaktī and Śiva appear to have been followed by the inhabitants.'[47] The Brahmanical remains at the site are terracotta plaques representing a goddess, probably Durgā, with four arms and with *ugra* or a fierce appearance, a female figure wearing a crown, another female figure with a child on her left waist touching the breast, probably a Mātṛkā,[48] an image of Gaṇeśa carved in yellowish stone, and a fragmentary image of baked clay representing the upper half of a woman with prominent breasts.[49] The terracotta image of Gaurī Śaṅkara from the site is dated to the fourth century AD.[50] Also recovered from the excavations were votive jars offered in religious ceremonies.[51] The Buddhist remains from the site include two small clay images—one of a *Bodhisattva* and the other of the Buddha,[52] dating to the fourth century AD,[53] and a number of fragmentary potsherds. The image of the Bodhisattva was recovered from the remains of a Buddhist structure on the northern fringes of the town.[54] Further evidence is from potsherds, which were fragments of vessels belonging to

FIGURE 6.7: Shamalaji: Viśvarūpa Viṣṇu currently worshipped as a goddess

monks. They contain fragmentary inscriptions, that seem to give the name of individuals or the localities they belonged to. Some of them read: Sri Gira [i]nagara, [V]ajapa, Sri Vighra, Sri Panda, Ghahta, Vakrumidrukaya,[55] indicating the presence of a Buddhist community at the site.

Another site that contains evidence of the coexistence of Buddhism and Brahmanism is Nagara. Excavations brought to light an image of Dhyāni Buddha, and of the twenty seals and sealings recovered from the site, three are inscribed, of which one has an oval die with four Brahmi letters, *Buddha Pyasa*.[56] In the excavations conducted on Hanuman Dhado, the images of the Buddha were seen along with the images of Brahma and Sūrya.[57] The sandstone-seated image of the Dhyāni Buddha measures 1.4 m high and 1.1 m wide, and the size suggests that the image would have been installed for purposes of worship and rituals. The lower portion of a standing deity and its fragmentary *vāhana* belonging to Period III, perhaps belonging to the eighth/ninth century AD[58] was also found. The image is of sandstone, and on its side panel is a wheel grasped by a lotus stalk. Another fragment of a lower portion of an unidentifiable image was also noticed.[59]

Yet another important site is Valabhi, which not only was the capital of the ruling Maitraka dynasty, but an important sacred centre as well. The archaeological, sculptural, and inscriptional data indicate the existence of not only the Brahmanical religion and Buddhism, but of Jainism as well. This is the only site for the period under study that provides evidence for the presence of all three religious communities. The copper plate grants provide vital data for the site being an important Buddhist centre, as they mention about fourteen vihāras that were located within and around Valabhi. Excavations at the basement of an ancient building, conducted by Father Heras (1934) brought to light parts of a damaged terracotta stūpa. Also found at the site were many Mahāyāna votive clay seals with images of the Buddha and a stūpa, inscribed with the Buddhist creed in characters of sixth to seventh centuries AD.[60] Recovered from the site were fragmentary stone slabs bearing words like *Tathāgata*, *Ratna traya*, and *Saṅgha*, as well as terracotta plaques with representation of a stūpa.[61] The images recovered from in and around the site include a life-size image of the Buddha from the nearby Islava hill,[62] a brass image of the Buddha from a field on the opposite side of river Ghelo

1.2 km west of Valabhi,[63] and five bronze images dating to the sixth century AD.[64]

The Brahmanical remains recovered from the sites are miniature Śivaliṅgas (first to fourth century AD),[65] images of Mahiṣāsuramardinī and Kṛṣṇa dated to the fourth century AD,[66] an image of the goddess Lajjāgaurī,[67] and a huge sandstone *Mānuṣaliṅga* (seventh century AD).[68] Among the ruins of Valabhi were seen a number of colossal liṅgas and images of Nandi, which imply the existence of several Śaiva temples.[69] Once again, inscriptional data here provides definite evidence for the presence of a temple at the site. An inscription of Suketuvarman dating to the Saka era 322 on a slab was recovered from this site. According to K.V. Ramesh, the only traces of the former greatness of the site are a ruined temple of Khaṇḍeśvara built of stones and mortar, and a ruined temple of Hanumān, which are located about 46 m east of the mamlatdar's office.[70] According to him, the ruined temple of Khaṇḍeśvara was the ancient temple of Koṭīśvara from where the epigraph must have been recovered.[71] It is dated to about fifth/sixth century AD, and records the installation of the deity Koṭīśvara by Siṁhadatta. The last line of the inscription contains a reference to the temple (*sthāna*)of Koṭīśvara, and this was the temple in which Siṁhadatta had installed the deity Koṭīśvara.[72] In the opinion of K.V. Ramesh, it is not unlikely that Vala was one of the seven ancient *Koṭīśvarasthāna*s on the west coast. If this is taken into consideration along with the finds of the colossal Nandis and Śivaliṅgas, and the fact that the rulers of the Maitraka dynasty claimed to be mostly *Paramamāheśvara*s, then it follows that the site was as important to the Brahmanical religion as to the Buddhists. The importance of the site also lies in the patterns of continuity as an important Brahmanical site beginning from the first century BC/AD (miniature Śivaliṅgas) to the seventh century AD (Lajjāgaurī), and its becoming an important Buddhist site in the sixth/seventh century AD. Evidence for the presence of the Jaina community is seen in the images recovered from the site and also the literary tradition that records that two synods were held at Valabhi, in AD 363, and between AD 513 and 516.[73]

This now brings us to sites that contain evidence of the presence of the Jaina and Brahmanical religions.

Jaina and the Brahmanical Remains

The essay will now discuss the sites of Vadodara and Akota (located within the city limits of Vadodara), which demonstrate the coexistence of Jainism and the Brahmanical religion. While no structural remains are found at the site, the inscriptions on the pedestal of the Jaina images provide important evidence. Also, this is the only site in Gujarat to have yielded such a large number of Jaina images. A total of 168 pieces were recovered from here, and sixty-eight different objects have been pieced together. These include two incense burners, a mango-shaped object, and a number of images or pedestals.[74] Eight images and an elephant-shaped incense burner are ascribed to the fifth/sixth century AD; a bell and fourteen images date to the seventh century AD; and belonging to the seventh/eighth century AD (Fig. 6.8) are an incense burner and thirteen images. Most of the inscriptions on the pedestals or back of the images indicate them to be gifts meant for installation. The continued donation of images over a period of time clearly suggests that either this site or one nearby was important to the Jaina community. These may have been buried here by the devotees to save them from mutilation, as in the case of the site of Kumbhariya, where the images are said to have been removed from the temples and secretly hidden when the area was invaded.

FIGURE 6.8: Akota: Seventh century Jina;
Eighth/ninth century Sarvānubhūti

Considering the number of images found at the site and the time frame covered by them, it seems plausible to suggest that they would have been housed in some type of structure, and the inscription on the image donated by Durginnī corroborates this. The inscription reads, 'This is the pious gift, in the Candrakula, of the female worshipper Durgginī, in the Rathavasatikā.'[75] In the opinion of Shah, Rathavasatikā was the name of the Jaina shrine in which the image was installed. He points out:

> In the first two centuries of the Christian era Ārya Vajra and his disciples and other great pontiffs visited different cities of western India such as Supāraka and Bhṛgukachha. Excavations have suggested that Akota was fairly well populated in the Kshatrapa age, and it is very likely that there was a Jaina temple here at that time. Since Akota was a district town on a caravan route from central India to Broach, it is possible that it was visited by Jaina monks. Ārya Ratha was a direct disciple of Ārya Vajra and came from Supāraka and the *vasatika* at Akota was probably named after him.[76]

The other explanation behind the name *ratha* is to see the shrine as a place from where annual procession (*rathayātrā*) was taken out. Shah points out that the Jaina texts mention the Mauryan ruler Samprati attending such a procession where a wooden image of Mahāvīra was taken out.[77]

The existence of a structure at the site is further strengthened by the presence of some mason marks on stones used for pavements in later repairs at the shrine of Bhīmanātha, situated to the north of Akota. According to Shah, 'As will be evident from Durgginī Pārśvanātha [one of the images from the site] there existed on the site a shrine called Rathavasatikā, probably named after *Ārya Ratha*, in the 2nd century AD.'[78] Excavations at the site of Akota brought to light a structure that has been dated to third/fourth century AD.[79] Remains of a township were traced from the Bhimnath Mahadeo temple in Sayajigunj.[80] The brick-built structures excavated at the site measured three furlongs, and one of these, measuring 21×12 m with its outer walls exposed to about 1.5 m, has been identified as a public building.[81] Perhaps this was the structure that housed a few of the bronzes excavated from the site, and hence the remnants of a religious structure that no longer exists. The finds of a bell[82] and incense burner[83] from the site further strengthen the case for that existence of a religious structure that may have been used for ceremonial purposes.

The Brahmanical remains at the site constitute mainly of Bhairava and Lakulīśa images dating mainly to the seventh/eighth century AD, mostly found at a single site in the region. Three images of Bhairava belong to the site and date to the seventh century AD, while one image of Lakulīśa dates to seventh/eighth century AD and another one dates to the eighth century AD. Also found was an eighth-century image of Viṣṇu. The site seems to have been important to a sect of the Śaivite community. Inscriptions give evidence of the existence of a temple at Vadodara. The Valabhi grant of Śilāditya I mentions the donation of land and a step-well to a temple of Mahādevā, or Śiva. This temple was located in Vātapadra or modern Vadodara, and was built by one Harinātha.[84] Grants were also made in the regions of Vadodara, testifying to the existence of agricultural activities in this area as well. The Maitraka ruler Śilāditya[85] granted land in Vātapadra, which corresponds to modern day Vadodara.

The vast number of Jaina images and some Śaiva images at the site, when seen along with the inscriptional data, point to the presence of religious structures of the Jaina and Saivite communities. The continued importance of the site can be judged by the find of Jaina bronze images that span four centuries. It is interesting to note here that temple sites of the medieval period in north Gujarat contain Jaina and Saiva shrines next to each other, and the site of Baroda/Akota demonstrates that the coexistence of these two religions had an earlier beginning in the region.

Besides the above-mentioned sites, others also demonstrate the coexistence of the Brahmanical religion with Buddhism or Jainism. From these, though, the only source of data is a limited number of images. There are two more sites I would like to mention that contain evidence, though limited, of Jainism and the Brahmanical religion. From the site of Mahudi was found a Jaina image of Pārśavanātha dating to sixth/seventh century AD, and a Brahmanical image of Bhadra of sixth century. Similarly, from the site of Khed Brahma, a Jaina image dates to the end of the sixth or beginning of the seventh century AD, and the continued association of the site with the Brahmanical religion is seen in the presence of an Ekamukhaliṅga of the fourth century AD, a life-size image of Śiva of the fourth/fifth century AD, and a temple belonging to the eighth century AD. Though these two sites do not contain much detailed evidence, they do demonstrate the coexistence of different religions at the site.

RESOURCE BASE OF THE SITES

It is noticed that at most of these sites a combination of two or more economic activities were being carried out (Table 6.1). Shamalaji, which lay in close proximity to Devnimori, was located on an inland route that connected Gujarat with Rajasthan and Ujjain, and it was an iron-manufacturing centre. Thus, the site would have acquired resources both from trade and manufacture. At present, one notices agricultural activities around both sites, and this may have been the case earlier too.

The site of Amreli is next in importance, because even though the evidence of religious remains is not as much, this site demonstrates that a one-to-one association cannot be made between Buddhism and trade, and the Brahmanical religion and agriculture. The archaeological data from the site amply demonstrates that it was a manufacturing centre besides being involved in trading activities. It thus has ample evidence to demonstrate the coexistence of Brahmanical religion and Buddhism, and the resource base was not primarily trade or agriculture, but included manufacturing activities as well. Besides its location near the Shetrunji river on a trade route,[86] the site was an urban centre, where all types of manufacturing was carried out, as seen from shell waste, beads of agate, carnelian, glass and crystal, inlay pieces, and bone dice.[87]

As for Vadodara/Akota, which reveal evidence of Śaivism and Jainism, the sites lay along the interior routes of communication. One of the trade routes that came from north and north-western India passed through Shamalaji and Karpatavanijya (Kapadvanj), Mahisaka Pathaka, and Kathlal, bifurcated near Nadiad, from where one of them crossed the Mahi and reached Broach via Ankottaka (Akota), while the other reached Nagara and Khambhat on the Gulf of Cambay.[88]

Not only was the site of Nagara located between two agriculturally fertile zones, but it was also involved in manufacturing activities and had trade links as well. Recovered from the site were 1,742 fragments of chank bangles,[89] and this industry flourished at the site for about a thousand years.[90] A total of 235 beads belonging to Period III were noticed, including those made of chalcedony, agate, carnelian, crystal, jasper, chert, lapis lazuli, terracotta, faience, glass, and chank.[91] The sheer number and variety of the beads found at the site is an unequivocal indicator of a bead-manufacturing industry.

Table 6.1: Buddhist and Brahmanical Remains, and Economic Activities at Sites

Site	Buddhist Remains				Brahmanical Remains		Period (AD)	Economic Activity		
	Vihāra	Stūpa	Images	Inscriptions	Images	Structures		Trade	Agriculture	Manufacturing
Devnimori		•	•	•	•	•	4th–7th/8th	•	•	•
Shamalaji					•	•	4th–7th/8th	•		•
Valabhi		•	•	•	•	Inscriptional reference	Mainly 6th–7th century	•	In nearby Hatab area	
Amreli	Find of a Buddhist structure		Terracotta	On potsherds	•		Kṣatrapa-Gupta	•		•
Nagara			Dhyānī Buddha	28 seals and sealings	•			Located at the head of Gulf of Khambat	•	•

• = Present

According to the excavation report, Nagara seems to have been a minor port at the tip of the Gulf of Cambay.[92] The site was also involved in agricultural activity, since 'available evidence indicates the existence of production of rice and *kodarva* as recorded in the excavations at Nagara and the site produces good rice even today. At Nagara small sections of a bund were exposed in the excavations, indicating that earthen bunds were used'.[93] Nagara was located at the junction of Bhal and Charotar, two important areas of agriculture in this area. It also lay on a trade route since, of the trade routes that came from north and north-western India, one of them crossed the Mahi and reached Broach via Ankottaka (Akota), while the other reached Nagara and Khambhat on the Gulf of Cambay.[94] Another trade route started from Nagara and entered Rajasthan via Vadnagar. Even though the archaeological evidence for the reconstruction of the religious landscape may be limited, the site amply demonstrates that it is difficult to associate a religion with a particular economic activity. Rather, the support base, for both Brahmanical religion and Buddhism, was a combination of trade, agriculture, as well as manufacturing activities.

CONCLUSION

A discussion of the sites makes it clear that the region of Gujarat demonstrates religious coexistence from the period covering the third/fourth to seventh/eighth centuries AD. The sites are located in varied niches, have varied archaeological remains, and vary in importance, but they all bear evidence of the presence of more than one religious tradition. While most historians address the question of origin and patronage as far as religious sites and structures are concerned, my study is an attempt to take the question a step further and look into issues such as the survivals and changes that occur over time at a site. Due to constraints of space, I shall briefly mention one site to illustrate this continuity of worship and survival. The site in question is that of Miyani, located at a creek in the coastal area of Saurashtra in Gujarat. Temples are found on either side of the creek and demonstrate continuity from the seventh/eighth century AD onwards. The latest temple, which throngs with pilgrims, is located at the base of a hill. The earliest temples at the site are seen on either side of the path leading to the top of the hill, where again a temple of a slightly later date is present. This temple is more elaborate than the earliest ones and seems to date to the Cālukyan period. On the other side of the creek is a single temple of the early medieval period and another two exquisitely carved ones dating to the Cālukyan period. Miyani is the only site where six temples (mostly in pairs) do not form a single temple complex and cover different periods of time. They bear testimony to the continued importance and sanctity of the site over a long period of time, and while at some sites the association may continue to remain the same, at others there is significant change. This is seen in the case of Shamalaji, which changes from a site dominated by Śaiva and Mātṛka worship to a Vaiṣṇava pilgrim centre.

It is also noticed that many of the sites carried out manufacturing activities, and the region demonstrates that a discussion of the support base of a religion minus manufacturing activities provides us with an incomplete picture. The sites with archaeological remains of Buddhism, for instance, carried out manufacturing and craft activities, as seen at Shamalaji and Devnimori (iron), Amreli (shell), and Nagara (bead and shell). Also, while discussing trading activities, it is noticed that these sites were generally located on trade routes connecting parts of Gujarat, or Gujarat with Rajasthan and Ujjain. Hence, these were not situated so much at places that were involved directly in trade with the Western world. The evidence clearly indicates that trade activity continued even after the decline in trade with the Roman world, as the sites demonstrate continuity beyond that period. While Jainism became a major religion in Gujarat in the medieval period, it is apparent that it had a presence prior to that period, and coexisted with other religious traditions. It also becomes clear that while studying religion, it is important to think of coexistence and interaction and to look for evidence of this, rather than think in terms of the existence of one religion at the cost of the other.

NOTES

1. Gavin Flood, 'Hinduism, Vaisnavism and ISKCON: Authentic Traditions or Scholarly Construct', www.iskcon.com.
2. Gauri Viswanathan, 'Colonialism and the Construction of Hinduism', in Gavin Flood (ed.), *The Blackwell Companion to Hinduism*, UK: Blackwell Publishing, 2003 (reprint), p. 25.
3. Ibid., p. 27.
4. Ibid.
5. Ibid., p. 25.
6. Ibid.

7. Gerard Colas, 'History of Vaiṣṇava Traditions: An Esquisse', Flood (ed.), *The Blackwell Companion to Hinduism*, p. 266.
8. Flood, 'Hinduism, Vaisnavism and ISKCON'.
9. Ibid.
10. R.S. Sharma, *Material Culture and Social Formations in Ancient India,* Delhi: MacMillan, 1983, p. 130.
11. D.D. Kosambi, *Culture and Civilization of Ancient India in Historical Outline*, London: Routledge and Kegan Paul, 1965, p. 185.
12. H. Kulke, *Kings and Cults: State Formation and Legitimisation in India and South East Asia*, Delhi: Manohar 2001 (reprint), p. 13.
13. B.D. Chattopadhyaya, *The Making of Early Medieval India*, New Delhi: Oxford University Press, 1999, p. 30.
14. Ibid., p. 203.
15. Vijay Nath, *Puranas and Acculturation: A Historic Anthropological Perspective*, Delhi: Munshiram Manoharlal, 2001, p. 37.
16. Ibid., p. 34.
17. Sara L. Scahstok, *The Samalaji Sculptures and 6th Century Art in Western India*, Leiden: E.J. Brill, 1985, List of Figures.
18. S.N. Chowdhary, 'Buddhist Monuments of Devnimori: North Gujarat', unpublished PhD thesis, Baroda: Department of Archaeology and Ancient History, Faculty of Arts, MS University, 1964, p. 19.
19. R.N. Mehta and S.N. Chowdhary, *Excavation at Devnimori (A Report of the Excavation Conducted from 1960 to 1963),* Baroda: Department of Archaeology and Ancient History, Faculty of Arts, MS University, 1966 p. 29.
20. Ibid., p. 10.
21. Ibid., p. 30.
22. Ibid., pp. 119–20.
23. Ibid., p. 34.
24. Chowdhary, 'Buddhist Monuments of Devnimori', p. 93.
25. Ibid., p. 93.
26. Ibid., p. 121.
27. Ibid., p.117.
28. Ibid., pp. 166–7.
29. Mehta and Chowdhary, *Excavation at Devnimori,* p. 3.
30. Ibid., pp. 186–7.
31. *Journal of Gujarat Research Society* (henceforth *JGRS*), XIV(1), 1952, p. 1.
32. V.L. Devkar, 'Sculptures from Samalaji & Roda', *Bulletin of Baroda Museum and Picture Gallery* (henceforth *BBMPG*), vol. 13 (Special no.), 1960, p. 136.
33. The field trip was undertaken to visit sites in north Gujarat. One of these was Shamalaji, and close to it was the site of Devnimori, where the Buddhist site is currently under water. The site has a small museum where some of the antiquities recovered from the site have been kept. Many of the Brahmanical images from the period under study are currently worshipped in newer shrines.
34. R.N. Mehta, 'Five Sculptures from Devnimori', *Journal of Indian Society of Oriental Art* (henceforth *JISOA*), (Special no.: Western Indian Art), 1965–6, p. 27.

35. Scahstok, *The Samalaji Sculptures*, List of Figures.
36. Ibid.
37. V.S. Parekh, 'The Iconography of Saiva Deities from Gujarat', unpublished PhD thesis, Baroda: MSU, 1978, Table on iconography of Śiva in Gujarat.
38. Scahstok, *The Samalaji Sculptures*, p. 16.
39. Ibid., List of Figures.
40. Devkar, 'Sculptures from Samalaji and Roda', pp. 35–6.
41. Ibid., pp. 52, 136.
42. Ibid., p. 52.
43. Ibid., p. 48.
44. H. Goetz, 'Gupta Sculptures from North Gujarat', *JGRS*, XIV(1), 1952, p. 2.
45. *Indian Archaeology: A Report* (henceforth *IAR*),1990–1, p. 6.
46. Haripriya Rangarajan, 'Wrong Identification of the Images of *Viśvarūpa* Viṣṇu from Gujarat', *Kala*, vol.VI, 1999–2000, p. 67.
47. S.R. Rao, *Excavation at Amreli, BBMPG,* vol. XVIII, 1966, p. 14.
48. *Annual Report: Archaeological Department*, Baroda State, 1936–7, p. 12.
49. *Annual Report: Archaeological Department,* 1935–6, p. 19.
50. Ravi Hazaris, 'Vrisha Sculptures in Gujarat', in C. Margabandhu, K.S. Ramachandran, A.P. Sagar, and D.K. Sinha (eds), *Indian Archaeological Heritage* (Agam Indological Series), no. 11, Delhi: Agam Kala Prakashan, 1991, p. 563.
51. Rao, *Excavation at Amreli*, p. 14.
52. *Annual Report: Archaeological Department*, 1935–6, p. 19.
53. Rao, *Excavation at Amreli*, p. 98.
54. Ibid., p. 14.
55. *Annual Report: Archaeological Department,* for year ending 31 July 1939, p. 5.
56. R.N. Mehta and D.R. Shah, *Excavation at Nagara*, Baroda: MS University, 1968, p. 107.
57. Le. Thi Lien, 'Buddhist Monuments and Antiquities of Gujarat', unpublished MA dissertation, Baroda: MS University, 1992, p. 89.
58. Mehta and Shah, *Excavation at Nagara*, p. 19.
59. Ibid., p. 127.
60. Le. Thi Lien, 'Buddhist Monuments and Antiquities of Gujarat', p. 91.
61. M.G. Dikshit, 'History of Buddhism in Gujarat', *JGRS*, vol. VIII, 1946, p. 109.
62. K.F. Sompura, *Buddhist Monuments and Sculptures in Gujarat: A Historical Survey*, Hoshiarpur: Vishveshvaranand Institute, 1965, p. 28.
63. M.K. Thakor, 'A Bronze Image of Buddha from Valabhipur', *Journal of Oriental Institute,* vol. XVI, pp. 79–85.
64. *Archaeological Survey of Western India*, for year ending 31 March 1915, p. 30.
65. *IAR*,1997–8, p. 24.
66. U.P. Shah, 'A Female Bust from Valabhi', *JISOA* (Special no.: Western Indian Art), 1965–6, p. 1.
67. Vasant Shinde, 'The Earliest Temple of *Lajjāgaurī*? The Recent Excavations at Padri in Gujarat', *East and West,* 44 (2–4), 1994, p. 484.

68. Parekh, 'The Iconography of Saiva Deities from Gujarat: Iconographic Chart of Lingas from Gujarat'.
69. K.F. Sompura, *Structural Temples of Gujarat*, Ahmedabad: Gujarat University, 1968, p. 83.
70. *Epigraphia Indica* (henceforth *EI*), 40(2), 1973, p. 51.
71. Ibid., p. 52.
72. Ibid., p. 53.
73. M.A. Dhaky and U.S. Moorti, *The Temples in Kumbhariya*, Gurgaon: American Institute of Indian Studies, 2001, p. 5.
74. U.P. Shah, *Akota Bronzes*, Bombay: Department of Archaeology, Government of Bombay, 1959, p. 4.
75. Ibid., p. 39.
76. Ibid., p. 40.
77. Ibid.
78. Ibid., p. 3.
79. Benapudi Subbarao, *Baroda Through the Ages*, Baroda: MS University, 1953, p. 14.
80. R.N. Mehta, 'Archaeology of the Baroda, Broach and Surat Districts upto 1300 AD', unpublished PhD thesis, Baroda: MS University, 1957, p. 67.
81. Ibid., p. 110.
82. Shah, *Akota Bronzes*, 1959, p. 49.
83. Ibid., pp. 31, 44.
84. *Indian Antiquary* (henceforth *IA*), vol. IX, p. 238.
85. Ibid., p. 237.
86. Atusha M. Bharuch, 'The Archaeology of Settlements of the Kshatrapa Period', unpublished PhD thesis, Pune: Deccan Post Graduate and Research Institute, 1997, p. 193.
87. Ibid., pp. 144–5.
88. Momin Kamarali Noormohmed, 'Archaeology of the Kheda District upto 1300 AD', unpublished PhD thesis, Baroda: MS University, 1979, p. 17.
89. Mehta and Shah, *Excavation at Nagara*, p. 129.
90. Ibid., p. 130.
91. Ibid., pp. 135–7.
92. Ibid., p. 166.
93. R.N. Mehta, 'Economic Pattern of India during the Early Iron Age (1000 BC – 100 AD)', *Puratattva*, vol. 9, 1977–8, p. 52.
94. Noormohmed, 'Archaeology of the Kheda District upto 1300 AD', p. 17.

REFERENCES

Annual Report: Archaeological Department, Baroda State, 1935–6, 1936–7, 1939.

Bharuch, Atusha M., 'The Archaeology of Settlements of the Kshatrapa Period', unpublished PhD thesis, Pune: Deccan Post Graduate and Research Institute, 1997.

Chattopadhyaya, B.D., *The Making of Early Medieval India,* New Delhi: Oxford University Press, 1999.

Chowdhary, S.N., 'Buddhist Monuments of Devnimori: North Gujarat', unpublished PhD thesis, Baroda: Department of Archaeology and Ancient History, Faculty of Arts, MS University, 1964.

Colas, Gerard, 'History of Vaiṣṇava Traditions: An Esquisse', in Gavin Flood (ed.), *The Blackwell Companion to Hinduism*, UK: Blackwell Publishing, 2003 (reprint), pp. 229–70.

Devkar, V.L., 'Sculptures from Samalaji and Roda', *Bulletin of Baroda Museum and Picture Gallery*, vol. XIII, Special no., 1960.

Dhaky, M.A. and U.S. Moorti, *The Temples in Kumbhariya*, Gurgaon: American Institute of Indian Studies, 2001.

Dikshit, M.G., 'History of Buddhism in Gujarat', *Journal of Gujarat Research Society*, vol. VIII, 1946.

Flood, Gavin, 'Hinduism, Vaiṣṇavism and ISKCON: Authentic Traditions or Scholarly Construct', http://www.iskcon.com.

Goetz, H., 'Gupta Sculptures from North Gujarat', *Journal of Gujarat Research Society*, vol. XIV, 1952, pp. 1–5.

Hazaris, Ravi, 'Vrisha Sculptures in Gujarat', in C. Margabandhu, K.S. Ramachandran, A.P. Sagar, and D.K. Sinha (eds), *Indian Archaeological Heritage* (Agam Indological Series), no.11. Delhi: Agam Kala Prakashan, 1991.

Kosambi, D.D., *Culture and Civilization of Ancient India in Historical Outline*, London: Routledge and Kegan Paul, 1965.

Kulke, H., *Kings and Cults: State Formation and Legitimisation in India and South East Asia*, Delhi: Manohar, 2001 (reprint).

Lien, Le. Thi, 'Buddhist Monuments and Antiquities of Gujarat', unpublished MA dissertation, Baroda: MS University, 1992.

Mehta, R.N., 'Archaeology of the Baroda, Broach and Surat districts upto 1300 AD', unpublished PhD thesis, Baroda: MSU, 1957.

——, 'Five Sculptures from Devnimori', *Journal of Indian Society of Oriental Art*, Special no.: Western Indian Art, 1965–6, pp. 27–9.

——, 'Economic Pattern of India During the Early Iron Age (1000 BC–100 AD)', *Puratattva*, vol. 9, 1977–8, pp. 52–6.

Mehta, R.N. and S.N. Chowdhary, '*Excavation at Devnimori (A Report of the Excavation Conducted from 1960 to 1963)*, Baroda: Department of Archaeology and Ancient History, Faculty of Arts, MS University of Baroda, 1966.

Mehta. R.N. and D.R. Shah, *Excavation at Nagara*, Baroda: Department of Archaeology and Ancient History, Faculty of Arts, MS University, 1968.

Nath, Vijay, *Puranas and Acculturation: A Historic Anthropological Perspective*, Delhi: Munshiram Manoharlal, 2001.

Noormohmed, Momin Kamarali, 'Archaeology of the Kheda District upto 1300 AD', unpublished PhD thesis, Baroda: MS University, 1979.

Parekh, V.S., 'The Iconography of Saiva Deities from Gujarat', unpublished PhD thesis, Baroda: MS University, 1978.

Rangarajan, Haripriya, 'Wrong Identification of the Images of *Viśvarūpa* Viṣṇu from Gujarat', *Kala*, vol. 6 , 1999–2000, pp. 67–70.

Rao, S.R., 'Excavation at Amreli: A Kshatrapa Gupta Town', *BBMPG*, vol. XVIII, 1966.

Scahstok, Sara L. *The Samalaji Sculptures and Sixth Century Art in Western India.* Leiden: E.J. Brill, 1985.

Shah, U.P., *Akota Bronzes*, Bombay: Department of Archaeology, Government of Bombay, 1959.

——, 'A Female Bust from Valabhi', *Journal of Indian Society of Oriental Art*, Special no.: Western Indian Art, 1965–6, pp. 1–2.

Sharma, R.S., *Material Culture and Social Formations in Ancient India*, Delhi: MacMillan, 1983.

Shinde, Vasant, 'The Earliest Temple of *Lajjāgaurī*? The Recent Excavations at Padri in Gujarat', *East and West*, 44 (2–4), 1994.

Sompura, K.F., *Buddhist Monuments and Sculptures in Gujarat: A Historical Survey.* Hoshiarpur: Vishveshvaranand Institute, 1965.

——, *Structural Temples of Gujarat*, Ahmedabad: Gujarat University, 1968.

Subbarao Benapudi, *Baroda Through the Ages*, Baroda: MS University, 1953.

M.K. Thakor, 'A Bronze Image of Buddha from Valabhipur', *Journal of Oriental Institute*, vol. XVI, pp. 79–85.

Viswanathan, Gauri, 'Colonialism and the Construction of Hinduism', in Flood (ed.), *The Blackwell Companion to Hinduism*, pp. 23–44.

7. Terracottas from Mathura and Ahichchhatra

An Archaeological Study (400 BC to Seventh/Eighth Century AD)

Shivani Agarwal

It is an indisputable fact that the expressions of art of a particular era are a true reflection of its social fabric and are inextricably linked to the society of the time. Anthropomorphic terracotta figurines have always been in use in the Indian subcontinent, right from the neolithic sites in Baluchistan and the Indus Civilization to the present day. The present essay uses the corpus of terracottas from the sites of Mathura and Ahichchhatra, (in Mathura and Bareilly districts, Uttar Pradesh respectively) pertaining to a time period between 400 BC and the seventh/eighth century AD, to explore the roles and functions that these objects fulfilled in their respective societies. Most scholars addressing this issue have clubbed the female terracotta figurines from the two regions under an undifferentiated and homogeneous category of the 'Mother Goddess', showing scant regard for the technical variations and stylistic peculiarities these objects exhibit. Moreover, these figurines have been isolated from their regional contexts as well as from the other objects and structures with which they were associated. The attempt, therefore, is to study the archaeological record according to the contexts of the objects found, namely, the association of terracotta figurines within their groups, and in relation to other artefacts and structural remains. Archaeological evidence has brought to light a very strong presence of regional cults at both Mathura and Ahichchhatra, and most of these objects could have been related to these. Therefore, any interpretation with regard to the nature and function of these figurines will have to move beyond the arbitrary 'Mother Goddess' tag.

There is a large corpus of scholarship pertaining to the terracotta figurines from the two sites. These figurines have commanded the interest of scholars from various fields: art history, social history, archaeology, and the history of ancient Indian religion. Some of the earliest outstanding works are by R.G. Bhandarkar,[1] John Marshall,[2] Stella Kramrisch,[3] Ananda Coomaraswamy,[4] and V.S. Agrawala,[5] among others. The 'Mother Goddess' as represented by the terracotta female figures, was defined as a fertility figure fulfilling the functions of procreation and sustenance of life. The genesis of these 'Goddesses' is traced to prehistoric societies where they controlled the realms of both animal and human fertility and, therefore, were venerated as cult figures. Gradually, these prehistoric goddesses lost out to the more dominant Aryan religion, and over a period of time, were assimilated and merged into the all-encompassing Brahmanical pantheon. As Coomaraswamy states:

> We can safely assert that the Indian nude goddess, was a goddess of fertility, for this is written unmistakably upon her image, that she was a popular and perhaps a household goddess, that she was one of the many non-Aryan feminine divinities who later on gradually and with difficulty, merged in the Brahmanical and Buddhist pantheons as Śaktīs.[6]

Therefore, the common presumption in most of these works is the overemphasis on the religious nature and function of these figurines.

Secondary writings analysing the nature and function of these figurines can be broadly differentiated into distinct phases on the basis of the source material utilized and the methodologies adopted for analysis. The earliest studies on ancient Indian religion began as early as the nineteenth century. In that period, religious history was constructed largely on the basis of literary texts and translations of Sanskrit texts by Indologists, who provided scholars with the material they needed to study ancient Indian religion. Most early studies on religion regarded Vedic literature as the starting point, followed by the Upaniṣads, and then the Purāṇas. The prevalence of goddess worship in ancient India became evident from Purāṇic sources, and was believed to have originated in close association with the development of Śaivism, later assuming the form of an independent cult of its own. Therefore, on the basis of textual data alone, scholars like Maurice Bloomfield,[7] Monier Williams,[8] and R.G. Bhandarkar,[9] to name a few, were able to outline a trajectory of the genesis and development of religion in ancient India. Archaeology had a minimal role in these studies.

THE MOTHER GODDESS IN ARCHAEOLOGICAL DATA

It was due to the pioneering works of Alexander Cunningham in the nineteenth century and John Marshall in the beginning of the twentieth, that archaeology firmly entered the realm of religious studies. Marshall's discovery of the Indus Civilization, and, more importantly, his excavations at the site of Mohenjodaro had far-reaching implications for the study of ancient Indian history. Not only did they push back the dates of ancient Indian civilization to as early as the third millennium BC; his interpretation of the archaeological data from the Indus Valley, particularly the female terracotta figurines in the light of the later Hindu beliefs and practices, encouraged scholars to trace back the genesis of Hindu religion to this civilization. The term 'Mother Goddess' was used during the initial excavations at Harappa and Mohenjodaro. On the basis of the material remains from these two sites, Marshall propounded a well-articulated theory of the cult of the Mother Goddess in India. To validate his theories, he had before him a corpus of writings on Hindu religion, as well as his previous experiences of large-scale excavations in Greece, southern Turkey, and Crete, and the archaeological material similar to the Indus Valley from these contemporaneous sites in West Asia and Europe. The female terracotta figurines unearthed from the Indus Valley were taken to represent a religious function, and Marshall drew cross-cultural parallels with similar figurines from West Asia and Europe. According to him,

> The correspondence between these figurines [the ones from West Asia and Europe] and those found on the banks of the Indus is such that it is difficult to resist the conclusion that the latter also represented a Mother or Nature Goddess and served the same purpose as their counterparts in the West.[10]

Marshall's methodology involved an intermixing of archaeological and textual data. His assumptions and conclusions on the terracotta figurines were adopted and applied by scholars working on the Ganga Valley sites. V.S. Agrawala, for instance, worked extensively on the terracotta figurines from this region, including Mathura and Ahichchhatra, dating from the fifth/sixth century BC to seventh/eighth century AD. Drawing inspiration from Marshall, he too interpreted female terracotta figurines as representations of goddesses and made a direct comparison of these figurines with the ones found at the pre-Harappan sites in Baluchistan, as well as the Indus Valley figurines. The parallels with Mother Goddess worship in distant parts of Asia and Europe were also taken as evidence to further strengthen the identification of these figurines as Goddesses. Agrawala also used the numerous references provided by the Vedas and the Purāṇas regarding the origin and prevalence of a belief in the Mother Goddess cult in India. The most evident flaw in such an approach is that not only do scholars mix up different cultures, but also move back and forth in time and space, with little regard for social, cultural, and chronological contexts.

While the Indus Valley terracotta figurines have been recently subjected to careful scrutiny and reassessment, and most of the earlier formulations have been questioned, such a study is lacking with respect to the Ganga Valley terracottas. Works by scholars like C. Jarrige,[11] Sharri Clark,[12] and A. Jansen[13] have criticized most of Marshall's theories, and have made clear the complexities of issues regarding these figurines, emphasizing the need to refocus and to look beyond simplistic explanations and tags. Jansen, through her quantification of Indus Valley data, has proved that most of the finds of female figurines are confined to the two sites of Harappa and Mohenjodaro alone and, therefore, it would be erroneous to talk about a pan-Indus Mother Goddess cult. Moreover, she feels that the iconographic diversity of these female figurines, and the range of other human and animal figurines associated with them, have to be accounted for and taken together, as these factors 'indicate an ideological sophistication that goes beyond the familiar fertility and maternity complex'.[14]

The corpus of figurines from the Indus Civilization is used by Clark to explore conceptions of sex, gender, and sexuality, as expressed in the representations of the body. In connection with the earlier held belief that nude female figurines with exaggerated hips and prominent breasts symbolized fertility and, therefore, were representations of fertility goddesses, Clark observes that these features usually associated with fertility are not typical of the majority of the Indus figurines. Cross-cultural comparisons have also been questioned by David Kinsley, who feels that comparing the Indus figurines with those of Europe and West Asia is problematic. He draws attention to the fact that very few of the Indus figurines have accentuated breasts, hips, or genital areas, physical attributes extremely common in the so-called Venus figurines from the sites of Europe and West Asia. In comparison to these, the Indus figurines are on the slim side and are often small breasted. Moreover, trade contacts with the West or the prevalence of some form of fertility cult are insufficient to suggest cultural similarities between the two civilizations.[15]

ETHNOGRAPHY AND THE WORSHIP OF THE GODDESS

Another dominant trend in studying the Mother Goddess cults in ancient Indian history is the use of ethnographic data. The pioneering work in this field was by D.D. Kosambi, who in his fieldwork in Maharashtra identified a number of local and tribal goddess cults that were gradually enrolled into the Brahmanical religious order. He used a combination of sources—archaeological, ethnographic, and literary—to work out an integration theory, according to which the process of Sanskritization that began after the coming of the Vedic Aryans resulted in the assimilation and integration of many folk and tribal cults into the mainstream Brahmanical religion. Kosambi's methodologies and his integration theory has perhaps been the most popular and readily accepted among scholars tracing the evolution of the goddess cult in India. The female terracotta figurines fit in perfectly as a representation of primitive local pre-Aryan goddesses that were later replaced by mainstream female divinities.

ECONOMIC DETERMINISM AND THE SOCIAL MILIEU OF THE TERRACOTTA FIGURINES

Apart from the religious associations made with regard to the terracottas, there have been some attempts to explore their social, economic, and political contexts. Stylistic peculiarities and patterns of production have been linked to political and economic changes, as well as urban developments. The chronological classification of the objects tends to follow a pattern of dynastic succession. With regard to Mathura, M.K. Dhavalikar links up the chronology of the production and style of terracottas with the rise and fall of political dynasties. Therefore, for him, the consolidation of the Mauryan Empire under a strongly unified rule ushered in a distinct cultural phase, which also resulted in a sudden spurt of artistic activity. The succeeding Kuṣāṇa period, on the other hand, saw the blending of the Graeco-Roman style of art, its main centres being Gandhara and Mathura. And in the Gupta period, terracotta art travelled with political power and, as a result, terracotta figures are found over a large part of the subcontinent.[16] Little wonder then that Dhavalikar's classification of the figurines include labels such as pre-Mauryan, Mauryan, Śuṅga, Kuṣāṇa, and Gupta terracottas.

There are others who link the production and distribution pattern of terracottas to economic changes and processes of urbanization. Devangana Desai summarizes her argument on terracotta art in this context. She argues that certain complex social conditions need to be fulfilled before one can talk about a large-scale production of terracotta figurines. And such a production is undertaken only when there is a demand arising either from institutionalized religious cults that require the use of clay figurines as votive offerings, magical charms, or household deities, or from a public who would buy secular figurines for the decoration of homes, as toys for children, or for other varied purposes. This demand, she asserts, was best fulfilled in urban societies, whose well-organized markets were a stimulus to the expansion of industries in general.[17] Therefore, the rise of terracottas in Indian history is associated with the rise and flourishing of urban cultures. The flourishing urban base of the Indus Civilization sustained a large-scale production of these objects, after which they made an appearance in large numbers only from the period of the second urbanization (that is, around 600 BC). Patterns of urban culture not only determined the production of terracottas, but also had a bearing on the themes and subjects depicted. Desai states that in the initial period (that is, *c.* 600 to 320 BC) the Mother Goddess cult had not developed fully and, therefore, the female figures were mostly handmade and simple in ornamentation. They were neither decorative nor artistic in intent, which was due to the fact that the process of urbanization had just begun and had not yet had much of an impact on cultural life.[18] Thereafter, urban character and tastes are reflected freely in the terracottas of the following periods. This urban sophistication can be seen in the female figurines that were now, in contrast to the primitive archaic goddesses, beautifully bedecked and bejewelled. The tastes of the leisured *nāgaraka* (a person belonging to the affluent urban social class in the cities) class can also be seen in the vast array of astounding themes depicted on the terracotta plaques including scenes of social gatherings, animal fights, and erotic acts. Active trade with the Romans and the consequent prosperity, as well as artistic influence, was also seen as the dominant cause for the spurt in the demand and production of terracotta objects. The production and distribution of terracottas in such studies is, therefore, linked directly to the growth of urbanization and the resultant demand it created.

Another interesting aspect to the discussion on the social base of terracotta figurines is the assumption that terracotta art is largely folk art, and that clay as a medium was used to express the social life and religious beliefs of the common people. Niharranjan Ray, in his study of Mauryan art, claims that there is a dichotomy between the refined court art on the one hand, which is largely represented by the elaborate stone sculptures and Ashokan pillars, and the cruder terracottas that represented the artistic expression of non-élite people. The succeeding Śuṅga art, on the other hand, reflected a period when the art of the folk and tribal affiliations came to be recognized and incorporated into the manifold artistic traditions. This, Ray argues, is clearly evident from the sculptures of Sanchi and Bodhgaya, where 'Gods of civilized conception as Sūrya, Lakṣmī and Indra mingled freely with the tribal deities as the yakṣas, yakṣiṇīs and apsarās of popular imagination'.[19] This, in some ways, follows from the integration theory that most scholars apply in the study of the female terracotta figurines.

The earlier part of this essay has already discussed how these figurines were seen as representing primitive local Mother Goddess cults, only to be subsequently incorporated into the larger Brahmanical pantheon. Most of these theories and conclusions, when applied to the study of terracotta figurines, are problematic, and a lot of assumptions that are made do not match with the actual data. It may be observed that almost all of these works tend to separate the archaeological data from its actual spatial/regional context and use it selectively to suit the requirements of their arguments.

As mentioned earlier, most of the female terracotta figurines from the two regions that form the focus areas of this study have been clubbed into an undifferentiated homogeneous category, and have been arbitrarily listed as Mother Goddesses. Also, in most of the theories, there are certain inherent contradictions that emerge. For instance, if we consider these figurines as fertility goddesses, as a lot of historians who club them as Mother Goddesses do, then how do we explain their fertility functions in the urban context of Mathura and Ahichchhatra? While studying the development of the various techniques and styles of terracotta production, there is a tendency to identify and associate certain stylistic features with a certain time period. Further, a linear progression is traced with regard to the techniques employed in terracotta production that get sophisticated with each succeeding period (therefore, we move from crude handmade figurines to the technically advanced mould-made specimens). Working on this premise, the appearance of a large number of crude and coarse terracottas during the Kuṣāṇa period poses a paradoxical situation for the social historian of art, as this was known to be a period of great prosperity, economically as well as artistically. The only explanation Desai attempts is that perhaps the Kuṣāṇa potters were preoccupied in the baking of bricks, tiles, and pots at the expense of terracottas (the former emerge in great numbers during this period). The argument does not seem very convincing, especially when one looks at the immense development of sculptural art during the Kuṣāṇa period, and the fact that Mathura was the main centre for this activity.

So far then, what becomes evident is that all these theories and methodologies have not been successful in establishing the nature and function of these figurines. Therefore, one needs to study them in their own right rather than making cross-cultural comparisons or looking into literary texts for their identification. Also, a detailed analysis of the regional contexts of these objects as well as their spatial distribution at the site is required. It has been observed in my study that most of these figurines exhibit immense diversity in style and technique that cannot be confined to particular time frames, and there are overlaps throughout. Most importantly, these figurines are accompanied by other objects, like animal figures, votive tanks, and ring stones, which occur along with them and, therefore, it becomes necessary to study the figurines in association with these objects. Due to constraints of space, it will not be possible to discuss each of these aspects in detail here, but in the following section, a brief mention is made of the main types of figurines that have been classified, and some arguments keeping in mind all the above-mentioned factors have been offered.[20]

CLASSIFICATION OF THE MAJOR TYPES OF FEMALE FIGURINES

The terracotta figurines from the sites of Mathura and Ahichchhatra can be classified into certain broad categories on the basis of their physical characteristics and techniques of production. The hand-

FIGURE 7.1: Hand-modelled terracotta figurine with animal-like appearance, Ahichchhatra

modelled ones with an animal-like appearance form the first category (Fig. 7.1). All of these figurines are hand-modelled, have an animal- or bird-like appearance, and in most cases have an elaborate triple rosette headdress, punched girdle, and a necklace. On the basis of their physical appearance, most of these figurines have been classified into an undifferentiated category of 'Mother Goddesses'. Due to the absence of any drapery, these figurines are assumed to fulfil certain fertility functions and, hence, the parallels drawn with the Venus figurines of Europe. Most of them make an appearance from 400 BC and continue till about 200 BC. Animal figurines also start occurring during this period.

The second category includes the partly hand-modelled and partly moulded figurines with increased ornamentation (Fig. 7.2). In these specimens, the face is pressed out of the mould, while the body is hand-modelled; the parts of the elaborate coiffure are applied separately to the moulded face. These figurines are especially depicted with heavy ornamentation, like the Pañcacūḍā headdress (Fig. 7.3), pearl strings, tassels, and elaborate drapery. These figurines are present both as free-standing specimens and as a part of Mithuna plaques.

FIGURE 7.2: Partly moulded, partly modelled figurine with increased ornamentation, Mathura

FIGURE 7.3: Terracotta female figurines with Pañcacūḍā headdress, Mathura

Some are depicted in different poses, like holding a child, feeding a parrot, or holding a bunch of flowers. The free-standing specimens in most cases, due to their ornamentation, have been identified as manifestations of some goddess. They make their appearance around 200 BC, and the moulded plaques continue throughout the period under study.

The next category includes 'mother and child' figures. These occur at both Mathura and Ahichchhatra from about 100 BC, and include a female figurine with an infant figure depicted in various poses—child on the lap, standing to the side, or touching the breast of the female figure. In some cases, these figures also form a part of a votive tank, and may be both hand-modelled or mould-made (Fig. 7.4). Archaeologists and historians have identified these figures as representations of goddesses fulfilling fertility functions, especially in cases where the infant is placed in the lap of the female figure or is shown touching her breast. In other cases, they are interpreted simply as mother and child figures, or as nurses in the royal household, as Agrawala identifies them in the case of Ahichchhatra figurines.[21] From this period onwards, there are a number of other types of figures that start occurring and continue throughout. The nude dwarfish figures, mostly mould-made, deserve special attention. Others include three-legged male and female figures from Ahichchhatra, and figures of couples riding.

There is a special category of female figurines from Ahichchhatra that deserve attention. These include twelve nude female figures,

FIGURE 7.4: Votive tank with female figures carrying child in lap, Mathura

single-moulded, with a bent body, and a dishevelled and disconsolate posture, which Agrawala takes to be representations of the south Indian goddess Koṭavī.[22] The others consist of approximately thirty-eight multi-headed female images, most having three heads arranged frontally in a row, two arms bent at the elbow and placed on the knee, and certain figurines holding a child, their breasts prominent with nipples depicted, and the signs of a bodice on the bust and skirts falling to the knees. These images are found in association with half a dozen Mahiṣāsurmardinī images, and are therefore identified as representing some goddess cult.

In an interesting study on the use of multiple limbs in religious iconography, Doris Srinivasan has highlighted that the first references to anthropomorphism and the representation of multiple heads and arms is in the Vedic texts, where the multiplicity convention is linked to the biological world view of creation.[23] The creator—God—creates by emitting forms that he contains within himself, and this view prepared the ground for the acceptance of a creator deity having multiple body parts. Srinivasan feels, therefore, that the theoretical base for the depiction of Brahmanical deities with multiple body parts was already present and was reflected later in the plastic arts. The case of the goddess Durgā, however, is intriguing, and perhaps an exception to this trend. The textual references to Durgā in her Mahiṣāsurmardinī form are not before the sixth century AD, whereas the depiction of this form in terracotta art is present as early as the Kuṣāṇa period from Sonkh in Mathura (Fig. 7.5). The presence of multi-headed female terracottas along with the Mahiṣāsurmardinī image, therefore, deserve greater attention. It is intriguing to note how the Vedic conception of multiplicity translates into the representation of the forms of a goddess for which no textual data is available. Also, what is to be carefully observed is that these female images belong to a time frame of AD 300 to 600, a period when we have the largest specimens of Brahmanical deities depicted on terracotta plaques from both Mathura and Ahichchhatra.

THE POSSIBLE NATURE AND FUNCTION OF TERRACOTTA FIGURINES

What is evident from the diversity of the previous data is that the nature and function of these figurines would have to be as varied as the figurines themselves. From both Mathura and Ahichchhatra, the first category of anthropomorphic figurines is the simple hand-

FIGURE 7.5: Terracotta Mahisāsuramardinī image, Mathura

modelled female terracottas that have been characterized as Mother Goddesses by scholars due to many reasons. The first is their hand-modelled, simple, and crude appearance; second, the fact that they display a nude body; and finally, that these figurines emerge earlier than the Brahmanical goddesses and, therefore, are to be seen as a precursor to the later Purāṇic goddesses.

On the basis of the data thus classified, one can question these assumptions effectively. First, not all the figurines share this set of physical characteristics. As for technique, all figurines that are grouped under the Mother Goddess category cannot be termed as 'crude' and 'simple' in appearance; on the contrary, they exhibit a lot of variation. These terracottas vary from hand-modelled specimens to a combination of moulded and modelled figurines, where the face is usually pressed out of a mould. Also, the animal-like appearance is limited only to very early specimens that later give way to proper and elegant facial features.

The decoration of these figurines is another element that shows variation. This varies from simple hairstyles to elaborate coiffures of trefoil headdresses decorated with rosettes and streamers, either punched out or in appliqué. Of particular importance is the Pañcacūḍā type of headdress, especially common in female figurines from

Ahichchhatra. Pañcacūḍā, literally meaning the five crests, referred to the five sacred symbols stuck on the headdress, namely, the arrowhead (*bāṇa*), the banner (*dhvaja*), the goad (*ankuśa*), the trident (*triśūla*), and a blade-like device, but the number of objects could vary from three to five. Kramrisch feels that the Pañcacūḍā symbolized sacred character and was usually associated with semi-divine characters like *apsarās*. In the case of Mathura and Ahichchhatra, figurines with the Pañcacūḍā headdress occur in large numbers, and probably these particular types were representations of some local goddess.[24] However, it can also be noted that such ornamentation with regard to the headdress was also a common feature of many figurines depicted in secular scenes on the Mithuna plaques and, therefore, the Pañcacūḍā headdress alone cannot be taken as an indicator of divinity, though the divine nature of some of the heavily ornamented, free-standing specimens cannot be entirely ruled out.

The nudity of these figurines is another important issue that needs to be addressed. The Mathura and Ahichchhatra figurines have been constantly compared with the Venus figurines from Europe to highlight the possible fertility function that they fulfilled. This comparison is totally ahistorical. We have to take into consideration the fact that the two sets of figurines are separated enormously in time and space and belong to completely different cultures, and also that visually the Venus figurines do not resemble the Mathura and Ahichchhatra terracottas in any way. The over-exaggerated sexual organs of the former stand in direct contrast to these rather proportionate, slim, and graceful terracottas. Moreover, nudity in itself does not signify eroticism and fertility. It can also be conjectured that these figurines may not have been nude at all; the depiction of belts and girdles may indicate the presence of a lower garment which, in the stone sculptures is frequently shown as diaphanous in nature, thereby exposing the genitals.

It may also be mentioned that a lot of these female figurines continue to be found along with images of Brahmanical goddesses. They, therefore, do not seem to be precursors of the later Brahmanical goddesses, nor can they be identified as proto-Durgā or proto-Lakṣmī. In fact, simple handmade and moulded figures continue to be unearthed in association with huge moulded plaques of gods and goddesses. The hand-modelled male and female goat-headed figures, the single-moulded nude female figures from Ahichchhatra, the nude dwarfish figures (Fig. 7.6), and other Yakṣa and small mother

FIGURE 7.6: Dwarf yakṣa image, Ahichchhatra

and child figures on votive tanks from both the regions are some examples.

If we take into account all the different varieties of other figurines that are found along with the female terracotta figures, then it seems that the so-called Mother Goddess figurines form a very small component of the entire data. There are only ten such figurines from Ahichchhatra, and the number from Mathura is not considerable either. These figurines, therefore, cannot be taken as conclusive evidence for the popular worship of an archaic Mother Goddess cult prevailing in the two regions. Also, one cannot completely overlook the possibility of a secular function that they may have fulfilled, as in some cases, the ornamentation of the individual female figures resembles those depicted on the Mithuna plaques, which are not necessarily religious in nature. Therefore, in some cases, the secular nature of these figurines is as evident as their religious function.

Even if one considers that some of these figurines fulfilled a religious function, it is not possible that all of them served the same purpose irrespective of their inherent differences. Religion itself operates at different levels, from elaborate Brahmanical rituals to local practices at regional shrines and everyday offerings to household deities. The diversity in archaeological remains from both Mathura and Ahichchhatra reflects great complexity with regard to religious practices and rituals, and fertility rites would have constituted a minor component in the compound whole. However, one can only speculate about the actual use of these figurines in local cultic practices or household rituals. The Archaeological Survey of India's report on the excavation of Mathura city mentions terracotta figurines being found in pits cut into the floor containing ash, fragments of animal bones, and sherds of Northern Black Polished Ware (NBPW) and full pots of fine Grey Ware.[25] Though some scholars have refuted ritualistic connections, they cannot be completely ruled out.[26] A similar example is mentioned in the excavation report of Sonkh, where two figurines belonging to Period II (400–200 BC) were recovered from residential structures. Though no animal bones or ash accompanied them, what is intriguing is that both resemble each other in style and decoration. Agrawala cites a similar example from Ahichchhatra, where three figurines of similar style and decoration were found in a refuse pit, which was filled with sweepings from the residential quarters of the Pañcāla period (100 BC–AD 100).[27] Again, all three were of a similar kind in terms of style and decoration. If used for religious purposes, it is possible that only a certain type of figurine was used in certain rituals and not all were cult objects. Also, since they were found from refuse pits and residential quarters, this might indicate their use in some seasonal domestic household rituals.

A valid question to ask is: Why are certain figurines mould-made while others are hand-modelled? One reason for the difference of technique could be due to the demand and area of circulation. Jayaswal, like Desai, on the basis of her ethnographic survey, reveals that there is a close connection between urban settlement and the prevalence of moulded terracotta techniques.[28] The quantitative demand for a particular occasion by a large section of society is an urban characteristic. Hence, the mass production of clay figurines during a comparatively short duration of time or interval in the annual cycle explains the use of moulds. Considering the urban contexts of both Mathura and Ahichchhatra, it is possible to talk about such occasions and festivals. The purpose for which the figurines were used must have defined their technique and production.

As far as the archaeological evidence regarding the place of production and distribution of these objects is concerned, there is little that can be said. Jayaswal shows that production centres for ritual figurines in the present areas of Uttar Pradesh and Bihar invariably continued to be located within the *Kumhāra-tolīs*, the residential areas of the potter communities. These tolis are usually situated at the outskirts of large settlements.[29] Any archaeological precedent for this ethnographic situation is absent. No single centre or workshop area of pottery production converging on the residential areas of potters has been thus recognized so far from any habitation in the Ganga Valley. The reasons may be that archaeological ruins of such concentration would be represented by equipment of a very general and perishable material. Clay lumps, ash pits, and potsherds from kiln remains may not form a distinctive or recognizable pattern to archaeologists. However, one such pit layer of pots and terracotta fragments has been unearthed from Ahichchhatra. Jayaswal feels that this pit represents similarities with present-day potter kilns and pits from archaeological horizons.[30] Careful analysis and minute contextual recording of actual articles, and comparisons with the accumulation debris in and around such pits may help one interpret the nature of terracotta-producing workshops of the ancient period.

But apart from the individual female figurines, there are many other types of terracottas that may point to many more local and regional practices. These include the hand-modelled nude female figures from Ahichchhatra, the mother and child figures, figures of dwarfs, and grotesque figurines. It is possible that the nude females could represent local cultic icons, and would have been used as offerings to ward off evil and ill luck. With reference to the multi-headed cult images that were found in association with the Mahiṣāsuramardinī images, it is possible that these were local cultic goddesses worshipped at a particular place. Jayaswal, in her ethnographic study, has highlighted the existence of many *devī-thāna*s and *bābā-thāna*s, which are local shrines consecrating male and female deities respectively. She suggests that though the local goddess here is seen in relation to the Śaktī cult, the custom originated essentially from local magico-religious practices.[31] The multi-headed images from Ahichchhatra may indicate the worship of local goddesses in many forms.

The mother and child images are also found in large numbers from both Mathura and Ahichchhatra. The figures from Sonkh in Mathura are hand-modelled on votive tanks. In most cases it seems that these votive tanks were used as offerings at some local shrine. However, the other individual figurines represented on plaques or as rounded figures could be objects for decoration, as most of the plaques have holes drilled into them, indicating that they were used as wall hangings.

The function of the grotesque and dwarfish figures, however, is speculative. Both Mathura and Ahichchhatra have yielded these in large numbers, and most of them are pressed out of double moulds.

They could be playthings for children, as some make sounds like rattles. On the other hand, judging from their facial features, they could have been used as magical charms to ward off evil spirits. Also, looking at the enormous variety of these figures, it is not certain whether all of them were used for the same purpose.

Both Mathura and Ahichchhatra have, from the very beginning, been centres of Buddhist, Jaina, and Brahmanical faiths, apart from the numerous local and regional cults that may have existed. The archaeological evidence reflects them all. The Buddhist and Jaina images are as prolific as the Brahmanical deities and simpler terracotta figurines. The presence of local cults is well attested to by the numerous *Nāga* (important serpent divinities in Buddhist, Jaina as well as Brahmanical pantheons) and *Yakṣa* (semi-divine beings that were associated with nature and fertility) images from both the regions. Apart from these, there are remains of many structures that would have marked the ancient landscape of these two regions and would have possibly housed these images. The earliest references to temple complexes in literary sources are found in the *Arthaśāstra* of Kauṭilya. It acknowledges the presence of *deśadevatā*s, which refer to the tutelary deity of a region or a kingdom. Kauṭilya also acknowledges the existence of local rituals and worship at local temples, and the fact that people stuck to the beliefs and practices that they were accustomed to.[32] There are two temple structures at Ahichchhatra. One can be clearly identified as a Śiva temple since a colossal *Śivaliṅga* surmounts the whole structure. The other is an apsidal structure that probably enclosed a *stūpa* at one end, as is indicated by the circular base, and the other corner has a monastic establishment consisting of many rooms.

At Sonkh, two apsidal temples have been unearthed belonging to the Kuṣāṇa period. The second temple is undoubtedly dedicated to the Nāga cult, as is evident from the architectural material. These include a lintel depicting a Nāga court scene, the voluted end pieces showing a *Makara* (literally 'alligator', used in the plastic arts as a decorative motif largely from the early historic period onwards) with a Nāga as his playmate, and the cubic block with two intertwined three-headed cobras. A pillar fragment with a Nāgarāja under a seven-headed cobra hood in the medallion and the stump of a Nāga image confirm the identification of the temple as belonging to that particular cult. The Nāga context is also indicated from the material found, which includes a Nāga hood, to which a hollow face and a

FIGURE 7.7: Terracotta Nāga image, Mathura

hand holding a flask fit in size, indicating a rather large terracotta figure of a Nāga deity. Five fragments of terracotta snakes also speak of the frequency and popularity of Nāga worship at the site (Fig. 7.7).[33]

The other finds are the numerous varieties of votive tanks unearthed from both Mathura and Ahichchhatra. Most of them have seated figures on them. From their structure and features, it is evident that most of them were intended to be filled with water, and the others have lamps that could be lit and were probably used as votive offerings in homes or shrines. The different varieties of tanks probably indicate their uses at different occasions or at different shrines (Fig. 7.8). It is possible that some of the anthropomorphic terracotta figurines and animal figurines would have accompanied these tanks in votive offerings.

The animal figurines from Ahichchhatra and Mathura are also numerous. From Ahichchhatra, as many as 234 terracotta animals have been recorded in the Central Antiquity Section of the Archaeological Survey of India, out of which 85 per cent are only

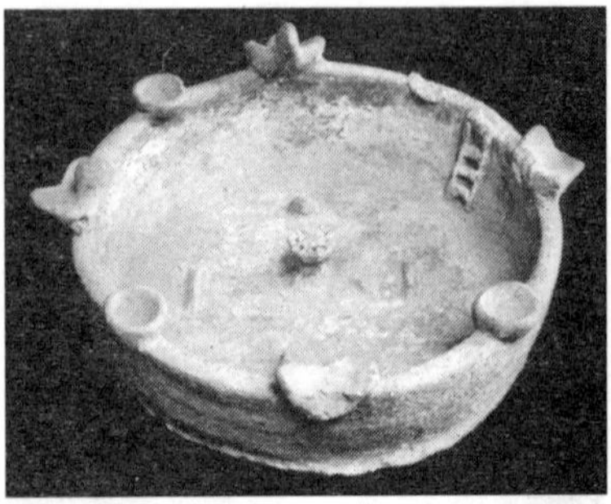

FIGURE 7.8: Terracotta votive tank, Mathura

of three animals, namely, the elephant, the bull, and the horse. The animal figurines from Sonkh total 306, and here too the elephant, bull, and horse predominate. Though it is tempting to attribute religious significance to them, like associating the bull with Śiva, or the tiger with Durgā, the animals could also have been used as toys by children. It is possible that some of the animal figurines could have been used as religious offerings at shrines or in household rituals. The religious nature of the bull is well attested at sites outside Mathura. Also, a number of Nāga terracotta figurines have been found from the apsidal temple at Sonkh. Animal figurines were probably also used as decorations, for example, the Makara, elephant, and birds that have been portrayed on various plaques.

Therefore, what emerges is that both Mathura and Ahichchhatra were multi-religious centres, and the diversity of terracotta figurines attests to that fact. The reliance on textual data cannot reveal the true nature of these figurines, as a number of smaller regional cults and practices prevailed outside the realm of Brahmanical literature. It is likely that the female figurines circulated at a local, regional, or household level, accompanied by votive tanks and animal figurines, co-existing with the Brahmanical deities representing the great tradition.

In conclusion, what really needs to be done is to explore newer methodologies through which the present archaeological data can be studied. Confining this exercise to the sites of Mathura and Ahichchhatra, I have argued that the earlier studies regarding the terracottas have been one-sided and, therefore, do not fully explain their nature and function. These limitations may not be due to the personal whims of scholars studying them, but were a reflection of the general trends in the studies of religion and archaeology.

The second issue is that most studies on terracottas have pulled these figurines out of their regional and spatial contexts and have interpreted them in the light of textual sources, or by making cross-cultural comparisons, or as part of theories tracing religious development, or as reflections of economic processes of trade and urbanization in ancient India. It may be noted that the nature and function of these figurines is evident only when they are studied in relation to the surroundings from which they have been unearthed. The identity of these terracottas is established by the socio-religious and cultural dynamics of the region in which they are found.

The most important aspect of terracotta art is that it functions at multiple levels, religious and secular. Therefore, while one set of terracotta objects might represent the tastes of the affluent urban class, another group may have fulfilled local cultic needs. The leading Brahmanical deities in temples were fashioned in terracotta, along with other objects like votive tanks and animal figurines that could have been utilized for religious offerings at shrines. What is more important is the dominance of local and regional cults, which are wrongly dismissed by scholars as mere tribal and folk cults of lesser importance, when compared with the Brahmanical tradition. The Nāga and Yakṣa cults are two such examples from Mathura and Ahichchhatra. The aim, therefore, should be to not to look into a limited section of archaeological data in isolation, but to take into consideration the whole of its spatial, chronological, and regional context.

NOTES AND REFERENCES

1. *Vaiṣṇavism, Śaivism and Minor Religious Systems*, Varanasi: Indological Book House, 1913.
2. John Marshall, *Mohenjodaro and the Indus Civilization*, London: Stephen Austin, 1931.
3. B.S. Miller (ed.), *Exploring India's Sacred Art: Selected Writings of Stella Kramrisch*, Philadelphia: University of Pennsylvania Press, 1983.
4. Ananda Coomaraswamy, *From the River Banks and the Sacred Places, Ancient Indian Terracottas*, Boston: Museum of Fine Arts, 1977. Also see his 'Intellectual Operation in Indian Art', *Journal of the Indian Society of Oriental Art*, 3 (1), 1935, pp. 1–12.
5. V.S. Agrawala, 'Terracotta Figurines of Ahicchatra, District Bareilly, UP', *Ancient India*, vol. 4, 1948, pp. 104–79. Also see V.S. Agrawala, *Mathurā Terracottas*, Varanasi: Prithvi Prakashan, 1984.
6. Coomaraswamy, *From the River Banks*, pp. 20–1.

7. Maurice Bloomfield, *The Religion of the Vedas: The Ancient Religion of India*, Delhi: Indological Book House, [1907] 1972.
8. William Monier, *Hinduism, Hinduism and its Sources*, New Delhi: Chaman Offset Printers, 1993 (Indian edition reprint).
9. Bhandarkar, *Vaiṣṇavism*.
10. Marshall, *Mohenjodaro*, pp. 49–50.
11. Catherine Jarrige, 'Terracotta Figurines from Nindowari', in Bridget Allchin (ed.), *South Asian Archaeology*, Cambridge: Cambridge University Press, 1981, pp. 129–34.
12. Sharri Clark, 'Representing the Indus Body, Sex, Gender and Sexuality, and the Anthropomorphic Terracotta Figurines from Harappa', *Asian Perspectives*, 42 (2), 2003, pp. 304–28.
13. A.A. Jansen, 'The Terracotta Figurines from Mohenjodaro: Consideration on Tradition, Craft and Ideology on the Harappan Civilization (*c.* 2400–1800 BC)', in S. Settar and Ravi Korisettar (eds), *Protohistory, Archaeology of the Harappan Civilization, Archaeology in Retrospect*, vol. 2, Delhi: Indian Council of Historical Research and Manohar, 2002, pp. 207–20.
14. Ibid., p. 219.
15. David Kinsley, *Hindu Goddesses: Visions of the Divine Feminine in the Hindu Religious Tradition*, Delhi: Archive Publishers, 1987, pp. 212–20.
16. M.K. Dhavalikar, *Mathura Art in Baroda Museum*, Baroda: Department of Museums, 1971, pp. 4–8.
17. Devangana Desai, 'The Social Milieu of Ancient Terracottas 600 BC–600 AD', in Amy Poster (ed.), *From the Indian Earth: 4000 Years of Terracotta Art*, New York: Brooklyn Museum, 1986, pp. 29–41.
18. Ibid., pp. 30–1.
19. Niharranjan Ray, *Maurya and Śuṅga Art: India Studies in Past and Present*, Calcutta: 1965, pp. 47–8.
20. Issues regarding chronology, technique, and stylistic classification of these terracotta figurines have been discussed in great detail in 'Terracotttas from Mathura and Ahicchatra: An Archaeological Study (400 BC–Seventh/Eighth Centuries AD', unpublished MPhil dissertation, Delhi: Jawaharlal Nehru University, 2004.
21. Agrawala, 'Terracotta figurines of Ahicchatra, District Bareilly, UP', pp. 104–79.
22. Ibid.
23. Doris Srinivasan, *Many Heads, Arms, and Eyes: Origin, Meaning, and Form of Multiplicity in Indian Art*, Brill: Leiden, 1997.
24. Miller (ed.), *Exploring India's Sacred Art*, pp. 75–6.
25. The details of the excavations on Mathura are provided in the volumes of the *Indian Archaeology: A Review*; 1966–7, 1969–70, pp. 42–3; 1970–1, pp. 39–40, 1972–3, pp. 33–4; 1973–4, pp. 31–2; 1974–5, pp. 48–50; 1975–6, pp. 53–5; 1976–7, pp. 54–6.
26. Joachim Bautze, 'Some Observation on the Female Maurya Terracotta Figurines', in Maurizio Taddei and Pierfrancesco Callieri (eds), *South Asian Archaeology*, Part 2, Rome: Instituto Italiano Per Il Medio Ed Estremo, 1987.

Bautze fails to see the ritual background to the find. According to him, the description of the find situation reminds one more of a dumping ground, though he does not rule out a possible ritual connection.

27. Agrawala, 'Terracotta figurines of Ahicchatra, District Bareilly, UP', pp. 104–79.
28. Vidula Jayaswal and Krishna Kalyan, *An Ethno-archaeological View of Indian Terracottas: A Comparative Study of Present and Past Terracotta Traditions of the Gangetic Plains*, Delhi: Agam Kala Prakashan, 1989.
29. Ibid., pp. 142–3.
30. Ibid.
31. Ibid., pp. 37–8.
32. R.P. Kangle, *The Arthaśāstra, Part III: A Study*, Bombay: University of Bombay, 1965, pp. 156–8.
33. H. Härtel, *Excavations at Sonkh: 2000 Years of a Town in Mathura District*, Berlin: Dietrich Reimer Verlag, 1993, p. 427.

8. Pleasure and Culture

Reading Urban Behaviour through Kāvya *Archetypes*

SHONALEEKA KAUL

OF ALL THE facets of early Indian urbanism, the one explored arguably the least, if at all, is the behavioural. How did urban men and women behave as social and sexual beings? That is to ask, did they act in any way peculiar to them as city dwellers? Did they operate within parameters dictated by traditional norms and institutions emphasizing control and regulation of gender interaction? Or did cities see the emergence of alternative modes and codes of public and private intercourse?[1]

These are questions intrinsic to developing a rounded grasp of urbanism as a complex and transforming historical experience. These are also questions that may elude definitive or comprehensive answers, not least because human behaviour—nebulous and ever divisible—lends itself to generalization only at some peril. Moreover, the dominant sources from early India that dwell on aspects of social conduct—such as the Dharmaśāstras—do so in a theoretical and prescriptive fashion, making it difficult to discern categorically what trends may have prevailed, perhaps at variance from what was prescribed. In any case, such literature does not distinctly address the city or issues arising out of living in one.

It is nonetheless possible to investigate these questions and arrive at broad tendencies that seem to stand out in characterizing urban gender behaviour. I propose to do this by exploring a body of literature that has yet to receive the historian's serious and appropriate attention, but which is uniquely endowed for an investigation of the kind I undertake. I refer to the *kāvya*, defined as literature as a form of art, as distinct from scripture (*āgama*), history (*itihāsa*), and technical treatise (*śāstra*).[2] This is the realm of Sanskrit creative literature that includes not only poetry (*mahākāvya* or *sargabandha*), but drama (*nāṭya*), tale (*kathā*), and biography (*ākhyāyikā*).[3] Among its defining elements is a linguistic and thematic deference to aesthetics (*alaṁkāra*) and emotion (*bhāva* rendered as *rasa*). The fictive-narrative character of kāvyas and their orientation to the erotic (*śṛngāra*) as the primary aesthetic give to this literature the space and the licence, as it were, to explore themes of socio-sexual behaviour.

What is more, the classical Sanskrit kāvya flourished in the first several centuries of the first millennium CE. As such, it was contemporary to early Indian city life and indeed a product of it. Many kāvya texts, abundantly locating themselves in cities, resonate with an urban situatedness and constitute themselves as primarily urban literature. Their depiction of behaviour in the city, then, can be said to come close to being the self-perception of an urban culture, albeit from a by-and-large elite vantage. This is particularly valuable for an investigation of the city because of what archaeologists and historians have found to be the 'endemic problem of definition', that is, the fact that a universally applicable idea of urbanism continues to elude us. The main reason for this could be that 'what is urbanism?' is a metaphysical, not scientific, query,[4] so that the answer would turn almost entirely on the question of perspective.[5] The kāvyas provide one such perspective.

This literary genre has, however, been underestimated as a source for exploring the past, chiefly on account of its overtly aesthetic and conventional nature, which is believed to render historical inquiry futile. But, as I have argued elsewhere,[6] literary aesthetics and conventions are not sterile constructs, and kāvyas can yield complex and enriching insights, provided they are handled in ways sensitive to the logic of literary modes of representation.

One of the major modes of representation recognizable in classical Sanskrit kāvyas is the construction of complex archetypes. An archetype, in the sense in which I use the word, is a recurrent motif. Its significance lies in its symbolizing potential. Kāvyas render experiences of perceived significance as eidetic[7] abstractions that are then recurrently employed to convey the sense of that experience. Developed with consistency yet complexity across texts, kāvya archetypes can be regarded as semantic codes, analysing the structure of which it is possible to access a wealth of meanings.

In keeping with this approach, this essay explores, in the main, two kāvya archetypes, the *nāgaraka* and the *gaṇikā*, which represent respectively masculine and feminine models of urban behaviour as textually portrayed. Working through them, I identify ideals that appear to distinguish the city's socio-sexual ethos. I also consider the contradictions and tensions these may entail with a view to developing a perspective on some of the dilemmas that seem to populate the city's moral universe.

This essay draws on a number of different kinds of kāvyas, several of these works of celebrated authors like Bhāsa, Kālidāsa, Bāṇa, Bhavabhūti, and Daṇḍin. It cites at length, primarily from the *Mṛcchakaṭikam* and *Caturbhāṇī,* and from the *Kāmasūtra.* Śūdraka's *Mṛcchakaṭikam* is a *prakaraṇa* play from the third/fourth century CE. A prakaraṇa is a fiction play with multiple acts that has a story usually dealing with bourgeois life.[8] The plot of the *Mṛcchakaṭikam* revolves around the love between a talented courtesan and a virtuous merchant who has fallen on bad days in the city of Ujjayini. The *Caturbhāṇī* is a set of four monologue plays, or *bhāṇa*, from the fifth/sixth century CE, namely, Vararuci's *Ubhayābhisārikā*, Īśvaradatta's *Dhūrtaviṭasaṁvāda*, Śūdraka's *Padmaprābhṛtaka,* and Saumillaka's *Pādatāḍitaka.* Set in various cities, enacted in each case by a *viṭa* who is a master eroticist and tutors prostitutes and lovers on the art and craft of love, these plays are classic specimens of erotic comedy in Sanskrit. Vātsyāyana's *Kāmasūtra* from about the fourth century CE is not a kāvya,[9] but being an urban treatise[10] on sexual pleasure, and displaying characters and concepts found in the kāvyas, it is an allied text of defining significance.[11]

*

The term nāgaraka is not common in the kāvyas; a character is hardly ever described or addressed as such. However, the attributes and pursuits that a nāgaraka epitomizes are amply evident in the characterization of male characters across texts like the *Mṛcchakaṭikam, Daśakumāracaritam, Mālavikāgnimitram, Caturbhāṇī, Avimāraka, Mālatīmādhava*, and *Kuṭṭanīmatam*. Before I look at some of these, let us turn to the *Kāmasūtra* to find out who a nāgaraka was and what being a nāgaraka meant. In the *Kāmasūtra*, the designation nāgaraka figures repeatedly and is given prominent treatment. A recent translation of the text renders the term as a 'man-about-town' who is 'a sophisticated connoisseur of the good life in general, of pleasure in particular, and of sex even more particularly'.[12] Chapter four of book I titled *Nāgarakavṛtti* ('The Avocation of the Nāgaraka') details in a prescriptive-cum-descriptive manner[13] all the signs of a nāgaraka, inscribing the full cultural connotation and urban(e) context of the term. It describes his daily routine thus:

I.4.5–6: He gets up in the morning, relieves himself, cleans his teeth, applies fragrant oils in small quantities, as well as incense, beeswax and red lac, looks at his face in a mirror, takes some mouthwash and betel, and attends to the things that need to be done. He bathes everyday, has his limbs rubbed with oil every second day, a foam bath every third day, his face shaved every fourth day, and his body hair removed every fifth or tenth day. All of this is done without fail. And he continually cleans the sweat from his armpits.

I.4.7–9: In the morning and afternoon he eats.... After eating he passes the time teaching his parrots and mynah birds to speak; he goes to quail-fights, cockfights, and ram-fights; engages in various arts and games; and passes the time with his libertine (*pīṭhamarda*), pander (*viṭa*) and clown (*vidūṣaka*). And he takes a nap. In the late afternoon, he gets dressed up and goes to salons (*goṣṭhī*) to amuse himself.

I.4.10,12–13: And in the evening, there is music and singing. After that, on a bed in a bedroom carefully decorated and perfumed by sweet-smelling incense, he and his friends await the women who are slipping out for a rendezvous with them.... And when the women arrive, he and his friends greet them with *gentle conversation and courtesies that charm the mind and heart* [emphasis added]. If rain has soaked the clothing of women who have slipped out for a rendezvous in bad weather, he changes their clothes himself, or gets some of his friends to serve them. This is what he does by day and night.

I.4.14, 19–22: He amuses himself by going to festivals, goṣṭhīs, drinking parties, picnics and group games.... A goṣṭhī takes place when *people of similar knowledge, intelligence, character, wealth, and age* [emphasis added] sit together in the house of a courtesan, or in a place of assembly, or in the dwelling place of some man, and engage in appropriate conversation with courtesans. There they *exchange thoughts about poems or works of art* [emphasis added], and in the course of that they praise brilliant women whom everyone likes.... They have drinking parties in one another's houses.

I.4.24–6: Picnics can be described in the same way. Early in the morning, men dress with care and go out on horse-back, attended by servants and accompanied by courtesans. They enjoy the daytime events there and spend the time at cockfights, gambling, theatrical spectacles... and then in the afternoon they go back in the same way, taking with them souvenirs of the pleasures of the picnic. And in the same way, in the summer, people enjoy water sports in pools built to keep out crocodiles.

It is possible to divide the nāgaraka's activities into four groups. The first relates to maintenance and enhancement of bodily hygiene and attractiveness; the second involves participation in sporting contests; the third refers to the communitarian cultivation of arts and recreation, including music, poetry, conversation, and theatre. The pīṭhamarda and viṭa among his hangers-on are also said to be 'skilled in the arts' and in teaching them.[14] The final aspect of his pursuits, presented somewhat teleologically as a grand finale or climax, is indulgence in amorous dalliance and sex.

It follows from this analysis that the ideal of the nāgaraka consisted in the careful cultivation of every aspect of human personality: body, mind, spirit, senses, and etiquette. Moreover, the nāgaraka was not envisaged as an exception or an isolated instance. He is seen to belong to like society—'people of similar knowledge, intelligence, character, wealth and age'—in which he circulates and interacts. In housing the man-about-town, then, the city houses an ideal community (ideal in *this* perspective)[15] that typically gathers at, and can therefore be identified as, the goṣṭhī or cultural conclave.

Significantly, underlying the various attributes and endeavours of nāgaraka and company are twin central concerns: pleasure and culture. These can be regarded as furnishing the primary principles of an urban behavioural code. Despite the fact that it must represent only a minority experience, that nāgarakavṛtti can indeed be equated with urban behaviour needs underlining. For, although it is obvious that only a man of means could afford to be a nāgaraka, the word literally means simply a man who lives in the city (*nagara*).[16] And in order to commence on the lifestyle of the nāgaraka, the *Kāmasūtra* expressly ordains habitation in one kind of urban settlement or another (*nagare-pattane-kharvaṭe vā*).[17] This urban contextualizing of the nāgaraka is echoed by the low opinion the text has of sexual and cultural activity in the village.[18] Altogether, the equation asserted seems confirmed as reasonable.

To elaborate on the close mixing of sexual pleasure and culture in the concept of the nāgaraka, as I have noted earlier, all his functions and activities through the day seem to be as if building up to the erotic rendezvous—the love ritual—at night. (It should be clarified at the outset that the sexual relations entailed are with public women/courtesans and perhaps secret paramours; the construct of the nāgaraka is not concerned with domestic sex.) The 'ritual' itself is explicated and demonstrated much like an art form in subsequent chapters of the *Kāmasūtra*.[19] But, as the nāgaraka list tells us, en route to the climactic act of pleasure are a host of other acts. And these are acts of culture (though not unproductive of pleasure in their own right).

I refer not merely to the making up or aestheticization of the body, or the music and singing, and the other arts the nāgaraka practises with his hangers-on or other nāgarakas. Significantly, it is with women themselves, their partners in the pleasure/sex rite, that the man-about-town is expected to make 'gentle conversation', 'exchange thoughts about poems and other works of art', enjoy 'theatrical spectacles', and show 'courtesies that charm the mind and heart'.[20] Further, a chapter in book V of the *Kāmasūtra* mentions a good conversationalist, a generous man who loves picnics and theatrical plays, and a man who dresses well and lives well—the nāgaraka, really—as a man 'sexually successful with women'.[21] Also, the chapter just preceding the one on the nāgaraka-vṛtti enlists literary work, music, make-up, and etiquette among the sixty-four arts 'that should be studied along with the *Kāmasūtra*'[22] by men and women alike. The compelling conclusion is that cultural expertise is seen as a complement to sexual expertise, and vice versa. The archetype of the nāgaraka epitomizes this evidently urban tendency to pursue art as pleasure and pleasure as art.

From the kāvyas we get examples of the different kinds of nāgarakas enumerated in the *Kāmasūtra*,[23] for instance Brāhmaṇas (Cārudatta,[24] Śaiśalaka[25]), kings and princes (Jayantaka,[26] Agnimitra,[27] Candrodaya,[28] Guptakula,[29] Upahāravarmā[30]), professionals and their sons (the judge and judge's son,[31] executive officer of the king,[32] general's son,[33] grammarian,[34] physician,[35] master-painter,[36], *vīnā* teacher[37]), and merchants and their sons, the largest group (a few examples are Dhanamitra, Dhanika, Kuberadatta, Samudradatta,[38] Kṛṣṇilaka,[39] Cārudatta[40]).[41] These protagonists are seen enacting different facets of nāgarakavṛtti, be it adeptness at arts of various kinds,[42] gambling,[43] hosting of hangers-on (the viṭa, *vidūṣaka*, and pīṭhamarda)[44] or attendance at goṣṭhīs,[45] appreciation and patronage of plays and classical recitals (*prekṣā, gāndharva, saṅgītaka*),[46] or falling in love and undertaking sexual exploits with courtesans and queens alike.[47]

The most complete and memorable nāgaraka in the kāvyas, albeit one fallen on poverty, is Cārudatta of the *Mṛcchakaṭikam*. In him not only do all the accomplishments and refinement of the nāgaraka's way of living come together, these are shown to be enhanced by a nature that is generous to a fault. Thus, Cārudatta is eulogized as 'handsome in appearance and speech' (*priyadarśa priyavādī*),[48] 'the ideal of the educated' (*ādarśaśikṣitānāṁ*),[49] 'ocean of seemly conduct' (*śīlavelasamudra*),[50] 'refined and magnanimous of spirit' (*dakṣiṇodārasattvo*),[51] 'treasure of all manly virtues' (*puruṣaguṇanidhīḥ*),[52] and, additionally, 'a wish-fulfilling tree for the needy' (*kalpavrikṣaḥ dīnānāṁ*) and 'the bridge for the good to cross over their miseries' (*sajjanadukhānāmuttaranasetuḥ*).[53] For all these qualities, Cārudatta is shown universally acclaimed as 'an adornment to Ujjayini' (*alaṁkṛtojjayinī*)[54] and 'the foremost in the city' (*nagarīpradhānabhūtaḥ*).[55]

Thus, Cārudatta clearly personified the urban ideal, albeit one which in the *Mṛcchakaṭikam* is qualified by the virtues of charity and magnanimity, something that is not explicitly a concern for the *Kāmasūtra*'s nāgaraka. Magnanimity apart, however, Cārudatta is true to the nāgaraka tendency to sexual and cultural good taste. The former is exemplified by his ardour for Vasantasenā, the best of the city's courtesans, and a beautiful and sophisticated woman. The latter, his commitment to culture, is highlighted in two episodes from the play. A late night vocal music recital leaves Cārudatta in raptures about the exponent's grasp of the nuances of his art that Cārudatta obviously follows well[56] (suggested also by the occurrence of musical instruments in his home).[57] Then, later in the same night when a thief breaks into his house, a hole dexterously excavated by the thief in the wall wins Cārudatta's admiration for the thief's mastery of *his* art ('*Aho! Darśanīyo ayaṁ saṅdhīḥ*! ... *kathamasminnapi karmaṇi kuśalatā*')![58]

However, the *Mṛcchakaṭikam* evidence on the phenomenon of the nāgaraka is complex. There are hints that Cārudatta's sophistication and inordinate aesthetic predisposition are the object of mild satire. For instance, when Cārudatta sings paens to the male vocalist's sweet, feminine voice, his vidūṣaka[59] Maitreya replies that he finds a woman reading Sanskrit and a man singing in a low, sweet tone hilarious and boring.[60] And when Cārudatta praises the thief's handiwork and expresses his regret that he found little to steal in his impoverished home, Maitreya's reaction strikes an honest chord: 'You're not sorry for that damn thief, are you?' he exclaims ('*Bhoḥ kathaṁ tameva caurahatakamanuśocasi*').[61] The vidūṣaka's responses are a foil to Cārudatta's gentility and make it out to be almost certainly overstated. Particularly in the theft episode, the author seems to be faintly ridiculing the hero, who, for all his cultural superiority (or because of it?), is a figure of self-induced pathos and absurdity (right down to the swoon he falls into when he later learns that jewellery left with him for his safekeeping had been stolen).[62] This could possibly be a veiled comment on the effects of (too much) refinement and 'culture' as espoused by the nāgaraka.

Be that as it may, it is Cārudatta's affair with Vasantasenā, a public woman, that comes in for serious disapproval from Maitreya (or the playwright?) who, in sounding a contrary note, goes against the grain of the *Mṛcchakaṭikam*'s (and generally the kāvya's) celebration of the theme of sexual love. Maitreya consistently expresses his distrust of and distaste for courtesans as mercenary, unreliable, and aggressive peddlers of their trade. Sometimes this is couched in sardonic humour. For instance, when Cārudatta agrees to keep safe Vasantasenā's ornaments and asks Maitreya to receive these from her, Maitreya refuses with his trademark reply he applied earlier in the act to the worship of gods: '*Na me śraddhā*' ('I don't have faith!').[63] He also likens himself in the proximity of a prostitute (among other mal-elements) to a mouse falling prey to a snake.[64]

At other times, Maitreya asserts the impropriety of a man associating with a courtesan by emphasizing the goodness and chastity of the man's wife (*satī, sadṛśadāra*) at home.[65] These are also the sentiments expressed in the *Kuṭṭanīmatam*[66] by relatives and well-wishers of male protagonists similarly attached to prostitutes. There is also seen in such men a corresponding sense of public shame at courting courtesans and a desire to conceal the fact.[67] This holds true for Cārudatta too, as I will presently discuss. The voice of satire in this case then seems to represent more than the voice of conscience, that of a countervailing social ideology in the city that does not sanction, let alone idealize, the nāgaraka's pleasure prescription. Instead, it seems to assimilate sexual permissiveness to social vice. I choose to broadly formulate the phenomenon as tension between *dharma* and *kāma* that, as Ludo Rocher has tracked with clarity,[68] is a concern in the *Kāmasūtra* as well. In accommodating this voice, the kāvyas allow a stepping back from the 'ideal' and hint at the complexities involved in the cultivation of sexual pleasure in the city.

The contours of both the erotic ideal and the normative counter-thrust[69] are clarified through a subsidiary kāvya character, the viṭa. The *Kāmasūtra* defines the viṭa as 'a man who has used up his wealth but has good qualities and is married. Well respected among courtesans and society people, he lives off them.'[70] In the *Kāmasūtra* and kāvyas alike, the viṭa is closely allied to the foremost among 'society people', the nāgaraka. He is not merely his aide and companion, but displays perhaps even more acutely than him his predilection for erotics and education. For instance, the *Nāṭyaśāstra,* the earliest extant treatise on Sanskrit dramaturgy, provides that the viṭa be skilled in pleasing prostitutes and be courteous, a poet, proficient in argumentation, bold, and shrewd.[71] In some kāvyas he is described in terms similar to those used for the nāgaraka, for example, 'the city's eternal spring season' ('*nagarasya sarvakāla vasantabhūtaḥ*'),[72] 'one whose flourish of clever speech has been witnessed by entire Pāṭalīputra' ('*pāṭalīputra yasya vacanalīlāṁ anubhavati*'),[73] or 'whose treasure is open to all supplicants' ('*apavṛtadhano yo nityamevārthiṣu*').[74] As the evidence suggests, there may indeed be little to distinguish viṭa from nāgaraka—except for their financial position—so much so that it is entirely possible that the viṭa is none other than a nāgaraka 'who has used up his wealth' in pursuit of his rather capital-intensive interests (courtesans, conviviality, good life).

Be that as it may, the viṭa is an uncompromising votary of the ideal of erotic pleasure, soliciting customers (for courtesans) and liaising with courtesans (for prospective lovers),[75] counselling lovers,[76] arbitrating love quarrels,[77] and deciding disputes, mostly of an amorous nature. He adds a significant dimension to the ideal when he insists, in the *Padmaprābhṛtaka*,[78] that the pursuit of sexual desire (by courting courtesans) be open, free, and without restraint or 'the armour of hypocrisy' (*mithyācāra-kañcukamudghāṭyatāṁ*). It can be argued that this clarion call strikes a blow for the pleasure principle in the 'clash' with the opposing voice of traditional social morality, at once addressing and challenging the latter.

In the *Dhūrtaviṭasaṁvāda* the viṭa is seen expounding in professorial detail on a host of erotic queries put to him by an aspiring or noviciate bon vivant. He is expressly requested to solve doubts regarding kāma-*tantra* (erotica) that have arisen in a goṣṭhī, since his views would be authoritative (*pramāṇaṃ bhaviṣyati*).[79] In the same vein, the viṭa of the *Ubhayābhisārikā,* aptly named Vaiśikācala or 'the mount of the courtesan's art', is commissioned to explicate the *vaiśika* śāstra (code of prostitution) to courtesans and their daughters.[80] The viṭa, then, is the authentic exponent of kāma in the city, more so than even the nāgaraka and the courtesan, for both of them he deigns to admonish. He is imaged as a scholar and something of an institution in his own right. Insofar as intellectual prowess is traditionally associated with austerity and asceticism, the city is remarkable in throwing up a master-eroticist as a model of learning. In the process, of course, the concept and content of 'learning' are themselves redefined.

Portentously, this role of the individual viṭa is seen expanded and extended to a whole community or assembly of leading viṭas in the *Pādatāḍitaka*. When Viṣṇunāga is kicked on the head in a love-match with a prostitute, he seeks to expiate the 'sin' (*pātakaṁ, kilviṣa*)[81]—his much-consecrated head being abused by a prostitute[82]—and consults the Brāhmaṇa *pīṭhīkā* (fraternity). They, however, find the issue *beyond the jurisdiction of the* Dharmaśāstras,[83] and refer him to the viṭa *samāja* (community of viṭas) instead as the more appropriate body.

The assembly of the viṭas, which could be as heterogeneously constituted as the ranks of the nāgaraka,[84] is duly convoked on this single-point agenda. The experts ponder over and debate the matter, raising fine points for and against, and considering different angles and schools of thought—and all this only after taking a duly administered oath that:

> May he who speak here what is improper never win anything in gambling, always meekly obey his parents, drink milk, and be the husband of a married wife… serve his superiors, forsake the clubs, be in youth modest like the old.[85] (*dyūteṣu mā sma vijayiṣta paṇaṃ kadācit, mātuḥ śṛnotu pitaraṃ vinayena yātu; kṣīraṃ sṛtam pibatu modakamattu mohat, vyudhapatirbhavatu yoatra vadedayuktaṃ.*)

From start to finish, this episode is heavy with irony and parallelism. Not only is the intellectual-discursive mode of functioning of the viṭa samāja analogous to that of the Brāhmaṇa pīṭhikā, the viṭa body is explicitly projected as a system *alternative to the traditional socio-legal authority*. Its composition, its issues, doubts, presiding figures, ideals, and punishments (howsoever tongue-in-cheek) are all external to the Dharmaśāstric purview—and starkly urban in their context. The city alone seems to be productive of such novel behaviour, situations, and solutions that can question the relevance of traditional authority.

Reading the subtext further, it is possible to argue from all that has preceded that the kāvyas present the city as a contested behavioural space, one that is claimed, as it were, by two opposing, unequal socio-sexual economies: one normative, dominant, repressive; the other inhabiting but a niche, contending the former's restrictions, and struggling to wrest for itself a de jure locus.[86] While the former maybe loosely designated as Dharmasastric, the latter, in its exclusively urban location, would correspond to the nāgaraka/viṭa's society, the goṣṭhī. At the heart of the tussle are attitudes to sexual pleasure. While the conflict is somewhat muted when the focus is on men, it erupts in sharp relief when women enter the picture.

*

The *Kāmasūtra* and kāvyas portray women in the city mainly in the context of pleasure, usually as heading for a rendezvous with lovers and dallying with them—in bedrooms, on terraces, in pleasure groves, pools, and rivers.[87] Chief among women so represented is the prostitute (*veśyā*) or courtesan (gaṇikā). The *Kāmasūtra* distinguishes common types of prostitutes from an elite counterpart over a graded hierarchy which culminates with the gaṇikā or courtesan de luxe[88] who is clearly the text's ideal. Similarly in the kāvyas, the female lead in the *Mṛcchakaṭikam*, Vasantasenā, is a gaṇikā just as Kāmamañjarī seems to be one in a tale in the *Daśakumāracaritam.*[89]

In fact, the gaṇikā can be regarded as the female counterpart to the nāgaraka. For one, just as the nāgaraka is identified with the city, so is the gaṇikā. She is described in one instance as '*nāgarīkā*'[90] and celebrated in another as 'the ornament of the city' (*nagarasya vibhūṣaṇaṁ*)[91] or 'the good fortune of the city' (*nagaraśrīḥ*).[92] Second, the gaṇikā shares in, indeed stars in, the nāgaraka's engagement with erotics or kāma, albeit as a matter of profession and not indulgence.[93] Texts describe their affair as 'illuminating the city'[94] in one case, and as 'a jewel uniting with a jewel'[95] in another.

Third, the gaṇikā too is seen as a paragon of artistic and other refinements. Hence, the comment in the *Pādatāḍitaka* that 'it is understood that the courtesans' quarter is associated with elegant manners' ('*veśo vilāsa ityutpannametat*').[96] So much so that it is claimed in the *Dhūrtaviṭasaṁvāda* that a man acquires 'self confidence, heroism, ready wit, elegant pose, brilliance of spirit, knowledge of psychology and an acquaintance with the arts by attaching himself to a courtesan'.[97] Elsewhere it is observed that 'courtesans who are rich in grace… utter measured words on proper occasions. Seldom do they speak anything harsh.'[98] And a comparison between the courtesan and a woman more ordinary is summed up in an analogy of a chariot and a bullock cart.[99] The *Kāmasūtra* lists an impressive range of arts to be learnt by the courtesan. This includes singing, dancing, playing instruments, painting, and decoration; preparing wines and other drinks; doing conjuring tricks, practising sleight of hand, telling jokes and riddles; completing words, reading aloud, improvising poetry, staging plays, knowledge of meter and literary work; gambling; and etiquette.[100]

This list appears addressed among women to courtesans de luxe and the daughters of kings and ministers of state, described as 'women whose understanding has been sharpened by the text'.[101] The grouping suggests that the gaṇikā is seen located within elite culture. The *Kāmasūtra* reiterates this impression with the words:

A courtesan who distinguishes herself in these arts
and who has a good nature, beauty, and good qualities,
wins the title of courtesan de luxe
and a place in the public assembly.
The king always honours her,
and virtuous people praise her.
Men seek her, approach her for sex,
and she is a standard for other courtesans to strive for. (emphasis added)[102]

Significantly, it appears that the combination of the cultural/intellectual with the sexual, represented by the gaṇikā, is publicly praiseworthy and respectable in the city. The addition of the cultural seems to have an at once emancipating and enhancing effect on the perception of sexual pleasure and of the stigmatized profession based on it. These are emancipated in that these seem to become respectable, and these are enhanced because, finally, after all the praise showered on her, it is the gaṇikā's status as a supplier of sex or a sex object that is promoted and reaffirmed. As such, the gaṇikā represents the harnessing of the concerns of civilization and culture in the service of the instincts of nature—and vice versa. Culture seems to negotiate nature (sexual desire) into a form that is socially acceptable.

Further, by virtue of the combination of pleasure and culture, the gaṇikā comes to share in the city's *male* ideal. She is witty and skilled, refined and elegant, and displays free and frank demeanour. Their common background of learning and behaviour qualifies the courtesan to interact with men—not only sexually as women are expected to do, but *socially*, as partners and companions at goṣṭhīs, picnics, and festivals, as the nāgaraka's timetable tells us. Thus, the erotico-cultural ideal milieu seems to render the city as a space for partially transcending traditionally confining norms of gender interaction outside of the family.[103] Crucially, it is the courtesan, a public woman, and not the wife or family woman—a man's socially legitimated partner—who can partake of this refashioned milieu.

The figure of the courtesan emerges as a signifier of urban life insofar as it points to the availability of opportunities in the city for free and feted access to (such) women.

Having said that, it would appear that the nature of her profession significantly qualifies the perception of the courtesan as the feminine symbol of pleasure and culture in the city, and of feminine sexual and intellectual freedom. Addressed to a courtesan, Anaṅgadattā, in love with an impoverished man, a verse from the *Ubhayābhisārikā* is rich in allusions in this regard. It goes:

Being addicted to the pleasure of lovesport, you overlooked the greed of your mother and disregarded the custom of courtesans, which for anyone of them is hard to ignore, and you went to the residence of your beloved man and enjoyed the sweet festival of love. By your merits you have done away with the stigma [of your profession].[104]

Among other things, the *Ubhayābhisārikā* verse points to the existence of a code for courtesans (*vaiśikaśāsanaṁ*), 'which for anyone of them is hard to ignore', and which consisted of variations on the same theme: profit, not real love or attachment, is the courtesan's object.[105] By corollary, to take a poor lover is taboo, as is retaining a paramour after reducing him to poverty, or establishing a relationship out of love or attraction for a man's charms or qualities—as Vasantasenā famously does with Cārudatta.[106] As the viṭa in the *Ubhayābhisārikā* puts it to another courtesan, Mādhavasenā, 'Exciting by every means the passion of a person [*sarvathā rāgamutpādya*], whether he is lovable or not [*vipriyasya priyasya vā*], one is merely to earn money. This is the confirmed view of the śāstra.'[107] He, however, recognizes that these cold, mercenary words are 'unwelcome advice' to a girl who is 'afflicted by the embrace of an undesirable person due to the greed of her mother'.[108]

Apart from other implications, there stands exposed from this discussion a contradiction within the compounded ideal of pleasure and culture we saw the city set up for the gaṇikā, like the nāgaraka, to pursue: there is an obvious clash between the cultural taste and refinement recommended to the courtesan de luxe and what is supposed to be her moving force, namely, the naked quest for money with little concern for any other criterion. The acuteness of the contradiction is heightened by the impression that the city can throw up characters/suitors always deficient in one of the two departments. Hence, the *Mṛcchakaṭikaṁ* dichotomy between the rich, powerful boor (Saṁsthānaka) and the poor, victimized gentleman (Cārudatta). These are the options before Vasantasenā, the gaṇikā. In an interesting psychological insight, the playwright makes Vasantasenā say: 'Cārudatta is poor. That is why I am in love with him. A courtesan in love with a poor man is not reproached.'[109] That Cārudatta's poverty was not really his sex appeal need hardly be stated. But if Vasantasenā still rationalizes her love for him in these terms, it shows that her sexuality was partially responding to social mistrust and castigation of the courtesan's role as a gold-digger. And sure enough, even Cārudatta, who loves her and knows of her love for him, is shown expecting that he would have to pay for her services.[110] (It is interesting that while the virtuous hero does not see any conflict between love and having to pay for it, a courtesan does; hence, her choice of a paramour incapable of paying.)

Much later, and well after having established a love relationship with Vasantasenā free of cost, Cārudatta is shown deeply embarrassed when he has to *publicly* acknowledge his association with the courtesan ('*mayā kathamīdṛśaṁ vaktavyaṁ yathā gaṇikā mam mitramiti*'),[111] despite Vasantasenā's cultural accomplishments and great prestige. He quickly tries to explain it away to himself as the fault of his youth, not character ('*yauvanamatraparādhyati na caritryaṁ*').[112] This sense of shame among men from reputed families at interacting with courtesans, and their desperate desire to conceal the fact, is found in more than one text and has already been referred to.[113] Moreover, it corresponds to the fairly low self-image of the courtesan as reflected in the *Mṛcchakaṭikam* and *Cārudattam*. For example, when an ordinary masseur apologizes to Vasantasenā in apprehension of having been rude to her, she responds with: 'Don't worry. I am (no doubt) a gaṇikā' ('*viśvastu bhavatāryaḥ gaṇikā-khalvaham*').[114] Similarly, on being queried by a monk who rescues her in a manhandled, bedraggled state, she describes her condition as 'what befits the profession of a courtesan' ('*yatsadṛśaṁ veśabhāvasya*').[115] Clearly, both incidents convey that a courtesan could expect insult and mistreatment.

Again, this militates against the distinct impression we earlier formed of the talented courtesan occupying a respected place in elite society. The confusion can be interpreted in different ways. At the very least, it is the reflection of a deeply ambivalent attitude to the courtesan in the city. Since she is a paragon of pleasure and culture combined, it can be argued that the ambivalence, taken to its logical end, shows up the combination of the two ideals as only a superficial one. Further, the ambivalence may be imagined as a function of social hypocrisy.

Insinuations to this effect are made in the *Padmaprābhṛtaka* where the son of a dispenser of dharma (*dharmāsanikaputra*), ironically named Pavitraka, poses in public as a man of uncompromising purity but secretly has a liaison with a prostitute. The viṭa appropriately calls him 'a holy devil' (*caukṣapiśāco*) who 'pretends to be fasting but keeps sipping milk' ('*pāyasopavāsamiva ka etat śraddhāsyati*').[116]

On another plane, it is possible to extrapolate from Cārudatta's 'character versus youth' dichotomy that the apparently conflicting portrayals of the courtesan in the kāvyas project, again, a behavioural dilemma on the city: having to choose between unfettered (pre- or extramarital) sexual indulgence and a social morality that disapproved of it.

Yet another way of seeing the evidence is that it posits the courtesan as at the centre of a series of paradoxes, which then defines the working complexity of what may be termed the urban socio-psychology of pleasure. She is regarded as mercenary and deceptive, yet desirable and sought after. She is coveted, but the act of coveting her is publicly a matter of shame. She is culturally accomplished and celebrated but socially degraded. Indeed, a connection is to be seen between the two limbs of the paradoxes: She is desirable (among other reasons) *because* she is available commercially and, therefore, freely (!) to any who can afford her. As Saṁsthānaka's viṭa puts it to Vasantasenā: 'You are like a creeper growing by the wayside. Your body is like merchandise to be purchased with money. Therefore, serve equally the man you love and the man you don't.'[117] Conversely, easy availability is general accessibility. A courtesan is available to many and not the preserve of any one. Thus, the *Dhūrtaviṭasaṁvāda* explains in the following way the pleasure a courtesan gives:

> Amorous passion is a kind of desire. Desire means solicitation. And solicitation occurs *when there is a chance of not getting a thing* [*prārthanā cāsamprāpterutpadyate*]. In courtesans it occurs even when she is under control... or *because she is accessible to many* [*sā ca veśyāyāṁ svadhīnaprāptāyāmapi mātsaryādutpadyate bahusādhāraṇatvāt*']. And jealousy also gives rise to cupidity. (emphasis added)[118]

Then, desiring the courtesan is an object of shame *because* she helps realize sexual desire and provides pleasure in an open and expert way outside socially constructed and controlled relations like marriage that are in this perspective a narrow and confining sensual experience.[119] Hence, the vita reacts thus to the news of the impending marriage of a young man attached to prostitutes: 'I indeed bewail with uplifted arms that (the man) leaves the wide road of courtesans [*veśyāmahāpatha*] for the narrow lane of a married life [*kulavadhūkumārga*].'[120] And elsewhere he says: 'No one leaves off a chariot to ride in a bullock cart' ('*na hi rathamatītya kaścid goyānena vrajet puruṣaḥ*').[121]

And, finally, the courtesan is socially degraded not only because she is a commercial sex worker, but because as such she is independent[122] and proactive in her relations with society in general and men in particular. Witness in this regard two of the several vivid synonyms used for the courtesan in the kāvyas: '*svādhīnayauvanā*' or 'mistress of her youth'[123] and '*prakāśanārī*' or 'the exposed woman'.[124]

Thus, the archetype of the gaṇikā emerges as a critical index of urban socio-sexual behaviour and the fault lines therein. Her sexual accessibility, facility, and proactivity characterize and highlight the city's ethic of unfettered pleasure, but also expose its dominant, normative structures that demand her social degradation, as being those of anti-pleasure. By 'anti-pleasure' I mean an approach to sexuality that firmly places social considerations over libidinal ones.[125] Chief among these structures appears to be the family, and the kāvya representation of the *kulastrī* or family woman, married or otherwise, completes the picture of feminine behavioural values that constitute the mainstay of anti-pleasure.

*

As a model of feminine behaviour, the family woman is supposed to be everything the courtesan is not.[126] While the courtesan was bold and gregarious, witty and vivacious, the family woman or wife in the kāvyas and *Kāmasūtra* alike is all humility and modesty. Her traits include slow movements, speaking little and in a low voice, never retorting or saying anything harsh, nor laughing loudly.[127] She 'treats her husband like a god',[128] 'talks while avoiding his gaze',[129] and always acts in ways compatible with and dependent on him and his parents.[130] She is also required to refrain from standing at the doorway or gazing from it, chatting in the park, and lingering in deserted places.[131] The ultimate mark of the *kulavadhū* is the veil (*avaguṇṭhana*),[132] that is, for example, bestowed on Vasantasenā immediately after the courtesan is decreed a *vadhū* or wedded wife by royal order.[133] The avaguṇṭhana symbolizes all the qualities associated with the wife that present such a contrast with the *svādhīnayauvanā* or *prakāśanārī*—she is timid and bashful, protected and dependent, controlled and subordinated.

Not just her demeanour, even the high-born woman's thinking is shown deferring to an overt moral code that prioritizes such considerations as modesty, propriety, and honour of the family. Thus, in the *Mālatīmādhava*, Mālatī repents over her love even for a worthy man in the following words:

> I alone am to blame in this matter who, degraded by immodesty, again and again looked (at him) with a heart... which was quite lost to all shame.... My noble father, my mother descended from a pure race, and my unblemished family are dear to me; neither this person nor my life.[134]

Similarly Kuraṅgī, the princess secretly in love with Avimāraka in the play of the same name, is expected to feel shame and fear, and to give a thought to family pride when she pines for her lover.[135] The cases of these women enact the family as the chief counterpoint to premarital sexual love and pleasure.[136] It is the arena where the conflicts induced by kāma (sexual desire) vis-à-vis dharma (socially defined and enforced considerations of morality/virtue) are 'resolved' in favour of the latter.

It is in the same light that we hear in the texts of the supposed naïveté and awkwardness, or indifference, of the wife in giving sexual pleasure,[137] and how it contrasts with the expertise and initiative of the courtesan, which are applauded. The grievance against the wife, as it were, can in fact be seen as a consequence and an inversion of a patriarchal truth, namely, that rites of marriage were designed to control the wife's sexuality, and, therefore, her sexual expression, so as to harness it for the specific purpose of legitimate childbearing within the caste and class arrangement that marriage signified.[138] In a remarkable display of sociological/gender insight, the *Dhūrtaviṭasaṁvāda* perhaps echoes this when it speaks of two kinds of feminine amorous desire (*strīnāṁ kāmitam*) : 'That which is open [*prakāśam*] befits courtesans.... That which is concealed [*pracchannam*] is proper for married ladies as well as courtesans.'[139] It is further said, 'Males not being easily accessible to them, married women may run after anyone, whoever he might be. But courtesans do not hanker after all men.'[140] The suggested freedom of the courtesan and desperation of the wife implies that a sexuality degraded by commercialization and commodification may yet exercise a greater say than one that is privileged and protected. It is a patriarchal irony that is visibly played out in the city in the types of the gaṇikā and the kulastrī. Cārudatta's wife Dhūtā epitomizes the chastity and silence that are expected of the wife, apart from her obvious redundance to her husband's quest for sexual love and her resignation in the face of it.

A spatial manifestation of the patriarchal value system is the *antaḥpura* or inner chambers, also signified by the *abhyantaracatuḥśālakam* or the inner quadrangle, of the family residence.[141] It was regarded as the domestic sanctum sanctorum to which the 'outer' world—with its corrupting (liberating/subverting?) influences—was not allowed. Thus when Vasantasenā entrusts Cārudatta with her necklace, he insists that the courtesan's jewels must not be taken into his inner residence.[142] However, in a necessary corollary, while the inner world must not be accessed by the outer, it may not access the outer world either. Hence, the powerful recurrent motif in our kāvyas of women beholding any special or mundane affair of the city, usually enacted on the royal road, through the windows, balconies, and terraces of their houses, the narrow openings of which they are invariably shown crowding.[143] The withholding of exposure to the public world[144] also meant denial of access to public opportunities, ensuring a woman's 'rightlessness'.

The connection between exposure and assertion of rights in the city, however, is a complex one in the world of the kāvyas. On the one hand, the 'exposed woman' has free access to public places (the streets of the city), public events (goṣṭhīs and saṅgītakas),[145] and public men (the king, nāgarakas, and so on). It is precisely because her business is public accessibility, however, that her basic rights to person and privacy are undermined, as we have seen. She also incurs social and moral stigma and reproach—the price for exposure.

On the other hand, the sexual and other behavioural restrictions laid out for the sequestered family woman did not necessarily pose an absolute obstacle between the inner and the outer world. Kāvyas show fairly routinely high-born women indulging in illicit love relationships with outsiders deep within (the bedroom) or high atop (the terrace) the antaḥpura edifice, or flirting with and seducing men on the street from their terraces.[146] The protected space was thus frequently breached and sub-spaces 'liberated' using the very qualities of seclusion and isolation to subvert the sequestration that these were meant to effect.

In the same context the *abhisārikā*, apparently a third feminine type in the city in the texts after the gaṇikā and the kulastrī, assumes significance. The abhisārikā was the beloved seen slipping out onto the streets well after dark for a secret tryst with her lover.[147] The

Nāṭyaśāstra tells us that the abhisārikā was the one who, having discarded modesty (*hitvā lajjām*), compelled by intoxication and lust, sets out to meet her lover.[148] Referred to in the kāvyas as abhisārikā (she who goes forth), *sundarī* (a beauty), or simply *yoṣitā* (a woman), the referent is in no instance revealed to be a courtesan. Who then but the sequestered kulastrī by day was the stealthy abhisārikā of the night? It is as if the forces of pleasure 'return' to undermine the structures of anti-pleasure, inscribing in the process a full-blooded moral and behavioural complexity in the city.

*

To sum up, pleasure and culture appear to be the leading values that orient public behaviour in the city, at least among the well-off echelons to which kāvya observations in this regard are more or less confined. It can be argued that the linking of the two ideals in the activities of the nāgaraka and the gaṇikā represents an urban behavioural strategy—an ingenious response to normative attitudes towards sex that seek to rule out all indulgence outside the contract of marriage and reorient it away from pleasure even within it. The pursuit of culture in common by (certain) men and women creates a uniquely urban zone where they can freely access each other socially and sexually, something that is denied by the traditional structure of society and its patriarchal-cum-caste ideology.[149] A niche public–private sphere of heterosexual interaction is thereby conjured in the city where the cultivation of culture provides the stage (and veneer?) for pleasure to play itself out. In this way avenues are created for satisfying behavioural needs and instincts unfulfilled by the traditional social set-up. The nāgaraka and the gaṇikā (in critical conjunction with the kulastrī) symbolize the tension between kāma and dharma—or ideologies of pleasure and anti-pleasure[150]—as well as the city's prescription for a partial resolution of that tension within a circumscribed arena.

NOTES

1. This question is located within the larger understanding that urbanism wrought radical change in the socio-economic order. The essay is concerned with only one, postulated manifestation of that change: a new public–private sphere that an urban environ occasions and an urban literature 'reports' and engages with, and against which a new socio-sexual discourse can be framed.
2. A.K. Warder, *Indian Kavya Literature, Vol. I: Literary Criticism*, Delhi: Motilal Banarsidass, 1989, p. x.

3. These four plus a fifth, lyric (*anibaddha* or *khaṅḍakāvya*), are laid down by Bhāmaha, the fifth century rhetorician, as the five main forms of kāvya. *Kāvyālaṁkara* I.18 cited in Warder, *Indian Kavya Literature*, p.122. Specifically on drama, the *Nāṭyaśāstra* from the second century CE, the earliest extant work to speak on 'kāvya composition', uses 'nāṭya' and 'kāvya' almost interchangeably (Warder, *Indian Kavya Literature*, p. 16), while Vamana, the eighth century rhetorician, calls nāṭya the highest form of kāvya (Warder, *Indian Kavya Literature*, p. 33).
4. This is quoted in a discussion of urbanism in Paul Wheatley, *The Pivot of the Four Quarters: A Preliminary Enquiry into the Origins and Character of the Ancient Chinese City*, Edinburgh: Edinburgh University Press, 1971, p. 398.
5. If the role of perspective is thus conceded, the absence of a universal definition need no longer be seen as a problem.
6. See Shonaleeka Kaul, 'The City in Early India: A Study of Literary Perceptions (First Millennium AD)', unpublished PhD thesis, New Delhi: Centre for Historical Studies, Jawaharlal Nehru University, 2005, 'Introduction'.
7. From the Greek word '*eidos*' meaning 'type'.
8. Warder, *Indian Kavya Literature*, p. 136.
9. However, Doniger (in Wendy Doniger and Sudhir Kakar (trans.), *Vātsyāyana Mallanāga* Kāmasūtra (new complete English translation of the Sanskrit text). Oxford and New York: Oxford University Press, 2002), p. xxv says that the the *Kāmasūtra* looks like a work of dramatic fiction more than anything else, a play in seven acts. As she points out, 'The man and the woman whose sex lives are described here are called the *nāyaka* and the *nāyikā* (male and female protagonists), and the men who assist the *nāyaka* are called the *pīṭhamarda*, *viṭa*, and *vidūṣaka* (the libertine, pander, and clown). All of these are terms for stock characters in Sanskrit dramas... according to yet another textbook, the one attributed to Bharata and dealing with dramatic writing, acting, and dancing, the *Nāṭyasāstra*.' See also Kaul, 'The City in Early India': A Study of Literary Perceptions (First Millennium AD)', unpublished PhD thesis and 'Women about Town: An Exploration of the Sanskrit Kāvya Tradition', *Studies in History*, 22 (1), 2006, pp. 59–76.
10. Doniger and Kakar (trans.), *Vātsyāyana Mallanāga* Kāmasūtra, 'Introduction', p. xii.
11. See Note 9. Also, Sheldon Pollock is of the opinion that the *Kāmasūtra* may have been but a sourcebook for poets composing erotic works, again suggesting the closeness of the text and the kāvya genre (cited in Doniger and Kakar (trans.), *Vātsyāyana Mallanāga* Kāmasūtra, 'Introduction', p. xxviii).
12. Ibid., p. 187, Note I.4.1.
13. Ibid., p. xvii.
14. *Kāmasūtra* (hereafter *KS*) I.4.31–2.
15. It would be a minority community, though.
16. This could be *any* man, irrespective of caste according to the *Kāmasūtra* (*KS* I.4.1) and irrespective of ethnicity according to descriptions of gatherings in the *Caturbhāṇī* (*Pāda*. pp. 113, 159). The only criterion for being a nāgaraka

was that he would have to be able to afford it (*KS* I.4.30). See also Note 41 later and its referent in the essay.

17. *KS* I.4.2.
18. *KS* I.4.2,36; V.1.52,54. For a discussion of the treatment of the village in the *KS* and kāvyas, see Kaul, 'The City in Early India', chapter 6.
19. *KS* II.1–10.
20. All the quotes are from the timetable from the *KS* quoted earlier.
21. *KS* V.1.50.
22. *KS* I.3.15.
23. *KS* I.4.1. See Jayamangala's commentary on this sūtra in Doniger and Kakar, *Vātsyāyana Mallanāga* Kāmasūtra, p. 17.
24. *Mṛccha.* 'Prologue', p. 9.
25. *Padma.* p. 67.
26. *Pāda.* pp.155–6.
27. *Mālavika.* I p.13.
28. *Padma.* p. 67.
29. *Pāda.* pp. 130, 135.
30. *Daśa.* III p. 73.
31. *Padma.* p. 80, *Pāda.* pp. 116, 143.
32. *Pāda.* pp. 103, 111, 129.
33. Ibid., p.102.
34. *Padma.* p. 79.
35. *Pāda.* p. 123.
36. Ibid., p. 137.
37. Ibid., p. 1.
38. All four names are from *Ubhaya*, p. 1.
39. *Dhūrta,* p. 25.
40. *Mṛccha.* 'Prologue', p. 9.
41. This again suggests that the nāgaraka model could represent the behaviour of a heterogeneous sweep of (affluent) urban society.
42. *Padma.* pp. 73, 79; *Pāda.* pp. 125, 130; *Ubhaya.* p.1; *Mṛccha.* III p. 117; *Daśa.* III p. 74.
43. *Dhūrta.* pp. 29, 31; *Padma.* pp. 83; *Daśa.* II pp. 53–4; *Mṛccha.* IV p. 173.
44. There are several examples from *Mṛccha., Avi., Mālavika., Kuṭṭani., Mālatī.*, etc.
45. *Pāda.* p. 112; *Dhūrta.* p. 42; *Kuṭṭani.* 209, 235, 795, 1013, pp. 158–9.
46. *Mṛccha.* III p. 105; *Kuṭṭani.* pp. 87, 68, 207; *Ubhaya.* pp. 3, 13, 19; *Cāru.* III p. 25–6; *Pāda.* p.148; *Mālatī.* I p. 4; *Daśa.* II p. 59; *Pratijña.* I p. 20.
47. Examples are embedded in the narrative of all the texts cited in the context of the nāgaraka.
48. *Mṛccha.* II p. 89.
49. *Mṛccha.* I p. 53, verse 48.
50. Ibid.
51. Ibid.
52. Ibid.
53. *Mṛccha.* X p. 359.

54. *Mṛccha.* I p. 49, II p. 89, X p. 359.
55. *Mṛccha.* X p. 355.
56. *Mṛccha.* III p. 105–7.
57. Ibid., p.117.
58. Ibid., p. 123.
59. The vidūṣaka was a jester-like hanger-on or sidekick of the nāgaraka or nāyaka (hero).
60. *Mṛccha.* III p. 105.
61. Ibid. p. 125. I have cited van Buitenen's evocative translation (*Two Plays of Ancient India*, Delhi: Motilal Banarsidass, 1971, p. 89).
62. *Mṛccha.* III p. 125.
63. *Cāru.* I p. 17.
64. *Mṛccha.*I p. 26.
65. *Mṛccha.* X p. 403; III p.129. It should be noted that the man (Cārudatta) being thus accused of all but wanton adultery occupies otherwise the ethical high ground, but sees no conflict in his behaviour.
66. *Kuṭṭani.* 301–24, p. 111. The *Kuṭṭanīmataṁ* is Dāmodaragupta's ninth century erotico-satirical prose-poem about a matron's advice to young prostitutes.
67. *Mṛccha.* IX p. 329; *Pāda.* p.146; *Padma.* p.80; *Kuṭṭanī.* 301–24, 411–24, 440, p.111.
68. Ludo Rocher, 'The Kāmasūtra: Vātsyāyana's Attitude toward Dharma and Dharmaśāstra', *Journal of the American Oriental Society*, 105 (3), 1985, pp. 521–9.
69. Note that the framing of the sentence reverses the usual, which is to speak of the normative as the ideal and any other ideology (in this case, the erotic) as the counter-thrust. This is in keeping with the location of the essay that is seeing things through the kāvya's eyes, as it were, and from what seems to be its standpoint.
70. *KS* I.4.32.
71. *Nāṭyaśāstra* XXXV.55, cited in Ajay Mitra Shastri, *India as Seen in the Kuṭṭani-Mata of Damodaragupta*, Delhi: Motilal Banarasidass, 1975, p. 123.
72. *Ubhaya.* p. 4. Spring here carries erotic undertones since the viṭa encourages lovers just as spring supposedly does.
73. Ibid., p. 23.
74. *Pāda.* p. 113.
75. *KS* I.4.34; *Mṛccha.*I p. 27, 31; *Padma.* p. 72.
76. *Ubhaya.* p. 23; *Padma.* p. 75.
77. *Ubhaya.* p. 3.
78. *Padma.* pp. 80–1.
79. *Dhūrta.* p. 42.
80. *Ubhaya.* pp. 9, 13.
81. *Pāda.* pp. 110, 112
82. Viṣṇunāga has the following to say to the prostitute about the sacredness of his head: 'Fie on you, O adulteress, who forgets her position and places a foot, without any care for its [the head's] high status, on this head where mother bound the *śikhaṅḍaka* [ritual top knot] with careful hands, father kissed on my

prostrating at his feet, saying "This is a good child", and on which brahmanas sprinkled water of peace and flower petals' (*Pāda*. p. 108, verse 9).

83. *Pāda*. p. 110. They put it like this: '*bhoḥ sādho avalokitavāṇ asmābhir manu-yaṃ-vasiṣṭha-gautama-bharadvāja-sankha-likhitāpastamb-hārīt-praceto-devala-vṛddhagargya-prabhṛtīnāṁ manīṣīnāṃ dharmaśāstrāṇi, naivamvidhasya mahataḥ pātakasya prāyaścittamavagacchāmaḥ iti*.'
84. For instance, the *Pādatāḍitaka* p. 113 lists as viṭas in the same breath a prince, a physician, a drummer, a royal officer, a hill man, an Ābhīra, a Parasava, a Maudgala, and so on. Heterogeneity was also no doubt ensured by the fact that these viṭas congregating in the city in question (appropriately called *sārvabhaumanagara*) came from different regions like Daśapura, Ānandapura, Surāṣtra, and Aparānta. The narrator viṭa addresses them as those who have 'come together from all parts of the country' (*sakalakṣititalasamāgataḥ*) (p. 159).
85. Ibid. p. 161, verses 124–5.
86. See Note 69.
87. *Megh*. I.25, 33, 37; *Raghu*. VI.75, XVI.12, 69; *HC* II.90; *Vāsav*. 194–5, p. 104; *Dhūrta*. p. 54; *Jātaka*. XXVIII p. 256; *Ṛtu*. I.3, 9–11, 28, IV.6, 12, V.2, 5, 10; *Śiśu*. VII, VIII; *Avi*. III. pp. 301–2, 311; *BC* II.31, IV.1–100. Other contexts in which women are seen associated with pleasure are the *madanamahotsava* and the ritual of kicking the *aśoka* tree for it to blossom at the onset of spring (known as *dohad*).
88. This is Doniger and Kakar's translation of the term '*gaṇikā*' (*Vātsyāyana Mallanāga* Kāmasūtra, p. 16).
89. The *Daśakumāracaritam* is Daṇḍin's eighth century *kathā* or tale about the heroic and amorous adventures of a bunch of princes. Also see *Daśa*. II p. 47.
90. *Kuṭṭanī*. 863, p. 111.
91. *Mṛccha*. VIII p. 277; *Daśa*. II p. 46.
92. *Mṛccha*. VIII p. 295.
93. I will discuss later in the section the contradictions her profession spawns in understanding the courtesan's position on kāma.
94. *Ubhaya*. p. 23.
95. *Mṛccha*. I p. 39.
96. *Pāda*. p. 125.
97. *Dhūrta*. p. 59.
98. Ibid., p. 57.
99. Ibid., p. 59.
100. *KS* I.3.15.
101. *KS* I.3.11.
102. *KS* I.3.17–18. The *Mṛcchakaṭikam* and an episode from the *Daśakumāra-caritam* echo the highlighted portions. For example, *Mṛccha*. IX p. 347, and *Daśa*. II p. 51.
103. The gender equation is not necessarily transformed since the gaṇikā's accomplishments are meant to cater to men, but she certainly seems to have greater elbow room in playing out her role vis-à-vis men.

104. *Ubhaya*. p. 7, verse 10.
105. *Ubhaya*. p. 9; *Daśa*. II p. 48; *KS* VI.1.19, etc.
106. She is described as *guṇānuraktā* gaṇikā (*Mṛccha*. I p. 9).
107. *Ubhaya*. p. 9.
108. Ibid.
109. *Cāru*. II p.19; *Mṛccha*. II p. 71.
110. *Cāru*. I p. 16; *Mṛccha*. I p. 59, V. p. 183.
111. *Mṛccha*. IX pp. 329.
112. Ibid.
113. *Dhūrta*. p. 58 spells it out: 'A person attached to a courtesan is not adored by people. His prestige is lost' ('*lokasya veśyāṁ prati sakto manuṣyaḥ pujyo na bhavati, sammatiśca tasya neṣṭā*').
114. *Cāru*. II p. 20.
115. *Mṛccha*. VIII p. 303.
116. *Padma*. pp. 80–1.
117. *Mṛccha*. I p. 37.
118. *Dhūrta*. p. 58.
119. Indeed, the gaṇikā represents the collapsing of the public and the private worlds, bringing pleasure out into the former, and divorcing it from the agenda of reproduction that characterizes the latter.
120. *Dhūrta*. p. 33.
121. *Dhūrta*. p. 59.
122. Of course, there are limits to her independence, as we have already seen.
123. *Mṛccha*. I p. 51.
124. *Mṛccha*. III p. 109.
125. Ortner and Whitehead speak of kinship-based societies in particular displaying 'the power of social considerations to override libidinal ones'. They are cited in Pat Caplan (ed.), *The Cultural Construction of Sexuality*, London and New York: Tavistock Publications, 1987, p. 17.
126. And vice versa.
127. *KS* IV.1.37; *Kuṭṭanī*. 848 p. 108.
128. *KS* IV.1.1.
129. *KS* IV.1.22.
130. *KS* IV.1.37.
131. *KS* IV.1.22.
132. *Kuṭṭanī*. 895 p.108; references also in the *Padma*., *Dhūrta*., *HC*, and *Mṛccha*.
133. *Mṛccha*. X p. 403.
134. *Mālatī*. II p. 20.
135. *Avi*. II p. 269.
136. This is ironical since pleasure is typically associated with the private realm, which is in most senses co-terminous with the family. However, there is at work a patriarchal logic behind the paradox, which is that the family ensures that only a certain kind of pursuit of sexual pleasure is indulged in that is controlled and channelized towards social reproduction that preserves caste and class arrangements. So the family is the private realm, but fundamentally

implicated in the affairs and agendas of the public or social realm. It is because the courtesan is located outside the family that she can be the locus for contravening social norms.

137. *Dhūrta*. pp. 33 and 58. Sample this: 'One should not think indeed of entering into the prison of a married wife [*kulavadhūkara*] who is, as it were, a beast in woman's form and who behaves during intercourse like one born blind, looks miserable, and speaks within her teeth, creates sorrow even for a happy person, and covered with the garment of bashfulness, she would never look to her private parts on any pretext whatsoever' (p. 33). Or the question: 'Why is there no such pleasure [*sukhaṁ*] from a gracious married wife as there is from a courtesan?' (p. 58).
138. Jaya S. Tyagi, 'Brahmanical Ideology on the Ritual Roles of the Grhapati and his Wife in the Gṛha: A Study of the Early Gṛhyasūtras (c. 800–500 BC', *Studies in History*, 18 (2), ns, p. 201.
139. *Dhūrta*. p. 53. In the text, however, these terms also carry the sense of distinguishing, respectively, affected desire [*kṛtakam*] from desire born out of 'real love' [*kevalamanurāgadutpadyate*].
140. Ibid. The original is: *durlabhatvādapi puruṣāṇāṁ kulavadhvastu yaṁ kañcit kāmyante, vesyayā tu na sarvaḥ kāmyate.*
141. *Mṛccha*. I p. 21, III p. 109.
142. *Mṛccha*. III p. 109.
143. *Buddha*.III.13,18,21, VIII.13; *Raghu*.VII.11, XI.93, XIV.13; *Mṛccha*.II.p.101; *Dhūrta*.p.32.
144. The *Kuṭṭanīmatam* (869, 889, 895, p. 108) and the *Harṣacaritam* (Bāṇa's seventh century biography of King Harṣa) (IV.142–4) suggest that festivals were an exception to this rule, for both high and low women (*āryā, anāryā*) participated publicly in these. However, unrestricted public festivities can also be interpreted as performing the function of temporary relaxation of control before the reimposition of taboos in full strength. For a discussion of this idea in the context of other systems of power, see Kaul, 'The City in Early India', chapter 4.
145. The goṣṭhī is a cultural conclave while the *saṅgītaka* is a musical performance.
146. *KS* V.6.6; *Avi*. III p.313; *Mālatī*. II p. 17; *Daśa*. IV p. 86, V p.102, VI p.117, VII p. 125; *Kuṭṭani*. 833 p. 110.
147. *Ṛtu*. I.10; *Megh*. I.37; *Raghu*. VI.75, XVI.12, XVII.69; *Kaumudi*. IV p. 79; *HC* II.90; *Dhūrta*. p. 54.
148. *NS* XXIV.216.
149. It has been argued that patriarchy is the ruling ideology even in a text like the *Kāmasūtra*, which is seen to be as prescriptive and normative as a Dharmaśāstric text. See Kumkum Roy, 'Unravelling the Kāmasūtra', in Janaki Nair and Mary E. John (eds), *A Question of Silence? The Sexual Economies of Modern India*, London and New York: Zed Books, 2000, pp. 60–6. Even if that is so, a reading of the *Kāmasūtra* leaves one with little doubt that *it sees itself* as departing from sexual arrangements ordained by the Dharmaśāstras. See Rocher ('The

Kāmasūtra') again on tell-tale signs of Vatsyayana's discomposure/ambivalence on the matter.

150. It should be noted that pleasure and anti-pleasure, in the sense in which the essay coins the concepts, are not antinomic but intersecting sets. Urban men could occupy the overlapping zone, whereas the courtesan at one end and the wife at the other belonged strictly to the mutually excluded realms of the intersecting sets. (Of course, the abhisārikā suggests that women too may have forded the divide.)

REFERENCES

Texts, Translations, and Editions Used

Avimāraka of Bhāsa

Menon, K.P.A. (trans.), *Complete Plays of Bhāsa* (text with English translation and notes), vol. III, Delhi: Nag Publishers, 2003.

Buddhacaritam of Aśvaghoṣa

Johnston, E.H. (trans.), *Aśvaghoṣa's Buddhacarita or Acts of the Buddha* (text and translation), Delhi: Motilal Banarsidass, 1992.

Cārudattam of Bhāsa

Devadhar, C.R. (trans.), *Charudatta* (text edited with introduction and translation), Poona: Poona Oriental Series No. 65, 1939.

Caturbhāṇī: *Ubhayābhisārikā* of Vararuci, *Dhūrtaviṭasaṁvāda* of Īśvaradatta, *Padmaprābhṛtaka* of Śūdraka, *Pādatāḍitaka* of Saumillaka.

Ghosh, M. (trans.), *Glimpses of Sexual Life in Nanda-Maurya India* (translation of the *Caturbhāṇī* with a critical edition of text), Calcutta: Manisha Granthalaya, 1975.

Daśakumāracaritam of Daṇḍin

Kale, M.R., *Daśakumāracarita of Daṇḍin* (text with Sanskrit commentary, English translation, critical notes, and introduction), Delhi: Motilal Banarsidass, 1979.

Harṣacaritam of Bāṇa

Cowell, E.B. and F.W. Thomas (trans.), *The Harṣacarita of Bāṇa*, Delhi: Motilal Banarsidass, 1968.

Jātakamālā of Āryaśūra

Speyer, J.S. (trans.), *The Jātakamālā: Garland of Birth Stories, of Aryasura* (translation based on text edited by Kern), Delhi: Motilal Banarsidass, 1971.

Kādaṁbarī of Bāṇa

Ridding, C.M. (trans.), *The Kādaṁbari of Baṇā* (translated with occasional omissions), New Delhi: Munshiram Manoharlal, 1974.

Kāmasūtra of Vātsyāyana Mallanāga

Doniger, Wendy and Sudhir Kakar (trans.), *Vātsyāyana Mallanāga Kāmasūtra* (new complete English translation of the Sanskrit text), Oxford and New York: Oxford University Press, 2002.

Kaumudīmahotsava of Vijayā

Shastri, Devadatt (trans.), *Kaumudī-Mahotsava Nāṭaka* (text and translation into Hindi), Delhi: na, 1953.

Kuṭṭanīmatam of Dāmodaragupta

Shastri, Ajay Mitra, *India as Seen in the Kuṭṭanī-Mata of Dāmodaragupta*, Delhi: Motilal Banarasidass, 1975.

Mālatīmādhava of Bhavabhūti

Kale, M.R. (trans.), *Bhavabhūti's Mālatīmādhava* (text with Sanskrit commentary, English translation, critical notes, and introduction), Delhi: Motilal Banarsidass, 1967.

Mālavikāgnimitram of Kālidāsa

Devadhar, C.R. (ed. and trans.), *Works of Kālidāsa*, vol. 1, Delhi: Motilal Banarsidass, 2002 (rpt of 1st edn).

Meghadūtam of Kālidāsa

Devadhar, C.R. (ed. and trans.), *Works of Kālidāsa*, vol. II, Delhi: Motilal Banarsidass, 2002.

Mṛcchakaṭikam of Śūdraka

Kale, M.R. (trans.), *Mṛcchakaṭikā of Śūdraka* (text with Sanskrit commentary, English translation, critical notes, and introduction), Delhi: Motilal Banarsidass, 1962.

van Buitenen, J.A.B., *Two Plays of Ancient India*, Delhi: Motilal Banarsidass, 1971.

Nāṭyaśāstra of Bharata

Ghosh, M. (trans.), *The Nāṭyaśāstra Ascribed to Bharata Muni*, vols 1 and 2, Calcutta: Manisha Granthalaya, 1967.

Raghuvaṁśam of Kālidāsa

Devadhar, C.R. (ed. and trans.), *Works of Kālidāsa*, vol. 2, Delhi: Motilal Banarasidass, 2002 (rpt of 1st edn).

Ṛtusaṁhāram of Kālidāsa

Devadhar, C.R. (ed. and trans.), *Works of Kālidāsa*, vol. 2, Delhi: Motilal Banarsidass, 2002.

Śiśupālavadham of Māgha

Shastri, Haragovinda, *Śiśupālavadham, Mahākavī Shrīmāghapraṇītam* (in Hindi), Benares: Chowkhamba Vidyabhawan Sanskrit Granthamala 8, 1955.

Vāsavadattā of Subandhu

Gray, Louis H. (trans.), *Vāsavadattā: A Sanskrit Romance by Subandhu* (translated with an introduction and notes), New York: Columbia University Press, 1965.

Other References

Caplan, Pat (ed.), *The Cultural Construction of Sexuality*, London and New York: Tavistock Publications, 1987.

Kaul, Shonaleeka, 'The City in Early India: A Study of Literary Perceptions (First Millennium AD)', unpublished PhD thesis, New Delhi: Centre for Historical Studies, Jawaharlal Nehru University, 2005.

———, 'Women about Town: An Exploration of the Sanskrit Kāvya Tradition', *Studies in History*, 22 (1), 2006, pp. 59–76.

Rocher, Ludo, 'The Kāmasūtra: Vātsyāyana's Attitude toward Dharma and Dharmaśāstra', *Journal of the American Oriental Society*, 105 (3), 1985, pp. 521–9.

Roy, Kumkum, 'Unravelling the Kāmasutra', in Janaki Nair and Mary E. John (eds), *A Question of Silence? The Sexual Economies of Modern India*, London and New York: Zed Books, 2000, pp. 52–76.

Tyagi, Jaya S., 'Brahmanical Ideology on the Ritual Roles of the Gṛhapati and his Wife in the Gṛha: A Study of the Early Grhyasutras (circa 800–500 BC)', *Studies in History*, 18 (2), n.s., 2002, pp. 189–208.

Warder, A.K., *Indian Kāvya Literature, Vol. I: Literary Criticism*, Delhi: Motilal Banarsidass, 1989.

Wheatley, Paul, *The Pivot of the Four Quarters: A Preliminary Enquiry into the Origins and Character of the Ancient Chinese City*, Edinburgh: Edinburgh University Press, 1971.

9. Gender Relations in Early Medieval Kashmir

DEVIKA RANGACHARI

EARLY MEDIEVAL Kashmir constitutes a discursive space that has been comprehensively delineated in terms of 'relevant' factors like its politics and topography. Yet, one of its most cardinal aspects—that of gender—remains in relative obscurity, an obscurity that is deepened by limited attempts to analyse this issue and by a general indifference towards women and their role in this time-span. Ironically, the very sources that are used for this seemingly all-inclusive yet gender-blind outline are the ones that lend themselves to a fruitful gender analysis and point to the extensive power and public presence enjoyed by royal and non-royal women in early medieval Kashmir. This essay discusses the potential of some of these sources for an understanding of gender relations in Kashmir between the seventh and the twelfth century AD. The focus here is on three literary sources that represent different genres of work—Kalhaṇa's *Rājataraṅgiṇī*, Kṣemendra's *Samayamātṛkā*, and the *Nīlamatapurāṇa*. The epigraphic evidence for this period in Kashmir is very inadequate and can, at best, be used as limited corroboration for textual material.

KALHAṆA'S *RĀJATARAṄGIṆĪ*[1]

The selected time-span of this study roughly corresponds to the historical subject matter provided by Kalhaṇa's *Rājataraṅgiṇī*, the most important and exhaustive source for this period. The text provides a sequential narrative of the rulers of Kashmir from the earliest period (for which only legendary traditions exist) till Kalhaṇa's own (AD 1149–50) in the form of a *kāvya* of 7,826 verses divided into eight books/*taraṅgas* of differing length. It owes its pivotal position in reconstructing Kashmir's history to several factors. On the one hand, it is the fullest and most authentic account of early Kashmir and is seen as a singular example of the genre of historical chronicles. In his endeavour to provide an authentic account of the history of Kashmir, Kalhaṇa consulted other types of evidence as well, such as sculptural and architectural remains, inscriptions, and coinage. Additionally, his lucidity, coherence, and attempts towards chronological precision imbue this text with great significance.

On the other hand, the text's treatment of women as historically relevant figures and the depiction of the immense formal and informal power wielded by them in this period indicates its lesser-known yet equally meaningful potential in the realm of gender studies.[2] Kalhaṇa's text highlights the power and agency of women in royal court culture in two essential ways—as sovereign rulers in their own right and as powers behind the throne. Power is wrested and exercised by them in what is essentially a patriarchal edifice, thus causing a certain amount of tension and ambiguity, not only in specific phases of Kashmir's history, but also in Kalhaṇa's portrayal of them. The contrast between the narrative and didactic sections of Kalhaṇa's text, evident in his alternate glorification and denigration of women, not only stresses their agency, but also reveals the complex power equations in the royal domain. This deliberate narrative style, however, has either been ignored or misinterpreted in secondary writings on Kashmir.

Women as Rulers

The *Rājataraṅgiṇī* reveals female rulership in Kashmir as an aspect that cut across time spans and dynasties, and, moreover, as culturally acceptable. The throne was a source of legitimate authority for both royal and non-royal women, either as direct rulers or as regents. This, naturally, posed a distinct challenge to prescriptive norms of succession that favoured the male and that denied women access to public roles of authority.

It may be pertinent to note here that the origin myths of Kashmir identify the land as Goddess Pārvatī's material manifestation. This is reiterated in the context of the definition of its rulership and is used, additionally, as justification for the rule of Yaśovatī (Gonanda dynasty, dates unknown), the first woman ruler of Kashmir.[3] Thus, although Yaśovatī herself has a shadowy presence, the rule of a woman is justified by Lord Kṛṣṇa's injunction that all occupants of the throne are portions of Śiva and, therefore, need to be obeyed, thereby providing a strong divine sanction to male and female rulership in Kashmir. The exercise of formal authority by women rulers of Kashmir is automatically validated by this comprehensive divine endorsement. A detailed description of Yaśovatī's reign is not available, but the paucity of details on her persona could be linked to the fact that her significance seems to lie in giving birth to the future heir, Gonanda II.

The reigns of Sugandhā and Diddā, the two most prominent women rulers of Kashmir, are based on much firmer historical ground. Sugandhā, daughter of King Svāmirāja of the northern region, appeared as a prominent figure in the last stages of the reign of her husband, Śaṁkaravarman, of the Utpala dynasty (AD 883–902). She accompanied him on a fatal military expedition, acquiesced in a bid to temporarily conceal the fact of his death for political reasons, and was spared from becoming a satī owing to the task of guardianship of their minor son, Gopālavarman, thrust upon her. Sugandhā eventually ascended the throne of Kashmir, backed by strong public approval, thereby testifying to her popularity. Thus, Kalhaṇa shows her role and influence to span Gopālavarman's reign (AD 902–4) and her own (AD 904–6).

Sugandhā's reign was marked by conflicts between rival military bodies, the *ekāṅgas* (royal bodyguards) and the *tantrins* (courtiers), interspersed with the growing influence of her lover, Prabhākaradeva, and her own forays into power politics, as, for instance, her determined attempt to crown her relative, Nirjitavarman, on the throne 'as he would follow her will'. Interestingly, Sugandhā was also implicated in Gopālavarman's death, apparently engineered by Prabhākaradeva. Subsequently thwarted by an open rebellion by the tantrins, who overruled her preference by crowning Nirjitavarman's minor son Pārtha instead, Sugandhā left the palace. Her abortive bid to regain power in AD 914 resulted in her imprisonment and eventual execution. Kalhaṇa's tone here is even-handed and he recounts the events of Sugandhā's reign in a largely objective manner.

Diddā, the third woman ruler of Kashmir, also commenced her pursuit of power as a regent. Daughter of Siṁharāja of Lohara and maternal granddaughter of the powerful Bhīma Śāhi of Udabhāṇḍa (who later built the magnificent Bhīmakeśava temple in Kashmir to underscore Diddā's power),[4] Diddā's formidable influence spanned the reigns of her husband Kṣemagupta of the Yaśaskara dynasty (AD 950–8), and that of their son and grandsons, until she herself ascended the throne in AD 980–1. Her influence on the largely ineffectual Kṣemagupta was amply proved by his coins where, unusually, the *di* prefixed to his name was intended as an abbreviation of hers.[5] Coins bearing Kṣemagupta's name alone are rare, whereas the other type with *di-kṣemagupta de(va)* are very common. Kalhaṇa provides corroborative information and reveals 'Diddākṣema' to have been Kṣemagupta's popular nickname. Kṣemagupta's death in AD 958 resulted in Diddā exercising total power as guardian during the reign of their son Abhimanyu (AD 958–72), displaying great political sagacity and fortitude.

As with Sugandhā, her growth to political maturity involved confrontations with rebellious factions and contenders to the throne. However, it was here that Diddā emerged triumphant, quelling her opposition with a sure hand, and soon dismissing the help of male councillors in her solitary pursuit of power. Interestingly, Diddā was physically disabled and was carried around by a porter-woman, Valgā, but she did not let this deter her in her quest for authority.

Kalhaṇa provides an account of the ministerial rivalries that faced the regent Diddā, prompting her to take unsound and impulsive decisions. However, with time her potential to rule surfaced and the shrewdness of her schemes for safeguarding her power, as in her alternate bribe-and-placation policy, is noteworthy. On the one hand she bribed the Brahmanas to rectify the impasse between her and the rebel grandsons of Parvagupta (Kṣemagupta's father), and bestowed offices on other malcontents. On the other hand, she destroyed the more intractable rebels by 'witchcraft', thereby exhibiting a ruthless streak that subsequently came to the fore. Minister Naravāhana, who gave Diddā sound advice and defended her against rebel forces, was of great help to her initially. However, she soon shook off his support and managed to get rid of her enemies in a systematic and ruthless purge.

After Abhimanyu's death, Diddā speedily disposed off her three grandsons, Nandigupta, Tribhuvana, and Bhīmagupta, in quick succession. She then assumed formal power and continued to rule Kashmir in a competent manner, providing peace and stability as well as a strong and effective administration. It is, perhaps, in Diddā's case alone that epigraphic evidence is of some relevance. Thus, the

Srinagar Buddhist image inscription of AD 989 and the Srinagar inscription of AD 992 refer to her by the masculine epithets of *deva* and *rājan*, respectively, rather than *devī* and *rājñī*, an interesting gender reversion.[6]

Interestingly, both Sugandhā and Diddā formed part of a succession of women who precipitated important dynastic changes in Kashmir's history. Thus, Sugandhā enabled her lover Prabhākaradeva's family to gain prominence in that Yaśaskara, his son, was later able to start his dynastic line. Likewise, Diddā bequeathed the throne to her maternal family from Lohara after a shrewd selection contest that her nephew Saṁgrāmarāja won. Consequently, on her death in AD 1003, the rule of Kashmir passed to the house of Lohara in undisputed succession, the latter holding sway until and beyond the date of the *Rājataraṅgiṇī*'s completion. Interestingly, Kalhaṇa lauds this 'third wonderful change' of dynasties caused 'by association with women'.[7]

Female rulership, therefore, was a strikingly significant feature of early medieval Kashmir, attesting the agency of its women in a very emphatic manner. Yet the evidence of the *Rājataraṅgiṇī* in this regard is routinely ignored or trivialized in secondary writings. Accounts of Sugandhā and Diddā are rife with uncritical portrayals. For instance, M.L. Kapur's endeavour to mould Sugandhā into a feminine stereotype of political ignorance, helplessness, and passivity militates against Kalhaṇa's deliberately ambivalent portrayal that portrays her as a puppet of various political factions on the one hand, but clearly indicates her ambition, shrewdness, and desire for power on the other.[8]

Kapur exonerates Sugandhā of any real desire for the throne. Nevertheless, the circumstances leading to her assumption of power and the cooperation of rival groups of ekāṅgas and tantrins in her reign, among other factors, are clear indicators of her diplomatic talents and ability to rule. Kapur further invests Sugandhā with a halo of martyrdom, noting that her comeback bid was due to her love for the people and her desire to free them from tantrin misrule. This, again, flies in the face of Kalhaṇa's evidence. The queen's reluctance to abandon the palace the first time around implies her reluctance to relinquish power. She was obviously not burdened by royal power, as Kapur believes, and was clearly interested in staking her claim to it more than once.

Kapur similarly tries to conventionalize Diddā's figure, although her rule is shown to parallel and even overshadow the impact of various male rulers.[9] Stressing her 'first impulse' to immolate herself on Kṣemagupta's death, he notes her intelligence and political talents but hastens to add that she was 'uncommonly voluptuous, profligate and dissolute' with a 'limitless' lust for power.[10]

Similarly, several historians like S.C. Banerjee, U.N. Ghoshal, and P.V. Kane focus on Diddā's cruelty and ambition—in short, her temerity in desiring total power. Epithets like 'dissolute', 'notorious', and 'self-indulgent' freely abound, while, ironically, male rulers who display the same ambition or cruelty are accepted as strong political figures who clearly did not vitiate the political atmosphere in the way these transgressive women figures did.[11] Ironically, Aurel Stein, the principal translator of the *Rājataraṅgiṇī*, is himself guilty of minimizing the text's potential by completely ignoring the presence of Kashmir's women rulers in the genealogical tables in his introductory preface.[12] Here, Yaśovatī, Sugandhā, and Diddā appear only as spouses, and not as rulers in their own right.

Interestingly, although the coinage of the women rulers of Kashmir can also be used as an entry point to study their power and presence, there is hardly any information or analysis available on this aspect in secondary works on Kashmir.[13] Both Sugandhā and Diddā issued coins in their capacity as sovereigns that refer to them by masculine epithets—as *śrī sugandhā deva* and *śrī diddā deva*, respectively. This is an important attestation of their power, raising the issue of the popular association of political authority with maleness, and whether women rulers needed to conform to this to gain acceptance. It is also notable that the copper issues of Sugandhā and Diddā (and those of their spouses) were common in Kashmir for several centuries. However, this is a fact that evokes very little interest.

Incidentally, this attitude of indifference not only permeates works dealing specifically with early medieval Kashmir, but also those that deal with royal life or social/political conditions in north India in this period. The overweening male focus, the factual errors, ambiguous references and dismissive statements with regard to women, and the desire to view them only within the parameters of 'social conditions' seem alarmingly consensual.[14] This is an offshoot of the overall tendency to view women as a peripheral, non-reactive, non-participatory group, whose 'status' or 'position' mechanically changes to reflect larger changes around them, rather than envisaging a certain degree of agency for women vis-à-vis historical processes.

M.K. Dhar's *Royal Life in Ancient India* is an illustrative case where women rulers form a part of 'social conditions', and Diddā's motives for ruling are completely distorted.[15] She is referred to as a queen (unnamed, with no mention of Kashmir) who killed her three grandsons for power. Dhar then makes the inexplicable observation that this was the result of Diddā's frustration with the king for neglecting her and bestowing favours on the principal queen and her children instead! As noted earlier, Diddā was Kṣemagupta's chief and most desired queen, and, in fact, was a widow by the time she felt the need to dispose off her grandsons. Likewise, Saroj Gulati who attempts a 'critical appraisal' of different social institutions/customs in north India and 'their influence on the position of women' dismisses Sugandhā and Diddā in a obscure reference and trivializes facts relating to women rulers in general.[16] B.N.S. Yadava too blames Kashmir's 'ambitious queens' rather than ambitious kings for ruining the political atmosphere, and is similarly dismissive of their rule and contributions.[17]

Vina Mathur's *The Role and Position of Women in the Social, Cultural and Political Life of Kashmir* that purports to undertake a pioneering study of the position of women in Kashmir and then proceeds to lambast Kalhaṇa's 'chauvinistic' attitude is another illuminating example.[18] What is missed in Mathur's intensely critical view is the fact of Kalhaṇa treating women as historically relevant figures and charting their rise to power with objectivity.

It should be noted that the examples cited here are only a few of the many inadequate analyses available on the women rulers of Kashmir. Works that appreciate their role and contributions are, predictably, minimal. Kumkum Roy's analysis, however, forms a welcome and notable exception to the trend of ignoring or explaining away the masterful presence of women in Kashmir.[19] Roy notes the existence 'of alternative socio-political norms' here and of the tension in the *Rājataraṅgiṇī* inherent in reconciling Śāstric norms with a situation that clearly did not conform to them.[20] She observes that the patrilineal (and patriarchal) ideal was only one among several contending power sources in Kashmir.

Another rare avowal is Ashvini Agrawal's work that notes the 'significant role' played by women in the political life of Kashmir 'from time to time'. The role of Sugandhā, Diddā, and other prominent queens 'as king-makers, sovereigns, mediators and diplomats' is conceded. However, Agrawal's work is more a straightforward rendition of details than an analytic exercise.[21]

Very few works, however, actually focus on the pertinent question of how the women of Kashmir were able to bypass ideological stipulations that associated political authority with maleness and emerge as powerful political figures. There are two ways of examining this problem. On the one hand, the prescriptions contained in the Dharmaśāstras and other texts can be juxtaposed with the actual exercise of political authority. A general survey of prescriptive and normative literature shows a distinct hostility to the idea of formal female authority. However, the prescriptions were clearly not inflexible/hegemonic, and could be subverted on occasion. The divergence of views among lawgivers itself strengthens this contention.[22] Female power in Kashmir can be traced to this gap between theory and practice.

What may also be kept in mind is that Sugandhā and Diddā are not entirely unrepresentative of the situation in early medieval India. Interesting parallels can be drawn with the Bhaumakara queens of Orissa, and other notable dowagers like Prabhāvatīguptā of the Vākāṭaka family (fourth century AD), and Vijayabhaṭṭārikā of the Cālukya house (seventh century AD) The evidence would indicate that women in ruling families, including the women rulers of Kashmir, had some familiarity with politics and administration.

On the other hand, Cynthia Talbot's study of early medieval India and Europe can be examined for its relevance.[23] Talbot considers women political leaders from three regions between the ninth and thirteenth century AD—Sugandhā and Diddā of Kashmir, the women rulers of the Orissan Bhaumakara dynasty (Gaurīmahādevī, Daṇḍīmahādevī, Vakulamahādevī, and Dharmamahādevī), and the four women rulers of Andhra (Rudramadevī, Gaṇapamadevī, Muppaladevī, and Vīryālā Nāgasānī). She then draws a parallel with medieval European women who possessed greatest political power in roughly the same period, pointing to the decentralized nature of the medieval European polity that associated political authority with particular families, thereby blurring the distinction between public and private spheres.

Claiming that medieval Kashmir, Andhra, and Orissa all resembled early medieval Europe in their lack of centralization, Talbot notes that women occupied a pivotal role in this decentralized situation where political power was personalized and could be embodied through marriage relations. Women were allowed to exercise political authority on several occasions to ensure the retention of a throne within the immediate kin group. Sugandhā's reign is a case in point. Thus, the centrality of the family in certain political cultures of the time could explain the phenomenon of ruling queens.

In addition, regency provided a justification for female authority. Talbot notes that the regent queen is shown as foregoing the 'attractive' option of self-immolation in order to fulfil her responsibilities towards her family and kingdom. Yet it is crucial to note here that both Sugandhā and Diddā used their regency as a stepping-stone towards acquiring power, and, hence, were not passive regents in the conventional sense.

The phenomenon of women exercising power in Kashmir, therefore, served to indicate constantly fluctuating social processes. Talbot stresses the flexibility of the prevalent gender ideology and construction of identity as well, whereby the gap between theory and practice could be reconciled through manipulation of gender imagery and privileging of maternal obligations. However, unlike rulers such as Rudramadevī and Raziya Sultan who deliberately adopted masculine clothing, styles, and titles to gain public acceptance, Kalhaṇa does not indicate any such attempt by the women rulers of Kashmir, except for the masculine titles on their coins. This indicates that women were tacitly accepted as legitimate wielders of power in the area.

One should also note that Talbot's theory cannot be rigidly applied to Kashmir. For instance, Diddā's bestowal of the throne to the Loharas was unorthodox in that the rights of her maternal family triumphed over that of the Yaśaskaras, her husband's family with whom the sovereignty was associated. Thus, her natal ties were given precedence over her husband's family. The formation of another dynasty, the Kārkoṭas, was similarly unusual in that the sovereignty was vested in the descendants of a king's daughter.[24] The specific conjunction of social and political circumstances that allowed women to exercise authority in Kashmir still remains a largely unexplored issue. One could, however, speculate that the strong tribal roots of this region, as also its geographical location that isolated it from the other kingdoms of north India, combined to produce a political and social climate that was conducive to the public presence of women with relatively unstructured gender roles.

WOMEN AS POWERS BEHIND THE THRONE

The *Rājataraṅgiṇī* shows power being exercised by royal and non-royal women of Kashmir in a range of situations as queens, courtesans, court participants, mediators, dynasty makers and destroyers, and other capacities, thereby stressing their access to the public domain of politics. Prominent among the powerful queens was Sūryamatī, daughter of Inducandra of Jālaṁdhara and wife of Anantavarman of the Lohara dynasty (AD 1028–63). She acquired supremacy by solving a financial crisis with her independent resources and acumen. Thereafter, she took over the administration, dictated orders to Ananta, and eventually forced him to abdicate in favour of their son Kalaśa. Despite Kalaśa's subsequent wayward behaviour, Sūryamatī restrained Ananta from punishing him, thereby prompting Ananta to kill himself. Sūryamatī's definitive political role was discernible even after her death in that Kalaśa's son Harṣa's initial survival in politics was due to her sage advice.

Another prominent queen was Kalhaṇikā, wife of Jayasiṁha of the Lohara dynasty (AD 1128–49), who dispelled a rebel threat by her mediation. Having become chief queen with public approval, Kalhaṇikā underscored her importance through her influential role as mediator, successfully effecting a reconciliation between Jayasiṁha and his rebel cousin Bhoja, and preventing an incipient *ḍāmara* rebellion.[25] Raḍḍādevī, Jayasiṁha's other wife, played an equally pivotal role in independently devising politically strategic marriages for her daughters. Other powerful queens included Śrīlekhā, Ananta's mother, who made an abortive bid for the throne, Śāradā, wife of Sussala, who legitimized a rebel scheme, and Sugalā, wife of Harṣa, who failed to kill him, but later boldly staked her claim as chief queen.

The vigorous participation of non-royal women in court politics was another striking feature of early medieval Kashmir. The diverse origin of queens was a clear indication that political power was a legitimate quest for non-royal women as well. In this context, the influence of courtesans and prostitutes on the throne was particularly noteworthy. For instance, Jayamatī, a temple dancer's ward 'of unknown origin' (VII.1460—...*kvāpi jātāṁ*...) and chief queen of Uccala of the Lohara dynasty (AD 1101–11), deliberately flouted his orders to kill Bhikṣācara, a future contender to the throne. She masterminded Bhikṣācara's escape and was, therefore, instrumental in enabling his accession to the throne at a later stage. Sāmbavatī, a courtesan and skilful mediator between political groups, and Kamalā, a temple dancer who was indirectly instrumental in the exiled Jayāpīḍa's resumption of power, were other stellar examples. So too was Jayādevī, a spirit distiller's daughter, whose hold over Lalitāpīḍa was used by her brothers to seize power, crown a series of puppet-kings, and eventually establish their own dynasty. There were numerous courtesans who appeared in the roles of dynasty makers/destroyers, power aspirants, court participants, and builders. Clearly, low origin was no barrier to their exercise of power in the public domain.

The *Rājataraṅgiṇī* provides other examples of prominent non-royal women in early medieval Kashmir. The role of the powerful ḍāmara-woman Chuḍḍā in charting political equations, challenging the reigning king, Sussala's might, and consolidating her son's power by becoming his guardian and protecting his interests was particularly noteworthy. So too was the role of Āsamatī, a relative of the Śāhi princesses, who changed the course of royal politics by thwarting Uccala's murderous designs, actively aiding Jayamatī in Bhikṣācara's escape, and at points seeming to be the more conniving of the two. In addition, one can consider Nonā, the rebel Bhoja's nurse, who played an important part in the reconciliation between him and Jayasiṁha by initially broaching the issue to the king. Sahajā, who mediated between Jayasiṁha and her rebel son Mallārjuna's forces, and Sillā, who commanded her son's troops in his absence, were other illustrative cases. Obviously, therefore, non-royal widows were not relegated to passive roles in the contemporary socio-political scenario, thereby indicating an important point of convergence with some of their royal counterparts.

Nevertheless, the familiar bias against female figures in secondary sources is once more in evidence. This finds expression in, for instance, attempts to conventionalize Sūryamatī's figure, grudging mentions of Kalhaṇikā's role, and summary dismissals of the intervention of royal and non-royal women in politics in general.[26] Corroborative details of Sūryamatī's power in Bilhaṇa's *Vikramāṅkadevacaritaṁ* (twelfth century AD) have been generally ignored, with the possible exception of the translators of the text who note that she was conversant with state policy.[27] Any attempt at a gender analysis or an acknowledgement of the light thrown on the contemporary socio-political scene is predictably missing.

Women as Builders/Donors

The building activities of men and women—as revealed by the *Rājataraṅgiṇī*—have important implications on a gender analysis of the politics and society of early medieval Kashmir. Royal and non-royal women are shown to parallel their male counterparts in this regard, indulging in building and donations not just for piety, but for other impelling motives as well. The power of women was made obvious in the physical landscape itself—in terms of the various towns, shrines, and buildings that usually bore their names (as, for instance, Kalyāṇadevī's Kalyāṇapura town and Diddā's Diddāsvāmin temple), and would have served as reminders to the people about their role and agency in a qualitatively visible sense. Although there is a clear linkage of power with the buildings of kings, this seemed to have been a driving factor for women too. The buildings of Sugandhā, Diddā, Sūryamatī, and other powerful queens like Ratnādevī (such as towns, *maṭhas*, temples, and *vihāras*) are a case in point. Prominent non-royal women builders included Sussala, the minister Rilhaṇa's wife, Valgā, Diddā's porter-woman, and the politically powerful courtesan, Sāmbavatī.

Thus, there were interesting variations in the social identities of builders and donors. Equally, there were disparate motives of donation. On the one hand there were instances of women perpetuating their name through their towns/buildings, as in Diddā's Diddāpura town. On the other hand there were women like Śrīlekhā, an eager aspirant for the throne, who built maṭhas in honour of her husband and son against whom she was, simultaneously, plotting treason. Predictably, however, this well-documented sphere of female agency is either ignored or misconstrued by most writers on Kashmir. M.L. Kapur's attempt to associate piety and grief with the buildings of Sugandhā is a case in point.[28] The buildings of Diddā, the most prolific woman builder (the Diddāsvāmin temple, Diddāpura town and maṭha, the Siṁhasvāmin shrine, and her vihāra for foreigners being notable examples, in this regard), are summarily dismissed. So too are the *gokula*, maṭha, and town built by Ratnādevī, Jayasiṁha's wife, which outranked others of the same type in size and splendour.

Female donation is closely linked with the control and extent of resources. Women donors in Kashmir were clearly not constrained by the norms of Dharmaśāstra texts in which their limited property rights and dependant religious identity precluded the possibility of their extensive/independent gift-giving. The Kashmir queens obviously had access to large amounts of money/resources that enabled them to finance constructions and make monetary donations towards buildings. Likewise, the possession of resources by non-royal women argues some amount of access and control in economic affairs.

Once again, one can draw attention to Talbot's study of thirteenth century Andhra inscriptions wherein she concludes that royal women indulged in donations as this was the only socially sanctioned public activity and prestige-enhancing opportunity open to them.[29] This view is largely untenable in the case of women in early medieval Kashmir who had manifold opportunities for public and political activity, and did not need building/donative activities to register their presence. Their involvement in it was, in fact, a mere affirmation of their status.

The immense potential of the *Rājataraṅgiṇī* for a gender analysis of early medieval Kashmir is, therefore, obvious. On the one hand, Kalhaṇa conveys a sense of the interaction and tension between male rulers and female consorts, ruling queens and male advisers, and other protagonists in the royal court culture. On the other hand, one also gets a sense of the potentials and pressures in the world of non-royal women as they sought to negotiate for their sons and husbands in the political arena, as also an idea of the common social ground occupied by royal and non-royal women. An appreciation of the text's gendered potential is vital owing to the fact that it is used almost exclusively as a source for this period in Kashmir.

KṢEMENDRA'S *SAMAYAMĀTṚKĀ*[30]

Although the *Rājataraṅgiṇī* provides significant examples of the role of prostitutes in early medieval Kashmir, it is Kṣemendra's *Samayamātṛkā* (eleventh century AD), a kāvya of 635 *śloka*s, which can be specifically related to Kashmir, that foregrounds their position and influence in a very effective manner. While its central idea of stressing the rapacity of the prostitute is reminiscent of Dāmodaragupta's *Kuṭṭanīmataṁ* (eighth century AD), its intrinsic potential for a gender analysis is greater—both in terms of the development of the story and in its overall characterization. The *Samayamātṛkā* essentially deals with a prostitute Kaṅkālī's ingenious means of survival and her timely adoption as a mother by a young prostitute Kalāvatī, whom she was instrumental in making wealthy by her judicious schemes. The numerous references to places in Kashmir as a part of Kaṅkālī's travels indicate a familiarity with its landscape and impart a tone of authenticity to the text.

The text traces the intelligent and resourceful Kaṅkālī's bid to survive by changing names, locales, and occupations, and simultaneously duping and controlling men with consummate ease. Sold at a tender age by her mother, Kaṅkālī (initially named Gargatikā) embarked on a trail littered with assumed names and pretended professions involving, among other things, fomenting trouble in a rich man's household to get rid of him and acquire his wealth, seizing the business of a horse-owner, bribing magistrates to fraudulently acquire property, cutting a jailor's tongue to escape imprisonment, pretending to be a businesswoman, a chief minister's daughter, and a spiritual adviser in turn, bearing a son and abandoning him after appropriating his jewels, assuming the identity of an ace gambler and astrologer, and duping and robbing kings, ministers, and fellow travellers. Her final successful endeavour was in helping Kalāvatī to ensnare a rich client, Śaṅkha, with clockwork precision, thereby justifying her selection as Kalāvatī's 'timely mother' (*Samayamātṛkā*).

As Kṣemendra's purpose was clearly to expose the cold-blooded aspects of prostitution, his stress is not so much on Kaṅkālī's resourcefulness and grit as on her deviousness and unscrupulousness. This translates into his harsh, and often exaggerated, portrayal of her character that is stripped of any redeeming feature. Her complete repudiation of motherhood underscores this. This makes an immediate point of contrast with the *Rājataraṅgiṇī* where the destructive potential of prostitutes is evoked along with their role as saviours and protectors, in a largely impartial manner.

Yet, ironically, Kṣemendra's stress on Kaṅkālī's rapacity actually underlines her strength, showing her to be a completely pragmatic survivor, and also indicating the possibilities and options open to a woman who was compelled by circumstances to live by her wits alone. Kaṅkālī's fluid adoption of various professions—most of which appear to be male prerogatives—further underscores the choices open to women who desired to lead unconventional lifestyles. Thus, she was alternately a businesswoman, manager of horses, astrologer, gambler, and maker of metal. The fact that people accepted her in these roles is an important comment on the contemporary social scene and corroborates Kalhaṇa's evidence on the public presence of women in early Kashmir. One might argue that prostitutes usually command a greater degree of freedom/licence than other women. However, Kaṅkālī always managed to conceal her actual trade from most of her associates. To them she was only an ordinary woman endeavouring to make a living.

Interestingly, Kṣemendra offers two varied motives for writing the *Samayamātṛkā*. He states at the outset that the text was intended to teach prostitutes the secret of their trade—a sarcastically worded intention, as his aim was clearly to teach the people about the threat posed by prostitutes.[31] The second motive, contained in the epilogue, was to provide the newly-crowned Ananta with ideas on the deployment of women in the enemy camp to effect the latter's downfall.[32] This is strongly reminiscent of Kalhaṇa's evidence of the destructive power of women and their potential to effect changes in rulership as, for instance, Cakravarman being murdered for his involvement with low-caste women, and Harṣa whose Śāhi wives egg him on to a self-destructive path. Ironically, while Kṣemendra strove to educate Ananta on the value of women as a political weapon, Ananta himself needed to be educated on political and other matters by his wife Sūryamatī, who took over the reins of administration from him.

Most secondary sources, once again, fail to exploit the *Samayamātṛkā*'s potential in revealing the specifics of a prostitute's status, and in indicating interesting points of convergence and divergence with Kalhaṇa's work among other things.[33] The bitterness of Kṣemendra's tone, viewed in conjunction with his intimate knowledge of prostitution, leads one to speculate whether it stemmed from some kind of personal experience and whether Kaṅkālī, one of the strongest female protagonists of contemporary literature, was based on an actual prostitute of his acquaintance. A more definite assessment cannot be made due to the lack of corroborative evidence. Nevertheless, the importance of prostitutes and their power, as attested by both the *Samayamātṛkā* and the *Rājataraṅgiṇī*, was a pivotal ingredient of the social and political history of early medieval Kashmir and, therefore, of a gender analysis of the time.

THE *NĪLAMATAPURĀṆA*

The *Nīlamatapurāṇa* (seventh/eighth century AD), a Purāṇa of unknown authorship that provides information on the legendary lore, topography, and customs of Kashmir, is another important source for this period, and is the earliest indigenous text for the history of Kashmir. It provides the 'social background' to Kalhaṇa's 'dynastic and political history', and also corroborates the *Samayamātṛkā* in certain aspects.[34] Written in the Purāṇic style of interwoven dialogues, it is the only source that provides an account of Kashmir's formation, the details of which Kalhaṇa borrowed in his work. It also talks of the identification of the land of Kashmir and its sovereign with Goddess Pārvatī (Umā), as part of Lord Kṛṣṇa's justification for crowning its first woman ruler, Yaśovatī.

The importance of this text lies in the fact that it corroborates on a social level Kalhaṇa's indications of the power wielded by non-royal women in the political sphere. Of particular note was the participatory nature of their involvement in socio-political functions. Ranging from the king's coronation ceremonies to pilgrimages and annual festivals marking the land's birth, the participation of men and women on a more or less equal plane is implied. Furthermore, there are interesting indications of the intermingling of both sexes at various levels. Women were enjoined to accept gifts from their husbands' friends, and wine and dine with them, as part of the ritual worship of certain deities. This suggests a degree of freedom and liberality in society at obvious divergence from prescribed norms that dictated regulation of contact between the sexes.

Not only are women shown as enjoying themselves in a relatively uninhibited manner in indoor and outdoor festivals with men, as in the worship of Goddess Śyāmā that involved a festival of singing and dancing, but they also participated in and performed certain rites along with them, as in the worship of Goddess Kaśmīrā. There are several other indications of their status as, for instance, the stress laid on honouring maternal relatives and those by marriage. Of equal weight is the specific prescription of *śrāddha* (death ceremony) days for women along with men, an indication of the importance accorded to each sex.[35] Likewise, there are repeated references to 'happy women—well-fed, well-dressed, well-scented, well-anointed and decorated with ornaments', to be 'pleased' on particular days and 'honoured', as on the day of the first snow.[36] The significance of these injunctions lies in the fact that they form a part of the 'good customs' laid down by Nīla, the patron snake deity of Kashmir, for the acquisition of prosperity and peace by the people.[37] Hence, the enjoining of respect towards women and their participation in contemporary affairs in this list is noteworthy.

Significantly, the *Nīlamatapurāṇa* corroborates Kalhaṇa's picture of the power wielded by courtesans. They are equated with prominent citizens and are enjoined to play important roles in royal ceremonies as well as ordinary festivals. Interestingly, if the text apparently reflects the attempt to combat Buddhism and restore Brahmanical practices in Kashmir,[38] this then raises the question of how to reconcile the space accorded to prostitutes who are otherwise condemned in Brahmanical prescriptive works.

At the same time, the *Nīlamatapurāṇa* indicates that the position of women may not have been so remarkably exalted. The worship of (married) women on various occasions—as in the Īramañjarī festival or on the full-moon night of *mārgaśīrśā*—which is a notable refrain of the text, and its eventual linkage with fertility, is a case in point. Such a stipulation does not necessarily imply that women had a powerful position, but often the reverse. Moreover, the preconditions for this worship indicate that widows and single women are proscribed categories. Clearly, ambiguous signals of the agency of non-royal women can be recovered from the *Nīlamatapurāṇa*. And yet the perception of women as a relevant and participatory category stresses their role in the contemporary socio-political milieu. Questions can be raised on the authorial stance, on whether this was a reflection of reality and, if so, whether this could have laid the ground for the assumption of power by various categories of women in subsequent ages and the general acceptance thereof. There are no clear answers, but the mere fact that such questions can be raised exemplifies the potential of these sources for constructing a gender-sensitive history of Kashmir.

Yet, the *Nīlamatapurāṇa*'s potential in this regard has not been fully appreciated. The views of Ved Kumari, the principal translator of the text, are an illustrative example. For instance, although she acknowledges the 'somewhat different and unconventional picture' of female life in this text, she completely trivializes Yaśovatī's rule, of which the text gives important evidence. The queen is mentioned in passing at the end of a discussion on 'Women in the Family' as a part of the 'Position of Women'.[39] Yaśovatī does not even find a place in

Kumari's discussion of the 'King and his Functions', despite being the first woman ruler of Kashmir and enabling the comprehensive definition of rulership in the kingdom. The potential of the text for a gender study is thereby effectively minimized.

Thus, that the same set of sources can be critically analysed to reveal a gendered perspective of early medieval Kashmir is undeniable. They reveal that royal and non-royal women of Kashmir seem to have wrested a distinct space for themselves within the contemporary society and polity. Their ability to subsume the patriarchal edifice in certain contexts and situations necessitates a rethinking of the negotiation of female identities within a patriarchal set-up.

As Roy notes, the rulers of Kashmir were evidently located within a social context that was less closely structured in hierarchical terms than the Śāstric ideal. Affinal kinsfolk could intervene to support/oppose rulers just as effectively as members of the patrilineage—and this was open to even relatively lower social categories like the *ḍombas* and *cāṅḍālas*. In such a situation, Roy opines that the rulers' conformity to Śāstric ideals would be superficial and their household would have contrasted with Śāstric norms at several levels. Domestic relations among non-royal groups would have been similarly loosely structured and divergent from the patrilineal model, thereby pointing to alternative forms of household organization in this region.

Women in Kashmir, therefore, clearly enjoyed a more equal status vis-à-vis men than those elsewhere and the assertion of their power seems to have been a fairly constant factor. One can contrast this with other parts of contemporary north India as, for instance, the kingdoms of Kanauj and Bengal-Bihar, where explorations of a similar nature reveal an intermittent expression of the role and influence of women over this time-span.[40] The question of woman's power is, consequently, a contextual one, calling for a careful analysis of available sources to glean pertinent information. The apparent irrelevance of women to the political and social order needs to be questioned and analysed, for this is often merely an erroneous projection by historical scholarship. In addition, it is necessary to explore the agency of different classes of women in any analysis rather than treating them as one amorphous whole. Thus, this essay has hopefully demonstrated the centrality of gender and its related explorations of female agency in any investigation of the society and polity of early medieval Kashmir.

NOTES

1. M.A. Stein (ed.), *Kalhaṇa's Rājataraṅgiṇī*, vol. III, Bombay: Motilal Banarsidass, 1988 (rpt); M.A. Stein (trans.), *Kalhaṇa's Rājataraṅgiṇī*, vols I and II, Delhi: Motilal Banarsidass, 1989 (third rpt).
2. For more information on this theme, Devika Rangachari, 'Gender and the Historical Chronicle: A Study of Kalhaṇa's *Rājataraṅgiṇī*', unpublished MPhil Dissertation, Delhi: Department of History, University of Delhi, 1997. See also Devika Rangachari, 'Kalhaṇa's *Rājataraṅgiṇī*: A Gender Perspective', *Medieval History Journal*, 5 (I), 2002, pp. 37–75.
3. Ved Kumari (trans.), *The Nīlamata Purāṇa*, vol. II, Srinagar: J&K Academy of Art, Culture and Languages, 1973, verse 246. Kalhaṇa does not provide dates for this period of Kashmir's history, but Gonanda III can be presumed to have ruled around 1182 BC. The Gonandas were apparently the first dynasty to rule Kashmir.
4. Bhīma Śāhi is mentioned in Alberuni's list of Hindu Shahiyas of Kabul as the successor of Kamalu. He is also known from his coins.
5. Stein, *Kalhaṇa's Rājataraṅgiṇī*, vol. I, VI.177. Also A. Cunningham, *Coins of Medieval India*. Varanasi: Oriental Books, 1967, p. 45, for details.
6. B.K. Kaul Deambi, *Corpus of Śāradā Inscriptions of Kashmir*, Delhi: Agam Kala Prakashan, 1982, pp. 97–8; K.N. Sastri, 'Srinagar Inscription of Queen Diddā', *Epigraphia Indica*, vol. XXVII, 1985 (rpt), pp.153–5. The first inscription records the consecration of a bronze statuette of the *bodhisattva* Padmapāṇi by Rājānaka Bhīmaṭa, a Buddhist devotee and son of Cāvata, and by the four brothers of Gaṅgā Devī. The second one mentions a certain Dharmāṇika honouring his mother by dedicating some religious institution or charitable work in her name.
7. Stein, *Kalhaṇa's Rājataraṅgiṇī*, vol. I, VI.366. Kalhaṇa's words are: *strī-saṁbandhena bhūpāla-vaṁśyānāṁ bhuvanādbhutaha, tṛitīya parivartoyaṁ vartate-mutra maṇḍale.*
8. M.L. Kapur, *Eminent Rulers of Ancient Kashmir*, Delhi: Oriental Publishers, 1975; M.L. Kapur, *The History and Culture of Kashmir*, Delhi: Anmol Publications, 1992 (2nd edn).
9. Kapur, *History and Culture of Kashmir*, p. 45.
10. Ibid., pp. 50, 53, 59–60. Also Kapur, *Eminent Rulers*, p. 68.
11. S.C. Banerji, *Cultural Heritage of Kashmir*, Calcutta: Sanskrit Pustak Bhandar, 1965, p. 51; U.N. Ghoshal, 'The Dynastic Chronicles of Kashmir', *The Indian Historical Quarterly*, vol. XVIII, 1985 (rpt), p. 323; P.V. Kane, *History of Dharmaśāstra*, vol. III, Poona: Bhandarkar Oriental Research Institute, 1946, p. 40.
12. Stein, *Kalhaṇa's Rājataraṅgiṇī*, vol. I, 'Introduction', Appendix II, pp. 139–44. Note that R.S. Pandit's translation of the *Rājataraṅgiṇī* is very literal and has an abundance of French terms. Moreover, his analysis of the text is sketchy, unlike Stein's well-structured and comprehensive one. See R.S. Pandit (trans.), *Rājataraṅgiṇī*, Delhi: Sahitya Akademi, 1935.
13. For instance, a seminal work on numismatics like P.L. Gupta's *Coins*, New Delhi: National Book Trust, 1969, has a pronounced male bias and only

fleetingly mentions associations of women with coins in early Indian history. For more information on the queens' coins, see Cunningham, *Coins of Medieval India*, p. 45; Devika Rangachari, 'Coinage and Gender: Early Medieval Kashmir', in H.P. Ray (ed.), *Coins in India: Power and Communication*, Mumbai: MARG, 2006, pp. 46–55.

14. For a critique of this, Uma Chakravarti and Kumkum Roy, 'In Search of Our Past: A Review of the Limitations and Possibilities of the Historiography of Women in Early India', *Economic and Political Weekly*, 23 (18), 1988, p. 2. See also B.D. Chattopadhyaya, 'General Editor's Preface', in Kumkum Roy (ed.), *Women in Early Indian Societies*, New Delhi: Manohar, 1999, p. ix; Kumkum Roy, 'Introduction', in Kumkum Roy (ed.), *Women in Early Indian Societies*, New Delhi: Manohar, 1999, p. 4.
15. M.K. Dhar, *Royal Life in Ancient India*, Delhi: Durga Publications, 1991, pp. 9, 44–5, 58–9.
16. Saroj Gulati, *Women and Society: Northern India in the 11th and 12th Centuries*, Delhi: Chanakya Publications, 1985, p. 28, where she mentions women rulers in one line. Also pp. 3, 39, 42.
17. B.N.S. Yadava, *Society and Culture in Northern India in the Twelfth Century*, Allahabad: Central Book Depot, 1973, p. 9.
18. Vina Mathur, *The Role and Position of Women in the Social, Cultural and Political Life of Kashmir: 7th century–16th century AD*, Jammu: Doron Publications, 1985.
19. For more information on the consistent attempt to 'invisibilize' women in history, Chakravarti and Roy, 'In Search of Our Past', pp. 2–10.
20. Kumkum Roy, 'Defining the Household: Some Aspects of Prescription and Practice in Early India', *Social Scientist*, 22 (1–2), 1994, pp. 3–18.
21. Ashvini Agrawal, 'Women in the Political Life of Kashmir (c. AD 650–1150)', in C.M. Agrawal (ed.), *Dimensions of Indian Womanhood*, vol. I, Almora: Shri Almora Book Depot, 1993, pp. 87–8.
22. For instance, while the *Majjhima Nikāya*, the *Arthaśāstra*, and the *Jātakas* stress the complete unsuitability of a woman for rulership and administration, the Śāntiparva of the Mahābhārata authorizes the coronation of a vanquished ruler's daughter in the absence of suitable male candidates. See A.S. Altekar, *State and Government in Ancient India*, Delhi: Motilal Banarsidass, 1958 (3rd edn), p. 87; A.K. Majumdar, *Concise History of Ancient India*, vol. 2, Delhi: Munshiram Manoharlal, 1980, p. 55; Beni Prasad and R.C. Majumdar, 'Political Theory and Administrative System', in R.C. Majumdar (ed.), *The Age of Imperial Unity*, Bombay: Bharatiya Vidya Bhawan, 1968 (4th edn), p. 303.
23. Cynthia Talbot, 'Rudrama-devī, the Female King: Gender and Political Authority in Medieval India', in David Shulman (ed.), *Syllables of Sky: Studies in South Indian Civilization in Honour of Velcheru Narayana Rao*, New Delhi: Oxford University Press, 1995, pp. 391–430.
24. For instance, Stein, *Kalhaṇa's Rājataraṅgiṇī*, vol. I, III.530.
25. Ḍāmaras were a class of feudal landholders that played an important part in the politics of Kashmir.

26. For instance, Ghoshal, 'Dynastic Chronicles of Kashmir', pp. 235–6; and Beni Prasad, *The State in Ancient India*, Allahabad: The Indian Press, 1974, pp. 327–8, for an inadequate and cursory treatment of Sūryamatī's role. Also B.P. Mazumdar, 'Role of the Dāmaras in Medieval Kashmir', in K.M. Shrimali (ed.), *Essays in Indian Art, Religion and Society*, New Delhi: Munshiram Manoharlal, 1987, pp. 27–36, where there is no mention of Chuḍḍā and her role in the discussion on the ḍāmaras.
27. S.C. Banerji and A.K. Gupta (trans.), *Bilhaṇa's Vikramāṅkadevacaritaṁ*, Calcutta: Sambodhi Publications, 1965, p. 11.
28. Kapur, *History and Culture of Kashmir*, p. 43.
29. Cynthia Talbot, 'Temples, Donors, and Gifts: Patterns of Patronage in Thirteenth-century South India', *Journal of Asian Studies*, 50 (2), 1991, p. 328.
30. R.S. Tripathi (ed. and trans.), *Samayamātṛkā of Mahākavi Kṣemendra*, Varanasi: Chowkhamba Vidyabhavan, 1967. Note that Kṣemendra's father was from a well-connected family in Kashmir and that his grandfather Narendra was a minister.
31. Ibid., I.3.
32. Ibid., 4.
33. For instance, Sukumari Bhattacharji, 'Prostitution in Ancient India', in Kumkum Roy (ed.), *Women in Early Indian Societies*, New Delhi: Manohar, 1999, pp. 211–12, where she points to Kaṅkālī's 'lack of proficiency' in any other profession (a statement that is directly contradicted by the text), and ignores the indications of her grit and intelligence.
34. Ved Kumari, *The Nīlamata Purāṇa*, vol. I, Srinagar-Jammu: J&K Academy of Art, Culture and Languages, 1968, p. v.
35. Kumari, *Nīlamata Purāṇa*, vol. II, verses 485–6.
36. For instance, ibid., verses 548, 557, 483–4.
37. Ibid., verses 225, 900–1.
38. Deambi, *Corpus of Śāradā Inscriptions*, p. 263.
39. Kumari, *Nīlamata Purāṇa*, vol. I, pp. 94–5, 131–4.
40. For more information on gender in early medieval north India, see Devika Rangachari, *Invisible Women, Visible Histories; Gender, Society and Polity in North India (Seventh to Twelfth Century AD)*, New Delhi: Manohar, 2009.

REFERENCES

Altekar, A.S., *State and Government in Ancient India*, Delhi: Motilal Banarsidass, 1958 (3rd edn).

Agrawal, Ashvini, 'Women in the Political Life of Kashmir (*c.* AD 650–1150)', in C.M. Agrawal (ed.), *Dimensions of Indian Womanhood*, vol. I, Almora: Shri Almora Book Depot, 1993, pp. 85–94.

Banerji, S.C., *Cultural Heritage of Kashmir*, Calcutta: Sanskrit Pustak Bhandar, 1965.

Banerji, S.C. and A.K. Gupta (trans.), *Bilhaṇa's Vikramāṅkadevacaritaṁ*, Calcutta: Sambodhi Publications, 1965.

Bhattacharji, Sukumari, 'Prostitution in Ancient India', in Kumkum Roy (ed.), *Women in Early Indian Societies*, New Delhi: Manohar, 1999, pp.196–228.

Chakravarti, Uma and Kumkum Roy, 'In Search of Our Past: A Review of the Limitations and Possibilities of the Historiography of Women in Early India', *Economic and Political Weekly*, 23 (18), 1988, pp. 2–10.

Chattopadhyaya, B.D., 'General Editor's Preface', in Kumkum Roy (ed.), *Women in Early Indian Societies*, New Delhi: Manohar, 1999, pp. ix–x.

Cunningham, A., *Coins of Medieval India,* Varanasi: Oriental Books, 1967.

Deambi, B.K. Kaul, *Corpus of Śāradā Inscriptions of Kashmir*, Delhi: Agam Kala Prakashan, 1982.

Dhar, M.K., *Royal Life in Ancient India*, Delhi: Durga Publications, 1991.

Ghoshal, U.N., 'The Dynastic Chronicles of Kashmir', *The Indian Historical Quarterly*, vol. XVIII, 1985 (rpt), pp. 195–207.

Gulati, Saroj, *Women and Society: Northern India in the 11th and 12th Centuries*, Delhi: Chanakya Publications, 1985.

Gupta, P.L. *Coins*, New Delhi: National Book Trust, 1969.

Kane, P.V., *History of Dharmaśāstra*, vol. III, Poona: Bhandarkar Oriental Research Institute, 1946.

Kapur, M.L., *Eminent Rulers of Ancient Kashmir*, Delhi: Oriental Publishers, 1975.

——, *The History and Culture of Kashmir*, Delhi: Anmol Publications, 1992 (2nd edn).

Kumari, Ved (trans.), *The Nīlamata Purāṇa*, vol. I, Srinagar-Jammu: J&K Academy of Art, Culture, and Languages, 1968.

—— (trans.), *The Nīlamata Purāṇa*, vol. II, Srinagar: J&K Academy of Art, Culture, and Languages, 1973.

Majumdar, A.K., *Concise History of Ancient India*, Delhi: Munshiram Manoharlal, 1980.

Mathur, Vina, *The Role and Position of Women in the Social, Cultural and Political Life of Kashmir: 7th century–16th century AD,* Jammu: Doron Publications, 1985.

Mazumdar, B.P., 'Role of the Dāmaras in Medieval Kashmir', in K.M. Shrimali (ed.), *Essays in Indian Art, Religion and Society*, New Delhi: Munshiram Manoharlal, 1987, pp. 27–36.

R.S. Pandit (trans.), *Rājataraṅgiṇī*, Delhi: Sahitya Akademi, 1935.

Prasad, Beni, *The State in Ancient India*, Allahabad: The Indian Press, 1974.

Prasad, Beni and R.C. Majumdar, 'Political Theory and Administrative System', in R.C. Majumdar (ed.), *The Age of Imperial Unity,* Bombay: Bharatiya Vidya Bhawan, 1968 (4th edn).

Rangachari, Devika, 'Gender and the Historical Chronicle: A Study of Kalhaṇa's *Rājataraṅgiṇī*', unpublished MPhil thesis, Delhi: Department of History, University of Delhi, 1997.

——, 'Kalhaṇa's *Rājataraṅgiṇī*: A Gender Perspective', *Medieval History Journal*, 5 (1), 2002, pp. 37–75.

——, 'Constructing Society and Polity in Early Medieval North India: 7th century AD–12th century AD: A Gender Perspective', unpublished PhD thesis, Delhi: Department of History, University of Delhi, 2004.

Rangachari, Devika, 'Coinage and Gender: Early Medieval Kashmir', in H.P. Ray (ed.), *Coins in India: Power and Communication*, Mumbai: MARG, 1996, pp. 46–55.

Roy, Kumkum, 'Defining the Household: Some Aspects of Prescription and Practice in Early India', *Social Scientist*, 22 (1–2), 1994, pp. 3–18.

——, 'Introduction', in Kumkum Roy (ed.), *Women in Early Indian Societies*, New Delhi: Manohar, 1999, pp.1–45.

Sastri, K.N., 'Srinagar Inscription of Queen Diddā', *Epigraphia Indica*, vol. XXVII, 1985 (rpt), pp.153–5.

Stein, M.A. (trans.), *Kalhaṇa's Rājataraṅgiṇī*, vols I and II, Delhi: Motilal Banarsidass, 1989 (3rd rpt).

—— (ed.), *Kalhaṇa's Rājataraṅgiṇī*, vol. III, Bombay: Motilal Banarsidass, 1988 (rpt).

Talbot, Cynthia, 'Temples, Donors, and Gifts: Patterns of Patronage in Thirteenth-century South India', *Journal of Asian Studies*, 50 (2), 1991, pp. 308–40.

——, 'Rudrama-devī, the Female King: Gender and Political Authority in Medieval India', in David Shulman (ed.), *Syllables of Sky: Studies in South Indian Civilization in Honour of Velcheru Narayana Rao*, New Delhi: Oxford University Press, 1995, pp. 391–430.

Tripathi, R.S. (ed. and trans.), *Samayamātṛkā of Mahākavi Kṣemendra*, Varanasi: Chowkhamba Vidyabhavan, 1967.

Yadava, B.N.S., *Society and Culture in Northern India in the Twelfth Century*, Allahabad: Central Book Depot, 1973.

Contributors

SHIVANI AGARWAL is pursuing her PhD from the Centre for Historical Studies, Jawaharlal Nehru University.

SHIBANI BOSE is pursuing her PhD from the Department of History, University of Delhi, and has taught at Miranda House, University of Delhi.

SANJUKTA DATTA obtained her MPhil from the Department of History, University of Delhi, and is teaching at St Stephen's College.

SHONALEEKA KAUL obtained her PhD from the Centre for Historical Studies, Jawaharlal Nehru University, and is teaching at Miranda House, University of Delhi.

NAYANJOT LAHIRI teaches archaeology as Professor at the Department of History, University of Delhi. She has authored and edited several books, including *Finding Forgotten Cities: How the Indus Civilization was Discovered* (2005). She is Member, Advisory Board of *World Archaeology* (UK) and Member, Editorial Board of *American Anthropologist* (USA)

DEVIKA RANGACHARI obtained her PhD from the Department of History, University of Delhi. Her recent publications include *Invisible Women, Visible Histories: Gender, Society and Polity in North India (Seventh–Twelfth Century AD)* (2009).

UPINDER SINGH is Professor at the Department of History, University of Delhi. Her recent publications include *The Discovery of Ancient India: Early Archaeologists and the Beginnings of Archaeology* (2004) and *A History of Ancient and Early Medieval India: From the Stone Age to the Twelfth Century* (2008).

UTHARA SUVRATHAN is pursuing her PhD in anthropological archaeology from the University of Michigan.

MUDIT TRIVEDI is pursuing his PhD from the Department of Anthropology, University of Chicago.

SUSAN VERMA MISHRA obtained her PhD from the Centre for Historical Studies, Jawaharlal Nehru University.

MEERA VISVANATHAN obtained her MPhil from the Centre for Historical Studies, Jawaharlal Nehru University, New Delhi.